WORKTEXT
for

AUTOMOTIVE STEERING, SUSPENSION, AND ALIGNMENT

Third Edition

James D. Halderman
Sinclair Community College

Chase D. Mitchell
Utah Valley State College

D0921522

Prentice
Hall

Upper Saddle River, New Jersey
Columbus, Ohio

10 9 8 7 6 5 4 3 2 1

Prentice
Hall

ISBN 0-13-048856-9

Preface

This worktext is designed to accompany the third edition of Automotive Steering, Suspension, and Alignment. The activity sheets enclosed cover 100% of the NATEF task lists for ASE content area A-4 – Suspension and Steering. Comprehensive appendixes include the following information.

Appendix 1 – Lug Nut Torque Specifications Chart

This chart includes all vehicle and gives the torque tightening specifications for wheel lug nuts.

Appendix 2 – Ride Height Chart

This chart lists all vehicles and gives the specified ride (trim) height specifications.

Appendix 3 – NATEF Task List and Correlation Chart

This chart lists all of the NATEF tasks along with the page number of the activity sheet(s) that correlates to the tasks. This chart makes it easy for students and instructors to keep track of progress. The NATEF tasks are grouped according to priority to make it easier to concentrate on high-priority tasks.

Explanation of NATEF Task List Numbering System

All NATEF tasks for Suspension and Steering are labeled A4, which is the designation for ASE test content covering suspension and steering.

TABLE OF CONTENTS

Wheel Alignment Diagnosis, Adjustment, and Repair

Wheel and Tire Diagnosis and Repair

Material Safety Data Sheet (MSDS)

Meets NATEF Task: Environmental Safety Practices for Suspension and Steering (A4)

Name _____ **Date** _____

Make/Model _____ **Year** _____ **Instructor's OK** [ ]

_____ **1.** Locate the MSDS sheets and describe their location_____

_____

_____ **2.** Select three commonly used chemicals or solvents. Record the following information
from the MSDS:

- **Product name** _____

    chemical name(s) _____

    Does the chemical contain "chlor" or "fluor" which may indicate hazardous

    materials? **Yes** _____ **No** _____

    flash point = _____ (hopefully above 140° F)

    pH _____ (7 = neutral, higher than 7 = caustic (base), lower than 7 = acid)

- **Product name** _____

    chemical name(s) _____

    Does the chemical contain "chlor" or "fluor" which may indicate hazardous

    materials? **Yes** _____ **No** _____

    flash point = _____ (hopefully above 140° F)

    pH _____ (7 = neutral, higher than 7 = caustic (base), lower than 7 = acid)

- **Product name** _____

    chemical name(s) _____

    Does the chemical contain "chlor" or "fluor" which may indicate hazardous

    materials? **Yes** _____ **No** _____

    flash point = _____ (hopefully above 140° F)

    pH _____ (7 = neutral, higher than 7 = caustic (base), lower than 7 = acid)

Fire Extinguisher

Meets NATEF Task: Safety Requirement for Suspension and Steering (A4)

Name _____ Date _____

Make/Model _____ Year _____ Instructor's OK [   ]

_____ 1. Describe the location of the fire extinguishers in your building or shop and note the

last inspection dates.

Type of Extinguisher	Location	Inspection Date
_____	_____	_____
_____	_____	_____
_____	_____	_____
_____	_____	_____

_____ 2. Do any of the fire extinguishers need to be charged?

_____ Yes (which ones) _____

_____ No

_____ 3. Where can the fire extinguishers be recharged? List the name and telephone number

of the company. _____ _____

_____ 4. What is the cost to recharge the fire extinguishers?

a. Water = _____

b. CO_2 = _____

c. Dry chemical = _____

Vehicle Hoisting

Meets NATEF Task: Safety Requirement for Suspension and Steering (A4)

Name _____ Date _____

Make/Model _____ Year _____ Instructor's OK [ ]

Getting Ready to Hoist the Vehicle

_____ 1. Drive the vehicle into position to be hoisted (lifted) being certain to center the vehicle in the stall.

_____ 2. Pull the vehicle forward until the front tire rests on the tire pad (if equipped).

> **NOTE:** Some long vehicles may have to be positioned forward of the pad and some short vehicles may have to be positioned behind the pad.

_____ 3. Place the gear selector into the park position (if the vehicle has an automatic transmission/transaxle) or in neutral (if the vehicle has a manual transmission/transaxle) and firmly apply the parking brake.

_____ 4. Lower the driver's side window before exiting the vehicle. (This step helps prevent keys from being accidentally being locked in the vehicle.)

_____ 5. Position the arms and hoist pads under the frame or pinch weld areas of the body.

Hoisting the Vehicle

_____ 6. Slowly raise the vehicle about one foot (30 cm) off the ground and check the stability of the vehicle by attempting to move the vehicle on the lift.

_____ 7. If the vehicle is stable and all pads are properly positioned under the vehicle, continue hoisting the vehicle to the height needed.
NOTE: Best working conditions are at chest or elbow level.

_____ 8. Be sure the safety latches have engaged before working under the vehicle.

Lowering the Vehicle

_____ 9. To lower the vehicle, raise the hoist slightly, then release the safety latches.

_____ 10. Lower the vehicle using the proper operating and safety release levers.

> **CAUTION:** Do not look away while lowering the vehicle. One side of the vehicle could become stuck or something (or someone) could get under the vehicle.

_____ 11. After lowering the hoist arms all the way to the floor, move the arms so that they will not be hit when the vehicle is driven out of the stall.

Safety Check

Meets NATEF Task: Safety Requirement for Suspension and Steering (A4)

Name _____ Date _____

Make/Model _____ Year _____ Instructor's OK [ ]

_____ 1. Check the headlights (brights and dim).

_____ 2. Check the taillights.

_____ 3. Check the side marker lights.

_____ 4. Check the license plate light.

_____ 5. Check the brake lights.

_____ 6. Check the turn signals.

_____ 7. Check the back-up lights with the ignition switch "on" (engine "off") and the gear selector in reverse.

_____ 8. Check the windshield wipers (all speeds) and wiper blades.

_____ 9. Check the heater-defroster fan (all speeds).

_____ 10. Check the condition of the tires (must have at least 2/32" of tread) and the tire pressure. Do not forget to check the spare tire!

_____ 11. Check for looseness in the steering wheel (less than 2" of play).

_____ 12. Check the 4-way emergency flashers.

_____ 13. Check the horn.

_____ 14. Listen for exhaust system leaks.

_____ 15. Check the parking brake (maximum 8-10 "clicks" and should "hold" in drive).

VIN Code

Meets NATEF Task: (A4-A-2) Locate and Interpret Vehicle Identification Numbers (P-1)

Name _____ Date _____

Make/Model _____ Year _____ Instructor's OK [　]

VIN Number _____

- The first number or letter designates the **country of origin** = _____

1 = United States	9 = Brazil	V = France
2 = Canada	J = Japan	W = Germany
3 = Mexico	K = Korea	Y = Sweden
4 = United States	L = Taiwan	Z = Italy
6 = Australia	S = England	

- The model of the vehicle is commonly the fourth or fifth character. **Model?**

  _____

- The eighth character is often the engine code. (Some engines cannot be determined

  by the VIN number.) **Engine code:** _____

- The tenth character represents the year on all vehicles. See the following chart.

Vin Year Chart   Year? _____

A = 1980	N = 1992	4 = 2004
B = 1981	P = 1993	5 = 2005
C = 1982	R = 1994	6 = 2006
D = 1983	S = 1995	7 = 2007
E = 1984	T = 1996	8 = 2008
F = 1985	V = 1997	9 = 2009
G = 1986	W = 1998	
H = 1987	X = 1999	
J = 1988	Y = 2000	
K = 1989	1 = 2001	
L = 1990	2 = 2002	
M = 1991	3 = 2003	

Suspension Problem Diagnosis

Meets NATEF Task: (A4-A-1) Identify and Interpret Suspension Concerns; Determine
Necessary Action (P-1)

Name _____ Date _____

Make/Model _____ Year _____ Instructor's OK [   ]

_____ 1. What is the stated customer concern? _____

_____ 2. Test drive the vehicle under the same conditions and road surface types as stated by
the customer when the problem occurs and check the following.

Tire-type noise?	**OK** ____	**NOT OK** ____
Clunks?	**OK** ____	**NOT OK** ____
Creaks?	**OK** ____	**NOT OK** ____
Tracks straight?	**OK** ____	**NOT OK** ____
Pull during braking only?	**OK** ____	**NOT OK** ____
Wandering (unstable)?	**OK** ____	**NOT OK** ____

Other concern (describe) _____

_____ 3. When does the fault or concern occur?

____ During turns or cornering to the right
____ During turns or cornering to the left
____ During turns or cornering both to the right or the left
____ While driving straight ahead
____ Only when driving on a rough road
____ Only when turning into or out of a driveway
____ Other (describe) _____

_____ 4. Based on the test drive, what components or systems could be the cause of the
suspension problem or concern?

_____

_____

_____ 5. What action will be needed to correct these concerns? _____

_____

_____

Steering Problem Diagnosis

Meets NATEF Task: (A4-A-1) Identify and Interpret Steering Concerns; Determine Necessary Action (P-1)

Name _____ Date _____

Make/Model _____ Year _____ Instructor's OK [＿＿]

_____ 1. What is the stated customer concern? _____

_____ 2. Test drive the vehicle under the same condition and road surface types as stated by the customer when the problem occurs and check the following.

Steers straight?	OK ____	NOT OK ____
Wanders?	OK ____	NOT OK ____
Noise during turns or corners?	OK ____	NOT OK ____
Hard steering when cold only?	OK ____	NOT OK ____
Hard steering when raining?	OK ____	NOT OK ____
Noise when steering?	OK ____	NOT OK ____
Looseness in steering wheel?	OK ____	NOT OK ____
Lack of steering control?	OK ____	NOT OK ____

Other concerns (describe) _____

_____

_____ 3. When does the fault or concern occur?

____ During turns or cornering to the right
____ During turns or cornering to the left
____ During turns or cornering both to the right or the left
____ While driving straight ahead
____ Only when driving on a rough road
____ Only when turning into or out of a driveway
____ Other (describe) _____

_____ 4. Based on the test drive, what components or systems could be the cause of the suspension problem or concern?

_____

_____

_____ 5. What action will be needed to correct these concerns? _____

_____

_____

Suspension and Steering System Information

Meets NATEF Task: (A4-A-2) Research Vehicle Information (P-1)

Name _____ Date _____

Make/Model _____ Year _____ Instructor's OK [   ]

Consult the service information and determine the following.

_____ **1.** List suspension-related technician service bulletins (TSBs).

      A. Topic _____ Bulletin Number _____

         Fault/Concern _____

         Corrective Action _____

      B. Topic _____ Bulletin Number _____

         Fault/Concern _____

         Corrective Action _____

_____ **2.** List all published service precautions from the service information.

         _____

         _____

_____ **3.** Research the vehicle's service history and record all suspension or steering service or repairs.

         _____

         _____

_____ **4.** Record all suspension and steering specifications.

         _____

         _____

Disable/Enable Airbag Systems

Meets NATEF Task: (A4-B-1) Disable and Enable Supplemental Restraint System (P-1)

Name _____ **Date** _____

Make/Model _____ **Year** _____ **Instructor's OK** ☐

_____ 1. Check the vehicle information for the specified steps and procedures that should be followed to disable and enable the supplemental restraint (airbag) system on the vehicle being serviced.

_____

_____

_____

_____ 2. Check all of the steps that are recommended.

    ___ Disconnect the battery negative cable
    ___ Remove the airbag circuit fuse
    ___ Disconnect the connector at the base of the steering column
    ___ Disconnect the connector for the passenger side airbag
    ___ Install the airbag inflator module load tool
    ___ Other (describe) _____

_____ 3. List the precautions stated in the service information when performing service work to the steering or suspension system around the components of the supplemental restraint system.

_____

_____

_____

Airbag System Coil (Clock Spring)

Meets NATEF Task: (A4-B-2) Steering Wheel Removal and Centering of SRS Coil (Clock Spring (P-1)

Name _____ Date _____

Make/Model _____ Year _____ Instructor's OK [ ]

_____ 1. Consult the service information and determine the specified procedures needed to remove and replace the steering wheel and to center/time the supplemental restraint system (SRS) coil (clock spring).

_____

_____

_____

_____

_____

_____ 2. List the tools or equipment needed.

A. _____

B. _____

C. _____

D. _____

_____ 3. List the safety precautions that are listed in the service information regarding these procedures.

A. _____

B. _____

C. _____

D. _____

3 1833 04592 3346

Steering Column Problem Diagnosis

Meets NATEF Task: (A4-B-3) Diagnose Steering Column Noises, Looseness, and Binding
Concerns and Determine Necessary Action (P-2)

Name _____ Date _____

Make/Model _____ Year _____ Instructor's OK [   ]

_____ 1. With the ignition key in the ignition (key on, engine off) and the steering column
unlocked, rotate the steering wheel.

Steering wheel turns without noise	**OK** ____	**NOT OK** ____
Steering wheel does not turn – still locked	**OK** ____	**NOT OK** ____

_____ 2. Check the service information and determine what service work is needed to correct?

_____

_____

_____ 3. If equipped, check for proper operation of the tilt and telescopic functions of the
steering column.

Works without excessive effort or looseness	**OK** ____	**NOT OK** ____
Does not work	**OK** ____	**NOT OK** ____
Works but is difficult to move or makes noise	**OK** ____	**NOT OK** ____
Works but has looseness in the column	**OK** ____	**NOT OK** ____

_____ 4. Test drive the vehicle and determine if the steering column is loose or makes noise
during normal driving.

OK ____   **NOT OK** ____

_____ 5. After the analysis, what service procedures should be performed to restore the proper
operation of the steering column?

_____

_____

Diagnose Power Steering Gear Problems

Meets NATEF Task: (A4-B-4) Diagnose Power Steering Gear Problems and Determine
Necessary Action (P-3)

Name _____ Date _____

Make/Model _____ Year _____ Instructor's OK [ ]

_____ 1. Start the engine and turn the steering wheel full left and full right. Check the
following items that apply.

      OK ____ **NOT OK** ____ Steering feels and operates as normal without any
abnormal noise, looseness, or binding.

      OK ____ **NOT OK** ____ Steering wheel is difficult to turn.

      OK ____ **NOT OK** ____ Steering feels loose or binds.

_____ 2. Perform a visual inspection of the power steering pump and steering gear and check
all that apply.

      OK ____ **NOT OK** ____ No leaks and drive belt appears to be serviceable.

      OK ____ **NOT OK** ____ Leak(s) detected. Describe the location _____
_____

      OK ____ **NOT OK** ____ Drive belt loose, defective, or worn. Describe the
fault _____

_____ 3. Test drive the vehicle and describe the operation of the power steering. _____

_____

_____

_____ 4. What actions are needed to correct the concern? _____

_____

_____

Power Steering System Test

Meets NATEF Task: (A4-B-4) Diagnose Power Steering and Determine Necessary
Action (P-3)

Name _____ **Date** _____

Make/Model _____ **Year** _____ **Instructor's OK** [ ]

(Using a Power Steering Pressure Tester)

Check the service information and/or pressure tester
instructions for the exact test procedure.

A typical procedure includes:

_____ 1. Start the engine. Allow the power steering
system to reach operating temperatures.

_____ 2. The pressure gauge should register 80 - 125 psi.
If the pressure is greater than 150 psi, check for
restrictions in the system including
the operation of the poppet valve located in the inlet of the steering gear.

_____ 3. Fully close the valve 3 times. All three readings should be within 50 psi of each other
and the peak pressure higher than 1,000 psi.

> **NOTE:** Do not leave the valve closed for more than 5 seconds!

_____ 4. If the pressure readings are high enough *and* within 50 psi of each other, the pump is
okay.

_____ 5. If the pressure readings are high enough, yet not within 50 psi of each other, the flow
control valve is sticking.

_____ 6. If the pressure readings are less than 1,000 psi, replace the flow control valve and
recheck. If the pressures are still low, replace the rotor and vanes in the power
steering pump.

_____ 7. If the pump is okay, turn the steering wheel to both stops. If the pressure at both stops
is not the same as the maximum pressure, the steering gear (or rack and pinion) is
leaking internally. **OK** _____ **NOT OK** _____

_____ 8. If not OK, what action is needed to restore proper operation?

_____

Diagnose Power Rack and Pinion Steering

Meets NATEF Task: (A4-B-5) Diagnose Power Rack and Pinion Steering Gear Problems and Determine Necessary Action (P-3)

Name _____ Date _____

Make/Model _____ Year _____ Instructor's OK [   ]

_____ **1.** Start the engine and turn the steering wheel full left and full right. Check the following items that apply.

      OK _____ **NOT OK** _____ Steering feels and operates as normal without any abnormal noise, looseness, or binding.

      OK _____ **NOT OK** _____ Steering wheel is difficult to turn.

      OK _____ **NOT OK** _____ Steering feels loose or binds.

_____ **2.** Perform a visual inspection of the power steering pump and steering gear and check all that apply.

      OK _____ **NOT OK** _____ No leaks and drive belt appears to be serviceable.

      OK _____ **NOT OK** _____ Leak(s) detected. Describe the location _____ _____

      OK _____ **NOT OK** _____ Drive belt loose, defective, or worn. Describe the fault _____

_____ **3.** Test drive the vehicle and describe the operation of the power steering. _____

_____

_____

_____ **4.** What actions are needed to correct the concern? _____

_____

_____

Steering Column Related Inspection

Meets NATEF Task: (A4-B-6) Inspect Steering U-Joints, Flexible Coupling(s) and Lock Cylinder Mechanism, and Steering Wheel; Perform Necessary Action (P-2)

Name _____ **Date** _____

Make/Model _____ **Year** _____ **Instructor's OK** [   ]

_____ **1.** Start the engine and turn the steering wheel full left and full right. Check the following items that apply.

        OK ____   **NOT OK** ____   Steering wheel is difficult to turn.
        OK ____   **NOT OK** ____   Steering feels loose or binds.
        OK ____   **NOT OK** ____   Steering feels and operates as normal without any
                                           abnormal noise, looseness, or binding.

_____ **2.** Perform a visual inspection and check the flexible coupling and intermediate shaft for excessive wear or damage.

        OK ____   **NOT OK** ____   Describe fault _____

_____ **3.** Check the operation of the lock cylinder.

        ____ Works smoothly
        ____ Key is difficult to remove/or install
        ____ Other concern (describe) _____

_____ **4.** Check the service information and determine needed action. _____

_____

_____

TO STEERING WHEEL

INTERMEDIATE SHAFT

FLEXIBLE COUPLING

Rack and Pinion Worm Bearing Adjustment

Meets NATEF Task: (A4-B-7) Adjust Rack and Power Worm Bearing Preload and Sector Lash (P-3)

Name _____ Date _____

Make/Model _____ Year _____ Instructor's OK [ ]

_____ **1.** Check the service information for the specified adjustment procedures and precautions for adjusting the worm bearing preload and sector lash.

    A. Recommended procedure: _____

    _____

    _____

    B. Precautions: _____

    _____

    _____

_____ **2.** Check the recommended method used to adjust the rack preload (pinion torque).

    _____ Shims (remove shims to increase torque, add shims to reduce torque)

    _____ Adjuster plug (usually tighten and loosen 60° to achieve proper torque)

    _____ Other (describe) _____

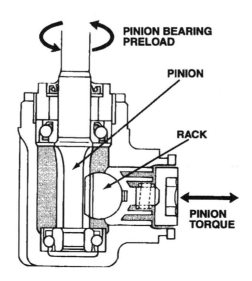

Rack and Pinion Steering Gear

Meets NATEF Task: (A4-B-8) Remove and Replace Rack and Pinion Steering Gear; Inspect Mounting Bushings and Brackets (P-1)

Name _____ Date _____

Make/Model _____ Year _____ Instructor's OK [ ]

_____ 1. Check the service information and write the specified procedure to follow when removing and replacing the rack and pinion steering gear.

_____

_____

_____

_____

_____

_____ 2. The following steps are usually specified by the vehicle manufacturer.

   A. Hoist the vehicle safely.

   B. Disable supplemental restraint system (SRS)

   C. Remove both front wheel assemblies.

   D. Disconnect both outer tie rods.

   E. Disconnect the intermediate shaft from the stub shaft of the rack and pinion steering gear.

   F. Disconnect the power steering lines from the gear assembly (if equipped with power steering).

   G. Remove the mounting brackets and remove the rack and pinion steering gear from underneath the vehicle.

_____ 3. Carefully inspect the rubber bushings and brackets for wear or damage.

   OK _____   NOT OK _____

_____ 4. Show the instructor the removed rack and pinion steering gear assembly.

   Instructor's OK _____

_____ 4. Reinstall the rack and pinion steering gear in the reverse order of disassembly.

Inner Tie Rod Ends and Bellows Boots

Meets NATEF Task: (A4-B-9) Inspect and Replace Rack and Pinion Steering Gear Inner Tie Ends (Sockets) and Bellows Boots (P-1)

Name _____ Date _____

Make/Model _____ Year _____ Instructor's OK [ ]

_____ 1. Check the service information and write the specified procedure to inspect and replace the inner tie rod ends.

_____

_____

_____

_____

_____ 2. Hoist the vehicle safely and visually check the condition of the inner tie rod end bellows boots.

_____ OK
_____ Cracked in places, but not all the way through (recommend replacement)
_____ Cracked open places (requires replacement)
_____ Missing

_____ 3. Most vehicle manufacturers recommend that the entire rack and pinion steering gear assembly be removed from the vehicle when replacing the inner tie rod ends (ball socket assemblies).

_____ **Yes** (recommend that rack be removed)
_____ **No** (the tie rod end can be removed with the rack in the vehicle)

_____ 4. Describe the method used to retain the inner ball sockets to the ends of the rack.

_____ Pin
_____ Rivet
_____ Stacked
_____ Other (describe) _____

_____ 5. List all precautions found in the service information regarding this procedure.

_____

_____ 6. Describe any problems _____

_____

Power Steering Fluid Inspection

Meets NATEF Task: (A4-B-10) Inspect Power Steering Fluid Level and Condition (P-1)

Name _____ **Date** _____

Make/Model _____ **Year** _____ **Instructor's OK** [ ]

_____ **1.** Check the service information and determine the specified type of fluid that should be used in the power steering system.

     ____ Power steering fluid
     ____ Dexron III ATF
     ____ Type F ATF
     ____ Other (specify) _____

_____ **2.** List any cautions or warnings as specified by the vehicle manufacturer.

_____

_____ **3.** With the engine off, raise the hood and locate the power steering fluid reservoir. Describe the location: _____

_____ **4.** Check the level of the power steering fluid.

     ____ OK (at the full mark that corresponds to the temperature of the fluid)
     ____ Overfilled
     ____ Underfilled
     ____ Empty

_____ **5.** Check the fluid for aeration (foaming), or contamination.

     ____ OK (like new)
     ____ Darker than new, but not aerated or contaminated
     ____ Silver color indicating contaminated with aluminum or other metal particles from the power steering system
     ____ Black and thick or smells rancid
     ____ Other (describe) _____

_____ **6.** What actions are necessary? _____

_____

_____

_____

Flush, Fill, and Bleed Power Steering

Meets NATEF Task: (A4-B-11) Flush, Fill, and Bleed Power Steering Systems (P-2)

Name _____ Date _____

Make/Model _____ Year _____ Instructor's OK [   ]

A power steering system that has air trapped in the system will cause a loud, whining noise. Use the following procedure to remove any air that could have been trapped in the system during a repair procedure.

_____ 1. Use a jack and safety stand or a lift and hoist the front wheels off the ground about one foot (30 cm).

_____ 2. Remove the cap from the power steering reservoir and rotate the steering wheel all the way one direction, then all the way the other direction with the engine off.

>   **NOTE:** As the steering wheel is being rotated, the fluid will be circulated through the system and the air will escape from the pump reservoir.

_____ 3. Add power steering fluid as needed to keep the reservoir filled.

_____ 4. Lower the vehicle and start the engine. Check for proper, quiet power steering gear operation.

>   **OK** _____   **NOT OK** _____

_____ 5. If not OK, repeat the procedure again.

_____ 6. After bleeding the system, fill the power steering reservoir to the proper level.

_____ 7. Carefully test drive the vehicle checking for proper operation of the power steering before returning the vehicle to the customer.

Diagnose Power Steering Fluid Leakage

Meets NATEF Task: (A4-B-12) Diagnose Power Steering Fluid Leakage; Determine
Necessary Action (P-2)

Name _____ Date _____

Make/Model _____ Year _____ Instructor's OK [   ]

_____ 1. Check the service information for the specified power steering fluid.

        _____ Power steering fluid

        _____ Dexron III ATF

        _____ Type F ATF

        _____ Other (specify) _____

_____ 2. Perform a visual inspection of the power steering system and determine the location of
any leaks. Hoist the vehicle if necessary. Check each area listed below that is found
to be leaking.

        _____ Pump shaft seal area

        _____ Reservoir cap

        _____ Reservoir

        _____ High-pressure line at the pump

        _____ High-pressure line between the pump and the gear

        _____ High-pressure line at the gear

        _____ Steering gear leak near the stub shaft

        _____ Steering gear leak at the inner tie rod end boots

        _____ Low-pressure hose leak (describe the location) _____

        _____ Other (describe) _____

_____ 3. What action is necessary to correct the leak(s)? _____

_____

_____

_____

Remove/Replace Power Steering Pump Belt

Meets NATEF Task: (A4-B-13) Remove, Inspect, Replace, and Adjust Power Steering Pump Belt (P-1)

Name _____ **Date** _____

Make/Model _____ **Year** _____ **Instructor's OK** [_____]

The proper operation of the power steering, as well as the air conditioning and charging system, depends on the accessory drive belt(s) being in good condition and properly tensioned.

_____ 1. Raise the hood and carefully inspect the accessory drive belt(s).

   CAUTION: Be sure the engine is off and pocket the ignition key to prevent the possibility that someone else could start the engine while you are inspecting the belt(s).

_____ 2. Record the number and type of accessory drive belts.

   _____ V-belt type
   _____ Flat serpentine (multigroove) type

_____ 3. Locate and record the vehicle manufacturer's specified belt tension and the actual tension for each belt:

   specification:_____ actual:_____

   NOTE: If a belt tensioner gauge is not available, press down on the belt between the pulleys with moderate force. Most vehicle manufacturers specify the deflection (movement) should be less than 1/2" (13 mm).

   OK _____   **NOT OK** _____

_____ 5. Check the tensioner for the tension mark location. Is it within the specified range according to the vehicle manufacturer's specifications?

   OK _____   **NOT OK** _____

_____ 6. Check the condition of the belt(s).

   _____ OK (like new)
   _____ Glazed (shiny) may need replacement if it is slipping or noisy
   _____ Cracked - may need replacement if more than three cracks are in any 3
   inch length per rib of the belt.   **OK** _____   **NOT OK** _____

Remove/Replace Power Steering Pump

Meets NATEF Task: (A4-B-14) Remove and Reinstall Power Steering Pump (P-3)

Name _____ Date _____

Make/Model _____ Year _____ Instructor's OK [ ]

_____ 1. Check the service information and write the specified procedure to follow for removing and reinstalling the power steering pump assembly.

_____

_____

_____

_____ 2. List all precautions as stated in the service information. _____

_____

_____ 3. Most removal and replacement procedures involve the following steps:

    A. Remove the drive belt
    B. Disconnect the high-pressure and low-pressure hoses at the pump.

    CAUTION: Dispose of the old power steering fluid according to federal, state, and local regulations.

    C. Remove the attaching bolts/nuts and remove the power steering pump assembly from the vehicle.
    D. Reinstall the replacement pump assembly in the reverse order of removal.
    E. Add the specified power steering fluid

_____ 4. Raise the front wheels of the vehicle off the ground and bleed the trapped air from the power steering system by rotating the steering wheel full left and full right several times.

_____ 5. Lower the vehicle and verify proper power steering operation.

Power Steering Pump Pulley

Meets NATEF Task: (A4-B-15) Remove and Reinstall Power Steering Pump Pulley; Check Pulley and Belt Alignment (P-3)

Name _____ Date _____

Make/Model _____ Year _____ Instructor's OK [   ]

_____ 1. Check the service information for the specified power steering pump pulley removal and installation procedure.

_____

_____

_____ 2. What special tools are needed? _____

_____

_____ 3. Most specified procedures include the following steps:

A. Remove the power steering drive belt

B. Use a puller to remove the pulley

C. Use an installation tool to install the pulley on the shaft

D. Reinstall the drive belt and check for proper alignment

E. Start the engine and check for proper operation

OK _____ NOT OK _____

MULTIPLE DRIVE BELTS
AIR CONDITIONER COMPRESSOR
ALTERNATOR
IDLER
WATER PUMP
POWER STEERING PUMP
CRANKSHAFT

SERPENTINE BELT
ALTERNATOR   TENSIONER   POWER STEERING PUMP
IDLER   WATER PUMP
AIR PUMP
CRANKSHAFT   AIR CONDITIONER COMPRESSOR

Inspect Power Steering Hoses and Fittings

Meets NATEF Task: (A4-B-16) Inspect and Replace Power Steering Hoses and Fittings
(P-2)

Name _____ Date _____

Make/Model _____ Year _____ Instructor's OK [ ]

_____ 1. Check the service information for the specified procedures, precautions, and torque specifications.

    A. Specified procedure: _____

    _____

    B. Specified precautions: _____

    _____

    C. Specified torque specifications _____

    _____

_____ 2. Check the reason why the hoses and/or fittings are being replaced.

    _____ Leaking

    _____ Worn outside cover

    _____ Possible restriction as determined by testing

    _____ Recommended when replacing pump or gear assembly

    _____ Other (specify) _____

    _____

_____ 3. Which hose(s) or fitting(s) was replaced?

    _____ High-pressure hose and fitting

    _____ Low-pressure hose and fitting

    _____ Other (specify) _____

    _____

Inspect and Replace Steering Components

Meets NATEF Task: (A4-B-17) Inspect and Replace Pitman Arm, Centerlink, Idler Arm and Steering Linkage Damper (P-2)

Name _____ Date _____

Make/Model _____ Year _____ Instructor's OK [ ]

_____ 1. Check the service information for the specified testing and inspection procedures and specifications.

    A. Specified testing procedures: _____

    _____

    B. Specifications: _____

    _____

_____ 2. Check the steering components listed and note their condition.

    Idler arm: _____

    _____

    Pitman arm: _____

    _____

    Centerlink: _____

    _____

    Steering linkage damper: _____

    _____

DIAL INDICATOR / MEASURE PLAY / IDLER ARM / SPRING SCALE

_____ 3. State the specified replacement procedure and list any specific tools needed.

    Idler arm: Procedure _____

        Tools _____

    Pitman arm: Procedure _____

        Tools _____

    Centerlink: Procedure _____

        Tools _____

    Steering linkage damper: Procedure _____

        Tools _____

Tie-Rod End Inspection and Replacement

Meets NATEF Task: (A4-B-18) Inspect, Replace, and Adjust Tie Rod Ends (Sockets), Tie Rod Sleeves and Clamps (P-1)

Name _____ Date _____

Make/Model _____ Year _____ Instructor's OK [   ]

_____ 1. Verify that the tie-rod end(s) requires replacement. Check all that apply.

      _____ Torn grease boot
      _____ Joint has side-to-side movement
      _____ Physically damaged
      _____ Other (specify) _____

_____ 2. Hoist the vehicle safely.

_____ 3. Compare the replacement tie-rod end with the original to be sure that the new end is correct.

_____ 4. Remove the retaining nut and use a tie-rod puller to separate the tie-rod end from the steering knuckle and/or center link.

    HINT: Often a hammer can be used to jar loose the tie-rod end especially if a downward force is exerted on the tie-rod while an assistant taps on the steering knuckle at the tie-rod end.

_____ 5. Measure the distance between the center of the tie-rod end and the adjusting sleeve and record this distance so the replacement tie-rod end can be installed in approximately the same location so that the wheel alignment (toe setting) will be close to being correct.

_____ 6. Unscrew the old tie-rod end and discard.

_____ 7. Install the replacement tie-rod end and adjust to the same distance as measured and recorded in #5.

_____ 8. Install the tie-rod end onto the steering knuckle and torque the retaining nut to factory specifications.

    Torque specifications for the tie-rod retaining nut = _____

_____ 9. Lower the vehicle and align the vehicle before returning it to the customer.

Electronically Controlled Steering Systems

Meets NATEF Task: (A4-B-19) Test and Diagnose Components of Electronically Controlled Steering Systems Using a Scan Tool; Determine Necessary Action (P-3)

Name _____ Date _____

Make/Model _____ Year _____ Instructor's OK [ ]

_____ 1. Check the service information for the exact testing procedure to follow when diagnosing an electronically controlled steering system.

Specified procedure: _____

_____

Specified scan tool or special tool: _____

_____

_____ 2. What scan tool was used? _____

_____ 3. Could the control valve or solenoid be operated by the scan tool?

Yes _____ No _____

_____ 4. What method(s) is specified to test the system if a scan tool is not available?

_____

_____ 5. The system being checked is: OK _____ NOT OK _____

_____ 6. If not OK, what action will be needed to correct the fault?

_____

_____

Diagnose SLA Suspension Concerns

Meets NATEF Task: (A4-C-1.1) Diagnose Short and Long Arm Suspension System Noises, Body Sway, and Uneven Riding Height Concerns; Determine Necessary Action (P-1)

Name _____ Date _____

Make/Model _____ Year _____ Instructor's OK [ ]

_____ 1. State the customer concerns:

_____

_____

_____

_____

_____

_____ 2. Perform a visual inspection of the vehicle including the following:

A. **Ride height**	Equal front and rear?	OK ____	NOT OK ____
B. **Ride height**	Left and right?	OK ____	NOT OK ____
C. **Tires**	Size and condition	OK ____	NOT OK ____

Describe: _____

D. **Front wheel alignment** look OK? OK ____ NOT OK ____

Describe any faults: _____

_____ 3. Test drive the vehicle and note any faults with the vehicle handling.

_____ OK
_____ Sways while cornering or turning
_____ Noise from suspension (describe when and type of noise) _____
_____
_____ Other (describe) _____

_____ 4. Check for any technical service bulletins (TSBs) that are suspension related.

_____

_____

Diagnose Strut Suspension Concerns

Meets NATEF Task: (A4-C-1.2) Diagnose Strut Suspension Noises, Body Sway, and Uneven
Riding Height Concerns; Determine Necessary Action (P-1)

Name _____ Date _____

Make/Model _____ Year _____ Instructor's OK [____]

_____ **1.** State the customer concerns:

_____

_____

_____

_____ **2.** Perform a visual inspection of the vehicle including the following:

    A. **Ride height**   Equal front and rear?   **OK** ____   **NOT OK** ____

    B. **Ride height**   Left and right?   **OK** ____   **NOT OK** ____

    C. **Tires**   Size and condition   **OK** ____   **NOT OK** ____

        Describe: _____

    D. **Front wheel alignment** look OK?   **OK** ____   **NOT OK** ____

        Describe any faults: _____

_____ **3.** Test drive the vehicle and note any faults with the vehicle handling.

    ____ OK
    ____ Sways while cornering or turning
    ____ Noise from suspension (describe when and type of noise) _____

        _____
    ____ Other (describe) _____

_____ **4.** Check for any technical service bulletins (TSBs) that are suspension related.

_____

_____

Suspension Identification

Meets NATEF Task: (A4-A-1) Identify and Interpret Suspension Concerns; Determine
Necessary Action (P-1)

Name _____ Date _____

Make/Model _____ Year _____ Instructor's OK

_____ **1.** Identify the type of front suspension. _____

_____ **2.** Locate and inspect the condition of the control arm bushings.

       OK _____ **NOT OK** _____

_____ **3.** Locate all ball-joints. Location = _____

_____ **4.** Is the vehicle equipped with strut rods?

       Yes _____   **No** _____

_____ **5.** Is the vehicle equipped with a stabilizer bar?

       Front - **Yes** _____ **No** _____

       Rear - **Yes** _____ **No** _____

_____ **6.** Locate and inspect the stabilizer links
and bushings. **OK** _____ **NOT OK** _____

_____ **7.** Locate and determine the condition of the shock absorbers. **OK** _____ **NOT OK** _____

_____ **8.** Identify the type of rear suspension. _____

UPPER BEARING MOUNT

COIL SPRING

STRUT HOUSING
(INCLUDES SHOCK ABSORBER)

KNUCKLE

DRIVE AXLE

LOWER CONTROL ARM
(TRANSVERSE LINK)

DISC ROTOR

Remove/Install Control Arm Components

Meets NATEF Task: (A4-C-1.3) Remove, Inspect, and Install Upper and Lower Control Arms, Bushings, Shafts, and Rebound Bumpers (P-3)

Name _____ Date _____

Make/Model _____ Year _____ Instructor's OK [ ]

_____ 1. Check the service information and determine the specified procedures to remove and install control arm bushings and related components.

_____
_____
_____
_____
_____
_____

_____ 2. Check the service information and determine the specified special tools needed to replace control arm bushings.

Tool part # _____ Description _____

Tool part # _____ Description _____

Tool part # _____ Description _____

Tool part # _____ Description _____

_____ 3. Inspect the rebound bumpers (describe the location): _____

_____

_____ OK (like new)
_____ Worn or damaged (describe location and fault) _____
_____
_____ Missing (describe location) _____

_____ 4. Based on a visual inspection, what action is necessary? _____

_____

Strut Rod Bushings

Meets NATEF Task: (A4-C-1.4) Remove, Inspect, and Install Strut Rods
(Compression/Tension Rods) and Bushings (P-2)

Name _____ Date _____

Make/Model _____ Year _____ Instructor's OK [   ]

_____ **1.** Which of the following symptoms are present requiring the replacement of the strut? rod bushings?

　　　　　_____ Pull to one side during braking only
　　　　　_____ Noise while driving
　　　　　_____ Noise (clunk) during braking
　　　　　_____ Other (describe) _____

_____ **2.** Check the location of the strut rod bushing.

　　　　　_____ Forward of the front wheels
　　　　　_____ Rearward of the front wheels

_____ **3.** Check the service information to determine the specified procedure for replacing strut rod bushings.

　　　　　_____
　　　　　_____

_____ **4.** List the special tools needed. _____

Ball-Joint Testing

Meets NATEF Task: (A4-C-1.1) Diagnose SLA Suspension System Noises, Body Sway and Uneven Riding Height Concerns; Determine Necessary Action (P-1)

Name _____ Date _____

Make/Model _____ Year _____ Instructor's OK [   ]

_____ 1. Determine the load-carrying ball-joint.

_____ upper _____ lower _____ both

_____ 2. Is this a wear indicator ball-joint? _____ **Yes** _____ **No** If yes, observe the area around the grease fitting with the vehicle weight on the ground.

A. Is it flush with the rest of the bottom of the joint? _____ **Yes** _____ **No**

B. Is it loose? _____ **Yes** _____ **No**

_____ 3. Position the floor jack correctly for testing. Describe: _____

_____

_____ 4. Locate and record the specification for axial play:

load-carrying = _____ follower = _____

_____ 5. Locate and record the specification for lateral play:

load-carrying = _____ follower = _____

_____ 6. Test both load-carrying and follower ball joints on both the left and the right side and record your results.

	Left	Right
Load-Carrying	_____	_____
Follower	_____	_____

OK _____ **NOT OK** _____

Ball-Joint Replacement

Meets NATEF Task: (A4-C-1.5) Remove, Inspect and Install Upper and/or Lower Ball Joints
(P-2)

Name _____ Date _____

Make/Model _____ Year _____ Instructor's OK [   ]

_____ 1. Check the service information and determine the specified ball-joint replacement
procedure. _____
_____

_____ 2. What special tools are needed? _____

_____ 3. A commonly recommended procedure includes:

_____ Hoist the vehicle safely.

_____ Remove the wheel/tire assembly.

_____ Remove the cotter key retaining
the ball-joint stud nut.

_____ Remove the ball-joint stud nut.

_____ Separate the ball-joint from the
control arm (or knuckle) following
the service information procedure
and tool(s).

_____ Using a C-clamp-shaped tool with
the proper adapter, press the ball-
joint from the control arm.

_____ 4. Show the instructor the removed ball-joint.

Instructor's OK _____

_____ 5. Replace the ball-joint using the proper adapters.

_____ 6. Reinstall the control arm (or knuckle) and reattach the ball-joint. Install the ball-joint
stud nut and torque to specifications.   Specifications = _____ lb.-ft.

_____ 7. Install a new cotter key.

NOTE: The vehicle wheels should be aligned after replacing the ball-joints.

Steering Knuckle Diagnosis

Meets NATEF Task: (A4-C-1.6) Remove, Inspect, and Install Steering Knuckle
Assemblies (P-3)

Name _____ Date _____

Make/Model _____ Year _____ Instructor's OK [ ]

_____ **1.** Check the service information for the specified procedure to follow to determine if the
steering knuckle is damaged or bent.

_____

_____

_____

The distance between the rotor and
the steering knuckle should be the
same on both sides of the vehicle.
Dimension "A" checks if the
steering arm is bent, and dimension
"B" checks if the spindle is bent.

Rotor
Steering Arm

B

A

_____ **2.** Because the steering arm and the steering knuckle are often an integral part, determine
the specified toe out on turn (TOOT).

Outside wheel = _____   Inside wheel = _____

_____ **3.** Measure the left and right side toe out on turns.

Left = _____   Right = _____

_____ **4.** Based on the inspection, what action is needed? _____

_____

Steering Knuckle Replacement

Meets NATEF Task: (A4-C-1.6) Remove, Inspect, and Install Steering Knuckle Assemblies (P-3)

Name _____ Date _____

Make/Model _____ Year _____ Instructor's OK [ ]

_____ **1.** Check the service information and determine the specified procedure.

_____

_____

_____ **2.** List the tools needed. _____

_____

_____ **3.** Show the instructor the removed steering knuckle. **Instructor's OK** _____

_____ **4.** List the torque specifications for all fasteners. _____

_____

_____ **5.** After replacing the steering knuckle assembly, the wheel alignment should be checked and corrected.

Coil Spring Replacement

Meets NATEF Task: (A4-C-1.7) Remove, Inspect, and Install Short and Long Arm Suspension Systems, Coil Springs, and Spring Insulators (P-2)

Name _____ Date _____

Make/Model _____ Year _____ Instructor's OK [   ]

_____ 1. Check the service information and determine the specified procedure for removing and installing front coil springs.

_____

_____

_____

_____

_____ 2. List the tools needed.

_____

_____

_____

_____

_____

_____ 3. List all precautions stated in the service information.

_____

_____

_____ 4. Show the instructor the removed spring(s).

Instructor's OK _____

_____ 5. List the torque specifications for the fasteners.

_____

_____

_____

COIL SPRING

FRAME

ISOLATOR

COIL SPRING

CONTROL ARM

Torsion Bar

Meets NATEF Task: (A4-C-1.8) Remove, Inspect, Install, and Adjust Suspension System
Torsion Bars; Inspect Mounts (P-3)

Name _____ Date _____

Make/Model _____ Year _____ Instructor's OK [ ]

_____ **1.** Check the service information for the specified removal and reinstallation procedure.

_____
_____
_____
_____

_____ **2.** List the tools needed.

_____
_____
_____
_____
_____

_____ **3.** Check the service information and describe the proper ride height adjustment procedure.

_____
_____
_____
_____
_____

TORSION BAR

TORSION BAR · ANCHOR ARM · SWIVEL · LOWER CONTROL ARM · HEIGHT ADJUSTMENT BOLT

_____ **4.** Inspect the torsion bar mounts.

OK ____   NOT OK ____

Describe the faults and needed action.

_____
_____

Stabilizer Bar Bushings

Meets NATEF Task: (A4-C-1.9) Remove, Inspect, and Install Stabilizer Bar Bushings, Brackets, and Links (P-2)

Name _____ Date _____

Make/Model _____ Year _____ Instructor's OK [ ]

_____ **1.** Check the service information and determine the specified procedure for replacing stabilizer bar bushings.

_____

_____

NOTE: Most vehicle manufacturers recommend that the bushings on both sides of the vehicle be replaced even if the bushings on only one side are worn or damaged.

_____ **2.** List any special tools needed. _____

_____

_____ **3.** List the torque specifications for the fasteners. _____

_____

_____ **4.** Check the brackets and links.　　**OK** _____　　**NOT OK** _____

If not OK, describe the condition and the action needed. _____

_____

_____

MacPherson Strut Service

Meets NATEF Task: (A4-C-1.10) Remove, Inspect, and Install Strut Cartridge or Assembly, Strut Coil Spring, Insulators (Silencers), and Upper Strut Bearing Mount (P-1)

Name _____ Date _____

Make/Model _____ Year _____ Instructor's OK [   ]

_____ 1. Check the service information for the specified service procedure.

_____

_____

_____

_____ 2. Safely support the vehicle on jacks and/or the lift.

_____ 3. Remove the upper and lower attaching bolts and nuts.

_____ 4. Carefully remove the MacPherson strut assembly from the vehicle.

_____ 5. Compress the coil spring with the proper equipment and replace the strut assembly.

Show the instructor the disassembled unit.

Instructor's OK _____

_____ 6. Reinstall the complete assembly.

NOTE: The vehicle should be aligned after replacing the strut assembly.

STRUT COVER

UPPER SPRING SEAT

DUST COVER

COIL SPRING

LATERAL LINK

TRAILING LINK

Suspension and Steering Lubrication

Meets NATEF Task: (A4-C-1.11) Lubricate Suspension and Steering
System (P-2)

Name _____ Date _____

Make/Model _____ Year _____ Instructor's OK [   ]

_____ **1.** Check the service information regarding lubrication points. Describe the location.

_____

_____

_____ **2.** What is the specified grease or lubricant? _____

_____

_____ **3.** How many sealed ball and socket joints are there that do not require lubrication?

_____

Rear Coil Springs

Meets NATEF Task: (A4-C-2.1) Remove, Inspect, and Install Coil Springs and
Spring Insulators (P-2)

Name _____   Date _____

Make/Model _____   Year _____   Instructor's OK [   ]

_____ 1. Check the service information for the specified rear coil spring removal and
installation procedure.

_____

_____

_____

FRAME

TRAILING
ARM

HANGER
BRACKET

_____ 2. List the tools and equipment needed as specified by the vehicle manufacturer.

_____

_____

_____

_____ 3. Show the instructor the removed coil spring(s). **Instructor's OK** _____

_____ 4. List all safety precautions. _____

_____

_____ 5. List the torque specifications for all fasteners. _____

_____

Transverse Suspension Links

Meets NATEF Task: (A4-C-2.2) Remove, Inspect, and Install Transverse Links, Control Arms, Bushings, and Mounts (P-2)

Name _____ **Date** _____

Make/Model _____ **Year** _____ **Instructor's OK** ☐

_____ **1.** Check the service information for the specified procedure to remove and replace transverse (lateral) links, bushings, and mounts.

_____

_____

_____

PIVOT BOLT — DIAGONAL BRACE — PANHARD ROD — BEAM AXLE — PIVOT BOLT

_____ **2.** List the tools and equipment needed. _____

_____

_____ **3.** Show the instructor the removed transverse link. **Instructor's OK** _____

_____ **4.** List the tightening torque specifications for the affected fasteners. _____

_____

Rear Leaf Springs

Meets NATEF Task: (A4-C-2.3) Remove, Inspect, and Install Leaf Springs, Leaf Spring
Insulators (silencers), Shackles, Brackets, Bushings, and Mounts (P-3)

Name _____ Date _____

Make/Model _____ Year _____ Instructor's OK [ ]

_____ 1. Check the service information for the specified procedure for the removal and
reinstallation of rear leaf springs.

_____

_____

_____

_____ 2. List the tools and equipment needed. _____

_____

_____ 3. Show the instructor the removed rear leaf spring(s). **Instructor's OK** _____

_____ 4. List the tightening torque specifications for the affected fasteners. _____

_____

Rear Strut Replacement

Meets NATEF Task: (A4-C-2.4) Remove, Inspect, and Install Strut Cartridge or Assembly, Strut Coil Spring, and Insulators (Silencers) (P-2)

Name _____ Date _____

Make/Model _____ Year _____ Instructor's OK [   ]

_____ 1. Check the service information for the specified procedure for the removal and reinstallation of rear struts.

_____

_____

_____

_____ 2. List the tools and equipment

needed. _____

_____

_____

_____

_____ 3. Show the instructor the removed

rear strut.

Instructor's OK _____

_____ 4. List the tightening torque

specifications for the affected

fasteners. _____

_____

_____

_____

_____

STRUT COVER

UPPER SPRING SEAT

DUST COVER

COIL SPRING

LATERAL LINK

TRAILING LINK

Front Shock Absorber Replacement

Meets NATEF Task: (A4-C-3.1) Inspect, Remove, and Replace
Shock Absorbers (P-1)

Name _____   Date _____

Make/Model _____   Year _____   Instructor's OK [   ]

_____ **1.** Verify that the front shock absorber requires replacement. Check all that apply:

        _____ bent or damaged shock or mounting hardware
        _____ shock absorber is leaking hydraulic fluid
        _____ excessively worn - causing tire wear or riding comfort problems
        _____ other (specify) _____

_____ **2.** Compare the replacement shocks to the original shocks to be sure that they are correct.
    OK _____   **NOT OK** _____

    NOTE: All shock absorbers should be replaced in pairs only. Do not replace just one shock absorber.

_____ **3.** Check the service information for the specified replacement procedure. _____
    _____
    _____

    HINT: Many shocks on rear-wheel-drive vehicles can be broken off using a deep-well socket and a long extension. By rocking the extension back and forth, the top of the shock will usually break off saving the time and effort it takes to remove a nut that is often rusted in place after many years of service.

_____ **4.** Safely hoist the vehicle.

_____ **5.** Remove the lower shock absorber retaining bolts (nuts) as per the service information instructions..

    CAUTION: Be ready to catch the shock absorber because it will likely fall after removing the last retaining bolt (nut).

_____ **6.** Show the instructor the removed shock absorber. **Instructor's OK** _____

_____ **7.** Extend the rod on the replacement shock and install the lower retaining bolts (nuts).

_____ **8.** Lower the vehicle and install the upper retaining fastener.

_____ **9.** Bounce the vehicle to check that the replacement shock does not interfere with any part of the suspension or frame.

_____ **10.** Test drive the vehicle before returning it to the customer.

Rear Shock Absorber Replacement

Meets NATEF Task: (A4-C-3.1) Inspect, Remove, and Replace
Shock Absorbers (P-1)

Name _____ Date _____

Make/Model _____ Year _____ Instructor's OK

_____ **1.** Verify that the front shock absorber requires replacement. Check all that apply:

     _____ bent or damaged shock or mounting hardware
     _____ shock absorber is leaking hydraulic fluid
     _____ excessively worn - causing tire wear or riding comfort problems
     _____ other (specify) _____

_____ **2.** Compare the replacement shocks to the original shocks to be sure that they are correct.
OK _____ **NOT OK** _____

     NOTE: All shock absorbers should be replaced in pairs only. Do not replace just one shock absorber.

_____ **3.** Check the service information for the specified replacement procedure. _____

_____

     NOTE: The upper shock mount may be located in the trunk or underneath the vehicle.

_____ **4.** Safely hoist the vehicle.

_____ **5.** Use tall safety stands to support the rear axle assembly.

_____ **6.** Remove the lower shock absorber retaining bolts (nuts).
     CAUTION: Be ready to catch the shock absorber because it will likely fall after removing the last retaining bolt (nut).

_____ **7.** Show the instructor the removed shock absorber. **Instructor's OK** _____

_____ **8.** Extend the rod on the replacement shock and install the lower retaining bolts (nuts).

_____ **9.** Lower the vehicle and install the upper retaining fastener.

_____ **10.** Bounce the vehicle to check that the replacement shock does not interfere with any part of the suspension or frame.

_____ **11.** Test drive the vehicle before returning it to the customer.

Wheel Bearing Service

Meets NATEF Task: (A4-C-3.2) Remove, Inspect, and Service or Replace Front and Rear Wheel Bearings (P-1)

Name _____ Date _____

Make/Model _____ Year _____ Instructor's OK [ ]

_____ 1. Remove the wheel cover and the hub dust cap (grease cap).

_____ 2. Remove and discard the cotter key.

_____ 3. Remove the spindle nut, washer and outer bearing.

_____ 4. Remove inner and outer bearing and grease seal.

_____ 5. Thoroughly clean the bearing in solvent and denatured alcohol or brake cleaner and blow it dry with compressed air.

_____ 6. Closely inspect the bearing for wear or damage.

_____ 7. Show the instructor the cleaned bearing.   **Instructor's OK** _____

_____ 8. Repack the bearing with the correct type of wheel bearing grease.

_____ 9. Install a new grease seal using a seal installing tool.

_____ 10. Correctly adjust the bearing preload:

_____ Install the spindle nut and while rotating the tire assembly, tighten (snug only, 12 to 30 lb.-ft.) with a wrench to "seat" the bearing correctly in the race.
_____ While still rotating the tire assembly, loosen the nut approximately 1/2 turn and then *hand tighten only*.
_____ Install a new cotter key (the common size is 1/8" diameter and 1.5 inches long).
_____ Bend the ends of the cotter key up and around the nut to prevent interference with the dust cap.

_____ 11. Install the hub dust cap (grease cap) and wheel cover.

Electronic Suspension Diagnosis

Meets NATEF Task: (A4-C-3.3) Test and Diagnose Components of Electronically Controlled Suspension Systems Using a Scan Tool; Determine Necessary Action (P-3)

Name _____ Date _____

Make/Model _____ Year _____ Instructor's OK [ ]

_____ **1.** Check the service information and determine the specified testing procedures.

_____

_____

_____

_____ **2.** Check the service information and compare normal scan tool readings of the electronically controlled suspension system to the actual readings obtained from the vehicle.

Parameter	Normal Reading	Actual Reading
_____	_____	_____
_____	_____	_____
_____	_____	_____
_____	_____	_____
_____	_____	_____
_____	_____	_____
_____	_____	_____
_____	_____	_____

_____ **3.** Based on the service information and the scan tool data, what is the necessary action?

_____

_____

_____

Steering and Suspension Concerns

Meets NATEF Task: (A4-D-1) Differentiate Between Steering and Suspension Concerns
Using Principles of Steering Geometry (Caster, Camber, Toe, etc.) (P-1)

Name _____ Date _____

Make/Model _____ Year _____ Instructor's OK [ ]

_____ **1.** Check the service information to determine the alignment specifications.

Camber = _____   Caster = _____   Toe = _____

_____ **2.** Hoist the vehicle on the alignment rack and install the wheel sensors.

_____ **3.** Compensate the wheel sensors.

_____ **4.** Lower the vehicle and jounce (bounce) to center the suspension.

_____ **5.** Read the rear camber and toe.

	LR	RR
Camber	_____	_____
Toe	_____	_____

Total rear toe = _____

_____ **6.** Read the front camber and toe.

	LF	RF
Camber	_____	_____
Toe	_____	_____

Total front toe = _____

_____ **7.** Perform a caster sweep to determine the front caster and SAI.

	LF	RF
Caster	_____	_____
SAI	_____	_____

Based on the alignment angles, what action is needed? _____

_____

_____

Vehicle Handling Diagnosis

Meets NATEF Task: (A4-D-2) Diagnose Vehicle Wander, Drift, Hard Steering, Bump Steer, Memory Steer, Torque Steer, and Steering Return Concerns; Determine Necessary Action (P-1)

Name _____ Date _____

Make/Model _____ Year _____ Instructor's OK [＿＿＿]

_____ **1.** Test drive the vehicle and check all of the following.

OK ____ NOT OK ____ Wander (unstable)

OK ____ NOT OK ____ Drift (pulls slightly to one side)

OK ____ NOT OK ____ Hard steering

OK ____ NOT OK ____ Bump steer (The vehicle travels left or right by itself, while driving without steering wheel input. Usually caused by unlevel steering linkage.)

OK ____ NOT OK ____ Memory steer (The vehicle pulls to the right after a right turn and pulls to the left after a left turn. Usually caused by a defective strut upper mount or stiff ball-joints.)

OK ____ NOT OK ____ Torque steer (front-wheel-drive vehicle only) (accelerates rapidly) (Does the vehicle pull to one side? Often caused by unequal tire pressures or a collapsed engine or transaxle mount.)

OK ____ NOT OK ____ Steering wheel returnability

_____ **2.** Based on the test drive, what actions are necessary to correct the concerns?

_____

_____

_____

_____

Pre-Alignment Inspection

Meets NATEF Task: (A4-D-3) Perform Prealignment Inspection; Perform Necessary Action (P-1)

Name _____ **Date** _____

Make/Model _____ **Year** _____ **Instructor's OK** ☐

_____ **1.** Check tires. Both front tires and both rear tires should be checked for the following:

    A. Correct tire pressure

    B. Same size and brand

    C. Same tread depth

    OK _____   **NOT OK** _____

_____ **2.** Perform a dry-park test to check for any looseness in the steering and suspension components such as:

    A. Tie rods

    B. Idler arms

    C. Ball-joints

    D. Control arm bushings

    E. Loose or defective wheel bearings

    OK _____   **NOT OK** _____

_____ **3.** Check for proper ride height.

    A. Front and rear

    B. Left and right

    OK _____   **NOT OK** _____

Alignment Specification

Meets NATEF Task: (A4-D-1 through 14) Necessary Information Needed to Perform
the Tasks Listed

Name _____ Date _____

Make/Model _____ Year _____ Instructor's OK [ ]

_____ **1.** Find the following alignment angle specifications for your vehicle:

Camber (left) preferred = _____ minimum _____ maximum _____

Camber (right) preferred = _____ minimum _____ maximum _____

Caster (left) preferred = _____ minimum _____ maximum _____

Caster (right) preferred = _____ minimum _____ maximum _____

Front toe preferred = _____ minimum _____ maximum _____

Rear camber preferred = _____ minimum _____ maximum _____

Total rear toe preferred = _____ minimum _____ maximum _____

_____ **2.** Determine the diagnostic angle specifications for your vehicle:

Toe-out on turn (TOOT) inside wheel = _____ degrees

outside wheel = _____ degrees

Maximum allowable variation = _____ degrees

Steering axis inclination (SAI) left = _____

right = _____

Maximum allowable difference = _____

Alignment Angle Readings

Meets NATEF Task: (A4-D-1 through 14) Necessary Information Needed to Perform the
Tasks Listed

Name _____ Date _____

Make/Model _____ Year _____ Instructor's OK [ ]

_____ 1. Hoist the vehicle on the alignment rack and install the wheel sensors.

_____ 2. Compensate the wheel sensors as per the alignment equipment manufacturer's
recommended procedure.

_____ 3. Lower the vehicle and jounce (bounce) to center the suspension.

_____ 4. Read the rear camber and toe.

	LR	RR
Camber	_____	_____
Toe	_____	_____
Total rear toe =	_____	

_____ 5. Read the front camber and toe.

	LF	RF
Camber	_____	_____
Toe	_____	_____
Total front toe =	_____	

_____ 6. Perform a caster sweep to determine the front caster and SAI.

	LF	RF
Caster	_____	_____
SAI	_____	_____

Describe what (if anything) is wrong with the present alignment.

_____

Ride Height Measurement

Meets NATEF Task: (A4-D-4) Measure Vehicle Riding Height; Determine Necessary Action
(P-1)

___

Name _____ Date _____

Make/Model _____ Year _____ Instructor's OK [　　]

_____ **1.** Check the service information or the chart in the appendix of this worktext and determine the specified vehicle riding height.

Specification for front = _____

Specification for rear = _____

_____ **2.** Measure the actual vehicle riding height.

Actual front = _____

Actual rear   = _____

OK _____ **NOT OK** _____ Describe the faults: _____

_____

_____ **3.** What necessary action is needed to restore proper riding height? _____

_____

_____

Front and Rear Camber

Meets NATEF Task: (A4-D-5) Check and Adjust Front and Rear Wheel Camber; Perform Necessary Action (P-1)

Name _____ Date _____

Make/Model _____ Year _____ Instructor's OK [   ]

_____ 1. Check with the service information and determine the specified camber angle for both front and rear wheels.

CAMBER

Front camber specification = _____

Rear camber specification = _____

POSITIVE   NEGATIVE

_____ 2. Following the alignment equipment manufacturer's recommended procedure, measure the camber angles.

	Left	Right
Rear camber	_____	_____
Front camber	_____	_____

_____ 3. Check the service information to determine the specified method for changing the rear and front camber angles.

Method	Rear Camber	Front Camber
No factory adjustment provided	_____	_____
Shims	_____	_____
Eccentric cams	_____	_____
Slots	_____	_____
Other (specify) _____	_____	_____

_____ 4. Perform the necessary camber angle adjustment to achieve specified camber angles for both front and rear wheels.

Check and Adjust Caster

Meets NATEF Task: (A4-D-6) Check and Adjust Caster; Perform
Necessary Action (P-1)

Name _____ Date _____

Make/Model _____ Year _____ Instructor's OK [   ]

_____ 1. Check the service information and determine the specified caster setting.

   Caster specification = _____

_____ 2. Following the alignment equipment manufacturer's
   recommended procedure, measure the caster
   angles.

   Left side actual caster angle = _____

   Right side actual caster angle = _____

_____ 3. Check the service information to determine the
   specified method for changing the caster angle(s).

   _____ No factory adjustment method is
      provided

   _____ Strut rods

   _____ Shims

   _____ Eccentric cams

   _____ Slots

_____ 4. Perform the necessary caster angle adjustment to
   achieve the specified angles on both front wheels.

ZERO CASTER

POSITIVE CASTER

NEGATIVE CASTER

Front Wheel Toe

Meets NATEF Task: (A4-D-7) Check and Adjust Front Wheel Toe; Adjust as Needed (P-1)

Name _____ **Date** _____

Make/Model _____ **Year** _____ **Instructor's OK** [ ]

_____ 1. Check the service information and determine the specified toe setting.

Front wheel toe specification = _____

_____ 2. Following the alignment equipment manufacturer's recommended procedure, measure the front wheel toe.

Left wheel toe = _____

Right wheel toe = _____

Total toe = _____

ZERO TOE

FRONT OF CAR

_____ 3. Check the service information to determine the specified method for changing front toe.

_____ Tie rod sleeve (one side only provided)

_____ Tie rod sleeves (one for each side)

_____ Lock nut and threaded tie rod

TOE-IN

TOE-OUT

_____ 4. Perform the necessary front wheel toe adjustment to achieve the specified toe angle on both front wheels and total toe.

Centering the Steering Wheel

Meets NATEF Task: (A4-D-8) Center Steering Wheel (P-1)

Name _____ **Date** _____

Make/Model _____ **Year** _____ **Instructor's OK** [ ]

_____ **1.** Check the service information for the specified method for centering the steering wheel.

        _____ Remove the steering wheel and reinstall.

        _____ Adjust the tie rods to straighten the steering wheel and maintain proper toe adjustment.

_____ **2.** Check the service information for the specified tolerance for centering the steering wheel. Most vehicle manufacturers recommend that the spoke angle be straight within ± 3°.

        Specified tolerance = _____

_____ **3.** Test drive the vehicle and mark the steering wheel or column with masking tape when the recommended vehicle is traveling straight on a straight, level road. How much out of align is the steering wheel?

        _____

_____ **4.** Following the alignment equipment manufacturer's recommended procedure, adjust the tie rods until the steering wheel is straight and the front toe is still within factory specifications.

Four-Wheel Alignment

Meets NATEF Tasks: (A4-D-1 through 14) Check Alignment Angle and Perform
Necessary Actions (P-1s)

Name _____ Date _____

Make/Model _____ Year _____ Instructor's OK [   ]

Specifications:	**Left**	**Right**
Camber	_____	_____
Caster	_____	_____
Toe (Total)	_____	
KPI/SAI	_____	
Rear Camber	_____	_____
Rear Toe	_____	_____
Rear Toe (Total)	_____	

Methods of Adjustment:

	Front	**Rear**
Camber	_____	_____
Caster	_____	
Toe	_____	_____

Reading Before Alignment: (Record here and attach the print out.)

	Left	**Right**
Camber	_____	_____
Caster	_____	_____
Toe (Total)	_____	
KPI/SAI	_____	
Rear Camber	_____	_____
Rear Toe	_____	
Thrust	_____	
Set Back	_____	

Reading After Alignment: (Record here and attach the print out.)

	Left	**Right**
Camber	_____	_____
Caster	_____	_____
Toe (Total)	_____	
KPI/SAI	_____	
Rear Camber	_____	_____
Rear Toe	_____	
Thrust	_____	
Set Back	_____	

Toe Out on Turns

Meets NATEF Tasks: (A4-D-9) Check Toe-Out-On Turns (Turning Radius); Determine
Necessary Action (P-2)

Name _____ Date _____

Make/Model _____ Year _____ Instructor's OK [   ]

_____ 1. Check the service information and determine the testing procedure and specifications
for toe out on turns.

     A. Testing procedure _____

         _____

     B. Specifications _____

_____ 2. Following the alignment equipment manufacturer's recommended procedure, measure
the left and right side toe-out-on-turns.

     Left side = _____

     Right side = _____

     OK ____   NOT OK ____

_____ 3. If the reading does not fall within the manufacturer's specifications, what action is
necessary?

_____

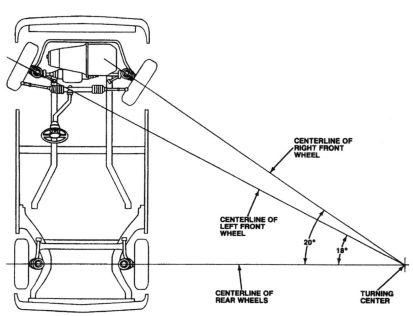

Steering Axis Inclination

Meets NATEF Tasks: (A4-D-10) Check SAI (Steering Axis Inclination) and Included Angle;
Determine Necessary Action (P-2)

Name _____ Date _____

Make/Model _____ Year _____ Instructor's OK [ ]

_____ 1. Check the service information and determine the specifications for SAI and included angle.

SAI = _____
Included angle = _____

_____ 2. Following the alignment equipment manufacturer's recommended procedure, measure the SAI and included angles.

Left SAI   = _____
Right SAI   = _____
Left included angle   = _____
Right included angle = _____
OK ____   NOT OK ____

_____ 3. Check the service information or the chart and determine necessary action if the SAI and/or included angle are not within factory specifications.

DIAGNOSING SAI, CAMBER, AND INCLUDED ANGLE			
SLA AND STRUT/SLA SUSPENSIONS			
SAI	**CAMBER**	**INCLUDED ANGLE**	**DIAGNOSIS**
CORRECT	LESS THAN SPECS	LESS THAN SPECS OR SPINDLE	BENT STEERING KNUCKLE
LESS THAN SPECS	GREATER THAN SPECS	CORRECT	BENT LOWER CONTROL ARM
LESS THAN SPECS	GREATER THAN SPECS	GREATER THAN SPECS	BENT LOWER CONTROL ARM AND STEERING KNUCKLE OR SPINDLE
GREATER THAN SPECS	LESS THAN SPECS	CORRECT	BENT UPPER CONTROL ARM
STRUT SUSPENSIONS			
SAI	**CAMBER**	**INCLUDED ANGLE**	**DIAGNOSIS**
CORRECT	LESS THAN SPECS	LESS THAN SPECS	BENT SPINDLE AND/OR STRUT
CORRECT	GREATER THAN SPECS	GREATER THAN SPECS	BENT SPINDLE AND/OR STRUT
LESS THAN SPECS	GREATER THAN SPECS	CORRECT	BENT CONTROL ARM OR STRUT TOWER OUT AT TOP
LESS THAN SPECS	GREATER THAN SPECS	GREATER THAN SPECS	BENT CONTROL ARM OR STRUT TOWER OUT AT TOP, ALSO BENT SPINDLE AND/OR STRUT
LESS THAN SPECS	LESS THAN SPECS	LESS THAN SPECS	BENT CONTROL ARM OR STRUT TOWER OUT AT TOP, ALSO BENT SPINDLE AND/OR STRUT
GREATER THAN SPECS	LESS THAN SPECS	CORRECT	STRUT TOWER IN AT TOP
GREATER THAN SPECS	GREATER THAN SPECS	GREATER THAN SPECS	STRUT TOWER IN AT TOP AND BENT SPINDLE AND/OR BENT STRUT
KINGPIN TWIN I-BEAM SUSPENSION			
SAI(KPI)	**CAMBER**	**INCLUDED ANGLE**	**DIAGNOSIS**
CORRECT	GREATER THAN SPECS	GREATER THAN SPECS	BENT SPINDLE
LESS THAN SPECS	GREATER THAN SPECS	CORRECT	BENT I-BEAM
LESS THAN SPECS	GREATER THAN SPECS	GREATER THAN SPECS	BENT I-BEAM AND SPINDLE
GREATER THAN SPECS	LESS THAN SPECS	CORRECT	BENT I-BEAM

Rear Wheel Toe

Meets NATEF Tasks: (A4-D-11) Check and Adjust Rear Wheel Toe (P-2)

Name _____ Date _____

Make/Model _____ Year _____ Instructor's OK [   ]

_____ **1.** Check the service information and determine the specifications for rear wheel toe.

      Total rear wheel toe specification = _____

      Left rear wheel toe specification = _____

      Right rear wheel toe specification = _____

_____ **2.** Follow the alignment equipment manufacturer's recommended procedure and measure the rear wheel toe.

REAR TOE ADJUSTMENT

      Left rear wheel toe   = _____

      Right rear wheel toe   = _____

      Total rear wheel toe   = _____

      OK _____   **NOT OK** _____

_____ **3.** Check the service information for the recommended rear wheel toe adjustment procedure.

      _____ Adjusting sleeves

      _____ Threaded tie rod(s)

      _____ Shims

      _____ Transverse (lateral) link adjustment

      _____ No factory adjustment

      _____ Other (describe) _____

_____ **4.** Adjust the rear wheel toe, if possible. Final toe readings:

      Left rear wheel toe = _____

      Right rear wheel toe = _____

Rear Wheel Thrust Angle

Meets NATEF Tasks: (A4-D-12) Check Rear Wheel Thrust Angle; Determine Necessary Action (P-2)

Name _____ Date _____

Make/Model _____ Year _____ Instructor's OK [ ]

_____ 1. Check the service information and determine the specification or tolerance for the rear wheel thrust angle.

Rear wheel thrust angle specification (tolerance) = _____

_____ 2. Following the alignment equipment manufacturer's recommended procedure, measure the rear thrust angle.

Rear thrust angle = _____

Positive (right) ? _____

Negative (left) ? _____

_____ 3. Check the service information and determine needed action. The difference in rear toe causes rear thrust angle, and therefore, the rear toe can often be adjusted to bring the thrust angle into specifications.

Rear toe adjustable? **Yes** _____ **No** _____

If the rear toe is not adjustable, determine what action is necessary to correct the rear thrust angle that is not within factory specifications.

_____

_____

Front Wheel Setback

Meets NATEF Tasks: (A4-D-13) Check for Front Wheel Setback; Determine
Necessary Action (P-2)

Name _____ **Date** _____

Make/Model _____ **Year** _____ **Instructor's OK** [   ]

_____ 1. Check the service information and determine the specification or tolerance for front
wheel setback.

   Specification (tolerance) for front wheel setback = _____

_____ 2. Following the alignment equipment manufacturer's recommended procedure, measure
the front wheel setback.

   Front wheel setback = _____

   OK _____ **NOT OK** _____

_____ 3. Consult the service information and
determine the necessary action, if the
front wheel setback is not within
specifications.

   _____

   _____

   _____

   _____

   _____

   _____

MEASURED IN DEGREES
FROM STRAIGHT ACROSS

RIGHT
WHEEL
SETBACK

0°

MEASURED
IN INCHES
BEHIND
LEFT WHEEL

Front Cradle Alignment

Meets NATEF Tasks: (A4-D-14) Check Front Cradle (Subframe) Alignment;
Determine Necessary Action (P-3)

Name _____ Date _____

Make/Model _____ Year _____ Instructor's OK [＿＿]

_____ 1. Check the service information and determine the procedure for checking front cradle alignment.

_____

_____

_____

_____ 2. Following the alignment equipment manufacturer's recommended procedure, measure the left side and right side camber, included angle, and SAI.

Left camber = _____ Right camber = _____

Left included angle = _____ Right included angle = _____

Left SAI = _____ Right SAI = _____

Most vehicle manufacturers specify that these angles be within 0.5 degrees of each other left to right.

OK _____ **NOT OK** _____

_____ 3. Check the service information and determine the necessary action to align the front cradle.

_____

_____

_____

Tire Wear Patterns

Meets NATEF Tasks: (A4-E-1) Diagnose Tire Wear Patterns;
Determine Necessary Action (P-1)

Name _____ Date _____

Make/Model _____ Year _____ Instructor's OK [   ]

_____ **1.** Hoist the vehicle safely.

_____ **2.** Inspect all four tires for the
following conditions:

    A. Excessive tire wear   **OK** ____   **NOT OK** ____

    B. Unequal tire wear on one side (incorrect camber or toe problem)
           OK ____   **NOT OK** ____

    C. Excessive wear in center of tread (overinflation)
           OK ____   **NOT OK** ____

    D. Excessive wear on both outside sides (underinflation)
           OK ____   **NOT OK** ____

    E. Cuts, bruises, or other physical damage (describe) _____
    _____ **OK** ____   **NOT OK** ____

_____ **3.** Determine necessary action. _____

_____

Tire Inspection and Inflation

Meets NATEF Tasks: (A4-E-2) Inspect Tires; Check and Adjust Air Pressure (P-1)

Name _____ Date _____

Make/Model _____ Year _____ Instructor's OK [   ]

_____ 1. Check the tire information placard on the driver's door or pillar and determine the recommended air pressure.

Recommended air pressure for front tires = _____

Recommended air pressure for rear tires = _____

Recommended air pressure for spare tire = _____

_____ 2. Check the air pressure on all of the tires and record the pressures.

Left front = _____

Right front = _____

Right rear = _____

Left rear = _____

Spare tire = _____

_____ 3. Visually check the tires for damage or excessive wear.

OK ____   **NOT OK** ____

_____ 4. Adjust the air pressures as needed.

Wheel/Tire Vibration Diagnosis

Meets NATEF Tasks: (A4-E-3) Diagnose Wheel/Tire Vibration, Shimmy, and Noise; Determine Necessary Action (P-2)

Name _____ Date _____

Make/Model _____ Year _____ Instructor's OK [ ]

_____ **1.** Test drive the vehicle and determine the following:

      Yes ___ **No** ___   Vibration is felt in steering wheel while driving.

      Yes ___ **No** ___   Vibration is felt in the seat while driving.

      Yes ___ **No** ___   Steering wheel shimmy is felt (back and forth motion).

      Yes ___ **No** ___   Excessive tire noise is heard.

_____ **2.** Check the service information for the specified steps to reduce or eliminate vibration due to wheels or tires.

    _____

    _____

    _____

_____ **3.** Perform a visual inspection and check all of the tires and wheels for excessive wear or damage.

      OK ___ **NOT OK** ___

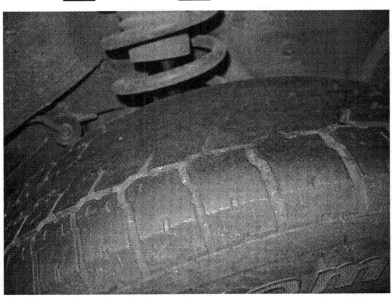

Tire Rotation

Meets NATEF Tasks: (A4-E-4) Rotate Tires According to Manufacturer's
Recommendations (P-1)

Name _____ **Date** _____

Make/Model _____ **Year** _____ **Instructor's OK** [   ]

_____ **1.** Check the service information for the recommended tire rotation method.

        _____ Cannot rotate tires on this vehicle
        _____ Modified X method
        _____ X method
        _____ Front to rear and rear to front

_____ **2.** Hoist the vehicle safely to a good working position (chest level).

_____ **3.** Remove the wheels and rotate them (if possible) according to the vehicle
manufacturer's recommendation.

_____ **4.** Check and correct the tire air pressures according to the service information on the
placard on the driver's door.

     Specified front tire air pressure = _____

     Specified rear tire air pressure = _____

_____ **5.** Lower the vehicle and move the hoist pads before driving the vehicle out of the
service stall.

Tire Runout Measurement

Meets NATEF Tasks: (A4-E-5) Measure Wheel, Tire, Axle, and Hub Runout;
Determine Necessary Action (P-2)

Name _____ Date _____

Make/Model _____ Year _____ Instructor's OK ☐

_____ **1.** Safely hoist the vehicle until all 4 tires are approximately 2" (5 cm) off the ground.

_____ **2.** Determine the specifications for radial and lateral runout.

Specification for radial runout = _____ (usually less than 0.060 inch).

Specification for lateral runout = _____ (usually less than 0.045 inch).

_____ **3.** Using a runout gauge, rotate the tire and record the radial runout (roundness of the tires) and the lateral runout (side-to-side movement) of the tires.

> **HINT:** Place masking tape over the tread of the tire to provide a smoother surface. This method makes it easier to read the dial indicator, especially on tires with an aggressive tread design.

Tire	Radial Runout	Lateral Runout
R.F.	_____	_____
R.R.	_____	_____
L.F.	_____	_____
L.R.	_____	_____

_____ **4.** Compare the specifications with the results.

OK ____   **NOT OK** ____

_____ **5.** Based on the measurements, what necessary action is needed?

_____

_____

Axle and Hub Runout Measurement

Meets NATEF Tasks: (A4-E-5) Measure Wheel, Tire, Axle, and Hub Runout; Determine Necessary Action (P-2)

Name _____   Date _____

Make/Model _____   Year _____   Instructor's OK [   ]

_____ **1.** Check the service information and determine the specifications for axle and hub runout.

_____

_____ **2.** Hoist the vehicle safely to a good working height (chest level).

_____ **3.** Remove the wheels.

_____ **4.** Using a dial indicator, measure the axle and the hub runout.

Hub runout   = _____   **OK** ____   **NOT OK** ____

Flange runout = _____   **OK** ____   **NOT OK** ____

CHECKING HUB RUNOUT

CHECKING MOUNTING FLANGE RUNOUT

_____ **5.** Check the service information and determine the necessary action. _____

_____

_____

Tire Pull Diagnosis

Meets NATEF Tasks: (A4-E-6) Diagnose Tire Pull (Lead) Problems;
Determine Necessary Action (P-2)

Name _____ Date _____

Make/Model _____ Year _____ Instructor's OK [ ]

_____ 1. Check and correct tire air pressures as per vehicle manufacturer's specifications.

_____ 2. Visually check the tires for faults.

         OK ____ **NOT OK** ____ (replace defective tires)

_____ 3. Test drive the vehicle on a straight, level road.

_____ 4. The vehicle pulls (leads) toward the:

         _____ Right

         _____ Left

_____ 5. A pull or lead can be due to tire conicity or ply steer. To diagnose if the pull or lead is tire related, rotate the front tires to opposite sides of the vehicle.

         OK ____ **NOT OK** ____

_____ 6. If not OK, rotate the rear tires to opposite sides of the vehicle.

         OK ____ **NOT OK** ____

_____ 7. If not OK, rotate the front tires to the rear and the rear tires to the front.

         OK ____ **NOT OK** ____

_____ 8. Based on the tests performed, what action is needed? _____

_____

_____

_____

Tire Balance

Meets NATEF Task: (A4-E-7) Balance Wheel and Tire Assembly
(Static and Dynamic) (P-1)

Name _____ Date _____

Make/Model _____ Year _____ Instructor's OK [　　]

_____ 1. Perform the pre-balance checks.

    A. Check tire pressure.

    B. Remove grease/dirt from inside

       of the rim.

    C. Remove stones from the tread.

_____ 2. Follow the tire balancing equipment
manufacturer's procedures.

_____ 3. Wheel width? _____ in.

_____ 4. Wheel diameter? _____ in.

_____ 5. Check balance before removing old weights.

    HINT: This will help in the diagnosis of a vibration knowing that one or more
wheels were not balanced.

_____ 6. Out of balance with old or no weights:

    inside = _____ outside = _____

_____ 7. Did the tire balance OK?

    OK _____ **NOT OK** _____

    If not OK, explain why: _____

    _____

    _____

Tire Changing

Meets NATEF Task: (A4-E-8) Dismount, Inspect, Repair, and Remount Tire on the Wheel (P-2)

Name _____ Date _____

Make/Model _____ Year _____ Instructor's OK [ ]

_____ 1. Be sure you are wearing approved safety glasses.

_____ 2. Slowly remove the Schrader valve using a tire valve tool and deflate the tire.

_____ 3. Place the tire against the tire changing machine and "break the bead" front and back following the tire machine manufacturer's instructions.

_____ 4. Secure the tire and wheel assembly onto the machine.

_____ 5. Remove the tire from the rim using the proper procedure.

_____ 6. Install the replacement tire on the rim using the proper procedure.

_____ 7. Inflate and seat the tire beads using the procedure.

CAUTION: Do not exceed 40 psi air pressure to seat the tire bead.

_____ 8. Install the valve core and check for leaks.

_____ 9. Inflate the tires to vehicle specifications.

Torque Wheel Lug Nuts

Meets NATEF Task: (A4-E-9) Reinstall Wheel; Torque Lug Nuts (P-1)

Name _____ Date _____

Make/Model _____ Year _____ Instructor's OK [ ]

_____ 1. Determine the vehicle manufacturer's specified lug nut torque specification.

_____ (usually between 80 and 100 lb-ft)

_____ 2. Use a hand-operated wire brush on the wheel studs to ensure clean and dry threads and check for damage.

OK _____ NOT OK _____ Describe fault: _____

_____ 3. Verify that the lug nuts are OK and free of defects.

CAUTION: Some vehicle manufacturers warn to not lubricate the wheel studs because this can cause the lug nuts to loosen while the vehicle is being driven, resulting in personal injury.

_____ 4. Install the wheel over the studs and start all lug nuts (or bolts) by hand.

_____ 5. Tighten the lug nuts a little at a time in a star pattern using an air impact wrench equipped with the proper torque limiting adapter or a torque wrench.

_____ Used a torque wrench

_____ Used an air impact with a torque limiting adapter

_____ 6. Tighten the lug nuts to final torque in a star pattern.

NOTE: "Tighten one, skip one, tighten one" is the usual method if four or five lug nuts are used.

Tire Repair

Meets NATEF Task: (A4-E-10) Inspect and Repair Tire (P-2)

Name _____ Date _____

Make/Model _____ Year _____ Instructor's OK [ ]

_____ 1. Locate the source of the leak by submerging the tire under water or by spraying the tire with soapy water. Describe the location of the leak.

_____

_____ 2. Remove the foreign object and use a reamer to clean the hole in the tire (tread area only).

_____ 3. Dismount the tire and buff the inside of the tire around the hole.

_____ 4. Apply rubber cement to the buffed area.

_____ 5. Insert the repair plug from the inside of the tire.

_____ 6. Pull the plug through the puncture from the outside of the tire.

_____ 7. Use a stitching tool to make sure the inside of the patch is well adhered to the inside of the tire.

_____ 8. Remove the tire and inflate to the air pressure specified by the vehicle manufacturer.

_____ 9. Check the repair for air leaks using soapy water.

OK ____ **NOT OK** ____

APPENDIX 1

Lut Nut Torque Specifications Chart

LUG NUT TIGHTENING TORQUE CHART

To be used as a guide only. Consult the factory service manual or literature for the exact specifications and exceptions for the vehicle being serviced.

NAME	MODEL	YEARS	LB. FT. TORQUE
Acura	All	86-99	80
American Motors	All	70-87	75
Audi	All	78-99	81
BMW	All except the following	78-99	65-79
	320I	77-83	59-65
	528L	79-81	59-65
Buick	All except the following	76-99	100
	Century	76-81	80
	Regal	78-86	80
	LeSabre	76-85	80
Cadillac	All except 1976 Seville	76-99	100
	Seville	1976	80
Chevrolet	Geo Prizm	92-99	100
	Geo Prizm	89-91	76
	Geo Storm	90-99	86.5
	Sprint	85-88	50
	Spectrum	85-88	65
	Chevette	82-87	80
	Chevette	76-81	70
	Nova	85-89	76
	Vega & Monza	76-80	80
	Cavalier	82-99	100
	Celebrity	82-90	100
	Citation	80-86	100
	Camaro	89-99	100
	Camaro	78-88	80
	Malibu & Monte Carlo	76-88	80
	Malibu Wagon	76-86	80
	Impala & Caprice Sedan	77-90	80
	Caprice	91-93	100

NAME	MODEL	YEARS	LB. FT. TORQUE
	Corvette	84-99	100
	Corvette	76-83	90
	Corsica & Beretta	87-98	100
Chevrolet/GMC Light Trucks & Vans			
	Geo Tracker	92-93	60
	Geo Tracker	89-91	37-58
	Lumina APV	90-99	100
	Astro/Safari Van	85-99	100
	S/10 & S/15 Pickup	80-88	80
	T/10 & T/15 Pickup	88-99	100
	C/K Pickup all except:	88-99	120
	C/K Pickup Dual Rear Wheels	88-99	140
	V10 (4WD Full Size) Suburban & Blazer (Aluminum Wheels)	88-89	100
	V10 (4WD Full Size) Suburban & Blazer (Steel Wheels)	88-89	90
	V10 (4WD Full Size) Suburban (All)	90-99	100
	R10 (2WD Full Size) Suburban & Blazer	1989	100
	R/V20 (2WD, 4WD Full Size) Suburban	1989	120
	G10, 20 (Full Size) Van	88-99	100
	G30 (Full Size) Van except:	88-99	120
	G30 (Full Size) Van (Dual Rear Wheels)	88-99	140
	El Camino/Caballero, Sprint	67-87	90
	Luv Pickup	76-82	90
	C/K10 Blazer & Jimmy	71-87	90
	Chevy & GMC Pickups 10/15, 20/25, 30/35 (Single Rear Wheel with 7/16 & 1/2 Studs)	71-87	90
	Chevy & GMC Pickups 10/15, 20/25, 30/35 (Single Rear Wheel with 9/16 Studs)	71-87	120
Chrysler	Concorde	93-99	95
	Chrysler T/C by Maserati	89-91	95
	Conquest	87-89	65-80
	LeBaron (FWD)	84-93	95
	LeBaron (FWD)	82-83	80
	New Yorker (FWD)	83-99	95
	Town & Country (FWD)	84-88	95
	Town & Country (FWD)	82-83	80

82

NAME	MODEL	YEARS	LB. FT. TORQUE
	Fifth Avenue (RWD)	83-90	85
	New Yorker (RWD	76-82	85
	New Yorker (FWD)	93-99	95
	Laser	84-86	95
	Limousine	85-86	95
	Executive Sedan	84-85	95
	E-Class	83-84	80
	Imperial	90-93	95
	Imperial (RWD)	81-83	85
	Cordoba	76-83	85
	LeBaron (RWD)	78-81	85
	Town & Country (RWD)	78-81	85
	Newport	76-81	85
Daihatsu	Charade	88-91	65-87
Daihatsu Light Trucks & Vans	Rocky (All)	90-91	65-87
Dodge	Intrepid	93-99	95
	Stealth	91-99	87-101
	Spirit	89-93	95
	Shadow	87-93	95
	Colt	76-93	65-80
	Lancer	85-89	95
	Aries	84-89	95
	Aries	81-83	80
	Charger	84-87	95
	Charger	82-83	80
	Daytona	84-93	95
	Omni	84-90	95
	Omni	78-83	80
	Vista	84-93	50-57
	600	84-88	95
	600	1983	80
	Diplomat	78-89	80
	Dynasty	88-93	95
	Monaco	90-91	54-72
	Conquest	1986	65-80
	Conquest	84-85	50-57
	400	82-83	80
	Challenger	78-83	51-58
	Mirada	80-83	85

NAME	MODEL	YEARS	LB. FT. TORQUE
	St. Regis	79-81	85
	Aspen	76-80	85
Dodge Light Trucks & Vans	Caravan, Ram Van (FWD)	84-99	95
	Rampage (FWD)	82-84	90
	Ramcharge AD, AW100	79-93	105
	Wagons B100/150	72-99	105
	Wagons B200/250	72-99	105
	Wagons B300/350 1/2" Studs	69-99	105
	Wagons B300/350 5/8" Studs	79-99	200
	D50 Pickup	78-86	55
	D50 Pickup	87-99	95
	D100/150 Pickup	72-99	105
	D200/250 Pickup	81-99	105
	D300/350 Pickup 1/2" Studs	79-99	105
	D300/350 Pickup 5/8" Studs	79-99	200
	W100/150 Pickup	79-99	105
	W200/250 Pickup	79-99	105
	W300/350 Pickup 1/2" Studs	79-99	105
	W300/350 Pickup 5/8" Studs	79-99	200
	Dakota	87-99	85
Ford	All except the following	84-99	85-105
	Probe	89-91	65-87
	Festiva	89-93	65-87
	Escort	81-83	80-105
	EXP	82-83	80-105
	Fiesta	78-80	63-85
	Mustang	79-83	80-105
	Pinto	76-80	80-105
	Fairmont	78-83	80-105
	Granada	76-82	80-105
	LTD	79-83	80-105
	LTD	76-78	70-115
	Torino	76-79	80-105
	LTD Crown Victoria	1983	80-105
	Country Sedan & Squire	79-83	80-105
	Thunderbird	80-83	80-105
	Thunderbird	76-79	70-115
Ford Light Trucks & Vans	E150/F150 & Bronco	88-99	100
	E250/E350, F250, F350	88-99	140

NAME	MODEL	YEARS	LB. FT. TORQUE
	Aerostar	86-99	100
	Bronco	88-93	135
	Bronco	72-87	100
	Explorer	91-99	100
	Club Wagon E100/150	75-87	100
	Club Wagon E200/250	76-87	100
	Club Wagon E300/350 (Single Rear Wheels)	76-87	145
	Club Wagon E300/350 (Dual Rear Wheels)	76-87	220
	Econoline Van E 100/150	75-81	100
	Econoline Van E200/250	76-87	100
	Econoline Van E300/350 (Single Rear Wheels)	76-87	145
	Econoline Van E300/350 (Dual Rear Wheels)	76-87	220
	Ranger Pickup	84-87	100
	Courier Pickup	77-83	65
	F100/150 Pickup	75-87	100
	F200/250 Pickup	76-87	100
	F300/350 Pickup (Single Rear Wheels)	76-87	145
	F300/350 Pickup (Dual Rear Wheels)	76-87	220
Honda	All except the following	84-99	80
	Civic All	73-83	58
	Accord All	82-99	80
	Accord All	76-81	58
	Prelude All	79-99	80
Hyundai	All except the following	90-99	65-80
	Excel	86-89	50-57
Infiniti	All	90-99	72-87
Isuzu	Stylus	1991	87
	Impulse	83-91	87
	I Mark	87-89	65
	I Mark	1986	90
	I Mark	1985	50
	I Mark	82-84	50
Isuzu Light Trucks & Vans	Pickup	91-99	72
	Pickup	1990	58-87
	Amigo	1991	72

NAME	MODEL	YEARS	LB. FT. TORQUE
	Amigo	89-90	58-87
	Rodeo	1991	72
	Trooper	84-91	58-87
Jaguar	All	89-91	65-75
	XJ6 & XJS	1988	75
	All	81-87	80
Eagle	Vision	1993	95
	Premier	89-91	54-72
	Talon	90-99	87-101
	Summit	89-91	65-80
	Medallion	1988	67
Jeep Light Trucks & Vans			88
	Grand Cherokee & Grand Wagoneer	92-99	
	Wrangler, YJ	90-99	80
	Cherokee, Comanche	84-91	75
	Wagoneer & Grand Wagoneer	84-91	75
	Trucks (under 8400 GVW)	84-89	75
	Trucks (over 8400 GVW)	84-89	130
	CJ Series	84-86	80
	CJ Series	81-83	65-80
	Cherokee, Wagoneer	81-83	65-90
	Trucks (under 8400 GVW)	81-83	65-90
	Trucks (over 8400 GVW)	81-83	110-150
Lexus	All	90-99	76
Lincoln	All	84-99	85-105
	Mark IV	80-83	80-105
	Continental	76-83	80-105
	Town Car	81-83	80-105
	Versailles	77-80	80-105
Mazda	All except the following	88-99	65-87
	Navajo	91-99	100
	323	86-87	65-87
	GLC	81-85	65-80
	GLC	77-80	65-80
	GLC Wagon	84-85	65-87
	626	84-87	65-87
	626	1983	65-80
	626	79-82	65-80

NAME	MODEL	YEARS	LB. FT. TORQUE
	Cosmo	76-78	65-72
	808	76-77	65-72
	RX7	84-87	65-87
	RX7	79-83	65-80
	RX7	76-78	65-72
	RX3	76-78	65-72
Mazda Light Trucks & Vans	B2600	87-99	65-87
	B2200	86-99	65-87
	B2000/B2200	80-85	72-80
Mercedes	All	76-99	81
Mercury	All	84-99	85-105
	All	76-83	80-105
Mitsubishi	Sigma V6	89-90	65-80
	Mirage	85-91	65-80
	Precis	87-89	51-58
	Cordia/Tredia	83-88	50-57
	Eclipse	90-99	87-101
	Galant	85-86	50-57
	Galant	1987	65-80
	Galant	88-99	65-80
	Starion	1983	50-57
	Starion	84-89	50-57
Mitsubishi Light Trucks & Vans	Van/Wagons	89-90	87-101
	Montero	89-91	75-87
	Pickups	89-91	72-87
	Pickups	83-87	65
	Montero	83-87	65
Nissan/Datsun	All	91-99	72-87
	Maxima	89-90	72-87
	Maxima	87-88	72-89
	Maxima	85-86	58-72
	Pulsar SE, SE	87-90	72-87
	Pulsar	83-86	58-72
	Sentra	83-86	58-72
	Stanza All	87-90	72-87
	Stanza	82-86	58-72
	210	79-82	58-72

NAME	MODEL	YEARS	LB. FT. TORQUE
	310	79-82	58-72
	510	78-81	58-72
	810	1981	58-72
	810	77-80	58-65
	200 SX All	87-88	87-108
	200 SX	80-86	58-72
	200 SX	77-79	58-65
	280 ZX	79-83	58-72
	300 ZX & ZX Turbo	1990	72-87
	300 ZX & ZX Turbo	87-89	87-108
	Axxess	1990	72-87
	240 SX	1989	72-87
Nissan/Datsun Light Trucks & Vans	All Pickups and Pathfinder	89-99	87-108
	Van	87-88	72-87
	Van	1990	72-87
Oldsmobile	All except the following	76-99	100
	Starfire	76-80	80
	Cutlass (RWD)	76-88	80
	Cutlass Supreme (FWD)	88-93	100
	Delta 88	77-85	80
Oldsmobile Light Trucks & Vans	Silhouette	90-99	100
	Bravado	92-99	95
Plymouth	Colt	83-93	65-80
	Sundance	87-93	95
	Acclaim	89-93	95
	Laser	90-91	87-101
	Caravelle	85-88	95
	Horizon	84-90	95
	Horizon	78-83	80
	Turismo	84-87	95
	Turismo	82-83	80
	Vista	84-91	50-57
	Reliant	84-89	80
	Reliant	81-83	80
	Gran Fury	80-89	85
	Conquest	1986	50-57
	Conquest	84-85	50-57
	Sapporo	78-83	51-58

NAME	MODEL	YEARS	LB. FT. TORQUE
	Champ	79-82	51-58
Plymouth Light Trucks & Vans	Voyager	84-99	95
Pontiac	All except the following	80-88	100
	T-1000	81-87	80
	Sunbird	76-80	80
	Firebird	76-88	80
	Grand Prix	76-87	80
	Lemans	89-93	65
	Catalina	76-86	80
	Bonneville	76-86	80
	Parisienne	83-86	80
Pontiac Light Trucks & Vans	Trans Sport	90-99	100
Porsche	All	79-99	94
Range Rover	All	91-99	90-95
Saab	All	88-99	80-90
	All	76-87	65-80
Saturn	All	91-99	100
Sterling	All	87-91	53
Subaru	All	76-99	58-72
Toyota	All except the following	84-99	76
	Celica	70-85	66-86
	Supra	79-85	66-86
	Corolla	80-83	66-86
	Corona	75-82	66-86
	Cressida	78-85	66-86
	Corona MK II	1976	65-94
	Tercel	80-85	66-86
	Starlet	81-85	66-86
Toyota Light Trucks & Vans	All except the following	88-99	76
	Land Cruiser	88-91	116
	Pickups	75-87	75
	Land Cruiser	75-84	75
	Van Wagon	84-86	75

NAME	MODEL	YEARS	LB. FT. TORQUE
Volkswagen	All except Van	88-99	81
	Golf	85-87	81
	Rabbit All	76-84	73-87
	Jetta	81-87	81
	Scirocco	76-84	73-87
	Quantum	82-86	81
	Dasher	76-81	65
	Scirocco	85-87	81
Volkswagen Light Trucks & Vans	Vanagon	80-99	123
	Pickups	79-84	81
	Transporter	77-79	95
Volvo	All	89-99	63
	740 Series	85-88	63
	760 Series	83-88	63
	GLE	76-82	72-94
	260 Series	75-84	72-95
	240 Series	81-88	63
	240 Series	75-80	72-95
Yugo	All with steel wheels	86-90	63
	All with alloy wheels	88-90	81

APPENDIX 2

Ride Height Chart

Vehicle Make and Model	Year	Front Measure Point	Rear Measure Point	Vehicle Loaded?	Loaded How?
Acura					
		Bottom of Front Bumper	Bottom of Rear Bumper		
2.3 CL	1998	7 1/2 - 8 1/2	7 3/4 - 8 3/4	No	Curb Weight
2.5 TL	1998	7 3/16 - 8 3/16	9 1/2 - 10 1/2	No	Curb Weight
3.0 CL	1998	7 1/2 - 8 1/2	8 1/2 - 9 1/2	No	Curb Weight
3.2 TL	1998	6 5/8 - 7 5/8	10 - 11	No	Curb Weight
3.5 RL	1998	8 - 9	7 3/4 - 8 3/4	No	Curb Weight
Integra (Hatchback)	1986 - 89	8 3/8 - 9 3/8	13 1/8 - 14 1/8	No	Curb Weight
Integra (Sedan)	1986 - 89	8 3/8 - 9 3/8	13 1/8 - 14 1/8	No	Curb Weight
Integra (Hatchback)	1990 - 93	7 1/4 - 8 1/4	12 1/4 - 13 1/4	No	Curb Weight
Integra (Sedan)	1990 - 93	7 1/4 - 8 1/4	12 1/2 - 13 1/2	No	Curb Weight
Integra	1994 - 97	5 13/16 - 6 13/16	9 11/16 - 10 11/16	No	Curb Weight
Integra (3 door)	1998	5 7/16 - 6 7/16	7 - 8	No	Curb Weight
Integra (4 door)	1998	5 7/16 - 6 7/16	6 3/4 - 7 3/4	No	Curb Weight
Legend (Coupe)	1986 - 90	7 3/8 - 8 3/8	12 1/8 - 13 1/8	No	Curb Weight
Legend (Sedan)	1986 - 90	8 1/2 - 9 1/2	11 - 12	No	Curb Weight
Legend (Coupe)	1991 - 95	7 3/8 - 8 3/8	11 5/16 - 12 5/16	No	Curb Weight
Legend (Sedan)	1991 - 95	7 3/4 - 8 3/4	11 5/16 - 12 5/16	No	Curb Weight
NSX (Coupe)	1991 - 97	5 3/4 - 6 3/4	8 11/16 - 9 11/16	No	Curb Weight
NSX	1998	5 3/16 - 6 3/16	7 29/32 - 8 29/32	No	Curb Weight
SLX	1998	15 1/2	16 15/16	No	Curb Weight
Vigor (Sedan)	1992 - 94	8 9/16 - 9 9/16	12 1/4 - 13 1/4	No	Curb Weight
American Motors					
		Bottom of Front Bumper	Bottom of Rear Bumper		
Eagle (Sedan)	1985	15 3/4 - 17 3/4	17 1/8 - 19 1/8	No	Curb Weight
Eagle (Wagon)	1985	15 3/4 - 17 3/4	17 1/8 - 19 1/8	No	Curb Weight
Eagle	1986 - 87	15 7/8 - 17 7/8	17 1/8 - 19 1/8	No	Curb Weight
Audi					
		Top of Front Wheel Opening	Top of Rear Wheel Opening		
80 (Quattro)	1988 - 92	25 1/8 - 25 3/8	25 1/4 - 25 1/2	No	Curb Weight
80 (all others)	1988 - 92	25 7/8 - 26 1/8	26 1/2 - 26 3/4	No	Curb Weight
90 (Quattro)	1988 - 91	25 3/8 - 25 5/8	25 7/8 - 26 1/8	No	Curb Weight
90 (all others)	1988 - 91	25 5/8 - 25 7/8	26 1/8 - 26 3/8	No	Curb Weight
100, 200	1988 - 91	26 - 26 1/4	25 1/4 - 25 1/2	No	Curb Weight
4000	1985 - 87	24 1/8 - 24 3/8	23 5/8 - 23 7/8	No	Curb Weight
4000 Quattro	1985 - 87	24 3/8 - 24 5/8	23 7/8 - 24 1/8	No	Curb Weight
5000 (all w/14" tires)	1984 - 88	25 5/8 - 25 7/8	24 3/4 - 25	No	Curb Weight
5000 (all w/15" tires)	1984 - 88	26 3/8 - 26 5/8	24 7/8 - 25 1/8	No	Curb Weight
Coupe	1985 - 87	24 7/8 - 25 1/8	24 1/8 - 24 3/8	No	Curb Weight
Quattro	1982 - 87	24 7/8 - 25 1/8	25 3/8 - 25 5/8	No	Curb Weight
BMW					
		Top of Front Wheel Opening	Top of Rear Wheel Opening		
318i	1983 - 87	22 15/16 - 23 3/4	22 3/8 - 23 1/8	No	Curb Weight
318i, 320i, 325, 325e, 325es, 325i, 325es, 325es, 325i, 325is, 325ix (Convertible)	1988 - 91	22 7/16	20 1/16	Yes	See footnote 1
318i, 320i, 325, 325e, 325es, 325i, 325is, 325ix (M-Tech. Suspension)	1988 - 91	21 11/16	19 5/16	Yes	See footnote 2
318i, 320i, 325, 325e, 325es, 325i, 325is, 325ix (all others)	1988 - 91	22 1/4	19 7/8	Yes	See footnote 2
318i, 318is, 325i, 325is, 328i, 328is (Convertible)	1992 - 97	22 7/16	20 1/16	Yes	See footnote 1
318i, 318is, 325i, 325is, 328i, 328is (M-Tech Suspension)	1992 - 97	22 1/16	20	Yes	See footnote 2
318i, 318is, 325i, 325is, 328i, 328is (all others)	1992 - 97	22 5/8	20 9/16	Yes	See footnote 2
325, 325e, 325es	1983 - 87	22 15/16 - 23 3/4	22 3/16 - 22 15/16	No	Curb Weight
5-Series (except M5) (w/14" wheels)	1983 - 87	23 5/16 - 23 11/16	20 11/16 - 21 1/2	No	Curb Weight
5-Series (except M5) (w/165 TR 390 wheels)	1983 - 87	23 7/8 - 24 5/8	20 11/16 - 21 1/2	No	Curb Weight
524td, 525i, 528e, 533i, 535i, 535is (M-Tech. Suspension)	1988 - 95	22 3/16	20 5/32	Yes	See footnote 2

Vehicle Make and Model

Vehicle Make and Model	Year	Front Measure Point	Rear Measure Point	Vehicle Loaded?	Loaded How?
524td, 525i, 525e, 533i, 535i, 535is (w/TR 415 wheels)	1988 - 95	22 11/16	20 11/16	Yes	See footnote 2
524td, 525i, 525e, 528e, 533i, 535i, 535is (all others)	1988 - 95	23 1/8	20 9/16	Yes	See footnote 2
525i, 525it, 530i, 530it, 540i (w/15" wheels)	1994 - 95	23 1/8	20 5/8	Yes	See footnote 2
525i, 525it, 530i, 530it, 540i (w/15" wheels M-Tech)	1994 - 95	22 3/16	20 3/16	Yes	See footnote 2
525i, 525it, 530i, 530it, 540i (w/15" wheels sport)	1994 - 95	22 7/16	20 1/8	Yes	See footnote 2
525i, 525it, 530i, 530it, 540i (w/TD390 wheels)	1994 - 95	23 5/16	20 11/16	Yes	See footnote 2
525i, 525it, 530i, 530it, 540i (w/TD390 wheels M-Tech)	1994 - 95	22 5/16	20 5/16	Yes	See footnote 2
525i, 525it, 530i, 530it, 540i (w/TD390 wheels sport)	1994 - 95	22 1/2	20 7/16	Yes	See footnote 2
525i, 525it, 530i, 530it, 540i (w/TR415 wheels)	1994 - 95	23 11/16	21 1/8	Yes	See footnote 2
525i, 525it, 530i, 530it, 540i (w/TR415 wheels M-Tech)	1994 - 95	22 11/16	20 11/16	Yes	See footnote 2
525i, 525it, 530i, 530it, 540i (w/TR415 wheels sport)	1994 - 95	22 15/16	20 11/16	Yes	See footnote 2
630CSi, 633CSi, 635CSi (w/14" wheels)	1983 - 87	22 15/16 - 23 11/16	22 - 22 13/16	No	Curb Weight
630CSi, 633CSi, 635CSi (w/165 TR 390 wheels)	1983 - 87	23 1/2 - 24 1/4	22 - 22 13/16	No	Curb Weight
630CSi, 633CSi, 635CSi (w/14" wheels)	1988 - 89	22 3/4	21 3/4	Yes	See footnote 2
630CSi, 633CSi, 635CSi (w/165 TR 390 wheels)	1988 - 89	23 5/16	21 7/8	Yes	See footnote 2
733i, 735i, 735iL, 740i, 740iL, 750iL (w/14" wheels)	1983 - 87	23	20 3/8	Yes	See footnote 3
733i, 735i, 735iL, 740i, 740iL, 750iL (w/165 TR 390 wheels)	1983 - 87	23 9/16	20 3/8	Yes	See footnote 3
733i, 735i, 735iL, 740i, 740iL, 750iL (w/TR415 wheels)	1988 - 93	23 11/16	21	Yes	See footnote 2
733i, 735i, 735iL, 740i, 740iL, 750iL (all others)	1988 - 93	23 1/8	20 9/16	Yes	See footnote 2
840Ci, 840i, 850CSi, 850Ci, 850i (w/M-Tech. Suspension)	1991 - 97	22 15/16	21 13/16	Yes	See footnote 2
840Ci, 840i, 850CSi, 850Ci, 850i (all others)	1991 - 97	23 17/32	22 13/32	Yes	See footnote 2
M3 (w/15" wheels)	1987 - 91	21 7/8	20 13/16	Yes	See footnote 1
M3 (w/16" wheels)	1987 - 91	22 3/8	20 7/8	Yes	See footnote 1
M3 (w/17" wheels)	1994 - 95	23	21 5/16	Yes	See footnote 1
M5	1987 - 89	23 1/8	20 9/16	Yes	See footnote 3
M5 (w/16" wheels)	1991 - 93	22 7/8	20 13/16	Yes	See footnote 1
M5 (w/17" wheels)	1991 - 93	23 15/32	21 7/16	Yes	See footnote 3
M6	1987 - 89	23 3/8	22 1/8	Yes	See footnote 3

Buick

Vehicle Make and Model	Year	Bottom of Front Bumper	Bottom of Rear Bumper	Vehicle Loaded?	Loaded How?
Century (Coupe)	1984 - 88	9 3/8 - 11 3/8	12 1/4 - 14 1/4	No	Curb Weight
Century (Sedan & Wagon)	1984 - 88	9 3/8 - 11 3/8	13 5/8 - 15 5/8	No	Curb Weight
Century (Coupe)	1989 - 93	9 3/8 - 11 3/8	12 1/4 - 14 1/4	No	Curb Weight
Century (Sedan & Wagon)	1989 - 93	9 3/8 - 11 3/8	13 1/2 - 15 1/2	No	Curb Weight
Century (Coupe)	1994 - 96	9 15/16 - 10 15/16	14 - 15	No	Curb Weight
Century (Sedan & Wagon)	1994 - 96	9 15/16 - 10 15/16	14 - 15	No	Curb Weight
Century	1997 - 98	9 7/32 - 10 7/32	13 1/2 - 14 1/2	No	Curb Weight
Electra	1985 - 88	14 1/4 - 16 1/4	14 3/4 - 16 3/4	No	Curb Weight
Electra	1989 - 90	8 5/8 - 10 5/8	13 1/8 - 15 1/8	No	Curb Weight
Estate Wagon	1983 - 85	12 3/4 - 14 3/4	11 1/2 - 13 1/2	No	Curb Weight
Estate Wagon	1986 - 90	12 3/4 - 14 3/4	11 1/2 - 13 1/2	No	Curb Weight
LeSabre (Coupe)	1983 - 85	12 3/4 - 14 3/4	12 3/4 - 14 3/4	No	Curb Weight
LeSabre (Sedan)	1983 - 85	12 3/4 - 14 3/4	12 3/4 - 14 3/4	No	Curb Weight
LeSabre	1986 - 88	13 1/2 - 15 1/2	15 3/4 - 17 3/4	No	Curb Weight
LeSabre	1989	8 5/16 - 10 5/16	14 3/8 - 16 3/8	No	Curb Weight
LeSabre	1990	8 3/8 - 10 3/8	13 1/2 - 15 1/2	No	Curb Weight
LeSabre	1991	8 3/8 - 10 3/8	13 1/2 - 15 1/2	No	Curb Weight
LeSabre	1992	9 - 11	12 5/16 - 14 5/16	No	Curb Weight
LeSabre	1993 - 97	8 15/16 - 10 15/16	13 1/16 - 15 1/16	No	Curb Weight
LeSabre (Custom)	1998	8 15/16 - 10 15/16	13 1/16 - 15 1/16	No	Curb Weight
LeSabre (Limited)	1998	8 15/16 - 10 15/16	13 1/16 - 15 1/16	No	Curb Weight
Reatta	1988	9 1/8 - 11 1/8	11 1/8 - 13 1/8	No	Curb Weight
Reatta	1989 - 90	9 1/8 - 11 1/8	15 - 17	No	Curb Weight

Vehicle Make and Model	Year	Front Measure Point	Rear Measure Point	Vehicle Loaded?	Loaded How?
Reatta	1991	15 5/16 - 17 5/16	12 1/8 - 14 1/8	No	Curb Weight
Regal	1985 - 87	11 1/2 - 13 1/2	12 3/4 - 14 3/4	No	Curb Weight
Regal	1988 - 89	13 3/8 - 15 3/8	12 13/16 - 14 13/16	No	Curb Weight
Regal (Coupe)	1990	13 3/8 - 15 3/8	12 3/4 - 14 3/4	No	Curb Weight
Regal (Sedan)	1990	13 3/4 - 15 3/4	11 1/8 - 13 1/8	No	Curb Weight
Regal (Coupe)	1991 - 94	13 3/8 - 15 3/8	12 7/8 - 14 7/8	No	Curb Weight
Regal (Sedan)	1991 - 94	13 7/8 - 15 7/8	11 1/8 - 13 1/8	No	Curb Weight
Regal	1995 - 96	14 - 15	13 5/16 - 14 5/16	No	Curb Weight
Regal	1997 - 98	10 1/8 - 11 1/8	12 7/8 - 13 7/8	No	Curb Weight
Riviera	1982 - 85	11 7/8 - 13 7/8	12 1/2 - 14 1/2	No	Curb Weight
Riviera	1986 - 88	12 7/8 - 14 7/8	13 - 15	No	Curb Weight
Riviera	1989 - 90	14 3/8 - 16 3/8	14 7/8 - 16 7/8	No	Curb Weight
Riviera	1991 - 93	13 3/8 - 15 3/8	14 - 16	No	Curb Weight
Riviera	1995 - 97	9 5/16 - 10 5/16	12 5/8 - 13 5/8	No	Curb Weight
Riviera	1998	9 5/16 - 10 5/16	12 5/8 - 13 5/8	No	Curb Weight
Roadmaster (Sedan)	1991 - 92	10 - 12	13 5/16 - 15 5/16	No	Curb Weight
Roadmaster (Wagon)	1991 - 92	10 1/2 - 12 1/2	12 1/2 - 14 1/2	No	Curb Weight
Roadmaster (Sedan)	1993 - 96	10 - 12	13 5/16 - 15 5/16	No	Curb Weight
Roadmaster (Wagon)	1993 - 96	10 7/16 - 12 7/16	12 1/2 - 14 1/2	No	Curb Weight
Park Avenue	1991	9 - 11	12 5/16 - 14 5/16	No	Curb Weight
Park Avenue	1992 - 97	9 - 11	12 5/16 - 14 5/16	No	Curb Weight
Park Avenue (Ultra)	1998	9 5/16 - 11 5/16	12 5/16 - 14 5/16	No	Curb Weight
Park Avenue (all others)	1998	9 13/32 - 11 13/32	12 5/16 - 14 5/16	No	Curb Weight
Skyhawk (Coupe & Sedan)	1982 - 86	13 1/4 - 15 1/4	13 1/4 - 15 1/4	No	Curb Weight
Skyhawk (Hatchback)	1982 - 86	13 1/4 - 15 1/4	13 1/4 - 15 1/4	No	Curb Weight
Skyhawk (Wagon)	1982 - 86	13 1/4 - 15 1/4	14 - 16	No	Curb Weight
Skyhawk (Wagon)	1987	7 1/2 - 9 1/2	14 1/4 - 16 1/4	No	Curb Weight
Skyhawk (all others)	1987	7 5/8 - 9 5/8	13 1/2 - 15 1/2	No	Curb Weight
Skyhawk (Coupe)	1988	7 5/8 - 9 5/8	13 5/16 - 15 5/16	No	Curb Weight
Skyhawk (Sedan)	1988	7 5/8 - 9 5/8	13 5/16 - 15 5/16	No	Curb Weight
Skyhawk (Wagon)	1988	7 1/2 - 9 1/2	13 5/16 - 15 5/16	No	Curb Weight
Skyhawk (Coupe)	1989	7 5/8 - 9 5/8	13 1/2 - 15 1/2	No	Curb Weight
Skyhawk (Sedan)	1989	7 5/8 - 9 5/8	13 1/2 - 15 1/2	No	Curb Weight
Skyhawk (Wagon)	1989	7 1/2 - 9 1/2	13 - 15	No	Curb Weight
Skylark	1980 - 85	13 - 15	14 1/4 - 16 1/4	No	Curb Weight
Skylark	1986	11 3/4 - 13 3/4	12 1/4 - 14 1/4	No	Curb Weight
Skylark	1987	7 1/8 - 9 1/8	12 3/4 - 14 3/4	No	Curb Weight
Skylark	1988	8 7/8 - 10 7/8	12 1/2 - 14 1/2	No	Curb Weight
Skylark	1989	7 3/8 - 9 3/8	12 1/2 - 14 1/2	No	Curb Weight
Skylark	1990 - 91	7 1/8 - 9 1/8	12 1/2 - 14 1/2	No	Curb Weight
Skylark	1992 - 94	9 - 11	10 11/16 - 12 11/16	No	Curb Weight
Skylark	1995 - 98	9 1/4 - 10 1/4	11 7/16 - 12 7/16	No	Curb Weight
Somerset	1985 - 86	12 1/2 - 14 1/2	12 1/4 - 14 1/4	No	Curb Weight
Somerset	1987	7 1/8 - 9 1/8	12 3/4 - 14 3/4	No	Curb Weight

Cadillac		Bottom of Front Bumper	Bottom of Rear Bumper		
Allante	1987 - 90	11 7/8 - 13 7/8	13 5/8 - 15 5/8	No	Curb Weight
Allante	1991 - 92	15 - 17	13 1/8 - 15 1/8	No	Curb Weight
Allante	1993	15 - 17	13 1/8 - 15 1/8	No	Curb Weight
Catera	1997 - 98	8 1/2 - 9 1/2	11 3/8 - 12 3/8	No	Curb Weight
Cimarron	1982 - 85	14 1/4 - 16 1/4	13 3/4 - 15 3/4	No	Curb Weight
Cimarron	1986 - 87	11 1/4 - 13 1/4	15 1/8 - 17 1/8	No	Curb Weight
Cimarron	1988	14 1/4 - 16 1/4	14 - 16	No	Curb Weight

Page 93

Vehicle Make and Model	Year	Front Measure Point	Rear Measure Point	Vehicle Loaded?	Loaded How?
Eldorado	1981 - 85	12 3/8 - 14 3/8	12 3/4 - 14 3/4	No	Curb Weight
Eldorado	1986 - 88	12 1/4 - 14 1/4	13 1/4 - 15 1/4	No	Curb Weight
Eldorado	1989 - 90	11 1/2 - 13 1/2	13 3/8 - 15 3/8	No	Curb Weight
Eldorado	1991	11 1/2 - 13 1/2	13 3/8 - 15 3/8	No	Curb Weight
Eldorado	1992 - 97	9 1/4 - 11 1/4	13 13/16 - 15 13/16	No	Curb Weight
Eldorado	1998	8 1/2 - 9 1/2	10 9/16 - 11 9/16	No	Curb Weight
DeVille	1985 - 87	12 1/4 - 14 1/4	13 - 15	No	Curb Weight
DeVille	1988	12 1/8 - 14 1/8	13 1/8 - 15 1/8	No	Curb Weight
DeVille (Coupe)	1989 - 90	10 5/8 - 12 5/8	12 7/8 - 14 7/8	No	Curb Weight
DeVille (Sedan)	1989 - 90	10 1/2 - 12 1/2	12 7/8 - 14 7/8	No	Curb Weight
DeVille (Coupe)	1991 - 93	10 9/16 - 12 9/16	12 7/8 - 14 7/8	No	Curb Weight
DeVille (Sedan)	1991 - 93	10 1/2 - 12 1/2	12 7/8 - 14 7/8	No	Curb Weight
DeVille (Concourse)	1994	9 1/8 - 10 1/8	13 5/8 - 14 5/8	No	Curb Weight
DeVille (all others)	1994	9 7/16 - 10 7/16	14 - 15	No	Curb Weight
DeVille	1995 - 97	8 3/4 - 9 3/4	13 7/16 - 14 7/16	Yes	See footnote 4
DeVille (Concourse)	1998	8 7/16 - 9 7/16	10 5/16 - 11 5/16	Yes	See footnote 5
DeVille (all others)	1998	8 3/4 - 9 3/4	10 5/8 - 11 5/8	Yes	See footnote 4
Fleetwood, Sixty Special (FWD)	1985 - 87	12 1/4 - 14 1/4	13 - 15	No	Curb Weight
Fleetwood, Sixty Special (FWD)	1988	12 1/8 - 14 1/8	13 1/8 - 15 1/8	No	Curb Weight
Fleetwood, Sixty Special (FWD) (Coupe)	1989 - 90	10 5/8 - 12 5/8	12 7/8 - 14 7/8	No	Curb Weight
Fleetwood, Sixty Special (FWD) (Sedan)	1989 - 90	10 1/2 - 12 1/2	12 7/8 - 14 7/8	No	Curb Weight
Fleetwood, Sixty Special (FWD) (Coupe)	1991 - 93	10 9/16 - 12 9/16	12 7/8 - 14 7/8	No	Curb Weight
Fleetwood, Sixty Special (FWD) (Sedan)	1991 - 93	10 1/2 - 12 1/2	12 7/8 - 14 7/8	No	Curb Weight
Fleetwood, Brougham (RWD) (2 door)	1985 - 87	11 7/8 - 13 7/8	12 1/4 - 14 1/4	No	Curb Weight
Fleetwood, Brougham (RWD) (4 door)	1985 - 87	11 7/8 - 13 7/8	12 1/4 - 14 1/4	No	Curb Weight
Fleetwood, Brougham (RWD)	1988 - 90	11 7/8 - 13 7/8	12 1/4 - 14 1/4	No	Curb Weight
Fleetwood, Brougham (RWD)	1991 - 92	11 3/4 - 13 3/4	12 1/4 - 14 1/4	No	Curb Weight
Fleetwood, Brougham (RWD)	1993	9 1/4 - 11 1/4	12 3/16 - 14 3/16	No	Curb Weight
Fleetwood, Brougham (RWD)	1994 - 96	9 1/4 - 11 1/4	12 3/16 - 14 3/16	No	Curb Weight
Seville	1981 - 85	13 - 15	12 1/8 - 14 1/8	No	Curb Weight
Seville	1986 - 88	12 1/4 - 14 1/4	13 1/4 - 15 1/4	No	Curb Weight
Seville	1989 - 90	11 1/2 - 13 1/2	13 3/8 - 15 3/8	No	Curb Weight
Seville	1991	11 1/2 - 13 1/2	13 3/8 - 15 3/8	No	Curb Weight
Seville (STS)	1992 - 93	8 3/8 - 10 3/8	13 3/16 - 15 3/16	No	Curb Weight
Seville (all others)	1994	10 1/2 - 11 1/2	10 1/2 - 13 1/2	No	Curb Weight
Seville	1995 - 97	8 3/8 - 10 3/8	14 5/16 - 15 5/16	Yes	See footnote 6
Seville (SLS)	1998	8 1/8 - 9 1/8	13 7/32 - 14 7/32	Yes	See footnote 5
Seville (STS)	1998	7 3/4 - 8 3/4	11 1/16 - 12 1/16	Yes	See footnote 5

Chevrolet

Vehicle Make and Model	Year	Bottom of Front Bumper	Bottom of Rear Bumper	Vehicle Loaded?	Loaded How?
Beretta (GT, GTZ)	1987 - 1991	13 5/16 - 15 5/16	14 - 16	No	Curb Weight
Beretta (all others)	1992	9 7/8 - 11 7/8	10 1/2 - 12 1/2	No	Curb Weight
Beretta (GT, GTZ)	1992	9 7/8 - 11 7/8	10 1/2 - 12 1/2	No	Curb Weight
Beretta (all others)	1993 - 94	10 3/8 - 11 3/8	10 15/16 - 11 15/16	No	Curb Weight
Beretta	1993 - 94	10 3/8 - 11 3/8	10 15/16 - 11 15/16	No	Curb Weight
Cavalier (Wagon)	1995 - 96	10 3/8 - 11 3/8	11 - 12	No	Curb Weight
Cavalier (all others)	1985 - 86	14 - 16	13 1/8 - 15 1/8	No	Curb Weight
Cavalier (Hatchback)	1985 - 86	14 - 16	13 1/2 - 15 1/2	No	Curb Weight
Cavalier (Notchback & Convertible)	1987	13 13/16 - 15 13/16	13 1/2 - 15 1/2	No	Curb Weight
Cavalier (Sedan)	1987	14 - 16	13 1/2 - 15 1/2	No	Curb Weight
Cavalier (Wagon)	1987	14 - 16	13 1/8 - 15 1/8	No	Curb Weight

Vehicle Make and Model	Year	Front Measure Point	Rear Measure Point	Vehicle Loaded?	Loaded How?
Cavalier (Convertible)	1988 - 89	8 3/8 - 10 3/8	10 11/16 - 12 11/16	No	Curb Weight
Cavalier (Coupe)	1988 - 89	8 11/16 - 10 11/16	10 11/16 - 12 11/16	No	Curb Weight
Cavalier (Sedan)	1988 - 89	8 11/16 - 10 11/16	10 11/16 - 12 11/16	No	Curb Weight
Cavalier (Wagon)	1988 - 89	8 13/16 - 10 13/16	12 5/8 - 14 5/8	No	Curb Weight
Cavalier (Coupe)	1990	8 11/16 - 10 11/16	10 11/16 - 12 11/16	No	Curb Weight
Cavalier (Sedan)	1990	8 11/16 - 10 11/16	10 11/16 - 12 11/16	No	Curb Weight
Cavalier (Wagon)	1990	8 13/16 - 10 13/16	12 5/8 - 14 5/8	No	Curb Weight
Cavalier (Coupe)	1991	9 - 11	10 9/16 - 12 9/16	No	Curb Weight
Cavalier (Sedan)	1991	9 - 11	10 9/16 - 12 9/16	No	Curb Weight
Cavalier (Wagon)	1991	9 1/8 - 11 1/8	9 7/8 - 11 7/8	No	Curb Weight
Cavalier (Coupe)	1992	9 - 11	10 9/16 - 12 9/16	No	Curb Weight
Cavalier (Sedan)	1992	9 - 11	10 9/16 - 12 9/16	No	Curb Weight
Cavalier (Wagon)	1992	9 1/8 - 11 1/8	9 7/8 - 11 7/8	No	Curb Weight
Cavalier (Coupe)	1993	9 - 11	10 9/16 - 12 9/16	No	Curb Weight
Cavalier (Sedan)	1993	9 - 11	10 9/16 - 12 9/16	No	Curb Weight
Cavalier (Convertible)	1994	9 - 11	10 9/16 - 12 9/16	No	Curb Weight
Cavalier (Coupe)	1994	9 - 11	10 9/16 - 12 9/16	No	Curb Weight
Cavalier (Sedan)	1994	9 - 11	10 9/16 - 12 9/16	No	Curb Weight
Cavalier (Wagon)	1994	9 1/8 - 11 1/8	10 7/16 - 12 7/16	No	Curb Weight
Cavalier	1995 - 96	9 1/8 - 11 1/8	13 - 14	No	Curb Weight
Cavalier (Convertible)	1997 - 98	9 1/2 - 10 1/2	13 - 14	No	Curb Weight
Cavalier (Coupe)	1997 - 98	9 1/2 - 10 1/2	13 - 14	No	Curb Weight
Cavalier (Sedan)	1997 - 98	9 1/2 - 10 1/2	13 - 14	No	Curb Weight
Camaro (IROC-Z, Z-28)	1985 - 87	13 1/8 - 15 1/8	12 1/2 - 14 1/2	No	Curb Weight
Camaro (all others)	1985 - 87	11 - 13	12 1/4 - 14 1/4	No	Curb Weight
Camaro	1988 - 90	13 1/8 - 15 1/8	12 1/2 - 14 1/2	No	Curb Weight
Camaro (Convertible)	1991 - 92	13 1/8 - 15 1/8	12 1/2 - 14 1/2	No	Curb Weight
Camaro (Coupe)	1991 - 92	13 1/8 - 15 1/8	12 1/2 - 14 1/2	No	Curb Weight
Camaro	1993 - 98	8 7/8 - 10 7/8	13 5/8 - 15 5/8	No	Curb Weight
Caprice, Impalla (Wagon)	1980 - 90	13 5/8 - 15 5/8	13 1/2 - 15 1/2	No	Curb Weight
Caprice, Impalla (all others)	1980 - 90	12 1/8 - 14 1/8	13 7/8 - 15 7/8	No	Curb Weight
Caprice, Impalla (Wagon)	1991	10 1/16 - 12 1/16	12 1/2 - 14 1/2	No	Curb Weight
Caprice, Impalla (all others)	1991	10 1/8 - 12 1/8	13 3/16 - 15 3/16	No	Curb Weight
Caprice, Impalla (Wagon)	1992	10 1/16 - 12 1/16	12 1/2 - 14 1/2	No	Curb Weight
Caprice, Impalla (all others)	1992	10 1/8 - 12 1/8	13 3/16 - 15 3/16	No	Curb Weight
Caprice, Impalla (Wagon)	1993 - 96	10 1/16 - 12 1/16	12 1/2 - 14 1/2	No	Curb Weight
Caprice, Impalla (all others)	1993 - 96	10 1/8 - 12 1/8	13 3/16 - 15 3/16	No	Curb Weight
Celebrity (Wagon)	1985 - 90	13 5/8 - 15 5/8	13 1/2 - 15 1/2	No	Curb Weight
Celebrity (all others)	1985 - 90	14 - 16	13 7/8 - 15 7/8	No	Curb Weight
Chevette	1981 - 86	13 - 15	12 1/4 - 14 1/4	No	Curb Weight
Chevette	1987	13 - 15	12 11/16 - 14 11/16	No	Curb Weight
Citation	1984 - 85	13 3/4 - 15 3/4	13 - 15	No	Curb Weight
Corsica	1987 - 91	12 1/4 - 14 1/4	14 5/8 - 16 5/8	No	Curb Weight
Corsica	1992 - 94	7 13/16 - 9 13/16	12 7/8 - 14 7/8	No	Curb Weight
Corsica	1995 - 96	8 5/16 - 9 5/16	13 3/8 - 14 3/8	No	Curb Weight
Corvette	1997 - 98	4 13/16 - 5 13/16	9 5/8 - 10 5/8	No	Curb Weight
El Camino	1981 - 87	13 5/8 - 15 5/8	13 5/8 - 15 5/8	No	Curb Weight
Lumina (Coupe)	1990	13 - 15	13 - 15	No	Curb Weight
Lumina (Sedan)	1990	13 - 15	13 5/8 - 15 5/8	No	Curb Weight
Lumina (Coupe)	1991 - 94	13 - 15	13 - 15	No	Curb Weight
Lumina (Sedan)	1991 - 94	13 - 15	13 - 15	No	Curb Weight
Lumina	1995 - 97	13 1/2 - 14 1/2	13 9/16 - 15 9/16	No	Curb Weight
Lumina	1998	13 1/2 - 14 1/2	14 - 15	No	Curb Weight

Vehicle Make and Model	Year	Front Measure Point	Rear Measure Point	Vehicle Loaded?	Loaded How?
Lumina APV	1990 - 91	9	12 3/4	Yes	See footnote 7
Lumina APV	1992 - 96	9 1/2	13 1/4	Yes	See footnote 7
Malibu	1997 - 98	7 27/32 - 8 27/32	8 13/32 - 9 13/32	No	Curb Weight
Metro (2 door)	1989 - 90	8 1/4 - 10 1/4	10 1/8 - 12 1/8	No	Curb Weight
Metro (2 door Turbo)	1989 - 90	6 7/8 - 8 7/8	9 1/4 - 11 1/4	No	Curb Weight
Metro (4 door)	1989 - 90	8 3/16 - 10 3/16	10 1/4 - 12 1/4	No	Curb Weight
Metro (2 door)	1991	8 1/4 - 10 1/4	10 1/8 - 12 1/8	No	Curb Weight
Metro (4 door)	1991	8 3/16 - 10 3/16	10 1/4 - 12 1/4	No	Curb Weight
Metro (Convertible)	1991	8 1/4 - 10 1/4	10 1/8 - 12 1/8	No	Curb Weight
Metro (2 door)	1992 - 94	7 5/8 - 9 5/8	9 7/16 - 11 7/16	No	Curb Weight
Metro (4 door)	1992 - 94	7 5/8 - 9 5/8	9 5/8 - 11 5/8	No	Curb Weight
Metro (Convertible)	1992 - 94	7 5/8 - 9 5/8	9 7/16 - 11 7/16	No	Curb Weight
Metro (Coupe)	1995 - 97	8 1/2 - 9 1/2	10 15/16 - 11 15/16	No	Curb Weight
Metro (Sedan)	1995 - 97	8 3/8 - 9 3/8	11 3/4 - 12 3/4	No	Curb Weight
Metro (Coupe)	1998	8 1/2 - 9 1/2	9 15/16 - 10 15/16	No	Curb Weight
Metro (Sedan)	1998	8 - 9	9 23/32 - 10 23/32	No	Curb Weight
Monte Carlo (SS)	1984 - 88	13 1/4 - 15 1/4	13 3/4 - 15 3/4	No	Curb Weight
Monte Carlo (all others)	1984 - 88	12 1/4 - 14 1/4	13 3/8 - 15 3/8	No	Curb Weight
		Rocker Behind Front Wheel	Rocker In Front of Rear Wheel		
Monte Carlo	1995 - 98	7 5/8	7 11/16	Yes	See footnote 7
		Bottom of Front Bumper	Bottom of Rear Bumper		
Nova	1985 - 87	14 1/2 - 16 1/2	14 3/4 - 16 3/4	No	Curb Weight
Nova (SL)	1988	14 1/8 - 16 1/8	15 - 17	No	Curb Weight
Nova (all others)	1988	14 1/2 - 16 1/2	14 3/4 - 16 3/4	No	Curb Weight
Prism	1989 - 90	8 3/4 - 10 3/4	11 3/8 - 13 3/8	No	Curb Weight
Prism (GSi)	1991 - 92	8 7/16 - 10 7/16	11 - 13	No	Curb Weight
Prism (all others)	1991 - 92	8 13/16 - 10 13/16	11 3/8 - 13 3/8	No	Curb Weight
Prism	1993 - 97	7 1/4 - 9 1/4	8 13/16 - 10 13/16	No	Curb Weight
Prism	1998	8 - 9	12 1/2 - 13 1/2	No	Curb Weight
Spectrum (Hatchback)	1985 - 86	9 1/2 - 11 1/2	9 7/8 - 11 7/8	No	Curb Weight
Spectrum (Notchback)	1985 - 86	9 1/2 - 11 1/2	9 3/4 - 11 3/4	No	Curb Weight
Spectrum (Hatchback)	1987 - 89	9 - 11	10 1/8 - 12 1/8	No	Curb Weight
Spectrum (Notchback)	1987 - 89	9 - 11	9 7/8 - 11 7/8	No	Curb Weight
Spectrum (Turbo Hatchback)	1987 - 89	8 - 10	10 1/8 - 12 1/8	No	Curb Weight
Spectrum (Turbo Notchback)	1987 - 89	8 - 10	9 7/8 - 11 7/8	No	Curb Weight
Sprint (2 door)	1985 - 86	14 - 16	15 1/2 - 17 1/2	No	Curb Weight
Sprint (4 door)	1985 - 86	14 - 16	15 3/8 - 17 3/8	No	Curb Weight
Sprint	1987 - 88	9 1/4 - 11 1/4	11 - 13	No	Curb Weight
Storm (w/DOHC)	1990 - 91	8 3/8 - 10 3/8	9 - 11	No	Curb Weight
Storm (w/SOHC)	1990 - 91	5 5/8 - 10 5/8	10 1/2 - 12 1/2	No	Curb Weight
Storm	1992 - 93	8 1/4 - 10 1/4	9 3/4 - 11 3/4	No	Curb Weight
Tracker (2 door, 2WD)	1998	10 11/16	12 13/32	No	Curb Weight
Tracker (4 door, 2WD)	1998	10 11/16	15	No	Curb Weight
Tracker (2 door, 4WD)	1998	11 13/32	13 1/2	No	Curb Weight
Tracker (4 door, 4WD)	1998	11 5/16	15 11/16	No	Curb Weight
Venture (Extended)	1997 - 98	8 1/2 - 9 1/2	10 7/8 - 11 7/8	No	Curb Weight
Venture (Regular)	1997 - 98	8 5/16 - 9 5/16	10 13/32 - 11 13/32	No	Curb Weight

Chrysler

Vehicle Make and Model	Year	Bottom of Front Bumper	Bottom of Rear Bumper	Vehicle Loaded?	Loaded How?
Cirrus	1995	6 9/32 - 7 9/32	11 3/16 - 12 3/16	No	Curb Weight
Cirrus	1996 - 98	6 9/32 - 7 9/32	11 3/16 - 12 3/16	No	Curb Weight
Concorde	1993 - 97	8 13/16 - 10 13/16	13 5/8 - 15 5/8	Yes	See footnote 6
Concorde	1998	6 11/16 - 7 11/16	9 - 10	No	Curb Weight

Vehicle Make and Model	Year	Front Measure Point	Rear Measure Point	Vehicle Loaded?	Loaded How?
Conquest	1985 - 89	13 - 15	13 1/2 - 15 1/2	No	Curb Weight
Imperial	1990	11 1/8 - 13 5/8	11 3/4 - 14 1/4	No	Curb Weight
Imperial	1991 - 93	11 1/8 - 13 5/8	11 3/4 - 14 1/4	No	Curb Weight
Laser	1984 - 86	9 1/2 - 12	12 7/8 - 15 3/8	No	Curb Weight
LeBaron (2 door, Convertible)	1985	11 5/8 - 14 1/8	13 3/8 - 15 7/8	No	Curb Weight
LeBaron (2 door, all others)	1985	11 7/8 - 14 3/8	13 1/4 - 15 3/4	No	Curb Weight
LeBaron (4 door, GTS)	1985	10 - 12 1/2	13 1/4 - 15 3/4	No	Curb Weight
LeBaron (4 door, all others)	1985	11 1/4 - 13 3/4	12 3/4 - 15 1/4	No	Curb Weight
LeBaron (Limo)	1985	12 1/4 - 14 3/4	13 3/8 - 15 7/8	No	Curb Weight
LeBaron (Town & Country Wagon)	1985	11 3/4 - 14 1/4	13 1/2 - 16	No	Curb Weight
LeBaron (2 door, Convertible)	1986	11 1/4 - 13 3/4	12 3/4 - 15 1/4	No	Curb Weight
LeBaron (2 door, all others)	1986	11 1/4 - 13 3/4	12 3/4 - 15 1/4	No	Curb Weight
LeBaron (4 door, GTS)	1986	10 - 12 1/2	13 1/4 - 15 3/4	No	Curb Weight
LeBaron (4 door, all others)	1986	11 1/4 - 13 3/4	12 3/4 - 15 1/4	No	Curb Weight
LeBaron (Limo)	1986	12 1/4 - 14 3/4	13 3/8 - 15 7/8	No	Curb Weight
LeBaron (Town & Country Wagon)	1986	11 1/8 - 13 5/8	13 3/8 - 15 7/8	No	Curb Weight
LeBaron (2 door Coupe)	1987 - 88	9 1/2 - 12	12 3/4 - 15 1/4	No	Curb Weight
LeBaron (4 door, GTS)	1987 - 88	12 - 12 1/2	13 1/4 - 15 3/4	No	Curb Weight
LeBaron (4 door, all others)	1987 - 88	11 1/4 - 13 3/4	12 3/4 - 15 1/4	No	Curb Weight
LeBaron (Convertible)	1987 - 88	9 1/2 - 12	12 3/4 - 15 1/4	No	Curb Weight
LeBaron (Town & Country Wagon)	1987 - 88	11 1/8 - 13 5/8	13 3/8 - 15 7/8	No	Curb Weight
LeBaron (2 door Coupe)	1989	9 1/2 - 12	12 3/4 - 15 1/4	No	Curb Weight
LeBaron (4 door, GTS)	1989	10 - 12 1/2	13 1/4 - 15 3/4	No	Curb Weight
LeBaron (Convertible)	1989	9 1/2 - 12	12 3/4 - 15 1/4	No	Curb Weight
LeBaron (2 door Coupe)	1990	9 1/2 - 12	12 3/4 - 15 1/4	No	Curb Weight
LeBaron (4 door)	1990	9 5/8 - 12 1/8	13 - 15 1/2	No	Curb Weight
LeBaron (Convertible)	1990	9 1/2 - 12	12 3/4 - 15 1/4	No	Curb Weight
LeBaron (2 door Coupe)	1991 - 92	9 3/8 - 11 7/8	12 1/4 - 14 3/4	No	Curb Weight
LeBaron (4 door)	1991 - 92	9 5/8 - 12 1/8	12 7/8 - 15 3/8	No	Curb Weight
LeBaron (Convertible)	1991 - 92	9 3/8 - 11 7/8	12 1/4 - 14 3/4	No	Curb Weight
LeBaron (2 door Coupe)	1993 - 95	9 5/8 - 11 5/8	13 - 15	No	Curb Weight
LeBaron (4 door)	1993 - 95	9 7/8 - 11 5/8	13 - 15	No	Curb Weight
LeBaron (Convertible)	1993 - 95	9 5/8 - 11 5/8	13 - 15	No	Curb Weight
LHS	1994 - 97	10 3/16 - 11 3/16	12 7/16 - 13 7/16	Yes	See footnote 6
New Yorker, E-Class	1985 - 87	11 7/8 - 14 3/8	13 3/8 - 15 7/8	No	Curb Weight
New Yorker, E-Class	1988	13 3/8 - 15 7/8	13 3/8 - 15 7/8	No	Curb Weight
New Yorker, Fifth Avenue	1990	11 1/8 - 13 5/8	11 3/4 - 14 1/4	No	Curb Weight
New Yorker, Fifth Avenue, Salon	1991 - 93	9 - 11 1/2	11 3/4 - 14 1/4	No	Curb Weight
New Yorker	1994 - 97	10 3/16 - 11 3/16	12 7/16 - 13 7/16	Yes	See footnote 4
Sebring Convertible	1996 - 98	7 5/16 - 8 5/16	12 - 13	No	Curb Weight
Sebring Coupe	1996	6 3/16 - 7 3/16	11 15/16 - 12 15/16	No	Curb Weight
Sebring Coupe (w/17" wheels)	1997 - 98	7 1/2 - 8 1/2	7 3/4 - 8 3/4	No	Curb Weight
Sebring Coupe (all others)	1997 - 98	7 1/16 - 8 1/16	7 3/8 - 8 3/8	No	Curb Weight
Town & Country (FWD)	1991 - 93	9 3/8	12 1/8	No	Curb Weight
Town & Country (FWD)	1994 - 95	9 3/8	12 1/8	No	Curb Weight
Town & Country (AWD)	1994 - 95	10 5/16	13 1/2	No	Curb Weight
Town & Country (LX FWD)	1996	9 5/8	13 5/8	No	Curb Weight
Town & Country (all others)	1996	9 5/8	13 5/8	No	Curb Weight
Town & Country (SX FWD)	1997 - 98	9 5/8	13 5/8	No	Curb Weight
Town & Country (all others)	1997 - 98	9 5/8	13 5/16	No	Curb Weight

Dodge

Vehicle Make and Model	Year	Front Measure Point	Rear Measure Point	Vehicle Loaded?	Loaded How?
		Bottom of Front Bumper	Bottom of Rear Bumper		
024, Charger	1985 - 87	9 7/8 - 12 3/8	11 7/8 - 14 3/8	No	Curb Weight

Vehicle Make and Model	Year	Front Measure Point	Rear Measure Point	Vehicle Loaded?	Loaded How?
600 (2 door Convertible)	1985	11 5/8 - 14 1/8	13 3/8 - 15 7/8	No	Curb Weight
600 (2 door all others)	1985	11 7/8 - 14 3/8	13 3/8 - 15 7/8	No	Curb Weight
600 (4 door)	1985	11 5/8 - 14 1/8	13 1/4 - 15 3/4	No	Curb Weight
600	1986 - 88	11 1/4 - 13 3/4	12 3/4 - 15 1/4	No	Curb Weight
Aries (Wagon)	1985 - 89	11 1/8 - 13 5/8	13 1/2 - 16	No	Curb Weight
Aries (all others)	1985 - 89	11 1/4 - 13 3/4	12 3/4 - 15 1/4	No	Curb Weight
Avenger	1995 - 96	6 1/4 - 7 1/4	12 - 13	No	Curb Weight
Avenger (w/17" wheels)	1997 - 98	7 1/2 - 8 1/2	7 3/4 - 8 3/4	No	Curb Weight
Avenger (all others)	1997 - 98	7 1/16 - 8 1/6	7 3/8 - 8 3/8	No	Curb Weight
Caravan	1991 - 93	8 7/8	11 5/8	No	Curb Weight
Caravan (FWD, Standard 5 Passenger)	1994 - 95	8 15/16	11 5/8	No	Curb Weight
Caravan (FWD, Standard 7 Passenger)	1994 - 95	8 15/16	11 5/8	No	Curb Weight
Caravan (FWD, Extended)	1994 - 95	9 3/8	12 1/8	No	Curb Weight
Caravan (AWD)	1994 - 95	10 5/16	13 1/2	No	Curb Weight
Caravan (FWD, Standard 5 Passenger)	1996 - 98	9 13/32	13 13/32	No	Curb Weight
Caravan (FWD, Standard 7 Passenger)	1996 - 98	9 13/32	13 13/32	No	Curb Weight
Caravan (FWD, Extended)	1996 - 98	9 13/32	13 3/32	No	Curb Weight
Caravan (AWD)	1996 - 98	9 5/8	13 5/16	No	Curb Weight
Colt (2 door, Hatchback)	1985 - 86	9 1/2 - 10 1/2	12 11/16 - 13 11/16	No	Curb Weight
Colt (4 door, Hatchback)	1985 - 86	9 3/8 - 10 3/8	12 3/8 - 13 3/8	No	Curb Weight
Colt (4 door, Sedan)	1985 - 86	9 3/8 - 10 3/8	13 1/8 - 14 1/8	No	Curb Weight
Colt (2 door)	1987 - 88	9 1/2 - 10 1/2	12 11/16 - 13 11/16	No	Curb Weight
Colt (4 door)	1987 - 88	9 5/16 - 10 5/16	13 1/16 - 14 1/16	No	Curb Weight
Colt (Wagon)	1987 - 88	9 15/16 - 10 15/16	13 1/4 - 14 1/4	No	Curb Weight
Colt (2 door, w/1.5L)	1989 - 90	9 1/4 - 10 1/4	11 1/8 - 12 1/8	No	Curb Weight
Colt (2 door, w/1.6L)	1989 - 90	8 1/4 - 9 1/4	11 1/8 - 12 1/8	No	Curb Weight
Colt (Wagon, 2WD)	1989 - 90	9 15/16 - 10 15/16	13 1/4 - 14 1/4	No	Curb Weight
Colt (Wagon, 4WD)	1989 - 90	11 1/2 - 12 1/2	16 1/4 - 17 1/4	No	Curb Weight
Colt	1991 - 92	9 1/4 - 10 1/4	11 1/8 - 12 1/8	No	Curb Weight
Colt	1993 - 94	6 1/4 - 7 1/4	12 - 13	No	Curb Weight
Colt Vista (2WD)	1985	12 1/2 - 13 1/2	13 1/2 - 14 1/2	No	Curb Weight
Colt Vista (4WD)	1985	16 5/8 - 17 5/8	17 - 18	No	Curb Weight
Colt Vista (2WD)	1986 - 91	14 1/2 - 15 1/2	14 1/2 - 15 1/2	No	Curb Weight
Colt Vista (4WD)	1986 - 91	17 - 18	17 - 18	No	Curb Weight
Daytona	1984 - 86	9 1/2 - 12	12 7/8 - 15 3/8	No	Curb Weight
Daytona (Shelby, Pacifica)	1987	8 - 10 1/2	12 3/8 - 14 7/8	No	Curb Weight
Daytona (all others)	1987	10 7/8 - 13 3/8	12 3/8 - 14 7/8	No	Curb Weight
Daytona (Shelby & Turbo)	1988 - 90	8 - 10 1/2	12 3/8 - 14 7/8	No	Curb Weight
Daytona (all others)	1988 - 90	10 7/8 - 13 3/8	12 3/8 - 14 7/8	No	Curb Weight
Daytona (Shelby & Turbo)	1991	8 1/8 - 10 5/8	12 3/8 - 14 7/8	No	Curb Weight
Daytona (all others)	1991	13 1/8 - 15 5/8	12 3/8 - 14 7/8	No	Curb Weight
Daytona (ES, IROC, & RT)	1992	8 1/8 - 10 5/8	12 3/8 - 14 7/8	No	Curb Weight
Daytona (all others)	1992	13 1/8 - 15 5/8	12 3/8 - 14 7/8	No	Curb Weight
Daytona (ES)	1993	8 9/16 - 10 9/16	9 9/16 - 11 9/16	No	Curb Weight
Daytona (IROC & RT)	1993	5 5/16 - 10 5/16	12 1/2 - 14 1/2	No	Curb Weight
Daytona (Standard)	1993	10 3/16 - 12 3/16	12 11/16 - 14 11/16	No	Curb Weight
Dynasty	1988 - 90	11 1/8 - 13 5/8	11 3/4 - 14 1/4	No	Curb Weight
Dynasty	1991 - 93	9 1/2 - 12	6 1/2 - 9	No	Curb Weight
Intrepid	1993 - 97	8 3/8 - 10 3/8	13 5/8 - 15 5/8	Yes	See footnote 6
Intrepid	1998	6 1/16 - 7 1/16	7 1/8 - 8 1/8	No	Curb Weight
Lancer	1985	10 - 12 1/2	13 1/8 - 15 5/8	No	Curb Weight
Lancer	1986	10 - 12 1/2	13 1/8 - 15 5/8	No	Curb Weight
Lancer (Shelby, Pacifica)	1987 - 89	9 1/2 - 12	12 5/8 - 15 1/8	No	Curb Weight

Vehicle Make and Model	Year	Front Measure Point	Rear Measure Point	Vehicle Loaded?	Loaded How?
Lancer (all others)	1987 - 89	10 - 12 1/2	13 1/4 - 15 3/4	No	Curb Weight
Monaco	1990 - 92	14 1/8 - 16 5/8	14 3/8 - 16 7/8	No	Curb Weight
Neon (Coupe)	1995 - 97	8 1/2 - 9 1/2	13 5/16 - 14 3/4	No	Curb Weight
Neon (Sedan)	1995 - 97	8 1/2 - 9 1/2	13 5/16 - 14 3/4	No	Curb Weight
Neon (Coupe)	1998	8 15/16	14 7/16	No	Curb Weight
Neon (Sedan)	1998	8 15/16	14 7/16	No	Curb Weight
Omni	1986 - 86	13 7/8 - 16 3/8	13 - 15 1/2	No	Curb Weight
Omni	1987	13 - 15 1/2	13 - 15 1/2	No	Curb Weight
Omni	1988 - 90	14 - 16 1/2	14 - 16 1/2	No	Curb Weight
Shadow	1987 - 90	9 1/8 - 11 5/8	12 1/4 - 14 3/4	No	Curb Weight
Shadow	1991	9 1/4 - 11 3/4	11 3/8 - 13 7/8	No	Curb Weight
Shadow (Convertible)	1992	9 1/4 - 11 3/4	11 3/8 - 13 7/8	No	Curb Weight
Shadow (Coupe & Sedan)	1992	9 1/4 - 11 3/4	11 3/8 - 13 7/8	No	Curb Weight
Shadow (Convertible)	1993 - 94	9 - 11	11 7/8 - 13 7/8	No	Curb Weight
Shadow (Coupe & Sedan)	1993 - 94	9 - 11	11 7/8 - 13 7/8	No	Curb Weight
Spirit	1989 - 90	9 5/8 - 12 1/8	13 - 15 1/2	No	Curb Weight
Spirit	1991 - 95	9 7/8 - 11 7/8	13 1/8 - 15 1/8	No	Curb Weight
Stealth (2WD, Base)	1992 - 93	9 5/8 - 10 3/8	11 1/4 - 12	No	Curb Weight
Stealth (2WD, R/T & ES)	1992 - 93	9 7/16 - 10 3/16	10 3/8 - 11 1/8	No	Curb Weight
Stealth (4WD R/T Turbo)	1992 - 93	9 7/16 - 10 3/16	10 3/8 - 11 1/8	No	Curb Weight
Stealth (2WD, Base)	1994 - 96	8 15/16 - 9 15/16	11 3/16 - 12 3/16	No	Curb Weight
Stealth (2WD, R/T & ES)	1994 - 96	7 7/16 - 8 7/16	9 5/8 - 10 5/8	No	Curb Weight
Stealth (4WD R/T Turbo)	1994 - 96	7 7/16 - 8 7/16	9 5/8 - 10 5/8	No	Curb Weight
Stratus (4 door, Sedan)	1996 - 98	6 1/4 - 7 1/4	11 3/16 - 12 3/16	No	Curb Weight
Stratus (ES, 4 door, Sedan)	1996 - 98	6 1/4 - 7 1/4	11 3/16 - 12 3/16	No	Curb Weight

Eagle

Vehicle Make and Model	Year	Bottom of Front Bumper	Bottom of Rear Bumper	Vehicle Loaded?	Loaded How?
Medallion (Sedan)	1988 - 89	9 - 11	13 - 15	No	Curb Weight
Medallion (Wagon)	1988 - 89	8 3/4 - 10 3/4	11 3/8 - 13 3/8	No	Curb Weight
Premier	1988 - 92	14 3/8 - 16 3/8	14 3/4 - 16 3/4	No	Curb Weight
Summit	1989 - 90	8 3/4 - 10 3/4	11 1/8 - 13 1/8	No	Curb Weight
Summit (2 door)	1991 - 92	8 3/4 - 10 3/4	10 5/8 - 12 5/8	No	Curb Weight
Summit (4 door)	1991 - 92	8 3/4 - 10 3/4	11 1/8 - 13 1/8	No	Curb Weight
Summit	1993 - 96	8 3/8 - 9 3/8	9 3/4 - 10 3/4	No	Curb Weight
Summit Wagon (FWD)	1992 - 96	10 3/8 - 11 3/8	13 3/16 - 14 3/16	No	Curb Weight
Summit Wagon (AWD)	1992 - 96	10 13/16 - 11 13/16	13 3/4 - 14 3/4	No	Curb Weight
Talon (FWD, w/Turbo)	1990 - 91	7 3/8 - 9 3/8	12 3/8 - 14 3/8	No	Curb Weight
Talon (FWD all others)	1990 - 91	8 1/2 - 10 1/2	12 5/8 - 14 5/8	No	Curb Weight
Talon (AWD)	1990 - 91	7 7/8 - 9 7/8	13 - 15	No	Curb Weight
Talon (FWD)	1992	8 - 10	10 - 12	No	Curb Weight
Talon (AWD)	1992	8 9/16 - 10 9/16	10 9/16 - 12 9/16	No	Curb Weight
Talon (FWD)	1993 - 94	7 3/4 - 9 3/4	12 13/16 - 14 13/16	No	Curb Weight
Talon (AWD)	1993 - 94	8 5/16 - 10 5/16	13 3/8 - 15 3/8	No	Curb Weight
Talon (ESi)	1995 - 98	5 5/16 - 6 5/16	9 - 10	No	Curb Weight
Talon (ESi; TSi, FWD)	1995 - 98	5 5/16 - 6 5/16	9 - 10	No	Curb Weight
Talon (TSi, AWD)	1995 - 98	5 13/16 - 6 13/16	9 1/2 - 10 1/2	No	Curb Weight
Vision	1993 - 97	13 1/2 - 15 1/4	13 9/16 - 15 9/16	Yes	See footnote 6

Ford

Vehicle Make and Model	Year	Bottom of Front Bumper	Bottom of Rear Bumper	Vehicle Loaded?	Loaded How?
Aspire	1994 - 97	9 11/16 - 10 11/16	13 3/16 - 14 3/16	No	Curb Weight
Contour	1995 - 98	8 1/2 - 9 1/2	11 29/32 - 12 29/32	No	Curb Weight
Escort (2 door)	1985	14 - 16 3/4	14 1/8 - 16 3/4	No	Curb Weight
Escort (4 door)	1985	14 - 16 3/4	14 1/8 - 16 3/4	No	Curb Weight

Vehicle Make and Model	Year	Front Measure Point	Rear Measure Point	Vehicle Loaded?	Loaded How?
Escort (Wagon)	1985	14 - 16 3/4	14 1/8 - 16 3/4	No	Curb Weight
Escort (2 door, GT)	1986 - 87	14 1/2 - 16 5/8	13 3/8 - 15 1/2	No	Curb Weight
Escort (2 door, all others)	1986 - 87	13 3/4 - 15 7/8	14 1/8 - 16 1/4	No	Curb Weight
Escort (4 door)	1986 - 87	13 3/4 - 15 7/8	14 1/8 - 16 1/4	No	Curb Weight
Escort (Wagon)	1986 - 87	13 3/4 - 15 7/8	14 - 16	No	Curb Weight
Escort (2 door, GT)	1988 - 89	9 11/16 - 11 11/16	11 1/2 - 13 1/2	No	Curb Weight
Escort (2 door, all others)	1988 - 89	10 1/8 - 12 1/8	11 7/8 - 13 7/8	No	Curb Weight
Escort (4 door)	1988 - 89	10 - 12	11 7/8 - 13 7/8	No	Curb Weight
Escort (Wagon)	1988 - 89	10 1/8 - 12 1/8	11 7/8 - 13 7/8	No	Curb Weight
Escort (2 door, GT)	1990	9 3/4 - 11 3/4	11 5/8 - 13 5/8	No	Curb Weight
Escort (2 door, all others)	1990	10 1/8 - 12 1/8	11 7/8 - 13 7/8	No	Curb Weight
Escort (4 door)	1990	10 1/8 - 12 1/8	11 7/8 - 13 7/8	No	Curb Weight
Escort (Wagon)	1990	10 1/8 - 12 1/8	11 7/8 - 13 7/8	No	Curb Weight
Escort (Wagon)	1991 - 96	Rocker Behind Front Wheel 5 15/16	Rocker In Front of Rear Wheel 5 15/16	Yes	See footnote 8
Escort (all others)	1991 - 96	Bottom of Front Bumper 8 7/8 - 9 5/8	Bottom of Rear Bumper 12 1/8 - 12 7/8	No	Curb Weight
EXP	1983 - 85	15 7/8 - 18 3/8	14 1/8 - 16 5/8	Yes - Front	See footnote 7
EXP	1986 - 87	14 1/8 - 16 5/8	14 - 16 1/2	Yes - Front	See footnote 7
EXP	1988	8 3/8 - 10 3/8	13 3/8 - 15 3/8	No	Curb Weight
Festiva	1988 - 93	9 5/16 - 10 1/16	11 15/16 - 12 1/16	No	Curb Weight
Full Size (Wagon)	1985	12 1/2 - 15 1/2	12 1/2 - 15 1/2	No	Curb Weight
Full Size (all others)	1985	12 5/8 - 15 5/8	12 5/8 - 15 5/8	No	Curb Weight
Full Size (Wagon)	1986	12 5/8 - 15 5/8	11 1/8 - 14 1/8	No	Curb Weight
Full Size (all others)	1986	13 - 16	13 - 16	No	Curb Weight
Full Size (Wagon)	1987	12 5/8 - 15 5/8	11 1/8 - 14 1/8	No	Curb Weight
Full Size (all others)	1987	12 7/8 - 15 7/8	12 7/8 - 15 7/8	No	Curb Weight
Full Size (Wagon)	1988 - 90	12 5/16 - 15 5/16	12 1/2 - 15 1/2	No	Curb Weight
Full Size (all others)	1988 - 90	12 11/16 - 15 11/16	12 13/16 - 15 13 16	No	Curb Weight
Full Size (Wagon)	1991	13 1/16 - 16 1/16	12 3/4 - 15 3/4	No	Curb Weight
Full Size (all others)	1991	13 3/8 - 16 3/8	12 1/4 - 15 1/4	No	Curb Weight
Full Size	1992	12 1/8 - 14 1/8	13 5/8 - 15 5/8	No	Curb Weight
Full Size	1993 - 97	14 7/16 - 16 7/16	13 5/8 - 15 5/8	No	Curb Weight
LTD (Sedan)	1985 - 86	12 1/2 - 15 1/4	12 1/4 - 15 1/8	No	Curb Weight
LTD (Wagon)	1985 - 86	12 1/2 - 15 1/4	12 - 14 7/8	No	Curb Weight
Mustang	1984 - 86	13 3/4 - 16 3/4	14 5/8 - 16 5/8	No	Curb Weight
Mustang	1987 - 90	13 7/8 - 16 7/8	14 5/8 - 16 5/8	No	Curb Weight
Mustang	1991 - 93	14 3/8 - 16 3/8	14 1/2 - 16 1/2	No	See footnote 9
Mustang (Cobra Convertible)	1994 - 97	6 1/2 - 7 1/2	13 11/16 - 14 11/16	No	Curb Weight
Mustang (Cobra Coupe)	1994 - 97	6 11/16 - 7 11/16	13 13/16 - 14 13/16	No	Curb Weight
Mustang (Convertible Base)	1994 - 97	6 11/16 - 7 11/16	13 3/16 - 14 3/16	No	Curb Weight
Mustang (Convertible GT)	1994 - 97	6 1/2 - 7 1/2	13 11/16 - 14 11/16	No	Curb Weight
Mustang (Coupe Base)	1994 - 97	6 15/16 - 7 15/16	13 5/16 - 14 5/16	No	Curb Weight
Mustang (Coupe GT)	1994 - 97	6 11/16 - 7 11/16	13 13/16 - 14 13/16	No	Curb Weight
Probe	1988 - 89	7 1/4 - 8	12 1/2 - 13 1/4	No	Curb Weight
Probe (GL)	1990	7 1/4 - 8	12 1/2 - 13 1/4	No	Curb Weight
Probe (GT)	1990	6 11/16 - 7 7/16	11 - 11 3/4	No	Curb Weight
Probe (LX)	1990	7 5/16 - 8 1/16	12 5/8 - 13 3/8	No	Curb Weight
Probe (GL)	1991 - 92	7 1/4 - 8	13 11/16 - 14 7/16	No	Curb Weight
Probe (GT)	1991 - 92	6 11/16 - 7 7/16	12 3/16 - 12 15/16	No	Curb Weight
Probe (LX)	1991 - 92	7 5/16 - 8 1/16	13 13/16 - 14 9/16	No	Curb Weight
Taurus (Sedan)	1986	13 1/8 - 13 7/8	13 3/4 - 14 1/2	No	Curb Weight
Taurus (Wagon)	1986	13 1/4 - 14	13 7/8 - 14 5/8	No	Curb Weight

Vehicle Make and Model	Year	Front Measure Point	Rear Measure Point	Vehicle Loaded?	Loaded How?
Taurus (Sedan)	1987	13 1/8 - 13 7/8	13 3/4 - 14 1/2	No	Curb Weight
Taurus (Wagon)	1987	13 1/4 - 14	13 13/16 - 14 9/16	No	Curb Weight
Taurus (Sedan)	1988	10 - 10 3/4	14 1/4 - 15	No	Curb Weight
Taurus (Wagon)	1988	10 1/8 - 10 7/8	14 1/8 - 14 7/8	No	Curb Weight
Taurus (Sedan)	1989	9 5/16 - 10 1/16	14 - 14 3/4	No	Curb Weight
Taurus (Wagon)	1989	9 1/2 - 10 1/4	14 1/8 - 14 7/8	No	Curb Weight
Taurus (Sedan)	1990	9 3/8 - 10 1/8	14 1/16 - 14 13/16	No	Curb Weight
Taurus (Wagon)	1990	9 1/2 - 10 1/4	14 1/8 - 14 7/8	No	Curb Weight
Taurus (Sedan)	1991 - 97	10 3/16 - 11 9-16	14 1/16 - 14 13/16	No	Curb Weight
Taurus (Wagon)	1991 - 97	9 1/2 - 10 3/8	14 1/8 - 14 7/8	No	Curb Weight
Taurus (Wagon)	1996 - 97	9 1/2 - 10 1/2	12 11/16 - 13 11/16	No	Curb Weight
Taurus (SHO)	1985	15 3/8 - 16 1/8	15 3/8 - 16 1/8	No	Curb Weight
Tempo	1986 - 87	14 1/2 - 15 1/4	14 1/2 - 15 1/4	No	Curb Weight
Tempo	1988	9 15/16 - 10 11/16	13 5/8 - 14 3/8	No	Curb Weight
Tempo	1989 - 91	9 3/4 - 10 1/2	13 9/16 - 14 5/16	No	Curb Weight
Tempo	1992 - 94	9 13/16 - 10 9/16	10 1/4 - 11	No	Curb Weight
Thunderbird	1983 - 86	12 3/4 - 15	12 1/4 - 14 1/4	No	Curb Weight
Thunderbird	1987 - 88	14 3/8 - 16 3/8	14 5/8 - 16 5/8	No	Curb Weight
Thunderbird	1989 - 93	14 3/16 - 16 3/16	14 5/8 - 16 5/8	No	Curb Weight
Thunderbird	1994 - 97	13 - 14	15 1/8 - 16 1/8	No	Curb Weight
Honda					
		Top of Front Wheel Opening	Top of Rear Wheel Opening		
Accord (w/A.C.)	1985	25 5/8 - 23 3/8	25 1/8 - 25 3/4	No	Curb Weight
Accord (all others)	1985	25 3/4 - 26 5/8	25 1/8 - 25 3/4	No	Curb Weight
Accord (Hatchback)	1986 - 87	25 5/8 - 26 1/4	25 5/8 - 26 1/4	No	Curb Weight
Accord (Sedan)	1986 - 87	25 5/8 - 26 1/4	25 5/8 - 26 1/4	No	Curb Weight
Accord (Coupe)	1988 - 89	25 5/8 - 26 1/4	25 5/8 - 26 1/4	No	Curb Weight
Accord (Hatchback)	1988 - 89	25 5/8 - 26 1/4	25 5/8 - 26 1/4	No	Curb Weight
Accord (Sedan)	1988 - 89	25 5/8 - 26 1/4	25 3/8 - 26	No	Curb Weight
Accord (Coupe)	1990 - 91	26 1/8 - 27 1/8	26 3/8 - 27 3/8	No	Curb Weight
Accord (Sedan)	1990 - 91	26 1/8 - 27 1/8	26 5/8 - 27 5/8	No	Curb Weight
		Bottom of Front Bumper	Bottom of Rear Bumper		
Accord (Wagon)	1990 - 91	8 1/16	9 11/16	Yes	See footnote 10
Accord (DX, LX)	1992 - 93	10 1/2 - 11 1/2	10 7/8 - 11 7/8	No	Curb Weight
Accord (EX, SE)	1992 - 93	8 11/16 - 9 11/16	10 7/8 - 11 7/8	No	Curb Weight
Accord (Wagon)	1992 - 93	8 - 9	11 1/2 - 12 1/2	No	Curb Weight
Accord	1994 - 97	5 5/8 - 6 5/8	9 15/16 - 10 15/16	No	Curb Weight
Accord Coupe (LX, EX)	1998	8 1/2 - 9 1/2	10 - 11	No	Curb Weight
Accord Coupe (LX-V6, EX-V6)	1998	9 - 10	11 - 12	No	Curb Weight
Accord Sedan (DX, LX, EX)	1998	8 3/4 - 9 3/4	10 1/2 - 11 1/2	No	Curb Weight
Accord Sedan (LX-V6, EX-V6)	1998	9 1/2 - 10 1/2	10 7/8 - 11 7/8	No	Curb Weight
T		Top of Front Wheel Opening	Top of Rear Wheel Opening		
Civic (CRX)	1984 - 85	24 3/4 - 26	24 5/8 - 25 1/4	No	Curb Weight
Civic (Hatchback)	1984 - 85	24 7/8 - 26	25 - 25 5/8	No	Curb Weight
Civic (Sedan)	1984 - 85	25 - 26 1/4	24 3/4 - 25 5/8	No	Curb Weight
Civic (Wagon)	1984 - 85	25 - 26 1/8	25 1/4 - 25 7/8	No	Curb Weight
Civic (CRX)	1986 - 87	24 3/4 - 26	24 5/8 - 25 1/4	No	Curb Weight
Civic (Hatchback)	1986 - 87	24 7/8 - 26	25 - 25 5/8	No	Curb Weight
Civic (Sedan)	1986 - 87	25 - 26 1/4	24 3/4 - 25 5/8	No	Curb Weight
Civic (Wagon, 2WD)	1986 - 87	25 - 26 1/8	25 1/4 - 25 7/8	No	Curb Weight
Civic (Wagon, 4WD)	1986 - 87	25 - 26 1/8	25 1/4 - 25 7/8	No	Curb Weight
Civic (CRX)	1988	25 1/8 - 26 3/8	26 1/8 - 26 3/4	No	Curb Weight
Civic (Hatchback)	1988	25 1/8 - 26 3/8	26 1/8 - 26 3/4	No	Curb Weight

Vehicle Make and Model	Year	Front Measure Point	Rear Measure Point	Vehicle Loaded?	Loaded How?
Civic (Sedan)	1988	25 1/8 - 26 3/8	26 1/8 - 26 3/4	No	Curb Weight
Civic (Wagon, 2WD)	1988	25 1/8 - 26 3/8	26 1/8 - 26 3/4	No	Curb Weight
Civic (Wagon, 4WD)	1988	25 7/8 - 27 1/8	26 3/4 - 27 3/8	No	Curb Weight
Civic (CRX)	1989	24 5/8 - 25 7/8	25 1/8 - 25 3/4	No	Curb Weight
Civic (Hatchback)	1989	24 5/8 - 25 7/8	25 1/8 - 25 3/4	No	Curb Weight
Civic (Sedan)	1989	24 5/8 - 25 7/8	25 1/8 - 25 3/4	No	Curb Weight
Civic (Wagon, 2WD)	1989	25 1/8 - 26 3/8	25 1/8 - 25 3/4	No	Curb Weight
Civic (Wagon, 4WD)	1989	25 7/8 - 27 1/8	26 3/4 - 27 3/8	No	Curb Weight
Civic (CRX)	1990 - 91	24 3/4 - 25 7/8	25 1/4 - 26 3/8	No	Curb Weight
Civic (Hatchback)	1990 - 91	24 3/4 - 25 7/8	25 1/4 - 26 3/8	No	Curb Weight
Civic (Sedan)	1990 - 91	24 3/4 - 25 7/8	25 1/4 - 26 3/8	No	Curb Weight
Civic (Wagon, 2WD)	1990 - 91	25 1/8 - 26 3/8	26 1/8 - 27 5/16	No	Curb Weight
Civic (Wagon, 4WD)	1990 - 91	25 7/8 - 26 1/8	26 13/16 - 28	No	Curb Weight
		Bottom of Front Bumper	Bottom of Rear Bumper		
Civic (Coupe)	1992 - 97	5 3/4 - 6 3/4	11 11/16 - 12 11/6	No	Curb Weight
Civic (del sol)	1992 - 97	7 1/16 - 8 1/16	11 13/16 - 12 13/16	No	Curb Weight
Civic (Hatchback)	1992 - 97	5 3/4 - 6 3/4	11 13/16 - 12 13/16	No	Curb Weight
Civic (Hatchback CX, DX, Si)	1992 - 97	5 3/16 - 7 3/16	11 13/16 - 12 13/16	No	Curb Weight
Civic (Sedan)	1992 - 97	6 3/4 - 7 3/4	11 11/16 - 12 11/6	No	Curb Weight
Civic (Hatchback)	1998	7 3/4 - 8 3/4	10 11/32 - 11 11/32	No	Curb Weight
Civic (Sedan)	1998	7 3/4 - 8 3/4	9 11/16 - 10 11/16	No	Curb Weight
CR-V	1997 - 98	11 3/32 - 13 3/32	14 1/2 - 16 1/2	No	Curb Weight
EV	1998	8 3/4 - 9 3/4	10 1/2 - 11 1/2	No	Curb Weight
Odyssey (LX, EX)	1998	10 - 11	10 1/2 - 11 1/2	No	Curb Weight
Odyssey (LX-7 Passenger)	1998	9 5/8 - 10 5/8	10 5/8 - 11 5/8	No	Curb Weight
		Top of Front Wheel Opening	Top of Rear Wheel Opening		
Prelude	1983 - 85	25 5/8 - 26 1/4	25 1/4 - 25 3/4	No	Curb Weight
Prelude (Si)	1986 - 87	25 5/8 - 28 1/4	25 1/4 - 25 3/4	No	Curb Weight
Prelude (all others)	1986 - 87	25 5/8 - 26 1/4	25 1/4 - 25 3/4	No	Curb Weight
Prelude	1988 - 90	25 3/4 - 26 7/8	25 1/2 - 26 3/4	No	Curb Weight
		Bottom of Front Bumper	Bottom of Rear Bumper		
Prelude	1991	7 11/16	9 11/16	Yes	Curb Weight
Prelude (Si, Si V-TEC)	1992 - 96	8 1/8 - 9 1/8	11 1/2 - 12 1/2	No	Curb Weight
Prelude (all others)	1992 - 96	10 1/16 - 11 1/16	11 1/2 - 12 1/2	No	Curb Weight
Prelude	1997 - 98	8 - 9	10 - 11	No	Curb Weight
Hyundai					
		Bottom of Front Bumper	Bottom of Rear Bumper		
Elantra	1992 - 95	8 1/2 - 9 1/4	10 3/16 - 10 15/16	No	Curb Weight
Excel	1986 - 89	9 3/4 - 10 3/4	13 1/2 - 14 1/2	No	Curb Weight
Excel (Hatchback)	1990 - 91	9 - 9 3/4	11 - 11 3/4	No	Curb Weight
Excel (Sedan)	1990 - 91	9 - 9 3/4	10 1/2 - 11 1/4	No	Curb Weight
Excel (Hatchback)	1992 - 94	8 11/16 - 9 7/16	9 13/16 - 10 9/16	No	Curb Weight
Excel (Sedan)	1992 - 94	8 11/16 - 9 7/16	9 3/16 - 9 15/16	No	Curb Weight
Sonata	1989	9 1/2 - 10 1/2	13 - 14	No	Curb Weight
Sonata	1990 - 91	10 5/16 - 11 1/16	10 1/2 - 11 1/4	No	Curb Weight
Sonata	1992 - 93	7 3/4 - 8 1/2	10 9/16 - 11 5/16	No	Curb Weight
S-Coupe	1991 - 92	8 9/16 - 9 5/16	10 - 10 3/4	No	Curb Weight
S-Coupe	1994 - 95	7 3/16 - 7 15/16	9 13/16 - 10 9/16	No	Curb Weight
Infiniti					
		Bottom of Front Bumper	Bottom of Rear Bumper		
G20	1991 - 96	7 15/16 - 8 11/16	9 15/16 - 10 11/16	No	Curb Weight
J30	1993 - 97	8 9/16 - 9 3/16	11 5/8 - 12 3/8	No	Curb Weight
M30	1990 - 92	9 7/16 - 10 15/16	10 7/8 - 12 3/8	No	Curb Weight

Vehicle Make and Model	Year	Front Measure Point	Rear Measure Point	Vehicle Loaded?	Loaded How?
Q45	1990	7 11/16 - 9 3/16	9 15/16 - 11 7/16	No	Curb Weight
Q45	1991 - 96	7 11/16 - 9 3/16	9 15/16 - 11 7/16	No	Curb Weight
Q45	1997	8 1/2 - 9 1/2	15 5/32 - 16 5/32	No	Curb Weight
Isuzu		Bottom of Front Bumper	Bottom of Rear Bumper		
I-Mark (2 door)	1983 - 85	15 7/8 - 16 5/8	15 7/8 - 16 5/8	No	Curb Weight
I-Mark (4 door)	1983 - 85	15 7/8 - 16 5/8	15 7/8 - 16 5/8	No	Curb Weight
I-Mark (2 door, RS)	1986 - 88	8 5/8 - 9 3/8	10 11/16 - 11 7/16	No	Curb Weight
I-Mark (2 door, all others)	1986 - 88	9 5/8 - 10 3/8	10 11/16 - 11 7/16	No	Curb Weight
I-Mark (4 door, RS)	1986 - 88	8 5/8 - 9 3/8	10 1/2 - 11 1/4	No	Curb Weight
I-Mark (4 door, all others)	1986 - 88	9 5/8 - 10 3/8	10 1/2 - 11 1/4	No	Curb Weight
I-Mark (2 door)	1989	8 3/8 - 9 1/8	9 7/8 - 10 5/8	No	Curb Weight
I-Mark (4 door)	1989	8 3/8 - 9 1/8	9 11/16 - 10 7/16	No	Curb Weight
Impulse	1983 - 89	14 7/8 - 15 5/8	16 3/8 - 17 1/8	No	Curb Weight
Impulse (Coupe)	1991 - 92	9 1/4 - 10	11 - 11 3/4	No	Curb Weight
Impulse (Hatchback)	1991 - 92	9 1/4 - 10	9 5/8 - 10 3/8	No	Curb Weight
Stylus	1991 - 93	8 3/8 - 9 1/8	9 7/8 - 10 5/8	No	Curb Weight
Jaguar		Bottom of Front Bumper	Bottom of Rear Bumper		
XJ-6	1994	12 1/2 - 13 1/2	15 7/16 - 16 7/16	No	Curb Weight
XJ-12	1994	12 1/2 - 13 1/2	15 7/16 - 16 7/16	No	Curb Weight
XJS (Convertible)	1994	14 1/2 - 15 1/2	15 1/4 - 16 1/4	No	Curb Weight
XJS (Coupe)	1994	14 1/2 - 15 1/2	15 1/4 - 16 1/4	No	Curb Weight
Lexus		Bottom of Front Bumper	Bottom of Rear Bumper		
ES 250	1990	10 1/4	13 3/4	No	Curb Weight
ES 250	1991	10 1-4	13 3/4	No	Curb Weight
ES 300	1992 - 96	10	13	No	Curb Weight
ES 300	1997 - 98	9 13/16	13 19/32	No	Curb Weight
GS 300	1993 - 97	8 11/16	13	No	Curb Weight
GS 300, GS 400	1998	7 29/32	11 5/8	No	Curb Weight
LS 400 (w/Air Suspension)	1990	9 7/8	13 3/4	No	Curb Weight
LS 400 (all others)	1990	9 7/8	14 15/16	No	Curb Weight
LS 400 (w/Air Suspension)	1991 - 92	9 7/16	13 3/4	No	Curb Weight
LS 400 (all others)	1991 - 92	9 7/16	14 15/16	No	Curb Weight
LS 400 (w/Air Suspension)	1993 - 94	10	14 3/8	No	Curb Weight
LS 400 (all others)	1993 - 94	10	15 9/16	No	Curb Weight
LS 400 (w/Air Suspension)	1995 - 98	8 7/8	11 13/32	No	Curb Weight
LS 400 (all others)	1995 - 98	9 7/16	12 3/16	No	Curb Weight
LX 470	1998	15 13/32	17 29/32	No	Curb Weight
RX 300	1999	13 19/32	17 1/8	No	Curb Weight
SC 300	1992 - 94	7 1/2	12 3/16	No	Curb Weight
SC 300	1995 - 97	7 1/2	12 13/32	No	Curb Weight
SC 300	1998	9 1/16	12 3/16	No	Curb Weight
SC 400	1992	7 11/16	12	No	Curb Weight
SC 400	1993 - 94	7 11/16	12 3/8	No	Curb Weight
SC 400	1995 - 97	7 11/16	12 13/32	No	Curb Weight
SC 400	1998	9 1/16	12 3/16	No	Curb Weight
Lincoln		Bottom of Front Bumper	Bottom of Rear Bumper		
Continental	1984 - 85	12 5/8 - 15 1/8	12 1/8 - 14 5/8	No	Curb Weight
Continental	1986 - 87	12 1/2 -15	12 7/8 - 15 3/8	No	Curb Weight
Continental	1988	9 9/16 - 12 1/16	11 5/8 - 14 1/8	No	Curb Weight

Vehicle Make and Model	Year	Front Measure Point	Rear Measure Point	Vehicle Loaded?	Loaded How?
Continental	1989 - 92	9 5/8 - 12 1/8	11 9/16 - 14 1/16	No	Curb Weight
Continental	1993 - 94	9 15/16 - 11 15/16	11 13/16 - 13 13/16	No	Curb Weight
Continental	1995 - 97	8 7/16 - 9 7/16	12 3/8 - 13 3/8	No	Curb Weight
Mark V, VI, VII, VIII	1984 - 89	13 3/4 - 15 3/4	13 7/8 - 16 3/8	No	Curb Weight
Mark V, VI, VII, VIII	1990	13 3/4 - 15 3/4	13 7/8 - 16 3/8	No	Curb Weight
Mark V, VI, VII, VIII	1991 - 92	13 9/16 - 16 1/16	13 7/8 - 16 3/8	No	Curb Weight
Mark V, VI, VII, VIII	1993 - 94	11 13/16 - 13 13/16	12 1/2 - 14 1/2	No	Curb Weight
Mark V, VI, VII, VIII	1995 - 97	12 5/16 - 13 5/16	13 - 14	No	Curb Weight
Town Car	1984 - 85	12 1/4 - 15 1/4	11 1/8 - 14 1/8	No	Curb Weight
Town Car	1986 - 89	12 - 15	10 7/8 - 13 7/8	No	Curb Weight
Town Car	1990 - 97	13 1/2 - 16 1/2	14 - 17	No	Curb Weight

Mazda

Vehicle Make and Model	Year	Front Measure Point	Rear Measure Point	Vehicle Loaded?	Loaded How?
323, Protégé (Hatchback)	1986 - 87	Center of Marker Light 25 1/8 - 25 1/2	Center of Marker Light 29 1/16 - 29 1/2	No	Curb Weight
323, Protégé (Sedan)	1986 - 87	25 3/8 - 25 3/4	27 1/2 - 27 15/16	No	Curb Weight
323, Protégé (Hatchback)	1988 - 90	24 3/4 - 25 3/4	28 3/4 - 29 3/4	No	Curb Weight
323, Protégé (Sedan)	1988 - 90	24 3/4 - 25 3/4	26 1/2 - 27 1/2	No	Curb Weight
323, Protégé (Hatchback)	1991	Bottom of Front Bumper 8	Bottom of Rear Bumper 10 7/16	Yes	See footnote 3
323, Protégé (Sedan, 4x2)	1991	8	10 7/16	Yes	See footnote 3
323, Protégé (Sedan, 4x4)	1991	8 15/16	10 3/4	Yes	See footnote 3
323, Protégé	1992 - 93	5 11/16 - 6 11/16	5 11/16 - 6 11/16	No	Curb Weight
626 (Coupe)	1983 - 85	Center of Marker Light 20 - 20 7/16	Center of Marker Light 30 11/16 - 31 1/16	No	Curb Weight
626 (Hatchback)	1983 - 85	20 1/16 - 20 1/2	29 1/8 - 29 1/2	No	Curb Weight
626 (Sedan)	1983 - 85	20 - 20 7/16	30 3/4 - 31 3/16	No	Curb Weight
626 (Coupe & Hatchback)	1986 - 87	20 3/16 - 20 9/16	29 1/4 - 29 5/8	No	Curb Weight
626 (Sedan)	1986 - 87	20 3/16 - 20 9/16	26 15/16 - 27 3/8	No	Curb Weight
626	1988 - 92	26 - 27	27 1/4 - 28 1/4	No	Curb Weight
929	1988 - 90	24 3/4 - 25 3/4	26 1/2 - 27 1/2	No	Curb Weight
929	1991	Bottom of Front Bumper 8 3/4	Bottom of Rear Bumper 12 9/16	Yes	See footnote 3
929	1992 - 93	8 5/16	11 3/8	Yes	See footnote 3
GLC (3 door, Hatchback)	1981 - 85	Center of Marker Light 24 3/8 - 25 1/8	Center of Marker Light 23 1/2 - 24 3/8	No	Curb Weight
GLC (4 door, Sedan)	1981 - 85	24 1/4 - 25	27 - 27 3/4	No	Curb Weight
GLC (5 door, Hatchback)	1981 - 85	24 1/4 - 25	23 1/4 - 24	No	Curb Weight
GLC (Wagon)	1981 - 85	26 5/8 - 27 1/2	24 1/8 - 24 7/8	No	Curb Weight
Miata	1990 - 93	15 5/8 - 16 3/8	17 7/8 - 18 5/8	No	Curb Weight
MPV (4x2, 5 Passenger)	1992 - 93	Bottom of Front Bumper 10 9/16	Bottom of Rear Bumper 10 7/8	No	Curb Weight
MPV (4x2, 7 Passenger)	1992 - 93	10 9/16	10 7/8	No	Curb Weight
MPV (4x4)	1992 - 93	13 5/16	13 5/8	No	Curb Weight
MPV (4x2, 7 Passenger)	1996	10 3/32 - 11 3/32	10 13/32 - 11 13/32	Yes	See footnote 11
MPV (4x4, 7 Passenger)	1996	12 11/16 - 13 11/16	13 1/8 - 14 1/8	Yes	See footnote 11
MX3 (GS)	1992 - 93	Center of Marker Light 6 - 7	Center of Marker Light 6 - 7	No	Curb Weight
MX3 (all others)	1992 - 93	6 - 7	6 - 7	No	Curb Weight
MX3 (GS)	1996	Bottom of Front Bumper 8 - 9	Bottom of Rear Bumper 12 9/32 - 13 9/32	No	Curb Weight
MX3 (all others)	1996	9 1/2 - 10 1/2	12 - 13	No	Curb Weight
MX6	1988 - 92	Center of Marker Light 18 1/2 - 19 1/2	Center of Marker Light 21 3/4 - 22 3/4	No	Curb Weight

Vehicle Make and Model	Year	Front Measure Point	Rear Measure Point	Vehicle Loaded?	Loaded How?
Protégé (DX, LX Sedan)	1997 - 98	6 1/2 - 7 1/2	8 - 9	Yes	See footnote 3
Protégé (ES Sedan)	1997 - 98	6 11/16 - 7 11/16	8 1/4 - 9 1/4	Yes	See footnote 3
		Center of Marker Light	Center of Marker Light		
RX7 (Manual Transmission)	1984 - 85	19 9/16 - 20	20 5/8 - 20 7/8	No	Curb Weight
RX7 (Automatic Transmission)	1984 - 85	19 7/8 - 20 1/4	20 1/2 - 20 3/4	No	Curb Weight
RX7	1986 - 88	18 1/4 - 18 11/16	19 7/16 - 19 3/4	No	Curb Weight
RX7	1989 - 91	19 1/8 - 20 1/8	20 - 21	No	Curb Weight
		Bottom of Front Bumper	Bottom of Rear Bumper		
RX7 (w/R-1 Package)	1993	5 7/16 - 6 7/16	5 3/16 - 6 3/16	No	Curb Weight
RX7 (all others)	1993	5 7/16 - 6 7/16	5 3/16 - 6 3/16	No	Curb Weight
Mercury					
		Bottom of Front Bumper	Bottom of Rear Bumper		
Capri	1984 - 86	13 3/4 - 16 3/4	14 5/8 - 16 5/8	No	Curb Weight
Capri (XR2)	1991 - 94	9 5/16 - 10 5/16	10 7/16 - 11 7/16	No	Curb Weight
Capri (all others)	1991 - 94	9 13/16 - 10 9/16	10 15/16 - 11 11/16	No	Curb Weight
Cougar	1983 - 86	12 3/4 - 15	12 1/4 - 14 1/4	No	Curb Weight
Cougar	1987 - 88	14 3/8 - 16 3/8	14 5/8 - 16 5/8	No	Curb Weight
Cougar	1989 - 93	14 3/16 - 16 3/16	14 5/8 - 16 5/8	No	Curb Weight
Cougar	1994 - 97	13 - 14	15 1/8 - 16 1/8	No	Curb Weight
Full Size (Wagon)	1985	12 1/2 - 15 1/2	12 1/2 - 15 1/2	No	Curb Weight
Full Size (all others)	1985	12 5/8 - 15 5/8	12 5/8 - 15 5/8	No	Curb Weight
Full Size (Wagon)	1986	12 5/8 - 15 5/8	11 1/8 - 14 1/8	No	Curb Weight
Full Size (all others)	1986	13 - 16	13 - 16	No	Curb Weight
Full Size (Wagon)	1987	12 5/8 - 15 5/8	11 1/8 - 14 1/8	No	Curb Weight
Full Size (all others)	1987	12 7/8 - 15 7/8	12 7/8 - 15 7/8	No	Curb Weight
Full Size (Wagon)	1988 - 90	12 3/16 - 15 3/16	12 1/2 - 15 1/2	No	Curb Weight
Full Size (all others)	1988 - 90	12 11/16 - 15 11/16	12 13/16 - 15 13/16	No	Curb Weight
Full Size (Wagon)	1991	13 - 16	12 11/16 - 15 11/16	No	Curb Weight
Full Size	1991	13 7/16 - 16 7/16	12 5/16 - 15 5/16	No	Curb Weight
Full Size	1992	12 1/16 - 14 1/16	13 5/8 - 15 5/8	No	Curb Weight
Full Size	1993 - 97	13 13/16 - 15 13/16	13 5/8 - 15 5/8	No	Curb Weight
Lynx (2 door)	1985	14 - 16 3/4	14 1/8 - 16 3/4	No	Curb Weight
Lynx (4 door)	1985	14 - 16 3/4	14 1/8 - 16 3/4	No	Curb Weight
Lynx (Wagon)	1985	14 - 16 3/4	14 1/8 - 16 3/4	No	Curb Weight
Lynx (2 door XR3)	1986 - 87	14 1/2 - 16 5/8	13 3/8 - 15 1/2	No	Curb Weight
Lynx (2 door all others)	1986 - 87	13 3/4 - 15 7/8	14 1/8 - 16 1/4	No	Curb Weight
Lynx (4 door)	1986 - 87	13 3/4 - 15 7/8	14 1/8 - 16 1/4	No	Curb Weight
Lynx (Wagon)	1986 - 87	13 3/4 - 15 7/8	14 - 16	No	Curb Weight
Marquis (Sedan)	1985 - 86	12 1/2 - 15 1/4	12 1/4 - 15 1/8	No	Curb Weight
Marquis (Wagon)	1985 - 86	12 1/2 - 15 1/4	12 - 14 7/8	No	Curb Weight
Merkur Scorpio	1988 - 90	10 1/8 - 10 7/8	11 - 11 3/4	No	Curb Weight
Merkur XR4Ti	1985 - 86	7 1/4 - 8	12 3/4 - 13 1/2	No	Curb Weight
Merkur XR4Ti	1987 - 89	7 1/4 - 8	8 3/4 - 9 1/2	No	Curb Weight
Mystique	1995 - 98	8 3/4 - 9 3/4	12 1/4 - 13 1/4	No	Curb Weight
Sable (Sedan)	1986	14 7/8 - 15 5/8	13 3/4 - 14 1/2	No	Curb Weight
Sable (Wagon)	1986	14 7/8 - 15 5/8	13 7/8 - 14 5/8	No	Curb Weight
Sable (Sedan)	1987	14 13/16 - 15 9/16	13 3/4 - 14 1/2	No	Curb Weight
Sable (Wagon)	1987	14 15/16 - 15 11/16	13 13/16 - 14 9/16	No	Curb Weight
Sable (Sedan)	1988	9 1/2 - 10 1/4	14 1/8 - 14 7/8	No	Curb Weight
Sable (Wagon)	1988	9 5/8 - 10 3/8	14 1/8 - 14 7/8	No	Curb Weight
Sable (Sedan)	1989	8 15/16 - 9 11/16	14 3/8 - 15 1/8	No	Curb Weight
Sable (Wagon)	1989	9 1/4 - 10	14 1/8 - 14 7/8	No	Curb Weight

Vehicle Make and Model	Year	Front Measure Point	Rear Measure Point	Vehicle Loaded?	Loaded How?
Sable (Sedan)	1990	8 15/16 - 9 11/16	14 7/16 - 15 3/16	No	Curb Weight
Sable (Wagon)	1990	9 5/16 - 10 1/16	14 1/8 - 14 7/8	No	Curb Weight
Sable (Sedan)	1991 - 92	9 3/16 - 9 15/16	14 5/8 - 15 3/8	No	Curb Weight
Sable (Wagon)	1991 - 92	9 3/16 - 9 15/16	14 1/8 - 14 7/8	No	Curb Weight
Sable (Sedan)	1993 - 95	9 7/8 - 10 5/8	13 15/16 - 14 11/16	No	Curb Weight
Sable (Wagon)	1993 - 95	10 - 10 3/4	14 1/2 - 15 1/4	No	Curb Weight
Sable (Sedan)	1996 - 97	10 - 11	13 9/16 - 14 9/16	No	Curb Weight
Sable (Wagon)	1996 - 97		13 - 14	No	Curb Weight
Topaz	1985	15 3/8 - 16 1/8	15 3/8 - 16 1/8	No	Curb Weight
Topaz	1986 - 87	14 1/2 - 15 1/4	14 1/2 - 15 1/4	No	Curb Weight
Topaz	1988	9 15/16 - 10 11/16	13 5/8 - 14 3/8	No	Curb Weight
Topaz	1989 - 91	9 3/4 - 10 1/2	13 9/16 - 14 5/16	No	Curb Weight
Tracer (Wagon)	1992 - 94	9 13/16 - 10 9/16	10 1/4 - 11	No	Curb Weight
Tracer (Wagon)	1988 - 89	9 13/16 - 10 9/16	14 1/8 - 14 7/8	No	Curb Weight
Tracer (all others)	1988 - 89	9 13/16 - 10 9/16	12 1/2 - 13 1/4	No	Curb Weight
Tracer (Sedan)	1991 - 96	9 - 9 3/4	10 5/8 - 11 3/8	No	Curb Weight
		Rocker Behind Front Wheel	Rocker In Front of Rear Wheel		
Tracer (Wagon)	1991 - 96	5 15/16	5 15/16	Yes	See footnote 8
		Bottom of Front Bumper	Bottom of Rear Bumper		
Villager (GS)	1993 - 97	9 5/16	10 9/16	No	Curb Weight
Villager (LS, 5 Passenger)	1993 - 97	9 7/16	10 3/4	No	Curb Weight
Villager (LS, 7 Passenger)	1993 - 97	9 1/4	11 1/4	No	Curb Weight
Mitsubishi		Bottom of Front Bumper	Bottom of Rear Bumper		
3000 GT (2WD)	1991 - 93	9 1/16	11 7/8	No	Curb Weight
3000 GT (4WD)	1991 - 93	9 1/16	11 7/8	No	Curb Weight
3000 GT	1994 - 96	8	11 5/16	No	Curb Weight
Cordia	1985 - 86	15 3/16	15 13/16	No	Curb Weight
Cordia	1987 - 88	15 9/16	15 13/16	No	Curb Weight
Diamante (Sedan, w/ECS Suspension)	1992 - 96	8 5/16	9 9/16	No	Curb Weight
Diamante (Sedan, all others)	1992 - 96	8 3/4	9 15/16	No	Curb Weight
Diamante (Wagon)	1992 - 96	9 15/16	11 15/16	No	Curb Weight
Eclipse (Turbo)	1990	7 15/16	13 5/8	No	Curb Weight
Eclipse (all others)	1990	9 1/2	13 5/8	No	Curb Weight
Eclipse (2WD)	1991	9 1/2	13 11/16	No	Curb Weight
Eclipse (4WD)	1991	8 7/8	14	No	Curb Weight
Eclipse (2WD)	1992 - 94	8 3/4	13 11/16	No	Curb Weight
Eclipse (4WD)	1992 - 94	9 5/16	14 1/16	No	Curb Weight
Expo (2WD)	1992 - 96	10 11/16	13 5/16	No	Curb Weight
Expo (4WD)	1992 - 96	11 1/4	13 13/16	No	Curb Weight
Expo LRV (2WD)	1992 - 94	10 7/8	13 11/16	No	Curb Weight
Expo LRV (4WD)	1992 - 94	11 5/16	14 1/4	No	Curb Weight
Galant	1985 - 87	9 1/8	11	No	Curb Weight
Galant	1988	10 3/8	12 3/8	No	Curb Weight
Galant (DOHC)	1989	9 13/16	11 3/8	No	Curb Weight
Galant (all others)	1989	9 3/8	8 1/2	No	Curb Weight
Galant (2WD, DOHC)	1990	9 13/16	11 13/16	No	Curb Weight
Galant (2WD, all others)	1990	8 1/8	12	No	Curb Weight
Galant (4WD)	1990	11	12 9/16	No	Curb Weight
Galant (2WD, DOHC)	1991 - 93	9 13/16	11 13/16	No	Curb Weight
Galant (2WD, all others)	1991 - 93	10 7/16	12	No	Curb Weight
Galant (4WD)	1991 - 93	11	12 9/16	No	Curb Weight
Galant	1994 - 96	8 3/16 - 9 3/16	11 1/2 - 12 1/2	No	Curb Weight

Vehicle Make and Model	Year	Front Measure Point	Rear Measure Point	Vehicle Loaded?	Loaded How?
Mirage (w/Air Dam)	1985 - 86	9 1/8	13 3/16	No	Curb Weight
Mirage (all others)	1985 - 86	10	13 3/16	No	Curb Weight
Mirage (2 door)	1987 - 88	10	13 3/16	No	Curb Weight
Mirage (4 door)	1987 - 88	9 13/16	13 9/16	No	Curb Weight
Mirage (2 door, DOHC)	1989 - 90	8 11/16	11 5/8	No	Curb Weight
Mirage (2 door, all others)	1989 - 90	9 3/4	11 5/8	No	Curb Weight
Mirage (4 door)	1989 - 90	9 3/4	12 1/8	No	Curb Weight
Mirage (2 door)	1991 - 92	9 3/4	11 5/8	No	Curb Weight
Mirage (4 door)	1991 - 92	9 3/4	12 1/8	No	Curb Weight
Mirage	1993 - 96	8 7/16	10 1/4	No	Curb Weight
		Rocker Behind Front Wheel	Rocker Behind Rear Wheel		
Precis	1987 - 89	8 3/4	9 1/4	Yes	See footnote 6
Precis	1990 - 91	6 1/8	5 1/4	Yes	See footnote 6
		Bottom of Front Bumper	Bottom of Rear Bumper		
Precis	1992 - 94	9 1/16	10 3/16	No	Curb Weight
Starion	1985 - 89	14	14 9/16	No	Curb Weight
Sigma	1989 - 90	11	15 15/16	No	Curb Weight
Tredia	1984 - 88	15 9/16	15 11/16	No	Curb Weight
Nissan/Datsun		Bottom of Front Bumper	Bottom of Rear Bumper		
200SX	1985 - 88	9 1/2 - 11 1/2	13 - 15	No	Curb Weight
240SX (Coupe)	1989 - 94	7 15/16 - 9 15/16	11 1/8 - 13 1/8	No	Curb Weight
240SX (Hatchback)	1989 - 94	7 13/16 - 9 13/16	11 1/4 - 13 1/4	No	Curb Weight
240SX (w/Front Spoiler)	1989 - 94	6 5/16 - 8 5/16	11 1/4 - 13 1/4	No	Curb Weight
240SX (w/Spoiler)	1995 - 96	6 11/16 - 7 11/16	11 1/2 - 12 1/2	No	Curb Weight
240SX (w/o Spoiler)	1995 - 96	9 3/8 - 10 3/8	11 1/2 - 12 1/2	No	Curb Weight
240SX (w/Spoiler)	1997	6 3/4 - 7 3/4	11 1/2 - 12 1/2	No	Curb Weight
240SX (w/o Spoiler)	1997	9 5/8 - 10 5/8	11 1/2 - 12 1/2	No	Curb Weight
300ZX (2+2)	1984 - 86	14 5/8 - 16 5/8	14 3/8 - 16 3/8	No	Curb Weight
300ZX (all others)	1984 - 86	14 1/2 - 16 1/2	14 1/2 - 16 1/2	No	Curb Weight
300ZX (2+2)	1987 - 89	14 5/8 - 16 5/8	14 1/2 - 16 1/2	No	Curb Weight
300ZX (all others)	1987 - 89	14 1/2 - 16 1/2	14 5/8 - 16 5/8	No	Curb Weight
300ZX (2+2)	1990 - 96	5 13/16 - 7 13/16	10 7/8 - 12 7/8	No	Curb Weight
300ZX (all others)	1990 - 96	5 3/4 - 7 3/4	10 7/8 - 12 7/8	No	Curb Weight
810, Maxima (Sedan)	1985 - 86	14 1/2 - 16 1/2	14 3/4 - 16 5/8	No	Curb Weight
810, Maxima (Wagon)	1985 - 86	13 7/8 - 15 7/8	12 - 14	No	Curb Weight
810, Maxima (Sedan)	1987 - 88	14 1/2 - 16 1/2	14 5/8 - 16 5/8	No	Curb Weight
810, Maxima (Wagon)	1987 - 88	13 3/4 - 15 3/4	12 - 14	No	Curb Weight
810, Maxima	1989 - 94	9 5/8 - 11 5/8	13 - 15	No	Curb Weight
Axxess (2WD)	1990	9 7/8 - 11 7/8	14 3/8 - 16 3/8	No	Curb Weight
Axxess (2WD, w/3rd Seat)	1990	9 7/8 - 11 7/8	14 3/8 - 16 3/8	No	Curb Weight
Axxess (4x2, 5 Passenger)	1990	10 13/16	15 3/8	No	Curb Weight
Axxess (4x2, 7 Passenger)	1990	10 13/16	15 3/8	No	Curb Weight
Axxess (4x4, 5 Passenger)	1990	11 3/16	15 3/8	No	Curb Weight
Axxess (4x4, 7 Passenger)	1990	11 3/16	15 3/8	No	Curb Weight
Altima	1993 - 97	9 7/16 - 10 3/16	13 5/8 - 14 3/8	No	Curb Weight
NX Coupe	1991 - 93	9 1/2 - 10 1/4	9 3/4 - 10 1/2	No	Curb Weight
Pulsar NX	1985 - 86	14 3/8 - 16 3/8	14 3/4 - 15 3/4	No	Curb Weight
Pulsar NX (SE)	1987 - 90	7 3/4 - 9 3/4	11 5/8 - 13 5/8	No	Curb Weight
Pulsar NX (XE)	1987 - 90	8 3/8 - 10 3/8	11 5/8 - 13 5/8	No	Curb Weight
Quest (Cargo Van)	1993 - 97	9 1/2	13 1/8	No	Curb Weight
Quest (GXE)	1993 - 97	9 5/16	10 9/16	No	Curb Weight
Quest (XE, 5 Passenger)	1993 - 97	9 1/4	11 1/4	No	Curb Weight

Vehicle Make and Model	Year	Front Measure Point	Rear Measure Point	Vehicle Loaded?	Loaded How?
Quest (XE, 7 Passenger)	1993 - 97	9 7/16	10 3/4	No	Curb Weight
Sentra	1983 - 86	13 3/4 - 15 3/4	15 3/4 - 17 3/4	No	Curb Weight
Sentra (Coupe)	1987 - 90	9 - 11	10 3/4 - 12 3/4	No	Curb Weight
Sentra (Hatchback)	1987 - 90	9 1/4 - 11 1/4	11 1/8 - 13 1/8	No	Curb Weight
Sentra (Sedan)	1987 - 90	9 1/4 - 11 1/4	11 - 13	No	Curb Weight
Sentra (Wagon, 2WD)	1987 - 90	9 1/4 - 11 1/4	11 - 13	No	Curb Weight
Sentra (Wagon, 4WD)	1987 - 90	9 1/4 - 11 1/4	12 - 14	No	Curb Weight
Sentra	1991 - 97	9 3/8 - 10 3/8	11 7/16 - 12 7/16	No	Curb Weight
Stanza (Wagon)	1983 - 86	15 3/4 - 17 3/4	15 3/8 - 17 3/8	No	Curb Weight
Stanza (all others)	1983 - 86	8 3/8 - 10 3/8	13 1/4 - 15 1/4	No	Curb Weight
Stanza (Wagon, 2WD)	1987 - 89	15 3/4 - 17 3/4	15 3/8 - 17 3/8	No	Curb Weight
Stanza (Wagon, 4WD)	1987 - 89	17 1/4 - 19 1/4	16 1/2 - 18 1/2	No	Curb Weight
Stanza (all others)	1987 - 89	13 3/4 - 15 3/4	`9 - 11	No	Curb Weight
Stanza	1990 - 92	9 1/16 - 11 11/16	10 7/16 - 12 7/16	No	Curb Weight
Van (Cargo Van)	1987 - 89	11 13/16	15 1/8	No	Curb Weight
Van (Passenger Van)	1987 - 89	11 5/8	14 15/16	No	Curb Weight

Oldsmobile

Vehicle Make and Model	Year	Front Measure Point	Rear Measure Point	Vehicle Loaded?	Loaded How?
88	1982 - 85	Bottom of Front Bumper 11 7/8 - 13 7/8	Bottom of Rear Bumper 13 3/8 - 15 3/8	No	Curb Weight
88, LSS	1986 - 87	Rocker Behind Front Wheel 9 3/8	Rocker In Front of Rear Wheel 9 11/16	Yes	See footnote 12
88, LSS	1988 - 89	Bottom of Front Bumper 9 1/8 - 11 1/8	Bottom of Rear Bumper 13 1/8 - 15 1/8	No	Curb Weight
88, LSS	1990	11 - 13	13 1/8 - 15 1/8	No	Curb Weight
88, LSS	1991	11 - 13	13 1/16 - 15 1/16	No	Curb Weight
88	1992	11 - 13	12 7/8 - 14 7/8	No	Curb Weight
88, LSS	1993 - 97	10 1/2 - 12 1/2	12 7/8 - 14 7/8	No	Curb Weight
98	1985 - 88	14 3/4 - 16 3/4	13 1/8 - 15 1/8	No	Curb Weight
98	1989 - 90	9 1/4 - 11 1/4	12 5/8 - 14 5/8	No	Curb Weight
98	1991 - 97	10 5/16 - 12 5/16	13 3/16 - 15 3/16	No	Curb Weight
Achieva	1992 - 94	8 9/16 - 10 9/16	9 1/16 - 11 1/16	No	Curb Weight
Achieva	1995 - 97	8 3/4 - 9 3/4	11 3/8 - 12 3/8	No	Curb Weight
Aurora	1995 - 97	9 - 10	13 1/2 - 14 1/2	No	Curb Weight
Custom Cruiser Wagon	1982 - 85	12 1/8 - 14 1/8	11 3/8 - 13 3/8	No	Curb Weight
Custom Cruiser Wagon	1986 - 90	12 1/8 - 14 1/8	11 3/8 - 13 3/8	No	Curb Weight
Custom Cruiser Wagon	1991 - 92	10 1/8 - 12 1/8	12 3/8 - 14 3/8	No	Curb Weight
Cutlass (2 door)	1984 - 86	12 3/4 - 14 3/4	12 3/4 - 14 3/4	No	Curb Weight
Cutlass (4 door)	1984 - 86	12 3/4 - 14 3/4	13 - 15	No	Curb Weight
Cutlass (2 door)	1987	12 7/8 - 14 7/8	12 3/4 - 14 3/4	No	Curb Weight
Cutlass (4 door)	1987	12 1/4 - 14 1/4	13 - 15	No	Curb Weight
Cutlass Calais	1985 - 86	14 1/2 - 16 1/2	17 3/8 - 19 3/8	No	Curb Weight
Cutlass Calais	1987 - 88	14 1/2 - 16 1/2	17 3/8 - 19 3/8	No	Curb Weight
Cutlass Calais	1989	8 - 10	12 7/8 - 14 7/8	No	Curb Weight
Cutlass Calais	1990 - 91	9 7/8 - 11 7/8	12 - 14	No	Curb Weight
Cutlass Ciera (Wagon)	1984 - 86	11 3/4 - 13 3/4	15 3/8 - 15 3/8	No	Curb Weight
Cutlass Ciera (all others)	1984 - 86	11 7/8 - 13 7/8	15 5/8 - 17 5/8	No	Curb Weight
Cutlass Ciera (Wagon)	1987	13 5/8 - 15 5/8	13 1/2 - 15 1/2	No	Curb Weight
Cutlass Ciera (all others)	1987	14 - 16	13 7/8 - 15 7/8	No	Curb Weight
Cutlass Ciera (Wagon)	1988 - 96	11 3/4 - 13 3/4	13 3/8 - 15 3/8	No	Curb Weight
Cutlass Ciera (all others)	1988 - 96	11 7/8 - 13 7/8	15 5/8 - 17 5/8	No	Curb Weight
Cutlass Supreme	1988	12 7/8 - 14 7/8	12 3/4 - 14 3/4	No	Curb Weight
Cutlass Supreme	1989	12 7/8 - 14 7/8	13 1/2 - 15 1/2	No	Curb Weight
Cutlass Supreme (Convertible)	1990	13 5/8 - 15 5/8	13 5/8 - 15 5/8	No	Curb Weight

Vehicle Make and Model	Year	Front Measure Point	Rear Measure Point	Vehicle Loaded?	Loaded How?
Cutlass Supreme (Coupe)	1990	13 5/8 - 15 5/8	13 5/8 - 15 5/8	No	Curb Weight
Cutlass Supreme (Sedan)	1990	13 5/8 - 15 5/8	13 3/4 - 15 3/4	No	Curb Weight
Cutlass Supreme (Convertible)	1991 - 96	12 7/8 - 14 7/8	13 1/2 - 15 1/2	No	Curb Weight
Cutlass Supreme (Coupe)	1991 - 96	12 7/8 - 14 7/8	13 1/2 - 15 1/2	No	Curb Weight
Cutlass Supreme (Sedan)	1991 - 96	13 11/16 - 15 11/16	13 13/16 - 15 13/16	No	Curb Weight
Cutlass Supreme (Coupe)	1997	13 13/32 - 14 13/32	14 - 15	No	Curb Weight
Cutlass Supreme (Sedan)	1997	14 3/16 - 15 3/16	14 3/16 - 15 3/16	No	Curb Weight
LSS	1992	10 1/2 - 12 1/2	12 7/8 - 14 7/8	No	Curb Weight
Silhouette	1990 - 91			Yes	Curb Weight
Silhouette	1992 - 96			Yes	Curb Weight
Toronado	1982 - 85	13 3/4 - 15 3/4	12 7/8 - 14 7/8	No	Curb Weight
Toronado	1986 - 87	14 1/4 - 16 1/4	13 - 15	No	Curb Weight
Toronado	1988 - 89	15 1/8 - 17 1/8	13 1/2 - 15 1/2	No	Curb Weight
Toronado	1990	15 1/8 - 17 1/8	13 1/2 - 15 1/2	No	Curb Weight
Toronado	1991 - 92	15 1/8 - 17 1/8	13 1/2 - 15 1/2	No	Curb Weight
Trofeo	1988 - 89	15 1/8 - 17 1/8	13 1/2 - 15 1/2	No	Curb Weight
Trofeo	1991 - 92	15 1/8 - 17 1/8	13 1/2 - 15 1/2	No	Curb Weight
Plymouth		Bottom of Front Bumper	Bottom of Rear Bumper		
Acclaim	1989 - 90	9 5/8 - 12 1/8	13 - 15 1/2	No	Curb Weight
Acclaim	1991 - 95	9 5/8 - 12 1/8	12 7/8 - 15 3/8	No	Curb Weight
Breeze	1996 - 97	6 1/4 - 7 1/4	11 3/16 - 12 3/16	No	Curb Weight
Breeze	1998	6 1/4 - 7 1/4	8 23/32 - 10 23/32	No	Curb Weight
Caravelle	1985	11 3/4 - 14 1/4	13 1/4 - 15 3/4	No	Curb Weight
Caravelle	1986 - 88	11 1/4 - 13 3/4	12 3/4 - 15 1/4	No	Curb Weight
Colt (2 door, Hatchback)	1985 - 86	9 1/2 - 10 1/2	12 11/16 - 13 11/16	No	Curb Weight
Colt (4 door, Hatchback)	1985 - 86	9 3/8 - 10 3/8	12 3/8 - 13 3/8	No	Curb Weight
Colt (4 door, Sedan)	1985 - 86	9 3/8 - 10 3/8	13 1/8 - 14 1/8	No	Curb Weight
Colt (4 door)	1987 - 88	9 1/2 - 10 1/2	12 11/16 - 13 11/16	No	Curb Weight
Colt (Wagon)	1987 - 88	9 5/16 - 10 5/16	13 1/16 - 14 1/16	No	Curb Weight
Colt (2 door, 1.5L)	1989 - 90	9 15/16 - 10 15/16	13 1/4 - 14 1/4	No	Curb Weight
Colt (2 door, 1.6L)	1989 - 90	9 1/4 - 10 1/4	11 1/8 - 12 1/8	No	Curb Weight
Colt (Wagon, 2WD)	1989 - 90	8 1/4 - 9 1/4	11 1/8 - 12 1/8	No	Curb Weight
Colt (Wagon, 4WD)	1989 - 90	9 15/16 - 10 15/16	13 1/4 - 14 1/4	No	Curb Weight
Colt	1989 - 90	11 1/2 - 12 1/2	16 1/4 - 17 1/4	No	Curb Weight
Colt	1991 - 92	9 1/4 - 10 1/4	11 1/8 - 12 1/8	No	Curb Weight
Colt	1993 - 94	7 15/16 - 8 15/16	9 3/4 - 10 3/4	No	Curb Weight
Colt Vista (2WD)	1985	12 1/2 - 13 1/2	13 1/2 - 14 1/2	No	Curb Weight
Colt Vista (4WD)	1985	16 5/8 - 17 5/8	17 - 18	No	Curb Weight
Colt Vista (2WD)	1986 - 91	14 1/2 - 15 1/2	14 1/2 - 15 1/2	No	Curb Weight
Colt Vista (4WD)	1986 - 91	17 - 18	17 - 18	No	Curb Weight
Colt Vista (2WD)	1992 - 94	10 3/8 - 11 3/8	13 3/16 - 14 3/16	No	Curb Weight
Colt Vista (4WD)	1992 - 94	10 13/16 - 11 13/16	13 3/4 - 14 3/4	No	Curb Weight
Horizon	1985 - 90	13 7/8 - 16 3/8	14 - 16 1/2	No	Curb Weight
Laser (FWD)	1990 - 91	8 3/4 - 10 1/4	12 7/8 - 14 3/8	No	Curb Weight
Laser (AWD)	1992 - 94	8 - 9 1/2	13 - 14 1/2	No	Curb Weight
Neon (Coupe)	1995 - 97	8 9/16 - 10 1/16	13 5/8 - 15 1/8	No	Curb Weight
Neon (Sedan)	1995 - 97	8 1/2 - 9 1/2	13 5/16 - 14 3/4	No	Curb Weight
Neon (Coupe)	1998	8 1/2 - 9 1/2	13 5/16 - 14 3/4	No	Curb Weight
Neon (Sedan)	1998	8 15/16	14 7/16	No	Curb Weight
Reliant (Wagon)	1985 - 89	11 1/8 - 13 5/8	13 1/2 - 16	No	Curb Weight
Reliant (all others)	1985 - 89	11 1/4 - 13 3/4	12 3/4 - 15 1/4	No	Curb Weight

Page 109

Vehicle Make and Model	Year	Front Measure Point	Rear Measure Point	Vehicle Loaded?	Loaded How?
Sundance	1987 - 90	9 1/8 - 11 5/8	12 1/4 - 14 3/4	No	Curb Weight
Sundance	1991	9 1/4 - 11 3/4	11 3/8 - 13 7/8	No	Curb Weight
Sundance (Convertible)	1992	9 1/4 - 11 3/4	11 3/8 - 13 7/8	No	Curb Weight
Sundance (Coupe & Sedan)	1992	9 1/4 - 11 3/4	11 3/8 - 13 7/8	No	Curb Weight
Sundance	1993 - 94	9 - 11	11 7/8 - 13 7/8	No	Curb Weight
Turismo, TC3	1985 - 87	9 7/8 - 12 3/8	11 7/8 - 14 3/8	No	Curb Weight
Voyager (5 Passenger)	1988 - 90	14 3/4	14 13/16	No	Curb Weight
Voyager (7 Passenger)	1988 - 90	14 3/4	14 13/16	No	Curb Weight
Voyager (Extended)	1988 - 90	14 3/4	14 7/8	No	Curb Weight
Voyager (FWD, 5 Passenger)	1991 - 93	8 7/8	11 5/8	No	Curb Weight
Voyager (FWD, 7 Passenger)	1991 - 93	8 7/8	11 5/8	No	Curb Weight
Voyager (FWD, Extended)	1991 - 93	9 3/8	12 1/8	No	Curb Weight
Voyager (AWD)	1991 - 93	10 5/16	13 1/2	No	Curb Weight
Voyager (FWD, 5 Passenger)	1994 - 95	8 15/16	11 5/8	No	Curb Weight
Voyager (FWD, 7 Passenger)	1994 - 95	8 15/16	11 5/8	No	Curb Weight
Voyager (FWD, Extended)	1994 - 95	9 3/8	12 1/8	No	Curb Weight
Voyager (AWD)	1994 - 95	10 5/16	13 1/2	No	Curb Weight
Voyager (FWD, 5 Passenger)	1996 - 98	9 13/32	13 13/32	No	Curb Weight
Voyager (FWD, 7 Passenger)	1996 - 98	9 13/32	13 13/32	No	Curb Weight
Voyager (FWD, Extended)	1996 - 98	9 13/32	13 13/32	No	Curb Weight
Voyager (AWD)	1996 - 98	9 5/8	13 5/16	No	Curb Weight

Pontiac

Vehicle Make and Model	Year	Bottom of Front Bumper	Bottom of Rear Bumper	Vehicle Loaded?	Loaded How?
1000	1981 - 87	12 1/8 - 14 1/8	12 3/4 - 14 3/4	No	Curb Weight
6000 (Wagon)	1982 - 91	12 1/8 - 14 1/8	13 1/4 - 15 1/4	No	Curb Weight
6000 (all others)	1982 - 91	12 1/8 - 14 1/8	12 7/8 - 14 7/8	No	Curb Weight
Astre, J2000, Sunbird (Wagon)	1984 - 85	9 1/4 - 11 1/4	14 - 16	No	Curb Weight
Astre, J2000, Sunbird (all others)	1984 - 85	9 1/4 - 11 1/4	13 3/4 - 15 3/4	No	Curb Weight
Astre, J2000, Sunbird (Wagon)	1986 - 87	9 1/4 - 11 1/4	14 1/4 - 16 1/4	No	Curb Weight
Astre, J2000, Sunbird (all others)	1986 - 87	9 1/4 - 11 1/4	13 3/8 - 15 3/8	No	Curb Weight
Astre, J2000, Sunbird (Convertible)	1988 - 89	9 1/8 - 11 1/8	11 1/2 - 13 1/2	No	Curb Weight
Astre, J2000, Sunbird (Coupe)	1988 - 89	9 1/8 - 11 1/8	11 1/2 - 13 1/2	No	Curb Weight
Astre, J2000, Sunbird (Sedan)	1988 - 89	9 1/8 - 11 1/8	11 1/2 - 13 1/2	No	Curb Weight
Astre, J2000, Sunbird (Convertible)	1990	9 1/8 - 11 1/8	11 1/2 - 13 1/2	No	Curb Weight
Astre, J2000, Sunbird (Coupe)	1990	9 1/8 - 11 1/8	11 1/2 - 13 1/2	No	Curb Weight
Astre, J2000, Sunbird (Sedan)	1990	9 1/8 - 11 1/8	11 1/2 - 13 1/2	No	Curb Weight
Astre, J2000, Sunbird (Convertible)	1991	8 1/8 - 10 1/8	11 1/2 - 13 1/2	No	Curb Weight
Astre, J2000, Sunbird (Coupe)	1991	8 1/8 - 10 1/8	11 1/2 - 13 1/2	No	Curb Weight
Astre, J2000, Sunbird (Sedan)	1991	8 1/8 - 10 1/8	11 1/2 - 13 1/2	No	Curb Weight
Astre, J2000, Sunbird (Convertible)	1992	8 1/8 - 10 1/8	11 1/2 - 13 1/2	No	Curb Weight
Astre, J2000, Sunbird (Coupe)	1992	8 1/8 - 10 1/8	11 1/2 - 13 1/2	No	Curb Weight
Astre, J2000, Sunbird (Sedan)	1992	8 1/8 - 10 1/8	11 1/2 - 13 1/2	No	Curb Weight
Astre, J2000, Sunbird (Convertible)	1993 - 94	8 1/8 - 10 1/8	11 1/2 - 13 1/2	No	Curb Weight
Astre, J2000, Sunbird (Coupe)	1993 - 94	8 1/8 - 10 1/8	11 1/2 - 13 1/2	No	Curb Weight
Astre, J2000, Sunbird (Sedan)	1993 - 94	8 1/8 - 10 1/8	11 1/2 - 13 1/2	No	Curb Weight
Bonneville	1984 - 86	13 3/4 - 15 3/4	13 - 15	No	Curb Weight
Bonneville	1987 - 89	13 1/2 - 15 1/2	13 1/8 - 15 1/8	No	Curb Weight
Bonneville (LE)	1990	12 3/8 - 14 3/8	12 - 14	No	Curb Weight
Bonneville (SE & SSE)	1990	7 3/4 - 9 3/4	10 1/8 - 12 1/8	No	Curb Weight
Bonneville (LE)	1991	12 3/8 - 14 3/8	12 - 14	No	Curb Weight
Bonneville (SE & SSE)	1991	7 11/16 - 9 11/16	11 3/16 - 13 3/16	No	Curb Weight
Bonneville (SE)	1992 - 97	9 3/8 - 11 3/8	12 5/8 - 14 5/8	No	Curb Weight
Bonneville (SSE & SSEi)	1992 - 97	7 15/16 - 9 15/16	11 3/16 - 13 3/16	No	Curb Weight

Vehicle Make and Model	Year	Front Measure Point	Rear Measure Point	Vehicle Loaded?	Loaded How?
Fiero (GT)	1984 - 88	11 3/8 - 13 3/8	11 3/4 - 13 3/4	No	Curb Weight
Fiero (all others)	1984 - 88	12 3/8 - 14 3/8	12 1/2 - 14 1/2	No	Curb Weight
Firebird	1982 - 90	11 - 13	13 7/8 - 15 7/8	No	Curb Weight
Firebird (Trans Am)	1991 - 92	11 - 13	13 7/8 - 15 7/8	No	Curb Weight
Firebird (all others)	1991 - 92	11 - 13	13 7/8 - 15 7/8	No	Curb Weight
Firebird	1993 - 95	8 11/16 - 10 11/16	11 7/8 - 13 7/8	No	Curb Weight
Firebird (Formula 1 LE)	1996	8 11/16 - 10 11/16	11 7/8 - 13 7/8	No	Curb Weight
Firebird (all others)	1996	8 11/16 - 10 11/16	11 7/8 - 13 7/8	No	Curb Weight
Firebird (Trans Am)	1997	9 1/2 - 10 1/2	10 13/16 - 11 13/16	No	Curb Weight
Firebird (all others)	1997	9 7/32 - 10 7/32	10 3/8 - 13 3/8	No	Curb Weight
Grand Am	1985 - 88	10 7/8 - 12 7/8	13 5/8 - 15 5/8	No	Curb Weight
Grand Am	1989 - 91	14 3/8 - 16 3/8	12 1/4 - 14 1/4	No	Curb Weight
Grand Am	1992 - 94	8 1/4 - 10 1/4	11 - 13	No	Curb Weight
Grand Am	1995 - 97	9 7/16 - 10 7/16	11 3/8 - 12 3/8	No	Curb Weight
Grand Prix	1982 - 87	11 3/4 - 13 3/4	12 3/4 - 14 3/4	No	Curb Weight
Grand Prix	1988 - 89	11 1/4 - 13 1/4	13 7/8 - 15 7/8	No	Curb Weight
Grand Prix (Coupe)	1990	13 5/8 - 15 5/8	13 1/2 - 15 1/2	No	Curb Weight
Grand Prix (Sedan)	1990	13 5/8 - 15 5/8	13 1/2 - 15 1/2	No	Curb Weight
Grand Prix (Coupe)	1991 - 92	11 5/16 - 13 5/16	13 7/8 - 15 7/8	No	Curb Weight
Grand Prix (Sedan)	1991 - 92	13 5/8 - 15 5/8	13 7/8 - 15 7/8	No	Curb Weight
Grand Prix (Coupe)	1994 - 96	11 5/16 - 13 5/16	13 7/8 - 15 7/8	No	Curb Weight
Grand Prix (Sedan)	1994 - 96	13 5/8 - 15 5/8	13 1/2 - 15 1/2	No	Curb Weight
Grand Prix (Coupe)	1997	10 - 11	10 5/32 - 11 5/32	No	Curb Weight
Grand Prix (Sedan)	1997	10 - 11	13 13/16 - 14 13/16	No	Curb Weight
LeMans	1988 - 90	Rocker Behind Front Wheel 7 11/16	Rocker In Front of Rear Wheel 7 1/2	Yes	Curb Weight
LeMans (Aerocoupe)	1991 - 92	Bottom of Front Bumper 8 9/16 - 10 9/16	Bottom of Rear Bumper 12 13/16 - 14 13/16	No	Curb Weight
LeMans (Sedan)	1991 - 92	8 7/16 - 10 7/16	13 3/8 - 15 3/8	No	Curb Weight
LeMans (Aerocoupe)	1993	8 9/16 - 10 9/16	12 13/16 - 14 13/16	No	Curb Weight
LeMans (Sedan)	1993	8 9/16 - 10 9/16	13 7/16 - 15 7/16	No	Curb Weight
Parisienne (Wagon)	1985 - 86	12 1/4 - 14 1/4	11 1/2 - 13 1/2	No	Curb Weight
Parisienne (all others)	1985 - 86	12 1/4 - 14 1/4	13 3/4 - 15 3/4	No	Curb Weight
Sunfire	1995	9 7/32 - 10 7/32	12 7/32 - 13 7/32	No	Curb Weight
Sunfire	1996	9 7/32 - 10 7/32	12 7/32 - 13 7/32	No	Curb Weight
Sunfire	1997	9 7/32 - 10 7/32	12 7/32 - 13 7/32	No	Curb Weight
Trans Sport	1990 - 91	7 3/16	13 3/16	Yes	See footnote 7
Trans Sport	1992 - 96	7 11/16	13 11/16	Yes	See footnote 7
Trans Sport (Extended)	1997	7 13/32 - 8 13/32	9 1/2 - 10 1/2	No	Curb Weight
Trans Sport (Regular)	1997	7 5/16 - 8 5/16	5 7/8 - 9 7/8	No	Curb Weight
Renault					
18i	1985 - 86	Bottom of Front Bumper 15 3/8	Bottom of Rear Bumper 16 11/16	No	Curb Weight
Alliance, Encore	1983 - 87	13 3/8 - 15 3/8	14 3/4 - 16 3/4	No	Curb Weight
Fuego	1982 - 85	10 3/4	15 11/16	No	Curb Weight
Saturn					
SC, SC1, SC2	1991 - 95	Rocker Behind Front Wheel 7 7/8 - 8 1/8	Rocker In Front of Rear Wheel 8 - 9 3/8	No	Curb Weight
SC1, SC2	1996	Bottom of Front Bumper 7 5/16 - 8 5/16	Bottom of Rear Bumper 8 7/8 - 9 7/8	No	Curb Weight
SC1, SC2	1997 - 98	9 3/8 - 10 3/8	10 1/8 - 11 1/8	No	Curb Weight
SL, SL1, SL2	1991 - 95	Rocker Behind Front Wheel 7 3/4 - 9	Rocker In Front of Rear Wheel 8 - 9 5/16	No	Curb Weight

Vehicle Make and Model	Year	Front Measure Point	Rear Measure Point	Vehicle Loaded?	Loaded How?
SL, SL1, SL2	1996 - 97	Bottom of Front Bumper 8 9/16 - 9 9/16	Bottom of Rear Bumper 8 13/16 - 9 13/16	No	Curb Weight
SL, SL1, SL2	1998	8 5/8 - 9 5/8	11 5/16 - 12 5/16	No	Curb Weight
SW2	1991 - 95	Rocker Behind Front Wheel 7 3/4 - 9	Rocker In Front of Rear Wheel 8 - 9 5/16	No	Curb Weight
SW1, SW2	1996 - 97	Bottom of Front Bumper 8 9/16 - 9 9/16	Bottom of Rear Bumper 8 13/16 - 9 13/16	No	Curb Weight
SW1, SW2	1998	8 1/2 - 9 1/2	11 5/16 - 12 5/16	No	Curb Weight
Sterling					
825, 827 (4 door)	1987 - 91	Bottom of Front Bumper 9 11/16	Bottom of Rear Bumper 10 3/16	Yes	See footnote 5
825, 827 (5 door)	1987 - 91	9 5/8	9 15/16	Yes	See footnote 5
Subaru					
DL, GL (2 door, 2WD)	1985 - 86	Bottom of Front Bumper 15 1/8	Bottom of Rear Bumper 15 3/8	No	Curb Weight
DL, GL (3 door, 2WD)	1985 - 86	15 1/8	15 3/8	No	Curb Weight
DL, GL (4 door, 2WD)	1985 - 86	15 5/8	16	No	Curb Weight
DL, GL (Wagon, 2WD)	1985 - 86	15 5/8	15 3/8	No	Curb Weight
DL, GL (2 door, 4WD)	1985 - 86	16 1/8	17 3/4	No	Curb Weight
DL, GL (3 door, 4WD)	1985 - 86	16 1/4	17 3/8	No	Curb Weight
DL, GL (4 door, 4WD)	1985 - 86	16 3/4	18	No	Curb Weight
DL, GL (Wagon, 4WD)	1985 - 86	16 3/4	16 1/2	No	Curb Weight
Forester	1998	11	12	No	Curb Weight
Impreza (2WD)	1993 - 95	9 7/16	12 13/16	No	Curb Weight
Impreza (4WD)	1993 - 95	9 3/4	13	No	Curb Weight
Impreza	1996 - 97	9 7/16	12 13/16	No	Curb Weight
Impreza	1998	9	10 29/32	No	Curb Weight
Justy	1987	9 1/4	12 7/8	No	Curb Weight
Justy (2WD)	1988 - 91	10 1/4	12 1/2	No	Curb Weight
Justy (4WD)	1988 - 91	9 5/8	9 5/8	Yes	See footnote 12
Justy	1992 - 94	10 1/4	12 9/16	No	Curb Weight
Legacy (Sedan)	1990 - 91	10	11 13/16	No	Curb Weight
Legacy (Wagon)	1990 - 91	9 5/8	12 5/8	No	Curb Weight
Legacy (Sedan, Turbo)	1992 - 94	9 7/16	13	No	Curb Weight
Legacy (Sedan, all others)	1992 - 94	10 13/16	12 9/16	No	Curb Weight
Legacy (Wagon, Turbo)	1992 - 94	9 7/16	12 13/16	No	Curb Weight
Legacy (Wagon, w/Air Suspension)	1992 - 94	10 7/16	12 13/16	No	Curb Weight
Legacy (Wagon, all others)	1992 - 94	10 7/16	13 3/8	No	Curb Weight
Legacy (GT Sedan)	1995 - 98	8 13/16	12	No	Curb Weight
Legacy (GT Wagon)	1995 - 98	8 5/8	12 3/16	No	Curb Weight
Legacy (Outback Wagon)	1995 - 98	10 3/16	14 3/16	No	Curb Weight
Legacy (Sedan, all others)	1995 - 98	9 5/8	12	No	Curb Weight
Legacy (Wagon, all others)	1995 - 98	9 7/16	12 3/16	No	Curb Weight
Loyale (2 door, 2WD)	1987 - 90	15 1/8	15 3/8	No	Curb Weight
Loyale (3 door, 2WD)	1987 - 90	15 1/2	15 3/4	No	Curb Weight
Loyale (4 door, 2WD)	1987 - 90	15 1/2	15 3/4	No	Curb Weight
Loyale (Wagon, 2WD)	1987 - 90	15 1/2	15 1/4	No	Curb Weight
Loyale (2 door, 4WD)	1987 - 90	10 3/4	14 1/4	Yes	See footnote 8
Loyale (3 door, 4WD)	1987 - 90	14 1/2	15 3/4	Yes	Sew footnote 8
Loyale (3 door, 4WD, RX)	1987 - 90	14 3/8	15 7/8	Yes	Sew footnote 8
Loyale (4 door, 4WD)	1987 - 90	14 7/8	16	Yes	Sew footnote 8
Loyale (4 door, 4WD, GL-10)	1987 - 90	14 1/8	15 7/8	Yes	Sew footnote 8
Loyale (Wagon, 4WD)	1987 - 90	14 1/2	14 1/4	Yes	See footnote 13

Page 112

Vehicle Make and Model	Year	Front Measure Point	Rear Measure Point	Vehicle Loaded?	Loaded How?
Loyale (Wagon, 4WD, GL-10)	1987 - 90	13 3/4	14 3/8	Yes	See footnote 13
Loyale (Sedan, 2WD)	1991 - 93	15 9/16	15 3/4	No	Curb Weight
Loyale (Wagon, 2WD)	1991 - 93	15 9/16	15 5/16	No	Curb Weight
Loyale (Sedan, 4WD)	1991 - 93	15 9/16	15 3/4	No	Curb Weight
Loyale (Wagon, 4WD)	1991 - 93	15 9/16	15 5/16	No	Curb Weight
Loyale	1994	15 9/16	15 5/16	No	Curb Weight
SVX	1992 - 97	8 11/16	9 5/8	No	Curb Weight
XT (DL)	1985 - 86	9 3/4	13 3/8	No	Curb Weight
XT (GL)	1985 - 86	9 3/4	13 3/8	No	Curb Weight
XT (GL-10, 2WD)	1985 - 86	7 5/8	13 3/8	No	Curb Weight
XT (GL-10, 4WD)	1985 - 86	8 3/4	15 1/8	No	Curb Weight
XT (2WD)	1987 - 91	9 3/4	13	No	Curb Weight
XT (4WD)	1987 - 91	11	14 5/8	No	Curb Weight
XT6 (2WD)	1987 - 91	8	12 3/4	No	Curb Weight
XT6 (4WD)	1987 - 91	9 1/4	15	No	Curb Weight

Suzuki

Vehicle Make and Model	Year	Bottom of Front Bumper	Bottom of Rear Bumper	Vehicle Loaded?	Loaded How?
Esteem	1996 - 97	8 1/2 - 9 1/2	10 - 11	No	Curb Weight
Swift (3 door, GT)	1989 - 91	7 3/8 - 8 3/8	9 3/4 - 10 3/4	No	Curb Weight
Swift (3 door, all others)	1989 - 91	8 11/16 - 9 11/16	10 3/4 - 11 3/4	No	Curb Weight
Swift (4 door)	1989 - 91	8 11/16 - 9 11/16	10 3/4 - 11 3/4	No	Curb Weight
Swift (3 door)	1992 - 94	7 3/4 - 8 3/4	9 15/16 - 10 15/16	No	Curb Weight
Swift (4 door)	1992 - 94	8 3/8 - 9 3/8	10 1/2 - 11 1/2	No	Curb Weight
Swift	1995	8 1/2 - 9 1/2	10 15/16 - 11 15/16	No	Curb Weight
Swift	1996 - 97	8 1/2 - 9 1/2	10 15/16 - 11 15/16	No	Curb Weight
X-90	1996 - 97	9 - 10	11 1/4 - 12 1/4	No	Curb Weight

Toyota

Vehicle Make and Model	Year	Bottom of Front Bumper	Bottom of Rear Bumper	Vehicle Loaded?	Loaded How?
Avalon	1995 - 97	11	13 3/8	No	Curb Weight
Avalon	1998	10 19/32	12 19/32	No	Curb Weight
Camry	1983 - 86	16 5/16	15 1/8	No	Curb Weight
Camry (Sedan 2WD)	1987 - 91	15 5/8	15 3/8	No	Curb Weight
Camry (Sedan 4WD)	1987 - 91	15 3/4	15 3/8	No	Curb Weight
Camry (Wagon)	1987 - 91	15 1/2	15 1/8	No	Curb Weight
Camry (Coupe, Sedan, 4 Cylinder)	1992 - 96	11 5/8	12 3/4	No	Curb Weight
Camry (Coupe, Sedan, 6 Cylinder)	1992 - 96	11 5/8	13 3/16	No	Curb Weight
Camry (Wagon, 4 Cylinder)	1992 - 96	11 3/8	13 3/16	No	Curb Weight
Camry (Wagon, 6 Cylinder)	1992 - 96	11 5/8	13 3/8	No	Curb Weight
Camry (4 Cylinder)	1997 - 98	9 19/32	13 3/16	No	Curb Weight
Camry (6 Cylinder)	1997 - 98	9 19/32	13 19/32	No	Curb Weight
Celica (GTS)	1985	16 1/8	15 15/16	No	Curb Weight
Celica (Coupe)	1985	16 1/8	15 15/16	No	Curb Weight
Celica (Liftback)	1985	16 1/8	16 5/16	No	Curb Weight
Celica (Sports Coupe)	1985	16 1/8	15 15/16	No	Curb Weight
Celica (Coupe)	1986 - 89	15 7/8	15 3/8	No	Curb Weight
Celica (Liftback, All Trac)	1986 - 89	8 7/8	11 3/4	No	Curb Weight
Celica (Liftback, all others)	1986 - 89	15 7/8	15 5/8	No	Curb Weight
Celica (4WD)	1990	15 15/16	13 3/4	No	Curb Weight
Celica (all others)	1990	15 15/16	13 3/4	No	Curb Weight
Celica (4WD)	1991 - 93	9 1/16	13 3/4	No	Curb Weight
Celica (all others)	1991 - 93	9 1/4	13 3/4	No	Curb Weight
Celica (1.8L)	1994 - 97	9 5/8	14 3/16	No	Curb Weight
Celica (Coupe, 2.2L)	1994 - 97	9 7/16	13 13/16	No	Curb Weight

Vehicle Make and Model	Year	Front Measure Point	Rear Measure Point	Vehicle Loaded?	Loaded How?
Celica (Sedan, 2.2L)	1994 - 97	9 7/16	14	No	Curb Weight
Celica (Convertible)	1998	9 1/2	14	No	Curb Weight
Celica (Coupe)	1998	9 1/2	13 13/16	No	Curb Weight
Corolla (Coupe DLX)	1985 - 86	14 3/8	15 3/8	No	Curb Weight
Corolla (GT-S)	1985 - 86	14 3/16	15 1/8	No	Curb Weight
Corolla (Sedan, Liftback)	1985 - 86	15 9/16	15 3/4	No	Curb Weight
Corolla (SR)	1985 - 86	14 9/16	15 9/16	No	Curb Weight
Corolla (DLX)	1987	14 3/8	15 3/8	No	Curb Weight
Corolla (FX)	1987	15 1/8	15 9/16	No	Curb Weight
Corolla (GT-S)	1987	14 3/16	15 1/8	No	Curb Weight
Corolla (Sedan, Liftback)	1987	15 9/16	15 3/4	No	Curb Weight
Corolla (SR5)	1987	14 9/16	15 9/16	No	Curb Weight
Corolla (Coupe)	1988	9 7/8	15 9/16	No	Curb Weight
Corolla (FX DLX)	1988	15 3/4	15 3/8	No	Curb Weight
Corolla (FX all others)	1988	15 1/8	15 9/16	No	Curb Weight
Corolla (Sedan)	1988	9 7/8	14	No	Curb Weight
Corolla (Wagon)	1988	9 7/8	13 3/8	No	Curb Weight
Corolla (Coupe)	1989 - 90	9 7/8	15 1/2	No	Curb Weight
Corolla (Sedan 4WD)	1989 - 90	10 7/16	14 9/16	No	Curb Weight
Corolla (Sedan all others)	1989 - 90	9 7/8	14	No	Curb Weight
Corolla (Wagon 4WD)	1989 - 90	10 7/8	14	No	Curb Weight
Corolla (Wagon all others)	1989 - 90	9 7/8	13 3/8	No	Curb Weight
Corolla (Coupe)	1991 - 92	9 13/16	15 9/16	No	Curb Weight
Corolla (Sedan)	1991 - 92	9 13/16	14	No	Curb Weight
Corolla (Wagon 4WD)	1991 - 92	10 13/16	13 3/8	No	Curb Weight
Corolla (Wagon all others)	1991 - 92	9 13/16	13 3/8	No	Curb Weight
Corolla (Sedan)	1993 - 97	9 5/8	12 3/16	No	Curb Weight
Corolla (Wagon)	1993 - 97	9 5/8	13	No	Curb Weight
Corolla	1998	8 1/2	13	No	Curb Weight
Cressida (Sedan w/14" Tires)	1985	15 15/16	16 1/8	No	Curb Weight
Cressida (Sedan w/15" Tires)	1985	15 3/4	15 15/16	No	Curb Weight
Cressida (Wagon)	1985	15 9/16	14 3/4	No	Curb Weight
Cressida (Sedan)	1986 - 87	15 3/4	15 7/8	No	Curb Weight
Cressida (Wagon)	1986 - 87	15 9/16	14 3/4	No	Curb Weight
Cressida	1988	15 3/4	15 15/16	No	Curb Weight
Cressida	1989	15 3/4	15 15/16	No	Curb Weight
Cressida	1990	15 3/4	15 15/16	No	Curb Weight
Cressida	1991 - 92	15 3/4	15 15/16	No	Curb Weight
MR2	1985 - 89	15 9/16	16 9/16	No	Curb Weight
MR2	1991 - 92	15 1/8	13 3/4	No	Curb Weight
MR2	1994 - 95	15 3/8	13 3/8	No	Curb Weight
Paseo	1992 - 97	9 13/16	11 13/16	No	Curb Weight
Previa (4x2)	1991 - 93	13	13 3/4	No	Curb Weight
Previa (4x4)	1991 - 93	13 3/8	14 3/16	No	Curb Weight
Previa (4x2)	1994 - 97	7 1/2	12 3/4	No	Curb Weight
Previa (4x4)	1994 - 97	7 7/8	15 5/32	No	Curb Weight
Sienna	1998	10	15 13/32	No	Curb Weight
Supra	1985	15 15/16	16 1/8	No	Curb Weight
Supra	1986 - 88	16 5/16	15 15/16	No	Curb Weight
Supra	1989 - 90	16 1/8	15 1/2	No	Curb Weight
Supra	1991 - 92	16 1/8	15 9/16	No	Curb Weight
Supra	1994 - 98	6 11/16	11 7/16	No	Curb Weight
Tercel (Sedan DLX)	1983 - 86	11	14 3/4	No	Curb Weight

Volkswagen

Vehicle Make and Model	Year	Front Measure Point	Rear Measure Point	Vehicle Loaded?	Loaded How?
Tercel (Sedan STD)	1983 - 86	10 13/16	14 9/16	No	Curb Weight
Tercel (Wagon 2WD)	1983 - 86	11	14	No	Curb Weight
Tercel (Wagon 4WD)	1983 - 86	12	14 3/4	No	Curb Weight
Tercel (3 door & 5 door)	1987	15 3/4	15 15/16	No	Curb Weight
Tercel (Wagon 2WD)	1987	11	14	No	Curb Weight
Tercel (Wagon 4WD)	1987	12	14 3/4	No	Curb Weight
Tercel (2 door)	1988	15 3/4	16 1/8	No	Curb Weight
Tercel (3 door & 5 door)	1988	15 3/4	15 15/16	No	Curb Weight
Tercel (Wagon)	1988	12	14 3/4	No	Curb Weight
Tercel (2 door)	1989 - 90	15 3/4	16 1/8	No	Curb Weight
Tercel (3 door & 5 door)	1989 - 90	15 3/4	15 15/16	No	Curb Weight
Tercel	1991 - 94	9 13/16	12 9/16	No	Curb Weight
Tercel	1995 - 98	9 1/4	11 1/4	No	Curb Weight
Van (4x2)	1989	13	12 3/8	No	Curb Weight
Van (4x4)	1989	15	14 3/8	No	Curb Weight
Cabriolet	1985 - 91	Top of Front Wheel Opening 23 7/8 - 24 1/8	Top of Rear Wheel Opening 24 1/8 - 24 3/8	No	Curb Weight
Cabriolet	1992 - 93	Bottom of Front Bumper 8 3/8 - 9 1/8	Bottom of Rear Bumper 10 - 10 3/4	No	Curb Weight
Corrado	1990 - 91	Top of Front Wheel Opening 24 1/8 - 24 7/8	Top of Rear Wheel Opening 25 - 25 3/4	No	Curb Weight
Corrado (G60)	1992 - 93	Bottom of Front Bumper 8 3/8 - 9 1/8	Bottom of Rear Bumper 9 7/8 - 10 5/8	No	Curb Weight
Corrado (SLC)	1992 - 93	8 1/2 - 9 1/4	10 - 10 3/4	No	Curb Weight
Fox (2 door)	1987 - 91	Top of Front Wheel Opening 24 3/8 - 24 5/8	Top of Rear Wheel Opening 24 1/8 - 24 3/8	No	Curb Weight
Fox (4 door)	1987 - 91	24 1/8 - 24 3/8	24 1/4 - 24 1/2	No	Curb Weight
Fox (Wagon)	1987 - 91	24 7/8 - 25 1/8	25 1/8 - 25 3/8	No	Curb Weight
Fox	1992 - 93	Bottom of Front Bumper 9 3/8 - 10 1/8	Bottom of Rear Bumper 8 - 8 3/4	No	Curb Weight
Golf	1985 - 91	Top of Front Wheel Opening 24 1/8 - 24 3/8	Top of Rear Wheel Opening 24 3/8 - 24 5/8	No	Curb Weight
Golf	1992	Bottom of Front Bumper 6 1/2 - 7 1/4	Bottom of Rear Bumper 9 1/4 - 10	No	Curb Weight
GTI	1985 - 91	Top of Front Wheel Opening 23 7/8 - 24 1/8	Top of Rear Wheel Opening 24 1/8 - 24 3/8	No	Curb Weight
GTI	1992	Bottom of Front Bumper 5 1/2 - 6 1/4	Bottom of Rear Bumper 9 1/4 - 10	No	Curb Weight
Jetta, GLI	1985 - 91	Top of Front Wheel Opening 24 3/8 - 24 5/8	Top of Rear Wheel Opening 23 7/8 - 24 1/8	No	Curb Weight
Jetta, GLI	1992	Bottom of Front Bumper 6 1/2 - 7 1/4	Bottom of Rear Bumper 10 - 10 3/4	No	Curb Weight
Passat (Sedan)	1990 - 91	Top of Front Wheel Opening 24 1/8 - 24 7/8	Top of Rear Wheel Opening 25 1/8 - 25 7/8	No	Curb Weight
Passat (Wagon)	1990 - 91	23 7/8 - 24 5/8	24 7/8 - 25 5/8	No	Curb Weight
Passat (Sedan)	1992 - 93	Bottom of Front Bumper 7 5/8 - 8 3/4	Bottom of Rear Bumper 9 1/4 - 10	No	Curb Weight
Passat (Wagon)	1992 - 93	7 5/8 - 8 3/4	9 1/8 - 9 7/8	No	Curb Weight
Quantum	1982 - 85	Top of Front Wheel Opening 23 3/4 - 25	Top of Rear Wheel Opening 25 - 25 1/4	No	Curb Weight
Quantum	1986 - 88	23 7/8 - 24 1/8	24 7/8 - 25 1/8	No	Curb Weight
Scirocco	1982 - 89	24 7/8 - 25 1/8	24 7/8 - 25 1/8	No	Curb Weight

Vehicle Make and Model	Year	Front Measure Point	Rear Measure Point	Vehicle Loaded?	Loaded How?
		Bottom of Front Bumper	Bottom of Rear Bumper		
Volvo					
240, 260	1984 - 93	14 5/8	14 3/8	Yes	See footnote 7
740, 760, 780	1982 - 86	14 7/8	15 1/2	No	Curb Weight
740	1987 - 92	14 7/8	15 1/2	No	Curb Weight
760	1987 - 92	16	14 1/2	No	Curb Weight
780	1987 - 92	16	16 1/2	No	Curb Weight
940, 960	1991 - 93	14 1/2	13	No	Curb Weight

Footnote 1: 150 pounds in the driver's seat, and the front passenger seat, and 30 pounds in the cargo area
Footnote 2: 150 pounds in the driver's seat, the front passenger seat, and the center of the back seat, and 50 pounds in the cargo area
Footnote 3: 150 pounds in the driver's seat, the front passenger seat, and the center of the back seat, and the cargo area empty
Footnote 4: 150 pounds in each of all 6 seats, and the cargo area empty
Footnote 5: 150 pounds in the driver's seat, the front passenger seat, and in each of the 3 back seats, and 100 pounds in the cargo area
Footnote 6: 150 pounds in the driver's seat, the front passenger seat, and in each of the 3 back seats, and the cargo area empty
Footnote 7: 150 pounds in the driver's seat and the front passenger seat, and the cargo area empty
Footnote 8: 150 pounds in the driver's seat, the front passenger seat, and in each of the 3 back seats, and 75 pounds in the cargo area
Footnote 9: Measured from the bottom of the bumper through a 1/4 inch hole
Footnote 10: 150 pounds in the driver's seat, the front passenger seat, and in each of the 3 back seats, and 200 pounds in the cargo area
Footnote 11: 150 pounds in the driver's seat, the front passenger seat, the 2 middle passenger seats, and in each of the 3 back seats
Footnote 12: 150 pounds in the driver's seat, the front passenger seat, and the 2 outside back seats, and 65 pounds in the cargo area
Footnote 13: 150 pounds in the driver's seat, the front passenger seat, and in each of the 3 back seats, and 150 pounds in the cargo area

APPENDIX 3

NATEF Correlation Chart

Steering and Suspension (A4)

NATEF TASK LIST

NATEF Task List	Page #	Date Completed	Instructor's OK
A. General Suspension and Steering Systems Diagnosis P-1:			
1. Identify and interpret suspension and steering concern; determine necessary action.	6, 7, 8, 29, 31		
2. Research applicable vehicle and service information, such as suspension and steering system operation, vehicle service history, service precautions, and technical service bulletins.	5, 8		
3. Locate and interpret vehicle and major component identification numbers (VIN, vehicle certification labels, calibration decals).	5, 8		
B. Steering Systems Diagnosis and Repair P-1:			
1. Disable and enable supplemental restraint system (SRS).	9		
2. Remove and replace steering wheel; center/time supplemental restraint system (SRS) coil (clock spring).	10		
3. Remove and replace manual or power rack and pinion steering gear; inspect mounting bushings and brackets.	17		
4. Inspect and replace manual or power rack and pinion steering gear inner tie rod ends (sockets) and bellows boots.	18		
5. Inspect power steering fluid levels and condition.	19		
6. Remove, inspect, replace, and adjust power steering pump belt.	22		
7. Inspect, replace, and adjust tie rod ends (sockets), tie rod sleeves, and clamps.	27		
B. Steering Systems Diagnosis and Repair P-2:			
1. Diagnose steering column noises, looseness, and binding concerns (including tilt mechanisms); determine necessary action.	11		

NATEF Task List	Page #	Date Completed	Instructor's OK
2. Inspect steering shaft universal-joint(s), flexible coupling(s), collapsible column, lock cylinder mechanism, and steering wheel; perform necessary action.	15		
3. Flush, fill, and bleed power steering system.	20		
4. Diagnose power steering fluid leakage; determine necessary action.	21		
5. Inspect and replace power steering hoses and fittings.	25		
6. Inspect and replace pitman arm, relay (centerlink/intermediate) rod, idler arm and mountings, and steering linkage damper.	26		
B. Steering Systems Diagnosis and Repair P-3:			
1. Diagnose power steering gear (non-rack and pinion) binding, uneven turning effort, looseness, hard steering, and fluid leakage concerns; determine necessary action.	12		
2. Diagnose power steering gear (rack and pinion) binding, uneven turning effort, looseness, hard steering, and fluid leakage concerns; determine necessary action.	14		
3. Adjust manual or power non-rack and pinion worm bearing preload and sector lash.	16		
4. Remove and reinstall power steering pump.	23		
5. Remove and reinstall power steering pump pulley; check pulley and belt alignment.	24		
6. Test and diagnose components of electronically controlled steering systems using a scan tool; determine necessary action.	28		
C. Suspension Systems Diagnosis and Repair 1. Front Suspensions P-1:			
1. Diagnose short and long arm suspension system noises body sway and uneven riding height concerns; determine necessary action.	29		
2. Diagnose strut suspension system noises body sway and uneven riding height concerns; determine necessary action.	30		
3. Remove, inspect, and install strut cartridge or assembly strut coil spring insulators (silencers) and upper strut bearing mount.	41		

NATEF Task List	Page #	Date Completed	Instructor's OK
C. Suspension Systems Diagnosis and Repair 　**1. Front Suspensions** 　**P-2:**			
1. Remove, inspect, and install strut rods (compression/tension) and bushings.	33		
2. Remove, inspect, and install upper and lower ball-joints.	34, 35		
3. Remove, inspect, and install steering knuckle assemblies.	36, 37		
4. Remove, inspect, and install short and long arm suspension system coil springs and spring insulators.	29, 38		
5. Remove, inspect, and install stabilizer bar bushings, brackets, and links.	40		
6. Lubricate suspension and steering systems.	42		
C. Suspension Systems Diagnosis and Repair 　**1. Front Suspensions** 　**P-3:**			
1. Remove, inspect, and install upper and lower control arms, bushings, shafts, and rebound bumpers.	32		
2. Remove, inspect, install and adjust suspension system torsion bars; inspect mounts.	39		
C. Suspension Systems Diagnosis and Repair 　**2. Rear Suspensions** 　**P-2:**			
1. Remove, inspect, and install coil springs and spring insulators.	43		
2. Remove, inspect, and install transverse links, control arms, bushings, and mounts.	44		
3. Remove, inspect, and install strut cartridge or assembly strut coil spring and insulators (silencers).	46		
C. Suspension Systems Diagnosis and Repair 　**2. Rear Suspensions** 　**P-3:**			
1. Remove, inspect, and install leaf springs, leaf spring insulators (silencers), shackles, brackets, bushings, and mounts.	45		
C. Suspension Systems Diagnosis and Repair 　**3. Miscellaneous Service** 　**P-1:**			
1. Inspect, remove, and replace shock absorbers.	47, 48		

NATEF Task List	Page #	Date Completed	Instructor's OK
2. Remove, inspect, and service or replace front and rear wheel bearings.	49		
C. Suspension Systems Diagnosis and Repair **3. Miscellaneous Service** **P-3:**			
1. Test and diagnose components of electronically controlled suspension systems using a scan tool; determine necessary action.	50		
D. Wheel Alignment Diagnosis, Adjustment, and Repair **P-1:**			
1. Differentiate between steering and suspension concerns using principles of steering geometry (caster, camber, toe, etc.).	51		
2. Diagnose vehicle wander, drift, pull, hard steering, bump steer, memory steer, torque steer, and steering return concerns; determine necessary action.	52		
3. Perform prealignment inspection; perform necessary action.	53, 54, 55		
4. Measure vehicle ride height; determine necessary action.	56		
5. Check and adjust front and rear wheel camber; perform necessary action.	57, 61		
6. Check and adjust caster; perform necessary action.	58, 61		
7. Check and adjust front wheel toe; adjust as needed.	59, 61		
8. Center steering wheel.	60, 61		
D. Wheel Alignment Diagnosis, Adjustment, and Repair **P-2:**			
1. Check toe-out-on-turns (turning radius); determine necessary action.	62		
2. Check SAI (steering axis inclination) and included angle; determine necessary action.	63		
3. Check and adjust rear wheel toe.	64		
4. Check rear wheel thrust angle; determine necessary action.	65		
5. Check for front wheel setback; determine necessary action.	66		
D. Wheel Alignment Diagnosis, Adjustment, and Repair **P-3:**			
1. Check front cradle (subframe) alignment; determine necessary action.	67		

NATEF Task List	Page #	Date Completed	Instructor's OK
E. Wheel and Tire Diagnosis and Repair P-1:			
1. Diagnose tire wear patterns; determine necessary action.	68		
2. Inspect tires; check and adjust air pressure.	69		
3. Rotate tires according to manufacturer's recommendations.	71		
4. Balance wheel and tire assembly (static and dynamic).	75		
5. Reinstall wheel; torque lug nuts.	77		
E. Wheel and Tire Diagnosis and Repair P-2:			
1. Diagnose wheel/tire vibration, shimmy, and noise concerns; determine necessary action.	70		
2. Measure wheel, tire, axle, and hub runout; determine necessary action.	72, 73		
3. Diagnose tire pull (lead) concern; determine necessary action.	74		
4. Dismount, inspect, repair, and remount tire on wheel.	76		
5. Inspect and repair tire.	78		

TABLES AND FIGURES

Tables

Figures

Foreward

The livestock and meat industry has played a significant role in the development and well-being of this nation for nearly 500 years. This role can be viewed from a historic, an economic and a health perspective.

A HISTORIC PERSPECTIVE

Agriculture is the largest industry in the nation today and it has been the largest industry since the time of the Revolutionary War. However, due to advances in technology, fewer people are needed to produce the food supply. When the Founding Fathers wrote the Declaration of Independence, 90 percent of the labor force was involved in farming. Today, the number is only 2.2 percent of the labor force.

Cattle

In the 1490s, Columbus brought cattle with him on his second trip to the West Indies. Soon after that, cattle were brought by ship to Florida and Texas. It was natural for these cattle, being from Spanish stock, to become acclimated to these dry, hot regions. Descendents of these early cattle evolved into the famous Texas Longhorns. Longhorns lived off the range and needed little care. The cattle business was on its way to becoming an important part of the American economy.

One of the reasons cattle thrived in Texas and other parts of the West was that the animals grew rapidly on forage as diverse as mesquite beans, prickly pear, weeds, shrubs and buffalo grass. Buffalo grass did not wither in hot weather or during drought periods. In winter, the grass stood straight and tall after drying, and if the stalks were covered by snow, the animals could feed on the grass, wild sage brush and other shrubs. Pork was the most common meat in this country from the early 1500s to the early 1800s but the desire for beef steadily increased during that time. By the mid-1800s the desire for beef was so great that cattle raised on family farms no longer met the demand, which resulted in the cattle drives.

Before the expansion of the railroads, the only way to get beef to consumers was to drive the cattle to packing plants located near population centers. Probably the most spectacular cattle drive was made by a man named Tom Ponting. He formed a herd of Texas Longhorns, trailed it to Illinois, fattened it on grass throughout the winter of 1853-1854, and then pushed on to market it in New York City.

The westward development of the railroad system shortened the cattle drives. The first rail-transported cattle were shipped from Abilene, Kansas in 1867. Other rail centers were soon established. Thereafter, thousands of animals were moved along the various cattle trails which led to these shipping points. The famous Chisholm trail led from South Texas north to Abilene, Kansas or Ogallala, Nebraska. The Shawnee Trail went from Fort Worth, Texas to Sedalia, Missouri; the Bozeman Trail from northeastern Colorado to Virginia City, Montana; and the hazardous Goodnight-Loving Trail from west Texas to Denver, Colorado and Cheyenne, Wyoming. As many as 2500 cattle in a drive would spend two to four months traveling to their destination. This was possible because the animals grazed upon the open land along the trail.

The open range, so vital to the 19th century livestock industry, began to disappear rapidly with the signing of the Homestead Act in 1862. With the increase in the number of farms which resulted from its enactment, along with the expansion of the population westward after the Civil War, the unobstructed cattle drives were no longer possible. However, by then the railroads had expanded closer to the farms and ranches, thus eliminating the need for *long* cattle drives.

Hogs

Hogs were easily transported to the New World, and they thrived in their new environment. They were first brought to Florida by Spanish explorers in 1539. The British shipped hogs to the colonies and as early as 1639, settlers of Virginia were supplying ham and bacon to England. In colonial days, pork was packed in barrels for shipment, giving rise to the term "meat packing." During the War of 1812, the United States government got its nickname, "Uncle Sam," from pork shipped to American soldiers in barrels stamped with the letters "US" and the name of the meat packer, Sam Wilson. The soldiers referred to the meat as Uncle Sam's meat.

Sheep

Columbus brought sheep on his second voyage to the New World in 1493. Spanish stock breeders subsequently established breeding centers in the Caribbean Islands, then in Mexico and in the Isthmus of Panama. In 1565 an expedition of men and livestock, including sheep and lambs, settled in St. Augustine, Florida.

The Spanish, wanting to bridge their settlements in Florida and Mexico, established missions in Texas, Arizona, and California. Thus, sheep raising spread throughout the Southwest because the animals provided both food and wool and were easily cared for.

Sheep raising was not as easily established in the British Colonies along the Eastern coast. The first sheep imported were consumed for food during the hard winter that followed. Then, as the British colonists' woolens began to wear thin, they were forced to send for more sheep to satisfy their need for wool clothing. By the mid-1700s, sheep were flourishing in the New England states.

In an attempt to maintain control of the wool trade, the British restricted the export of sheep to America and forbade the import of woolens from the colonies. Therefore, the Colonists passed laws forbidding the use of sheep for food in order to preserve the flocks for wool. As a result, a strong woolen industry developed after the Revolutionary War.

Packing/Processing Industry

The expanding rail system and development of refrigerated rail cars marked the beginning of a new era. Cattlemen began to breed animals for the quality of meat, rather than for their stamina to survive the long drives. In fact, by 1880, the United States was exporting beef to England, which had long claimed to have the best beef in the world.

The first successful refrigerated rail car service was established by the Chicago meat packer, Gustavus Swift. Not far behind in utilizing this new form of distribution was another Chicago meat packer, Philip Armour. The ingenuity of Swift and Armour also turned meat processing into a mechanized industry. The Union Stockyards became the nation's major livestock marketing facility, earning Chicago the reputation (described by Carl Sandburg) of "hog butcher for the world."

By the beginning of the 20th century, meat packing was by far the nation's largest industry. Its one billion dollar annual sales exceeded the total yearly budget of the United States government.

Responding to growing demand, methods for processing huge quantities of meat evolved rapidly, creating major safety and sanitation concerns. In 1906, Upton Sinclair's book, *The Jungle*, dramatized these problems, aroused the public and caused meat sales to drop significantly. A campaign to correct the purported abuses resulted in the passage of the Meat Inspection Act in 1906 and inspired the formation of the American Meat Packers Association (1906), now known as the American Meat Institute, the main trade organization for the meat packing industry.

Initially, the meat packing industry was extremely wary of federal interference in its operations, but it soon accepted the government's role in assuring that all federally inspected meat was wholesome and unadulterated. When the 1906 Meat Inspection Act was updated and modified by the Wholesome Meat Act of 1967, the meat industry was one of its main supporters.

National Live Stock and Meat Board

In 1922, representatives of the major livestock and meat organizations formed the National Live Stock and Meat Board as a consumer marketing coalition. The entire industry from farm/ranch to table is represented in this coalition of producers, feeders, packers, processors, retailers and food service operators. The Meat Board conducts market development programs of research, education, information and promotion to fulfill its mission of protecting and improving consumer demand for beef, veal, pork, lamb and deli/prepared meats. The first checkoff from the receipts of livestock sales for market development programs in American agriculture was initiated in 1922 to finance the Meat Board. Today, the Meat Board continues to be funded through livestock and meat industry checkoffs conducted by the Beef Promotion Research Board, the federation of state beef councils, the National Pork Board, the voluntary checkoff on sheep and lambs and voluntary investments by packers and processors.

Land Use

The U.S. comprises 2.3 billion acres of land. Of that 2.3 billion acres, 1.783 billion acres (77 percent of the total of all U.S. land) is used for agricultural purposes. Of these, 718 million acres are forest, 600 million are pastureland and rangeland, and 465 million are used to grow crops. See Figure F-1.

Pastureland and Rangeland—The beef and lamb segments of the meat industry give cash value to the 600 million acres of U.S. pastureland and rangeland because grasses and shrubs which grow on this land are used as the primary source of food for cattle and sheep during the first half of their lives. Because the cost to use this land is minimal, the cost of feeding livestock is less than if the rancher had to purchase feed for each lamb or steer during its entire lifetime. This keeps the price of U.S. meat affordable to consumers as compared to costs of meat in other parts of the world.

The vast majority of the nation's pastureland and rangeland is too rugged, too arid, too wet or too high to cultivate crops of any kind. However, cattle and sheep are able to convert the otherwise unusable cellulose in the grasses and shrubs which grow on this land into a food with high nutrient density. If it were not for these ruminant (four-stomach) animals, this 600 million acres of land would not have productive use for the U.S. economy.

Cropland—During the latter part of their lives, livestock are fed a high-energy grain ration. Ingredients of such rations are primarily soybeans and corn (in some geographic areas, milo or barley are used) which are grown on the 465 million acres of U.S. land classified as cropland. As a result, there are economic benefits to farmers who produce grains for use by livestock producers.

Some of those who are concerned about the problem of world hunger argue that livestock production uses grain that could otherwise be used to feed the world's hungry people. However, the grain that is fed to livestock is mostly "feed" grain, for which there is limited use as human food. Although the land on which feed grains are grown could be used to grow other crops for use as human food, they will not be unless there is a market for such crops. Farmers will grow the crops from which they believe they can make a profit and growing feed grains is profitable because there is currently a market for these grains.

7

AN ECONOMIC PERSPECTIVE

Agriculture is the number one income-producing sector of the U.S. economy. As is true of agriculture in general, the production of livestock for food plays an important role in the nation's economy. Cattle and sheep production give cash value to land that would otherwise be unproductive. Cattle, hog and sheep production requires input from other parts of the economy, giving cash value to croplands and supporting millions of jobs in addition to those of the farmers and ranchers themselves. Export of meat, meat products and breeding animals helps to offset the imbalance of trade which the U.S. suffers.

Figure F-1
Total U.S. Land Use

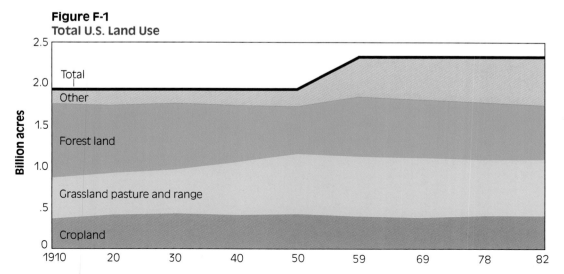

Sources: 1959-1982, Statistical Abstract of the United States: 1988.
1910-1950, Historical Statistics, Colonial Times to 1970.

Many of the feedstuffs given to animals are the by-products of processing other crops which are grown primarily for food and fiber for humans. For instance, cottonseed, citrus fruit pulp (from the processing of orange juice) and potato skins (from the processing of potatoes to make frozen products), are used to feed cattle in certain southeastern and western states. The use of these by-products of food and fiber production to feed livestock gives added value to the land on which the original crops were grown and their use helps to lower the cost of meat to the consumer because they are inexpensive sources of feed for the farmer or rancher.

Jobs

In order to provide consumers with an adequate supply of meat, an extensive system of production, processing and distribution is required, all of which contribute significantly to the U.S. economy in terms of the labor force. In addition to those individuals who are involved in raising and feeding livestock, more than 200,000 persons are employed in the meat-packing industry. Numerous people are involved in the business of transporting livestock and meat to and from packing houses. Thousands more are in the business of producing the equipment and electrical power used in the meat industry. The hundreds of thousands of other people who work in grocery stores and supermarkets, as well as in fast-food outlets and restaurants, all depend in total, or in part, on the meat industry for employment.

Exports

Meat, as well as live animals which are used for breeding, are exported to other nations. Some countries, such as Korea, buy breeding cattle raised by U.S. ranchers. Other countries, such as China, buy U.S. hogs to improve their swine population. The U.S. is a good source of cattle and hogs for this purpose because our ranchers and farmers have utilized technological advances to improve the genetic makeup of livestock and they have the advantage of a long history of livestock breeding. The export of breeding animals and meat helps, in part, to offset the imbalance of trade which exists between the U.S. and foreign countries. The 1987 dollar value of exported animals and products was at an all-time high of 5.2 billion dollars. It has climbed steadily since 1970, when the dollar value was 900 million (less than one-fifth of the 1987 figure).

Trends

The number of livestock production operations on farms and ranches has been declining. In recent years there has been approximately a 3 percent annual reduction in the number of cattle operations, a 6 percent reduction in the number of hog operations and about a 2 percent reduction in the number of sheep operations.

Food stores numbered 192,000 units as little as 10 years ago and now number fewer than 160,000. When one takes into account the increase in population, the trend is even more impressive. These structural changes in the food industry are driven by the need for higher levels of productivity in order to be competitive.

Nutrient Density

Of particular interest is meat's nutrient density, which is reflected in its contribution to specific nutrient needs relative to its energy contribution (as calories) to the diet. If the contribution of a food in supplying certain nutrients is large in comparison to that food's contribution of calories, then that food is said to be "nutrient dense." Viewing meat as a "single" food, it is nutrient dense for an adult male for protein, iron, zinc, thiamin, niacin and vitamin B_{12}. Since meat, as ingested, is nutrient dense for more than four nutrients, it is among the foods described as "nutritious." When lean meat cuts, trimmed of fat, are eaten in amounts recommended by health authorities (five to seven ounces per day), meat easily fits into diets recommended to prevent or treat heart disease.

Per-capita Meat Consumption

Much confusion exists with regard to the actual amount of meat ingested by Americans. Statistics have been reported by the USDA since the early 1900s on the amount of meat "consumed" annually, using carcass weight as the basis for the data, but "consumption" grossly overestimates "ingestion." The total of the weight of all carcasses produced by the U.S. meat industry was divided by the total population in the U.S. in order to determine estimated "consumption" per person.

The data derived from such a calculation are a means of tracking trends and making comparisons about the food supply over a period of time. However, such data do not accurately reflect the amount of actual meat each person in the U.S. "ingests" each year because

the numbers include significant amounts of bone and fat which are removed before the meat is eaten. Nevertheless, health authorities have used these "consumption" data to determine how much meat is eaten per person per year and they have incorrectly concluded that Americans eat far more than the amount now recommended by health professionals.

The USDA has other means of reporting food supply data. One of these, edible portion weights, comes closer to reflecting ingested weight than the data based on carcass weight. However, edible portion weight still represents a significantly higher amount of meat than people actually eat because edible portion weight includes fat, which most consumers remove before eating, and fat which is subsequently lost during cooking. (Meat loses an average of 25 percent of its weight during cooking due to evaporation and loss of fat in drippings.) Edible portion weight also fails to account for the meat that is left on the plate in households and in restaurants and the amount of meat which spoils before it is used.

When all of the losses in weight that occur in the stages of slaughter, packing, retail preparation and food preparation (along with cooking losses, plate waste and spoilage) are taken into consideration, the actual amount of meat (beef, veal, pork, lamb and processed meat from beef, pork, etc.) that is eaten ("ingested") is just under 91.0 pounds per person* per year or 3.99 ounces per person* per day. This is well below the five to seven ounces recommended (by the USDA Human Nutrition Information Service and many health organizations) per day from the meat group (meat, poultry, fish, eggs, nuts and legumes).

9

---

*The number of people used to calculate the per person data excludes people who do not eat meat.

The major component of a cut of meat, as it appears in the market, is its muscle. Depending on how the cut was prepared for sale, adipose tissue, connective tissue and skeletal tissue may also be present. An understanding of both the visible composition and the micro-structure of meat is essential to understanding how meat is cut, prepared, priced, cooked and served. The composition of meat will be covered in two sections: physical and chemical.

PHYSICAL COMPOSITION

This classification applies to components of meat that can be physically separated. They are muscle, fibrous connective tissues, fat (those three are intertwined) and skeletal tissues, mainly bone.

Muscle and Fibrous Connective Tissues

Muscle tissue can be of three types: skeletal, cardiac, and smooth. Skeletal muscle is attached directly or indirectly to the bone and facilitates movement and/or gives support to the body. From an economic standpoint, skeletal muscle is the most important and it is the major component of the carcass. Cardiac, as the name implies, is the muscle which forms the heart. Smooth muscles, also called visceral muscles, are found in the digestive and reproductive tracts as well as throughout the blood vessels, capillaries and arteries of the circulatory system.

Skeletal muscles differ in length, in depth and in thickness. Each muscle is interspersed with connective tissue and fat and is surrounded by connective tissue (called the epimysium or muscle sheath) which may vary in thickness over different parts of the muscle.

A single muscle is made up of many "bundles" (or fasciculi) of muscle cells or fibers held together by connective tissue (perimysium) (Figure 1-1). The size of the bundles varies in different muscles in the same animal and in different species. When the fiber bundles are small, the meat has a fine grain.

The muscle fibers which make up the bundles are elongated, multinucleated cells which have an outer covering known as the sarcolemma. Muscle fibers vary greatly in length and have an average diameter of about 0.0002 inch.

Figure 1-1
A Muscle

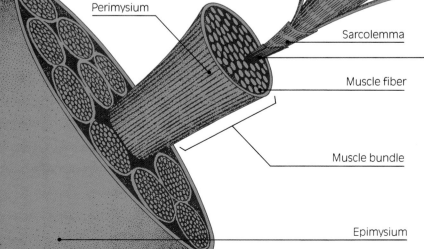

Myofilament

Myofibril

Sarcomere

Perimysium

Sarcolemma

Endomysium

Muscle fiber

Muscle bundle

Epimysium

Striated Muscle

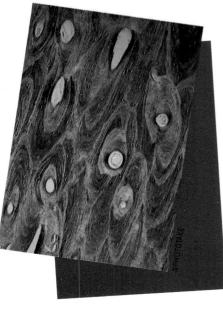
Bone Tissue

Muscles that are used for locomotion and power (e.g., in the legs and shoulders) have more connective tissue and yield less tender meat. The muscles of support (e.g., those in the back—rib and loin) move less, are not as important for locomotion or power, and are more tender. Other muscles, such as those in the portion of the shoulder nearest the rib, in the rump, and in the upper portion of the hind leg, provide moderately tender meat.

Adipose Tissue

The amount of adipose tissue differs widely among carcasses. The amount of fat stored in adipose tissue and the total quantity of adipose tissue increase rapidly as animals mature (if they are on a high plane of nutrition) and can be affected by the amount and type of feed fed to the animal, hormone balance and genetics. As an animal "fattens," fat is first deposited in the adipose tissues around the kidney and heart, and in the pelvic canal area; body cavity fat is more prevalent in dairy cattle than in beef cattle. External or subcutaneous adipose tissue is the second site of fat deposition. Located just beneath the skin, the subcutaneous adipose tissue is often referred to as "finish." The third site in which fat is deposited is between muscles (intermuscular or seam fat). The fourth area is within the muscles (as intramuscular fat or marbling). Intramuscular fat (marbling) is deposited, if and only if, needs of the adipose tissue sites of higher priority for fat deposition have been satisfied (e.g., around the organs, under the skin, and between the muscles). The amount of marbling is an important factor in determining the USDA quality grade for beef. The role of marbling in determining cooked-meat palatability is discussed at length in Chapter 5.

The muscle's capacity to accumulate increasing quantities of intramuscular fat is partially related to animal age (increasing as the animal matures) but is almost entirely (given that the animal is on a high plane of nutrition) determined by genetics (hereditary predisposition to deposit fat as marbling). Although there are differences among species, the general tendency is for the percentage of fat in the body to increase with age, particularly after the major stage of muscle growth has been completed. In addition, site and amount of fat accumulation in adipose tissues differs among individual animals of the same species, depending substantially upon their genetic makeup.

Bone and Skeletal Tissue

Skeletal tissue, a type of connective tissue, consists of bone, tendons, ligaments and cartilage. Unlike other connective tissue, bone is ossified; and, cartilage becomes ossified as the animal matures. The skeleton protects vital organs and provides a structural framework upon which muscles are distributed.

Bones, like all tissues, are dynamic and contain cells and structures that are constantly being degraded and rebuilt. Maturation of bones (the degree of conversion of cartilage to bone) can serve as an indication of the chronological and physiological age of the animal. The USDA uses degree of ossification in animal bones as an indication of relative maturity in assigning quality grades to veal/calf/beef and lamb/mutton carcasses, recognizing that tenderness is highly influenced by age at slaughter (maturity). Generally, tenderness decreases with increased chronological age. See the discussion of meat grading in Chapter 5.

Anatomically, the same bones from each of the four species of meat animals are almost identical in shape, but different in size. With a few exceptions, the same bones from each of the four species also have identical scientific names. The consumer can use the shapes and sizes of bones to identify retail cuts of meat (Chapter 3).

CHEMICAL COMPOSITION

The most abundant chemical constituent in meat is water. Next is protein, then fat. Nitrogenous extractives, carbohydrates, minerals and vitamins occur in much smaller amounts, but nevertheless are very important metabolically and nutritionally. These components are analyzed by chemical methods, which are more detailed than the physical separations discussed above.

Water

Adipose tissue contains little moisture; therefore, the fatter the animal, the lower the total water content of its carcass or cuts. Beef muscle from mature and relatively fat animals may contain as little as 45 percent moisture, while veal muscle from very youthful and relatively lean animals may contain as much as 72 percent moisture. Texture, color and flavor of muscle are affected by the amount of water in muscle tissue.

A large percentage of the water in muscle tissue exists as free molecules within the muscle fibers; a smaller percentage is located in the connective tissue. It is possible for some of the water to remain (during storage, curing and heat treatment) within muscle fibers because of the three-dimensional structure of the fibers; water retained under forces of pressure and temperature increase is termed "bound water;" that which is lost is called "free water." The water-holding capacity of the muscle can be decreased by disruptions of muscle structure. Grinding, chopping, freezing, thawing, salting, degradation of connective tissue by enzymatic or chemical means, application of other chemicals or organic additives that change acidity (pH), and heating are treatments that can affect the final water content of meat products.

Protein

Muscle tissue contains many different proteins with many different functions. Meat proteins are grouped in three general classifications: (1) myofibrillar, (2) stromal, and (3) sarcoplasmic. Each class of proteins differs as to the functional properties it contributes to meat.

Myofibrillar Proteins—Muscle fibers, the muscle cells which are grouped into muscle bundles, are composed of myofibrils (Figure 1-1). The proteins that comprise the myofibril, including actin and myosin and several more, are collectively called the myofibrillar proteins. The myofibrillar protein components most important for muscle fiber structure are actin and myosin. They are the most abundant proteins in muscle and are directly involved in the ability of muscle to contract and to relax.

The orderly arrangement of the protein molecules, actin and myosin and other myofibrillar proteins, forms the myofilaments. When viewed through an electron microscope these filaments form a pattern of cross striations, seen as alternating light and dark bands (Figure 1-1). The bands will differ in length depending upon the state of contraction or relaxation of the muscles. During contraction, actin and myosin filaments slide together to form a more complex protein known as actomyosin. Where these filaments overlap, darker bands occur in the striation pattern. Pre-slaughter and postmortem handling are extremely important in controlling the state of muscle contraction as it relates to muscle tenderness. If muscles are contracted (if the bands overlap) when the meat is prepared for eating, it will be less tender.

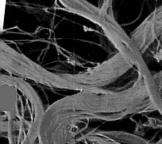

Collagen Fibers

©PHOTOTAKE

Stromal Proteins—Connective tissue is composed of a watery substance into which is dispersed a matrix of stromal-protein fibrils; these stromal proteins are collagen, elastin and reticulin.

- **Collagen**—Collagen is the single most abundant protein found in the intact body of mammalian species, being present in horns, hooves, bone, skin, tendons, ligaments, fascia, cartilage and muscle. Collagen is a unique and specialized protein which serves a variety of functions. The primary functions of collagen are to provide strength and support and to help form an impervious membrane (as in skin). In meat, collagen is a major factor influencing the tenderness of the muscle after cooking. Collagen is not broken down easily by cooking except with moist-heat cookery methods. Collagen is white, thin and transparent. Microscopically, it appears in a coiled formation which softens and contracts to a short, thick mass when it is heated, helping give cooked meat a plump appearance. Collagen itself is tough; however, heating (to the appropriate temperature) converts collagen to gelatin which is tender.

- **Elastin**—Elastin is found in the walls of the circulatory system as well as in connective tissues throughout the animal body and provides elasticity to those tissues. Elastin is sometimes referred to as "yellow" connective tissue due to its color. The ligamentum nuchae (heavy gristle) present in chuck blade and rib roasts and steaks, is almost pure elastin. Unlike collagen, elastin is not degraded by moist-heat cookery methods and should be removed from cuts where it exists. Fortunately, muscle tissue from young animals contains relatively little elastin.

- **Reticulin**—Reticulin is present in much smaller amounts than either collagen or elastin. It is speculated that reticulin may be a precursor to either collagen and/or elastin as it is more prevalent in younger animals.

Older animals can, but do not necessarily, have more connective tissue per unit of muscle than do younger animals. Cross-linkages between the collagen molecules increase (decreasing susceptibility of collagen to heat-induced solubilization) in older animals yielding tougher muscles than those found in muscle from more youthful animals. In general, the less connective tissue a cut of meat contains, the more tender it will be.

Sarcoplasmic Proteins—The sarcoplasmic proteins include hemoglobin and myoglobin pigments and a wide variety of enzymes.

- **Pigments** from hemoglobin and myoglobin help to contribute the red color to muscle. Hemoglobin carries oxygen from the lungs to the tissues—including muscle. Myoglobin is present in muscle and it stores the oxygen transported to the muscle via the blood by hemoglobin until it is utilized in metabolism. The carbon dioxide produced during cell metabolism diffuses out of the cells (including those of the muscle) and is transported as the bicarbonate ion to the lungs where it is exhaled as carbon dioxide. Myoglobin is present in the sarcoplasm, or bathing fluid, of the muscle cell; hemoglobin is the protein found in red blood cells or erythrocytes. In meat, there is a substantial quantity of hemoglobin because not all blood is removed from capillaries, arterioles and venules during slaughter and dressing.

The color of muscle can influence the USDA quality grade of beef carcasses. Color also plays a role in the aesthetic appeal of meat in the market display case. The color range of pinks to reds found in muscle is partially dependent on the amount of myoglobin present and partially due to the chemical state (and free binding-site occupant) of the heme in myoglobin and hemoglobin.

Differences in myoglobin concentration are related to species, age and sex of the animal, and type of muscle. Cattle have more myoglobin in their muscles than pigs; mature sheep more than lambs; bulls more than cows; and the constantly operating muscles of the *diaphragm* have more myoglobin than less frequently used muscles, like the *longissimus dorsi*.

When exposed to the air, the pigments (myoglobin and hemoglobin) on the surface of the muscles are oxygenated. Oxygenation forms oxymyoglobin, which is bright red. The interior of the muscle will remain purple because oxygen cannot penetrate to the center portion of the muscle. Store-packaged meat (wrapped in oxygen-permeable plastic film) is usually bright red, while vacuum-packaged meat is purplish-red due to decreased oxygen permeability of the packaging film. Ground beef is normally packaged for retail sale in oxygen-permeable clear film, allowing the exterior to become bright red. When these packages are opened and the unit is broken apart, the interior of the chub or patty will be dark brown or purple, but that too will brighten up in a few minutes upon exposure to the oxygen in the air. Prolonged exposure to oxygen causes the oxymyoglobin to oxidize and form metmyoglobin, which is an unappealing brownish-red color. While the palatability of such meat, after cooking, may be satisfactory, brown muscle will become rancid and unpalatable more quickly than will bright-red muscle if further storage occurs (prior to cooking).

In the curing process, myoglobin unites loosely with nitric oxide to form nitrosomyoglobin. Upon cooking, nitrosomyoglobin is converted to nitrosohemochrome, which is characteristically cured-pink in color and which is sensitive to light. For this reason, cured meat (e.g., slices of ham) are often displayed in the meat case with the meat (on its foam tray) turned face down.

Although sensitive to light, nitrosohemochrome is heat-stable. As a result, reheating of cured meat does not further alter its color. In contrast, fresh meat turns brownish-red when cooked because denatured globins, hemichrome and hemochrome are formed.

- **Enzymes** which occur naturally in muscle tissue, continue to function during the aging of meat. *Proteolytic* enzymes are those that degrade protein, *amylolytic* enzymes degrade carbohydrates, and *lypolytic* enzymes degrade fats. During aging, proteolytic enzymes break down myofibrillar proteins, thereby contributing to the tenderness of meat. The enzymes (e.g., calcium-activated proteases and cathepsins) responsible for tenderization are sensitive to time and temperature—the longer meat remains at the temperature optimal for enzyme activity, the more complete will be the enzyme degradation of myofibrilla proteins.

Nitrogenous Extractives—Another group of substances that are related to proteins (but are not true proteins) are the nitrogenous substances and nucleopeptides. These water-soluble components excite the flow of gastric juices when cooked meat is ingested. Along with fat, they (especially the nucleotides and nucleosides, and their metabolic by-products—xanthine and hypoxanthine) provide much of the aroma and flavor of meat. Examples of this group of substances are creatine, creatinine, the purines and free amino acids. Greater quantities of nitrogenous extractives are present in muscle from older animals, and they are more abundant in the more active muscles that occur in the less tender cuts. Nitrogenous extractives, in part, are responsible for the so-called "gamey (intense) flavor" of meat from wild animals.

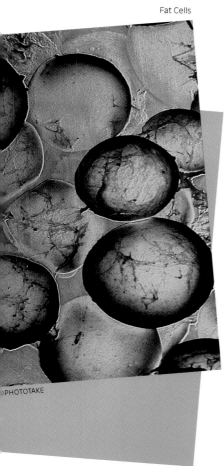

PHOTOTAKE

Fats

The characteristics of fats (triglycerides) in the adipose tissues differ most because of differences in carbon-chain length and the degree of saturation/unsaturation of the fatty acids. External depots (e.g., subcutaneous adipose tissue) contain more unsaturated fatty acids than do internal depots (e.g., the adipose tissue capsule around the kidneys). This is due in part, to the need to maintain fluidity of the fats in the outer layers of adipose tissues in the live animal at low ambient temperatures. As saturation of a fatty acid increases, the fat and the adipose tissue become firmer. Lamb fat, which is more saturated than beef fat, is relatively hard, while pork fat, which is less saturated than beef fat, is relatively soft. See Chapter 2 for a discussion of saturated fat.

Carbohydrates

The primary carbohydrate reservoir of the animal body is the liver. That organ contains about one-half of the carbohydrates found in the body. Carbohydrates are stored as glycogen in the liver and in muscles. The remaining 50 percent of carbohydrates are distributed throughout the body, largely in the muscles, but with substantial quantities in the blood (usually as glucose) and in other tissues, organs and glands.

The changes that occur in energy metabolism, e.g., the conversions of glycogen to glucose and glucose to lactic acid, are complex; all such changes are controlled and mediated by enzymes and hormones. The lactic acid content of the muscles in a carcass increases during initial stages of aging *or ripening*, lowering the pH (muscle acidity). The pH of muscle considered "normal" is 5.6 (pH is the negative log of the hydrogen ion concentration; the higher the pH, the less acidic is the muscle). Muscle color, texture, water-holding capacity and tenderness are influenced by pH.

If an animal experiences vigorous stress or exercise of the muscles immediately prior to slaughter and has no opportunity to restore its normal glycogen levels, the glycogen content within the muscles at slaughter will be reduced substantially. Because so little glycogen is available to be converted (after death) to lactic acid, a higher ultimate pH (e.g., a final pH of 6.2) will occur in this animal's muscles after slaughter, and the muscles will be dark, firm and dry (DFD). This is a reasonably rare occurrence in beef (perhaps 2 percent of carcasses are affected) and those carcasses are termed "dark cutters." The DFD condition also occurs in pork and lamb carcasses. It is thought that the dark color of muscles with a high pH is due to its higher water-holding capacity, which causes muscle fibers to be swollen. The swollen state of the fibers causes more incident light to be absorbed, rather than reflected, by the meat surface, and thus the color appears to be darker. "Dark cutters" are severely discounted in price by packers and retailers, due to poor consumer appeal of this meat; therefore, stress and rough handling of animals is minimized prior to slaughter.

A too-rapid postmortem (after death) drop in muscle pH (to a final pH of 5.1, for example) is associated with the pale, soft, and exudative (PSE) conditions that are somewhat common in pork muscle. PSE muscle is characterized by soft and mushy texture, low water-holding capacity and pale muscle color. The looser muscle structure of PSE muscle associated with its lower water-holding capacity is responsible for a greater reflectance of incident light and hence it has a pale color.

Minerals and Vitamins

In addition to protein and fat, meat (beef, veal, pork and lamb) is a significant source of several other nutrients in the U.S. diet. These include the minerals iron and zinc, and most of the B-vitamin complex (B_1, B_2, niacin, B_6 and B_{12}). See Chapter 2 for a complete discussion of meat in the diet.

Chapter 2

*T*his chapter focuses on the nutrients provided by meat and the role of meat in a balanced diet. The information is not intended to be a comprehensive overview of human nutrition. For that reason only 10 of the 17 nutrients for which there are quantified recommendations are discussed in this chapter. These 10 nutrients are those for which meat is a significant source. See Appendix for nutrient data on beef, veal, pork, lamb and processed meat.

DIETARY RECOMMENDATIONS

Recommendations for daily intake of food and nutrients have been made in the form of the Recommended Daily Dietary Allowances (RDA), food grouping systems and dietary guidelines. The RDA specify amounts of individual nutrients for different age/sex categories. Food grouping systems suggest amounts and types of foods that will meet the RDA for nutrients. Dietary guidelines address problem areas in nutrition in terms of foods and nutrients that are known to be overconsumed or underconsumed in the "typical" American diet.

Recommended Dietary Allowances

Recommendations for daily intake of components of the diet are established by the Food and Nutrition Board of the National Academy of Sciences, National Research Council. Approximately every five years, the Board publishes the Recommended Daily Dietary Allowances (RDA). The most recent set of recommendations was published in 1989 (see Table 2-1).

The RDAs are defined as the levels of intake of essential nutrients considered to be adequate to meet the known nutritional needs of nearly all healthy individuals. The "allowances" are the average needs of each population group plus a margin of safety. One exception to this definition is the allowance for energy (calories). A calorie allowance sufficient to cover the energy needs of nearly all healthy individuals in a specific group would result in excess energy for most of the group and would consequently promote obesity. The Food and Nutrition Board also publishes a table of recommended energy intake which is based on mean age, weight, height and sex (See Table 2-2).

The recommended energy intake for males (age 25-50) is 2900 calories per day. The recommended daily energy intake for females in the same age category is 2200 calories. Smaller or less active women require less, while taller or physically active women require more. Additional calories are needed during periods of growth such as throughout childhood, during adolescence and during pregnancy.

Table 2-1
Recommended Daily Dietary Allowances[a]
Revised 1989

	Age (years)	Weight (kg)[b]	Weight (lbs)[b]	Height (cm)	Height (in)	Protein (g)	Vitamin A (μg RE)[c]	Vitamin D (μg)[d]	Vitamin E (mg α TE)[e]	Vitamin K (μg)	Vitamin C (mg)	Thiamin (mg)	Riboflavin (mg)	Niacin (mg NE)[f]	Vitamin B6 (mg)	Folacin (μg)	Vitamin B12 (μg)	Calcium (mg)	Phosphorus (mg)	Magnesium (mg)	Iron (mg)	Zinc (mg)	Iodine (μg)	Selenium (μg)
Infants	0.0-0.5	6	13	60	24	13	375	7.5	3	5	30	0.3	0.4	5	0.3	25	0.3	400	300	40	6	5	40	10
	0.5-1.0	9	20	71	28	14	375	10	4	10	35	0.4	0.5	6	0.6	35	0.5	600	500	60	10	5	50	15
Children	1-3	13	29	90	35	16	400	10	6	15	40	0.7	0.8	9	1.0	50	0.7	800	800	80	10	10	70	20
	4-6	20	44	112	44	24	500	10	7	20	45	0.9	1.1	12	1.1	75	1.0	800	800	120	10	10	90	20
	7-10	28	62	132	52	28	700	10	7	30	45	1.0	1.2	13	1.4	100	1.4	800	800	170	10	10	120	30
Males	11-14	45	99	157	62	45	1000	10	10	45	50	1.3	1.5	17	1.7	150	2.0	1200	1200	270	12	15	150	40
	15-18	66	145	176	69	59	1000	10	10	65	60	1.5	1.8	20	2.0	200	2.0	1200	1200	400	12	15	150	50
	19-24	72	160	177	70	58	1000	10	10	70	60	1.5	1.7	19	2.0	200	2.0	1200	1200	350	10	15	150	70
	25-50	79	174	176	70	63	1000	5	10	80	60	1.5	1.7	19	2.0	200	2.0	800	800	350	10	15	150	70
	51+	77	170	173	68	63	1000	5	10	80	60	1.2	1.4	15	2.0	200	2.0	800	800	350	10	15	150	70
Females	11-14	46	101	157	62	46	800	10	8	45	50	1.1	1.3	15	1.4	150	2.0	1200	1200	280	15	12	150	45
	15-18	55	120	163	64	44	800	10	8	55	60	1.1	1.3	15	1.5	180	2.0	1200	1200	300	15	12	150	50
	19-24	58	128	164	65	46	800	10	8	60	60	1.1	1.3	15	1.6	180	2.0	1200	1200	280	15	12	150	55
	25-50	63	138	163	64	50	800	5	8	65	60	1.1	1.3	15	1.6	180	2.0	800	800	280	15	12	150	55
	51+	65	143	160	63	50	800	5	8	65	60	1.0	1.2	13	1.6	180	2.0	800	800	280	10	12	150	55
Pregnant						60	800	10	10	65	70	1.5	1.6	17	2.2	400	2.2	1200	1200	320	30	15	175	65
Lactating 1st 6 months						65	1300	10	12	65	95	1.6	1.8	20	2.1	280	2.6	1200	1200	355	15	19	200	75
2nd 6 months						62	1200	10	11	65	90	1.6	1.7	20	2.1	260	2.6	1200	1200	340	15	16	200	75

a The allowances, expressed as average daily intakes over time, are intended to provide for individual variations among most normal persons as they live in the United States under usual environmental stresses. Diets should be based on a variety of common foods in order to provide other nutrients for which human requirements have been less well defined.

b Weights and heights of Reference Adults are actual medians for the U.S. population of the designated age, as reported by NHANES II. The median weights and heights of those under 19 years of age were taken from Hamill et al. (1979). The use of these figures does not imply that the height-to-weight ratios are ideal.

c Retinol equivalents. 1 retinol equivalent = 1 μg retinol or 6 μg β-carotene.

d As cholecalciferol. 10 μg cholecalciferol = 400 I.U. of vitamin D.

e α-Tocopherol equivalents. 1 mg d-α tocopherol = 1 α-TE.

f 1 NE (niacin equivalent) is equal to 1 mg of niacin or 60 mg of dietary tryptophan.

Source: Recommended Dietary Allowances, Revised 1989.

Table 2-2
Mean Heights and Weights and Recommended Energy Intakes
for Adult Males and Females

	Age (years)	Weight (kg)	Weight (lb)	Height (cm)	Height (in)	Energy Needs (kcal)
Males	25-50	79	174	176	70	2900
Females	25-50	63	138	163	64	2200

Source: Recommended Dietary Allowances, Revised 1989.

In order to determine the nutrient contributions of a food to daily nutrient needs or to compare nutrition contributions between foods, the percent RDA is computed as follows:

$$\left[\frac{\text{(Amount of a nutrient in one serving of a specific food)}}{\text{(RDA for that nutrient)}}\right] = \underline{\hphantom{xx}} \times 100 = \underline{\hphantom{xx}} \%$$

For example: Percent RDA for cooked, trimmed beef tenderloin is computed as follows:

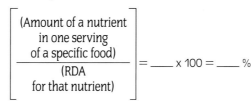

$$\left[\frac{\begin{array}{c}24.01g\\ \text{(protein in 3 ounces)}\end{array}}{\begin{array}{c}50.00g\\ \text{(protein RDA for women)}\end{array}}\right] = .48 \times 100 = 48\%$$

Food Grouping Systems

Foods which provide significant amounts of similar nutrients can be combined into "food groups." Various systems of food groupings have been used since the early 1900s. Food groupings help consumers translate the technical information from the RDA into practical information for meal planning. The current grouping recommended by the United States Department of Agriculture (USDA) is shown in Table 2-3.

Most nutrition experts agree that eating a wide variety of foods is the best way for humans to be sure of proper nutrition. People who emphasize one food or food group in diet planning while de-emphasizing others will find it difficult to meet daily nutrient requirements.

Dietary Guidelines

A number of organizations have published dietary guidelines. The most widely used guidelines were developed by the USDA and the United States Department of Health and Human Services (HHS). There have been three editions of the USDA/HHS guidelines. The most recent revision was published in 1990 and recommends the following guidelines: eat a variety of foods; maintain healthy weight; choose a diet low in fat, saturated fat, and cholesterol; choose a diet with plenty of vegetables, fruits, and grain products; use sugars only in moderation; use salt and sodium only in moderation; and if you drink alcoholic beverages, do so in moderation.

Table 2-3
USDA Food Groups and Suggested Daily Servings

Food Group	Suggested Daily Servings
Breads, Cereals and Other Grain Products Whole-grain Enriched	**6 to 11 servings** Include several servings a day of whole-grain products.
Fruits Citrus, melon, berries Other fruits	**2 to 4 servings**
Vegetables Dark-green leafy Deep-yellow Dry beans and peas (legumes) Starchy Other vegetables	**3 to 5 servings** Use all types regularly; use dark-green leafy vegetables, dry beans and peas several times a week.
Meat, Poultry, Fish and Alternates Eggs, dry beans and peas, nuts and seeds	**2 to 3 servings — total 5 to 7 oz. lean**
Milk, Cheese and Yogurt	**2 servings** 3 servings for teens and women who are pregnant or breastfeeding. 4 servings for teens who are pregnant or breastfeeding.
Fats, Sweets and Alcoholic Beverages	Avoid too many fats and sweets. If you drink alcoholic beverages, do so in moderation.

Source: USDA Human Nutrition Information Service
Nutrition and Your Health, Dietary Guidelines for Americans.
Home and Garden Bulletin Number 232-1, Washington, D.C.:
U.S. Government Printing Office, April 1986.

Food calories come from four sources of fuel: carbohydrates, fats, proteins and alcohol. Calories are not provided by vitamins or minerals. However, vitamins and minerals are important cofactors in energy metabolism. Carbohydrates such as sugars and starches, which generally are about 98 percent digested and fully oxidized by humans, provide about 4 kcal/g. Most fats are generally digested to the extent of 95 percent yielding 9 kcal/g. Proteins, due to incomplete digestion and oxidation, generally yield an energy equivalent of 4 kcal/g. Thus, on an equal-weight basis, fat generally yields 2.25 times as many calories as protein or carbohydrates.

The calories from meat are provided primarily by protein and fat. As noted in Chapter 1, there is only a small amount of carbohydrate stored in the liver in the form of glycogen (animal starch). Since meat is not a good carbohydrate source, carbohydrate is not discussed in this chapter. If wine or other sources of alcohol are added to meat during cooking, the alcohol burns off and does not contribute calories to the meat when it is consumed.

ENERGY VALUE OF MEAT

The energy value of foods is measured in heat units called kilocalories. A kilocalorie is the amount of heat required to raise the temperature of one kilogram of water one degree centigrade (e.g., from 14.5° to 15.5°C). The kilocalorie (1000 calories) is the scientific unit used in expressing energy values of foods. Hereafter, in this publication, the common term "calorie" will denote the scientific term, kilocalorie.

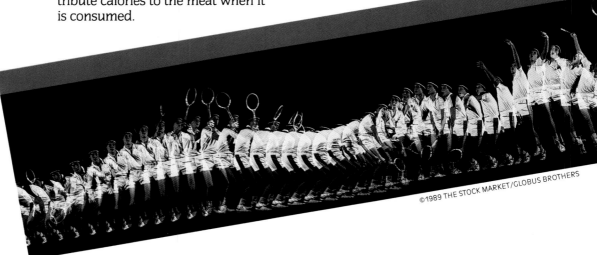

©1989 THE STOCK MARKET/GLOBUS BROTHERS

Table 2-4
Energy Value of Food

Calories Per Gram	In Laboratory*	In Human Body**
Carbohydrate	4.10	4.00
Protein	5.65	4.00
Fat	9.45	9.00
Alcohol	7.00	7.00

*Physical or specific food value
**Physiologic fuel value

Figure 2-1
Contribution to RDA for Women Aged 25-50
3 oz. Cooked, Lean Meat

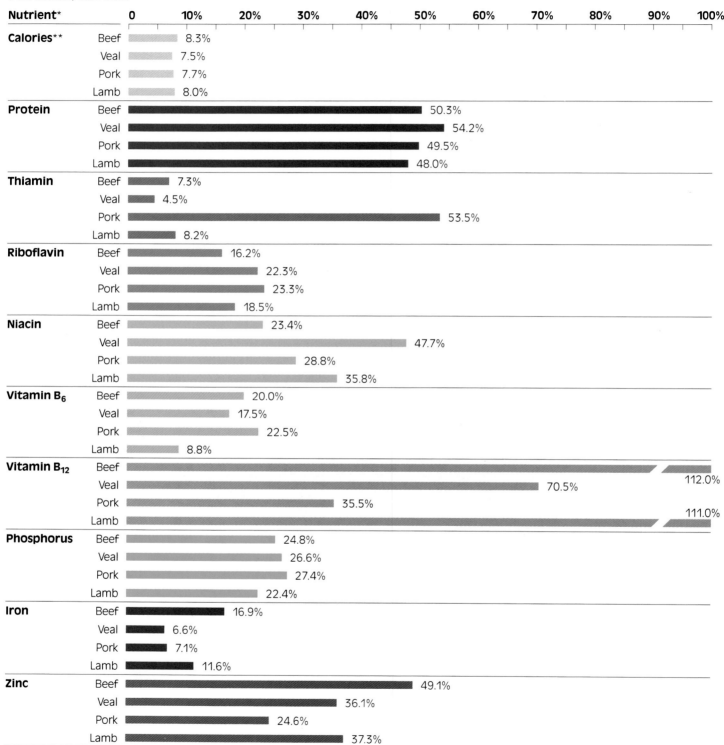

Nutrient*		0	10%	20%	30%	40%	50%	60%	70%	80%	90%	100%

Calories**
- Beef 8.3%
- Veal 7.5%
- Pork 7.7%
- Lamb 8.0%

Protein
- Beef 50.3%
- Veal 54.2%
- Pork 49.5%
- Lamb 48.0%

Thiamin
- Beef 7.3%
- Veal 4.5%
- Pork 53.5%
- Lamb 8.2%

Riboflavin
- Beef 16.2%
- Veal 22.3%
- Pork 23.3%
- Lamb 18.5%

Niacin
- Beef 23.4%
- Veal 47.7%
- Pork 28.8%
- Lamb 35.8%

Vitamin B$_6$
- Beef 20.0%
- Veal 17.5%
- Pork 22.5%
- Lamb 8.8%

Vitamin B$_{12}$
- Beef 112.0%
- Veal 70.5%
- Pork 35.5%
- Lamb 111.0%

Phosphorus
- Beef 24.8%
- Veal 26.6%
- Pork 27.4%
- Lamb 22.4%

Iron
- Beef 16.9%
- Veal 6.6%
- Pork 7.1%
- Lamb 11.6%

Zinc
- Beef 49.1%
- Veal 36.1%
- Pork 24.6%
- Lamb 37.3%

*Vitamins A and C and the mineral calcium, although essential to the diet, are not listed on this chart because meat is not a significant source of these nutrients.
**Based on 2200 calories per day.

Source: Beef, veal and lamb data are based on USDA *Composition of Foods.* Agriculture Handbook No. 8-13 and 8-17, respectively. Pork data for calories, protein, fat, and cholesterol is from Buege, D.R., et.al., "A nationwide Survey of the Composition and Marketing of Pork Products at Retail," University of Wisconsin, Madison, Wisconsin, 1990. Conducted in cooperation and with the guidance of the U.S. Department of Agriculture to provide the data base for the revision of USDA Agriculture Handbook 8-10, which will be published in 1991. All other pork data is from the current USDA Handbook 8-10, last revised in 1983.

Figure 2-2
Contribution to RDA for Men Aged 25-50
3 oz. Cooked, Lean Meat

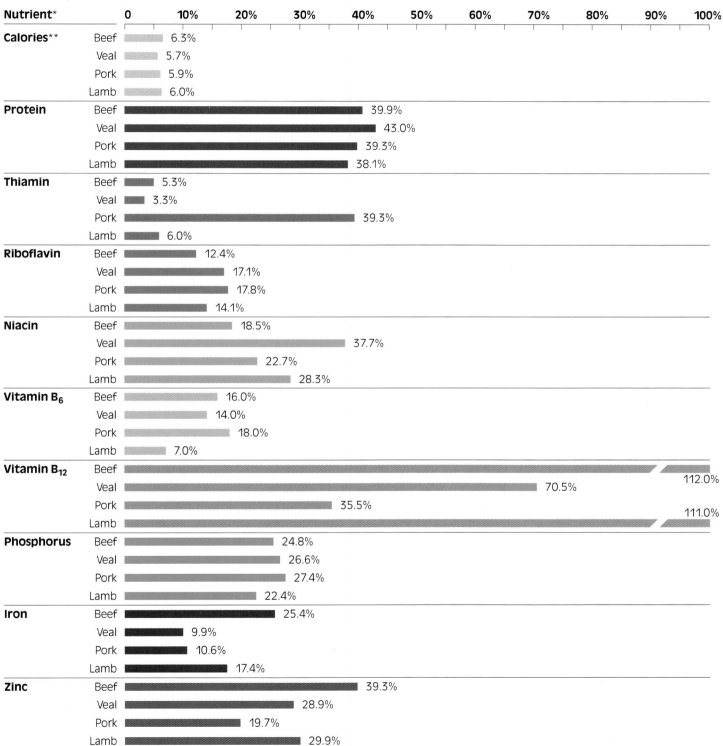

Nutrient*		0	10%	20%	30%	40%	50%	60%	70%	80%	90%	100%
Calories**	Beef	6.3%										
	Veal	5.7%										
	Pork	5.9%										
	Lamb	6.0%										
Protein	Beef					39.9%						
	Veal					43.0%						
	Pork					39.3%						
	Lamb					38.1%						
Thiamin	Beef	5.3%										
	Veal	3.3%										
	Pork					39.3%						
	Lamb	6.0%										
Riboflavin	Beef	12.4%										
	Veal	17.1%										
	Pork	17.8%										
	Lamb	14.1%										
Niacin	Beef	18.5%										
	Veal				37.7%							
	Pork	22.7%										
	Lamb	28.3%										
Vitamin B$_6$	Beef	16.0%										
	Veal	14.0%										
	Pork	18.0%										
	Lamb	7.0%										
Vitamin B$_{12}$	Beef											112.0%
	Veal								70.5%			
	Pork				35.5%							
	Lamb											111.0%
Phosphorus	Beef	24.8%										
	Veal	26.6%										
	Pork	27.4%										
	Lamb	22.4%										
Iron	Beef	25.4%										
	Veal	9.9%										
	Pork	10.6%										
	Lamb	17.4%										
Zinc	Beef					39.3%						
	Veal	28.9%										
	Pork	19.7%										
	Lamb	29.9%										

*Vitamins A and C and the mineral calcium, although essential to the diet, are not listed on this chart because meat is not a significant source of these nutrients.
**Based on 2900 calories per day.
Source: Beef, veal and lamb data are based on USDA *Composition of Foods*. Agriculture Handbook No. 8-13 and 8-17, respectively. Pork data for calories, protein, fat, and cholesterol is from Buege, D.R., et.al., "A nationwide Survey of the Composition and Marketing of Pork Products at Retail," University of Wisconsin, Madison, Wisconsin, 1990. Conducted in cooperation and with the guidance of the U.S. Department of Agriculture to provide the data base for the revision of USDA Agriculture Handbook 8-10, which will be published in 1991. All other pork data is from the current USDA Handbook 8-10, last revised in 1983.

NUTRIENTS IN MEAT

In a varied diet, meat makes a significant contribution towards the RDA for several nutrients as indicated in Figures 2-1 and 2-2.

Protein

The word protein comes from the Greek word meaning "first" or "of primary importance." Every living cell contains protein, whether the cell is found in skin, muscle, blood, organs or any other component of the body. Protein is a vital nutrient in the growth process—for building and maintaining body tissues. Body proteins help to regulate acid/base balance, are components of hormones and enzymes, and are integral in the functioning of the immune system.

The protein in meat is high in both quality and quantity. The main determinant of protein quality is the type and arrangement of amino acids, the basic building blocks of all proteins. Of the approximately 20 different amino acids found in protein, nine are essential for adults. Essential amino acids cannot be made in adequate quantities in the human body and must be supplied by food. Non-essential amino acids, if not provided in the diet, can be synthesized when adequate essential amino acids and energy are available. Both essential and non-essential amino acids are used to build, repair and replace body cells every minute of the day.

Proteins in food which contain all of the essential amino acids in amounts and proportions that can be recycled into body proteins are described as having high "biological values." Animal foods, including beef, veal, pork and lamb, have high biological value.

The proteins in most grains, fruits and vegetables are incomplete proteins. They have fair to low biological values. For efficient use of the amino acids, plant foods must be consumed with other foods that complete their amino acid mix and balance. These combinations are called complementary proteins. Animal foods, containing complete proteins, can complement plant proteins, and certain plant proteins can complement other plant proteins when combined in specific ways (grains with legumes, grains with nuts/seeds, legumes with nuts/seeds).

Individuals who choose to limit their intake of animal foods will need to plan their meals carefully. Dietary guidance and counseling may be needed to learn about protein combinations needed to assure a nutritionally complete diet.

The quantity of protein required to meet the RDA is typically expressed in grams. The total grams of protein a person needs is influenced by the quality of the dietary protein. If all the protein consumed has a high biological value, less is required than if all or some of the food proteins are of low biological value. The RDAs for protein (Figure 2-3) are based on the assumption that individuals consume a combination of animal and vegetable proteins.

The values in Figure 2-3 are for cooked, lean, boneless portions of meat which have been trimmed of fat.

Figure 2-3
Recommended Daily Dietary Allowances for Protein in Grams

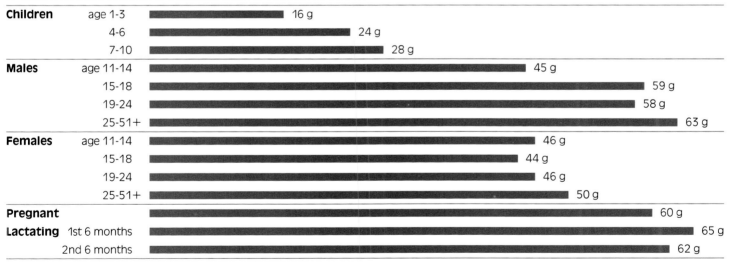

Children	age 1-3	16 g
	4-6	24 g
	7-10	28 g
Males	age 11-14	45 g
	15-18	59 g
	19-24	58 g
	25-51+	63 g
Females	age 11-14	46 g
	15-18	44 g
	19-24	46 g
	25-51+	50 g
Pregnant		60 g
Lactating	1st 6 months	65 g
	2nd 6 months	62 g

Grams of Protein in Various Meat Sources*

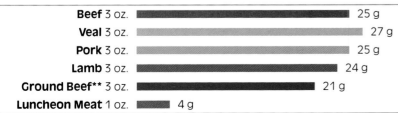

Beef 3 oz.	25 g
Veal 3 oz.	27 g
Pork 3 oz.	25 g
Lamb 3 oz.	24 g
Ground Beef** 3 oz.	21 g
Luncheon Meat 1 oz.	4 g

*All meat source values are for cooked, trimmed boneless portions.
**Lean

24

Type of Fat in the U.S. Diet

The total amount of fat in the U.S. food supply has increased since the early 1900s. The increase is attributed to fat from vegetable sources, which has more than tripled — from 17.1 to 54.7 pounds per capita between 1909-13 and 1981. In 1981, the amount of fat from animal sources was 6.4 pounds less per capita than in 1909-13.

Between 1965 and 1985, the total fat content of the food supply increased by 16.3 pounds per capita. The shift from animal to vegetable sources has been even more dramatic: fat from animal sources decreased 3.6 pounds per capita and fat from vegetable sources increased 19.9 pounds per capita during these 20 years.

Fat

The Food and Nutrition Board of the National Academy of Sciences (NAS) has not established Recommended Daily Dietary Allowances for fat in the diet. Recent recommendations, in other publications from the NAS, suggest limiting fat consumption so that no more than 30 percent of total calories in the diet are from fat. The National Cholesterol Education Program (NCEP) of the National Heart, Lung and Blood Institute (NHLBI), the American Dietetic Association (ADA) and the American Heart Association (AHA) all also recommend a dietary fat intake not to exceed 30 percent of total calories.

Fats are important components of a balanced diet. Dietary fats add flavor, appetite appeal and satiety value to foods. They are a concentrated source of calories, providing nine calories per gram compared to carbohydrates and protein which provide four calories per gram. They provide essential fatty acids and aid in the absorption of the fat-soluble vitamins A, D, E and K.

Figure 2-4
Total Fat Content of the Food Supply, 1985

Pounds Per Capita Per Year

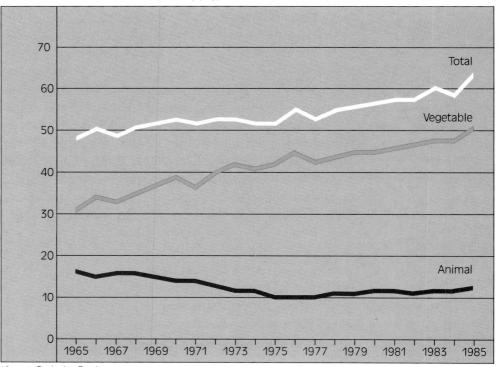

*Source: *Designing Foods*.

Fatty Acids—Edible fats and oils are basically triglycerides. Triglycerides are composed of three fatty acids attached to glycerol. Most of the fatty acids have an even number of carbon atoms arranged in a long straight chain. The fatty acids may be saturated, that is, each carbon atom in the chain is linked by single bonds to other adjacent carbon atoms or to hydrogen atoms; or they may be unsaturated, having two or more adjacent carbon atoms in the chain joined by double bonds. Unsaturated fatty acids are further classified as monounsaturated, having one double bond in the carbon chain, or polyunsaturated, having two or more double bonds in the carbon chain.

Animal fats and vegetable oils contain mixtures of both saturated and unsaturated fatty acids. It is the proportion of saturated to unsaturated fatty acids attached to the glycerides that gives fats and oils their individual physical properties. Fats which contain more of the saturated, than unsaturated, fatty acids, are typically solid at room temperature. Fats which contain more unsaturated than saturated, fatty acids, are typically liquid at room temperature. Exceptions to this rule are tropical oils (palm oil and coconut oil) which contain purified saturated fatty acids yet are liquid at room temperature. Regardless of the type, saturated or unsaturated, all fatty acids provide the same number of calories per gram (nine) when metabolized in the body for energy.

Figure 2-5
Saturated and Unsaturated Fatty Acids

Saturated

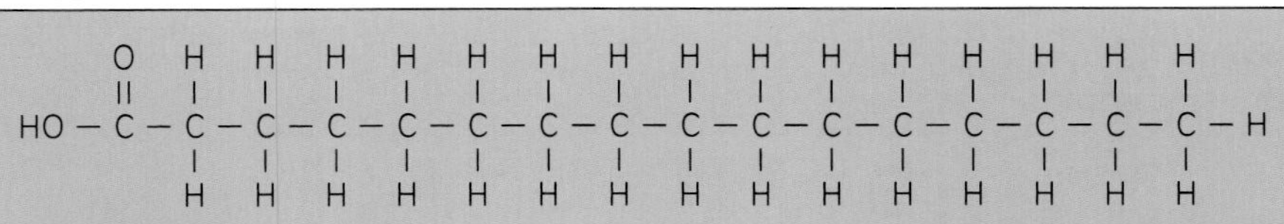

(Palmitic Acid, $C_{16}H_{32}O_2$)

Monounsaturated

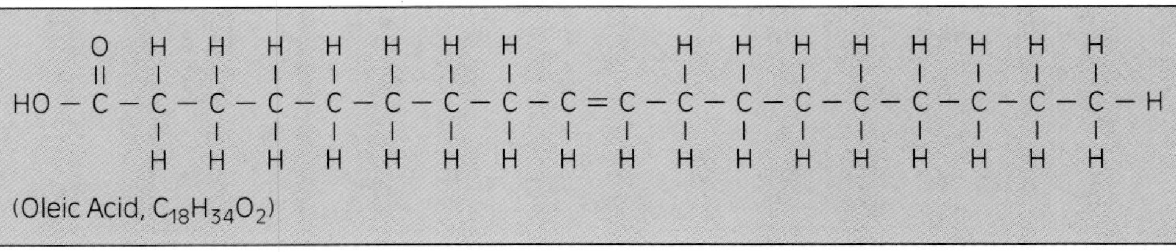

(Oleic Acid, $C_{18}H_{34}O_2$)

Polyunsaturated

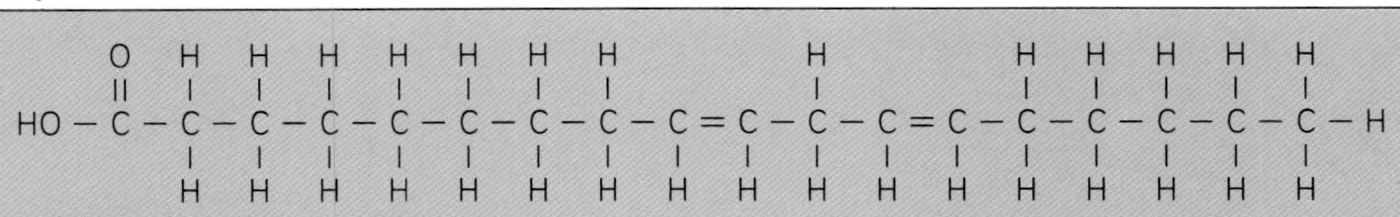

(Linoleic Acid, $C_{18}H_{32}O_2$)

Table 2-5
Lipid Components of Certain Foods

Cooking Fats and Oils[1]

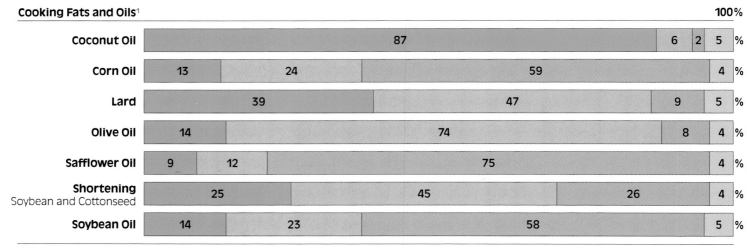

100%

Food	Saturated	Monounsaturated	Polyunsaturated	Other Lipids
Coconut Oil	87	6	2	5 %
Corn Oil	13	24	59	4 %
Lard	39	47	9	5 %
Olive Oil	14	74	8	4 %
Safflower Oil	9	12	75	4 %
Shortening (Soybean and Cottonseed)	25	45	26	4 %
Soybean Oil	14	23	58	5 %

Foods[1]

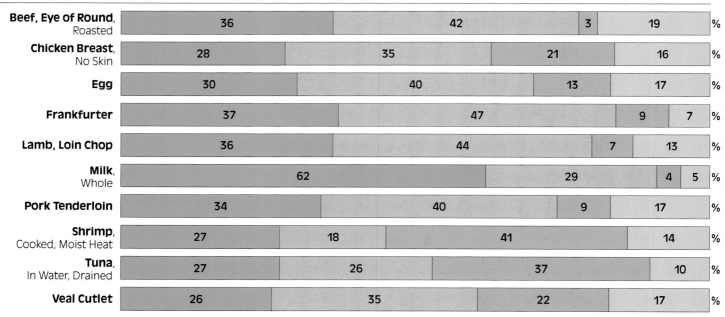

Food	Saturated	Monounsaturated	Polyunsaturated	Other Lipids
Beef, Eye of Round, Roasted	36	42	3	19 %
Chicken Breast, No Skin	28	35	21	16 %
Egg	30	40	13	17 %
Frankfurter	37	47	9	7 %
Lamb, Loin Chop	36	44	7	13 %
Milk, Whole	62	29	4	5 %
Pork Tenderloin	34	40	9	17 %
Shrimp, Cooked, Moist Heat	27	18	41	14 %
Tuna, In Water, Drained	27	26	37	10 %
Veal Cutlet	26	35	22	17 %

Spreads[1]

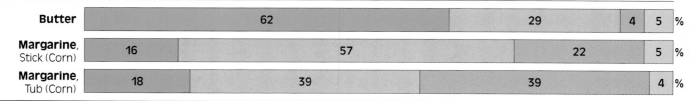

Food	Saturated	Monounsaturated	Polyunsaturated	Other Lipids
Butter	62	29	4	5 %
Margarine, Stick (Corn)	16	57	22	5 %
Margarine, Tub (Corn)	18	39	39	4 %

[1]USDA Composition of Foods — Raw, Processed, Prepared. USDA Human Nutrition Information Service, Agriculture Handbook No. 8 Series (8-1, 8-4, 8-5, 8-9, 8-10, 8-13, 8-15, 8-17). Washington, D.C.: U.S. Government Printing Office. Pork data for calories, protein, fat, and cholesterol is from Buege, D.R., et.al., "A nationwide Survey of the Composition and Marketing of Pork Products at Retail," University of Wisconsin, Madison, Wisconsin, 1990. Conducted in cooperation and with the guidance of the U.S. Department of Agriculture to provide the data base for the revision of USDA Agriculture Handbook 8-10, which will be published in 1991.

Fatty Acids

Saturated   Monounsaturated   Polyunsaturated   Other Lipids

Minerals

Meat is a major dietary source of three important minerals: iron, zinc and phosphorus. Meat is not a good source of calcium, iodine or magnesium.

Iron—A 1984 report based on data from the Second National Health And Nutrition Examination Survey (HANES II: 1976-1980) found that iron deficiencies were occurring with sufficient frequency among older infants, women between the ages of 15 and 44, and males in pre- and early-teens to warrant study and surveillance. While these population segments show the highest incidence of iron deficiency, no group is risk-free. As many as 10 percent of all U.S. citizens may be consuming less iron than they need. Significant lack of iron results in iron-deficiency anemia (reduced amount of hemoglobin in the blood), which is characterized by paleness, listlessness, irritability, shortness of breath and fatigue.

Iron is found in hemoglobin, the pigment which gives color to red blood cells. Hemoglobin transports oxygen and carbon dioxide throughout the body. Another important function of iron is as a constituent of enzymes associated with energy metabolism. Iron is also a component in myoglobin (a compound similar to hemoglobin), which gives meat its red color.

Figure 2-6
Recommended Daily Dietary Allowances for Iron in Milligrams

Children	age 1-10	10 mg
Males	age 11-18	12 mg
	19-51+	10 mg
Females	age 11-50	15 mg
	51+	10 mg
Pregnant		30 mg
Lactating	1st 6 months	15 mg
	2nd 6 months	15 mg

Milligrams of Iron in Various Meat Sources*

Beef	3 oz.	2.54 mg
Veal	3 oz.	1 mg
Pork	3 oz.	1 mg
Lamb	3 oz.	2 mg
Ground Beef**	3 oz.	1.79 mg
Luncheon Meat	1 oz.	.24 mg

*All meat source values are for cooked, trimmed boneless portions.
**Lean

Dietary iron occurs in two forms—heme iron and nonheme iron. Heme iron comes from the myoglobin and hemoglobin of meat, fish and poultry, and is so named because the iron atom is complexed in the center of a porphyrin ring, called the "heme group." Heme iron accounts for about 50-60 percent of the iron in beef, lamb and chicken and 30-40 percent of that in pork, liver and fish. Nonheme iron accounts for the remaining iron in animal foods and all the iron in grains, fruits and vegetables. The human body can absorb heme iron at a rate about five to ten times higher than it absorbs nonheme iron.

At present, two dietary factors are known to enhance the absorption of nonheme iron when consumed along with other food sources of iron: ascorbic acid (vitamin C) and an unidentified factor associated with all muscle foods known as the "meat factor."

The enhancing effect of the meat factor occurs only in the presence of muscle tissue. Other animal proteins such as those found in milk, cheese and eggs do not have the same positive effect on nonheme iron absorption.

The nature of the meat factor has not been positively identified, but the amino acid cysteine appears to be a key component. Evidence suggests that this amino acid is released during digestion and binds to iron forming a soluble complex. These soluble complexes pass more readily into the mucosal cells of the intestinal wall than does the unsolubilized iron.

Dietary factors known to inhibit absorption of nonheme iron include: tannins in tea; polyphenols in coffee; phosviten in egg yolk; phytates in whole grains, bran and soybeans; oxalates in spinach, rhubarb and chocolate; EDTA (ethylene-diamine tetra-acetic acid), which is used as a preservative; and antacids when consumed in large amounts. Otherwise, the composition of the meal does not appear to affect the absorption of heme iron.

Meat contains a significant amount of iron. Liver, poultry, seafood and eggs are other good providers of iron from animal sources. Legumes, dried apricots and prunes, whole grains, enriched and fortified cereals and breads, dark green vegetables and nuts can be good iron sources depending on the quantity consumed and if they are consumed with absorption enhancers.

Figure 2-7
Iron Absorption of Various Food Sources

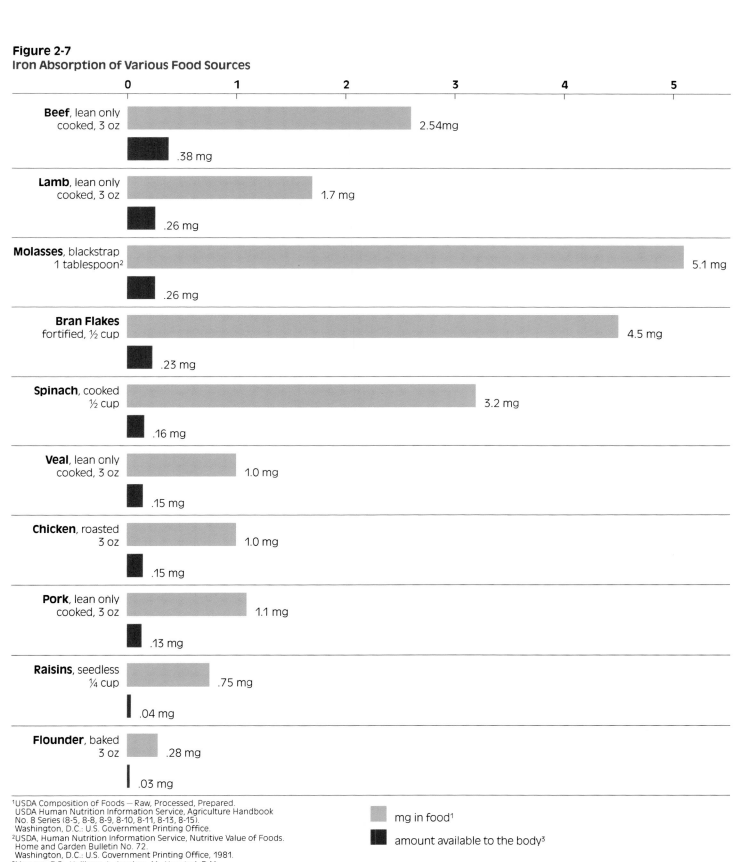

[1]USDA Composition of Foods — Raw, Processed, Prepared.
USDA Human Nutrition Information Service, Agriculture Handbook
No. 8 Series (8-5, 8-8, 8-9, 8-10, 8-11, 8-13, 8-15).
Washington, D.C.: U.S. Government Printing Office.
[2]USDA, Human Nutrition Information Service, Nutritive Value of Foods.
Home and Garden Bulletin No. 72.
Washington, D.C.: U.S. Government Printing Office, 1981.
[3]Monsen, E.R.; Hallberg, L.; Layrisse, M.; Hegsted, D.M.;
Cook, J.D.; Mertz, W.; and French, C.A.
Estimation of available dietary iron.
Am. J. Clin. Nutr. 31:131-141, 1978.

mg in food[1]

amount available to the body[3]

Zinc—Zinc is a co-factor for enzymes involved in many metabolic pathways. It plays an important role in DNA synthesis, is essential for protein synthesis and is necessary for growth and repair of tissues.

A mild deficiency of zinc, occurring at any age, may cause a slow rate of wound-healing and decrease ability to taste. There is evidence that moderate zinc deficiencies occur more often in growing children and the elderly.

The availability of zinc varies among food sources. Meat, liver, eggs and shellfish are excellent sources of this essential element. Zinc is more readily absorbed from animal, than from vegetable, sources. Vegetable products, particularly grains, contain phytate and dietary fiber which are believed to depress the availability of zinc and of other trace elements.

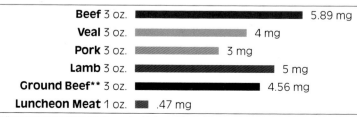

Figure 2-8
Recommended Daily Dietary Allowances for Zinc in Milligrams

Children	age 1-10	10 mg
Males	age 11-51+	15 mg
Females	age 11-51+	12 mg
Pregnant		15 mg
Lactating	1st 6 months	19 mg
	2nd 6 months	16 mg

Milligrams of Zinc in Various Meat Sources*

Beef 3 oz.	5.89 mg
Veal 3 oz.	4 mg
Pork 3 oz.	3 mg
Lamb 3 oz.	5 mg
Ground Beef* 3 oz.	4.56 mg
Luncheon Meat 1 oz.	.47 mg

*All meat source values are for cooked, trimmed boneless portions.
**Lean

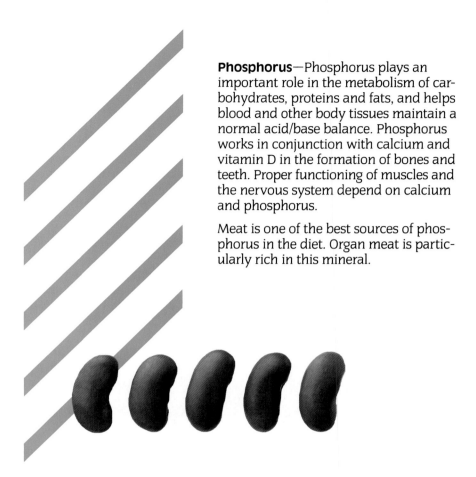

Phosphorus—Phosphorus plays an important role in the metabolism of carbohydrates, proteins and fats, and helps blood and other body tissues maintain a normal acid/base balance. Phosphorus works in conjunction with calcium and vitamin D in the formation of bones and teeth. Proper functioning of muscles and the nervous system depend on calcium and phosphorus.

Meat is one of the best sources of phosphorus in the diet. Organ meat is particularly rich in this mineral.

Figure 2-9
Recommended Daily Dietary Allowances for Phosphorus in Milligrams

Children	age 1-10	800 mg
Males	age 11-24	1200 mg
	25-51+	800 mg
Females	age 11-24	1200 mg
	25-51+	800 mg
Pregnant		1200 mg
Lactating	1st 6 months	1200 mg
	2nd 6 months	1200 mg

Milligrams of Phosphorus in Various Meat Sources*

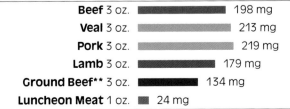

Beef 3 oz.	198 mg
Veal 3 oz.	213 mg
Pork 3 oz.	219 mg
Lamb 3 oz.	179 mg
Ground Beef** 3 oz.	134 mg
Luncheon Meat 1 oz.	24 mg

*All meat source values are for cooked, trimmed boneless portions.
**Lean

Vitamins

Meat is a major dietary source of five of the B-complex vitamins: thiamin, riboflavin, niacin, vitamin B_6 and vitamin B_{12}. Meat is not a good source of folacin but it does contain biotin and pantothenic acid. The B-vitamins are found in a wide variety of other foods.

Thiamin—Thiamin acts in conjunction with other B-vitamins to promote and regulate the many chemical reactions necessary to promote growth and maintain health. Thiamin plays an essential role in regulating the metabolic reactions necessary to produce energy, particularly from carbohydrates. Low intakes of thiamin may cause fatigue, loss of appetite, constipation, depression and irritability.

Most meat is a very good source of thiamin. Pork, in recommended serving sizes, provides more thiamin than any other food commonly eaten. Brewer's yeast, fish and legumes are also sources of thiamin.

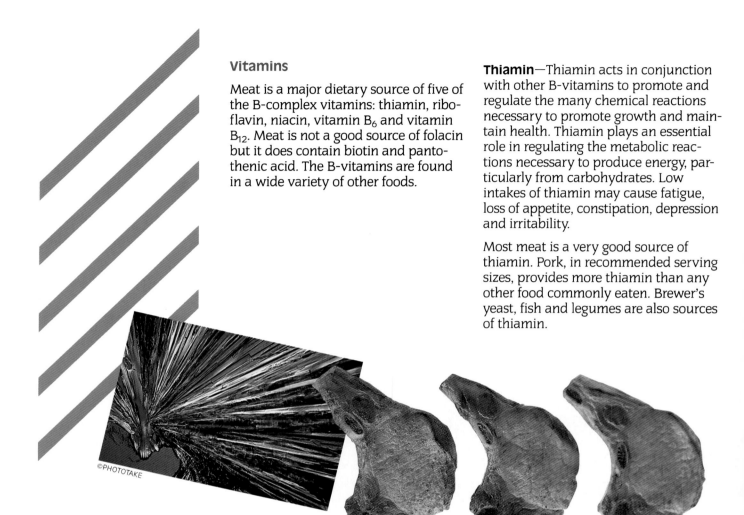

©PHOTOTAKE

Figure 2-10
Recommended Daily Dietary Allowances for Thiamin in Milligrams

Children	age 1-3	0.7 mg
	4-6	0.9 mg
	7-10	1.0 mg
Males	age 11-14	1.3 mg
	15-50	1.5 mg
	51+	1.2 mg
Females	age 11-50	1.1 mg
	51+	1.0 mg
Pregnant		1.5 mg
Lactating	1st 6 months	1.6 mg
	2nd 6 months	1.6 mg

Milligrams of Thiamin in Various Meat Sources*

Beef 3 oz.	0.08 mg
Veal 3 oz.	0.05 mg
Pork 3 oz.	0.59 mg
Lamb 3 oz.	0.09 mg
Ground Beef** 3 oz.	0.04 mg
Luncheon Meat 1 oz.	0.09 mg

*All meat source values are for cooked, trimmed boneless portions.
**Lean

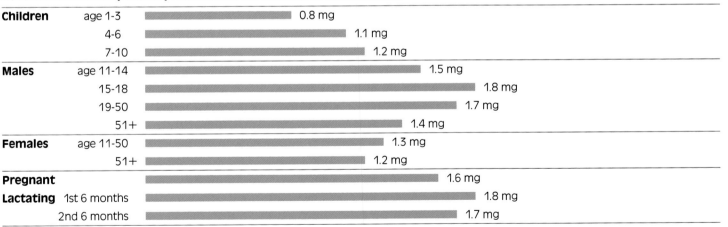

Riboflavin—Riboflavin is essential for the release of energy from carbohydrates, fats and proteins. It helps maintain good vision and healthy skin. Riboflavin is also needed for the conversion of tryptophan (an amino acid) to niacin. Adequate riboflavin in the diet is believed to promote iron absorption and utilization.

Liver and brewer's yeast are the best food sources of riboflavin. Other meat, poultry, milk, yogurt, cheese and green leafy vegetables are also good sources.

Figure 2-11
Recommended Daily Dietary Allowances for Riboflavin in Milligrams

Children	age 1-3	0.8 mg
	4-6	1.1 mg
	7-10	1.2 mg
Males	age 11-14	1.5 mg
	15-18	1.8 mg
	19-50	1.7 mg
	51+	1.4 mg
Females	age 11-50	1.3 mg
	51+	1.2 mg
Pregnant		1.6 mg
Lactating	1st 6 months	1.8 mg
	2nd 6 months	1.7 mg

Milligrams of Riboflavin in Various Meat Sources*

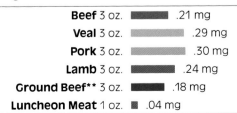

Beef 3 oz.		.21 mg
Veal 3 oz.		.29 mg
Pork 3 oz.		.30 mg
Lamb 3 oz.		.24 mg
Ground Beef** 3 oz.		.18 mg
Luncheon Meat 1 oz.		.04 mg

*All meat source values are for cooked, trimmed boneless portions.
**Lean

Niacin—Together with other B-vitamins, niacin functions in a variety of intracellular enzyme systems, including those involved in energy production.

"Niacin equivalents" are the measure of actual niacin present in a food plus the potential niacin from the conversion of tryptophan. (Tryptophan, an essential amino acid, is a precursor for niacin formation. Approximately 1 mg of niacin is produced by the body from every 60 mg of dietary tryptophan.) All complete proteins (meat, poultry, fish, eggs, milk) provide niacin and tryptophan.

©PHOTOTAKE

Figure 2-12
Recommended Daily Dietary Allowances for Niacin in Milligrams

Children	age 1-3	9 mg
	4-6	12 mg
	7-10	13 mg
Males	age 11-14	17 mg
	15-18	20 mg
	19-50	19 mg
	51+	15 mg
Females	age 11-50	15 mg
	51+	13 mg
Pregnant		17 mg
Lactating	1st 6 months	20 mg
	2nd 6 months	20 mg

Milligrams of Niacin in Various Meat Sources*

Beef 3 oz.	3.51 mg
Veal 3 oz.	7.2 mg
Pork 3 oz.	4.3 mg
Lamb 3 oz.	5.4 mg
Ground Beef** 3 oz.	4.39 mg
Luncheon Meat 1 oz.	.8 mg

*All meat source values are for cooked, trimmed boneless portions.
**Lean

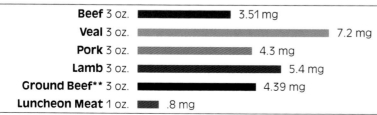

Vitamin B₆—Vitamin B₆ is a component in the enzyme system that converts the amino acid tryptophan to niacin.

The active form of vitamin B₆ is pyridoxal phosphate. Pyridoxal phosphate functions as a coenzyme in numerous biochemical reactions, most of which involve amino acids. For this reason, human requirements for the vitamin are related to protein intakes.

Good sources of pyridoxine include meat, whole grain breads and cereals, beans, peas, poultry, fish and fresh vegetables.

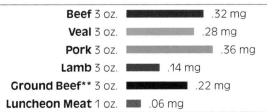

©PHOTOTAKE

Figure 2-13
Recommended Daily Dietary Allowances for Vitamin B₆ in Milligrams

Children	age 1-3	1.0 mg
	4-6	1.1 mg
	7-10	1.4 mg
Males	age 11-14	1.7 mg
	15-51+	2.0 mg
Females	age 11-14	1.4 mg
	15-18	1.5 mg
	19-51+	1.6 mg
Pregnant		2.2 mg
Lactating	1st 6 months	2.1 mg
	2nd 6 months	2.1 mg

Milligrams of Vitamin B₆ in Various Meat Sources*

Beef 3 oz.	.32 mg
Veal 3 oz.	.28 mg
Pork 3 oz.	.36 mg
Lamb 3 oz.	.14 mg
Ground Beef** 3 oz.	.22 mg
Luncheon Meat 1 oz.	.06 mg

*All meat source values are for cooked, trimmed boneless portions.
**Lean

Vitamin B₁₂ (Cobalamin)—Vitamin B_{12} is necessary for the synthesis of DNA deoxyribonucleic acid), the gene-containing component of cell nuclei, and is essential for growth and development.

Vitamin B_{12} is found only in foods of animal origin, therefore, vegans (strict vegetarians who consume no animal products) may need to supplement their diets with this vitamin. Individuals who do not consume vitamin B_{12} or who have pernicious anemia (the inability to absorb vitamin B_{12} from food) can be treated successfully with injections of the vitamin.

Veal (calf) liver, beef and lamb are especially high in B_{12}; some other sources are fish, oysters, cheese and egg yolk.

Other Vitamins—Vitamin A is a fat-soluble vitamin necessary for the maintenance of healthy tissues and for maintaining normal vision. Green and yellow vegetables provide most of the vitamin A consumed in the U.S. It occurs in the form of carotene (a precursor which the body converts to vitamin A). Milk and margarine are often fortified with vitamin A. Liver is the greatest single food source of vitamin A on a per-portion basis (783 RE in a three-ounce portion of veal liver).

Liver is also a good source of the fat soluble vitamins D and K. However, meat is not an important source of vitamin E and, with the exception of liver, is not a particularly good source of fat-soluble vitamins.

©PHOTOTAKE

Figure 2-14
Recommended Daily Dietary Allowances for Vitamin B₁₂ in Micrograms

Children	age 1-3	0.7 mcg
	4-6	1.0 mcg
	7-10	1.4 mcg
Males	age 11-51+	2.0 mcg
Females	age 11-51+	2.0 mcg
Pregnant		2.2 mcg
Lactating	1st 6 months	2.6 mcg
	2nd 6 months	2.6 mcg

Micrograms of Vitamin B₁₂ in Various Meat Sources*

Beef	3 oz.	2.24 mcg
Veal	3 oz.	1.41 mcg
Pork	3 oz.	.71 mcg
Lamb	3 oz.	2.22 mcg
Ground Beef**	3 oz.	2.00 mcg
Luncheon Meat	1 oz.	.36 mcg

*All meat source values are for cooked, trimmed boneless portions.
**Lean

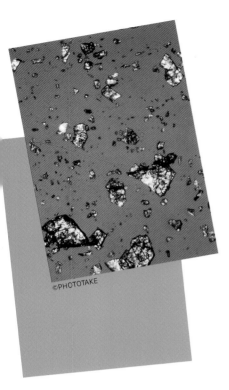
©PHOTOTAKE

Cholesterol and Sodium

Cholesterol—The Food and Nutrition Board of the NAS has not established RDAs for cholesterol in the diet. However, the National Cholesterol Education Program (NCEP) and the American Heart Association (AHA) recommend that cholesterol intake not exceed 300 mg per day.

Cholesterol is associated with fats (lipids) because it is a fat-like sterol in its chemical structure. Found only in animal tissues, cholesterol is an integral part of the structure of cell membranes, particularly in the brain and nervous system. Cholesterol plays an important role in the synthesis of bile acids, adrenal hormones and sex hormones. A derivative of cholesterol found in the skin is converted by sunlight to the active form of vitamin D.

Most cholesterol in the body is made in the liver and is not from dietary sources, although synthesis is influenced in part by the amount of cholesterol obtained from the diet. The body can manufacture from 800 to 1500 mg of cholesterol daily, even if none is consumed in the diet. The relationship between dietary cholesterol from foods and serum cholesterol in humans is variable and not fully understood. The wide variation in the way individuals manufacture (in their body) cholesterol and respond to dietary intakes of cholesterol is influenced by genetics and other physiological factors.

Beef, pork and lamb muscles are not significantly higher in cholesterol than many other common foods of animal origin, such as chicken, turkey or many varieties of fish. Three ounces of cooked lean beef and cooked lean pork contain 73 mg and 72 mg of cholesterol, respectively (Figure 2-15). A three-ounce serving of roast chicken, with the skin removed, contains 76 mg of cholesterol. These figures are 24 percent, 24 percent, and 25 percent, respectively, of the AHA recommendations for the upper limit of daily cholesterol consumption (300 mg).

Figure 2-15
Cholesterol Content of Some Commonly Eaten Animal Foods

	Total mg[a]	Percent of 300 mg[b]
Veal (Calf), **Liver**, Cooked, Pan-fried, 3 oz.	280 mg	93%
Egg yolk, 1	213 mg	71%
Shrimp, Cooked, Moist heat, 3 oz.	166 mg	55%
Veal (lean only), Cooked, 3 oz.	100 mg	30%
Lamb (lean only), Cooked, 3 oz.	78 mg	26%
Chicken (lean only), Roasted, 3 oz.	76 mg	25%
Ground Beef (80% lean), Cooked, 3 oz.	74 mg	25%
Beef (lean only), Cooked, 3 oz.	73 mg	24%
Pork (lean only), Cooked, 3 oz.	72 mg	24%
Flounder or **Sole**, Cooked, Dry heat, 3 oz.	58 mg	19%
Tuna, White, Canned in water, 3 oz.	35 mg	11%
Whole Milk, 1 cup	33 mg	11%
Cheddar Cheese, 1 oz.	30 mg	10%
2% Milk, 1 cup	18 mg	6%
Skim Milk, 1 cup	4 mg	2%

[a]USDA Composition of Foods — Raw, Processed, Prepared. USDA Human Nutrition Information Service. Agriculture Handbook 8 Series (8-1, 8-5, 8-10, 8-13, 8-15, 8-17). Washington, D.C.: U.S. Government Printing Office. Pork data for calories, protein, fat, and cholesterol is from Buege, D.R., et.al., "A nationwide Survey of the Composition and Marketing of Pork Products at Retail," University of Wisconsin, Madison, Wisconsin, 1990. Conducted in cooperation and with the guidance of the U.S. Department of Agriculture to provide the data base for the revision of USDA Agriculture Handbook 8-10, which will be published in 1991.
[b]National Institutes of Health (NIH) recommends no more than 300 mg/day.

Sodium—There is no RDA for sodium; however, the Food and Nutrition Board suggests an estimated minimum requirement of 500 mg per day for healthy adults.

Sodium works with potassium and chloride to help regulate fluids and the acid/base balance of the body. Sodium and potassium contribute to the functioning of the nervous system and muscles.

Sodium levels in fresh meat are naturally low, ranging from 55 to 80 mg per three-ounce serving. Sodium levels in processed meat are higher than in fresh meat because, as in the case of most prepared foods, sodium compounds are used to perform a number of important functions in the final product, such as preservation (for food safety) and flavor enhancement. These functions are discussed in Chapter 4.

However, a wide variety and ever-increasing number of reduced-sodium meat is currently available in the marketplace.

NUTRITIVE VALUE OF PROCESSED MEAT

Processed meat provides the same nutrients as the cooked meat from which it is made. The protein quality, degree of fatty acid saturation and cholesterol levels are in the same range as fresh meat. Processed meat is higher in sodium than fresh meat and some processed meat is also higher in fat.

Braunschweiger and liverwurst are exceptional sources of vitamin A, because this vitamin is stored in the liver from which these products were made. When vitamin C is present in processed meat, it reflects the use of ascorbic acid as an additive.

Heat processing (as in smoking or cooking of processed meat) has little or no effect on the niacin or riboflavin of meat, but may reduce the retention of thiamin, vitamin B_6 and B_{12} and pantothenic acid, depending upon the amount of heat used. In most cases, the loss of nutrients due to processing is less than the losses from home cooking of fresh meat.

Some processed meat may have as much as .75 percent of calcium if made from meat which has been mechanically deboned. When meat is mechanically removed from bones during processing, a small amount of bone is removed by the boning machine and ground into a fine powder. When this powder is mixed with muscle tissue, it contributes to the calcium content of the final product.

Sodium content differs among processed meat products depending on the amount of salt incorporated in processing. Salt is used because it functions in preservation, emulsion stabilization, myosin extraction and flavor enhancement. It is possible to reduce the salt content somewhat, but such products are more perishable, requiring careful storage. Meat scientists are seeking ways of reducing salt in meat processing while retaining flavor, texture and food safety.

Processed meat, like all foods, should be eaten in moderation. An individual can eat processed meat and stay well within the Food and Nutrition Board's recommendation for sodium and the American Heart Association's guidelines for fat if consumption of processed meat is balanced in the diet with other low fat, low sodium foods. Those who have been advised to reduce their intake of cholesterol, saturated fat, calories or salt should follow the advice of a registered dietitian or their physician when selecting processed meat.

Studies of the effects of cooking and other methods of processing report no significant alterations in the protein value of meat. However, cooking at too high a temperature for long periods of time can slightly decrease the biological value of meat proteins.

Fat, and consequently the caloric value of meat, can change substantially depending on cooking method and time. Methods such as broiling will reduce final fat content because the meat is cooked on a rack which allows the fat in the meat to drip off as it melts. Methods such as frying increase final fat content because the meat is cooked in added fat and the fat naturally present in the meat does not drip away as it does in broiling.

Thiamin is one of the least stable vitamins and reported retentions are from 90 percent (for fried beef) to about 30 percent (for pressure-cooked stew). The average retention of thiamin in cooked meat is about 65 percent. Values stated in food composition tables reflect the thiamin level after cooking. Generally, more thiamin is retained in meat cooked by dry heat, rather than by moist heat methods because, being water-soluble, it tends to leach into the cooking liquid.

The longer cooking time needed for moist heat methods also increases the amount of thiamin lost. However, if the meat drippings are consumed with the meat, the total amount of thiamin is about the same as before cooking. Meat cooked to lower internal temperatures usually retains more thiamin than meat cooked to higher internal temperatures.

Other B-vitamins are fairly heat-stable, but may also be transferred to the drippings or cooking liquids during preparation.

Niacin is the most stable of the B-vitamins. It is relatively unaffected by heat, light, oxygen, acids or alkalis.

Because minerals such as iron and zinc are heat-stable, cooking *temperatures* do not appear to reduce the quantity or availability of minerals in meat. However, *methods* of food preparation can affect the iron content of food both positively and negatively. Research findings suggest a five-fold increase in the iron content of foods, particularly acidic foods, cooked in cast-iron pots. Using iron cookware could be a simple and practical way of increasing dietary iron. However, fewer and fewer consumers are using iron cookware.

The major cause for the loss of iron during food preparation is cooking in liquid because iron will dissolve in the liquid. If cooking meat in liquid is the chosen method, the liquid should be simmering, not boiling; the pieces should be relatively large; the amount of liquid used should be small; and the meat should not be overcooked. However, if the cooking liquid is consumed, the dissolved iron is not lost. As mentioned above, temperature does not appear to affect iron content since this mineral is relatively heat-stable.

NUTRIENT RETENTION DURING COOKING

Cooking time, temperature and technique can influence the nutrient content of meat.

DIET AND DISEASE PREVENTION

Reports from several leading private and public health organizations have linked dietary fat and cholesterol to several major chronic diseases. Because meat is a source of both fat and cholesterol in the diet, and because it is a major part of the U.S. diet, meat consumption has been implicated as a possible risk factor for these diseases. However, recent research indicates that beef, veal, pork and lamb are very similar to poultry in fat and cholesterol content.

Coronary Heart Disease

Several factors relate to an individual's risk of developing coronary heart disease. Age, sex and genetic factors cannot be altered but several other factors, termed "environmental" risk factors, can be. These include cigarette smoking, high blood pressure, obesity, lack of physical activity and diet.

The level of cholesterol in the blood is influenced by dietary cholesterol as well as the quantity and degree of saturation of dietary fat. (See page 25 for an explanation of fatty acids.)

Because a correlation has been established between serum cholesterol levels and the incidence of coronary heart disease, this marker has been used to identify those individuals who may be at risk. Individuals who are identified as having a blood cholesterol level above 200 mg/dl are classified as borderline high and should have a lipoprotein analysis. A lipoprotein analysis will characterize how serum cholesterol is being transported within the body and it is a more reliable predictor of heart disease risk than is the total amount of blood cholesterol.

Lipoproteins are complexes of lipid and protein which are synthesized in the liver and which transport fat-soluble substances throughout the blood system to and from various tissues. Lipoproteins are composed of proteins, phospholipids, triglycerides and cholesterol, and are classified by their physical properties.

Three forms of lipoproteins commonly identified in the blood are: VLDL (very low density lipoproteins), LDL (low density lipoproteins) and HDL (high density lipoproteins). High levels of LDL (higher than 160 mg/dl) are associated with an increased risk for coronary artery disease. Low levels of HDL (lower than 40 mg/dl) may also increase the risk of coronary artery disease.

Dietary cholesterol and the quality and quantity of dietary fat, appear to have significant influences on both the amount of cholesterol in the blood and the types of lipoproteins formed. Studies have shown that dietary cholesterol appears to increase the total amount of LDL cholesterol in the blood. However, individuals differ significantly in the way their bodies respond to increases or decreases in dietary cholesterol.

The role of saturated fatty acids in increasing blood cholesterol and the role of polyunsaturated fatty acids in lowering blood cholesterol have been known for many years. Until recently, the role of monounsaturated fatty acids was thought to be neutral, having no effect on blood cholesterol levels. However, researchers now suggest that monounsaturated fatty acids lower blood cholesterol by decreasing LDL cholesterol and maintaining HDL cholesterol.

Further research in the area of fatty acids shows that not all of the saturated fatty acids increase blood cholesterol levels. A recent study suggests that stearic acid (found in beef, veal, pork, lamb and poultry fats and in cocoa butter) lowers blood cholesterol levels as much as do the monounsaturated fatty acids when either replaces the saturated fatty acid, Palmitate, in persons fed a liquid diet. The reason stearic acid did not raise blood cholesterol in this study may be due to the fact that stearic acid, after ingestion, is rapidly changed to a monounsaturated fatty acid in the body. Further research in this area is currently underway. Meat's contribution of fatty acids and cholesterol to the diet can be seen in Table 2-5 and Figure 2-15, respectively.

Experts disagree about why and for whom fat intakes should be reduced. Many believe the beneficial vs. detrimental effects of a dietary change among children and adults who have normal weight and have no risk factors for developing coronary heart disease need to be examined. Virtually all authorities agree with reducing dietary fat for purposes of personal body-weight control and with modifying both the type and proportion of fat for individuals who are at risk of heart disease.

If total fats are to be reduced, all sources of fat, including fat added in food preparation and serving, must be considered. Techniques such as substituting reduced-fat products, trimming visible fat, avoiding fatty toppings and avoiding fried foods of all types will reduce dietary fat.

Cancer

Excess dietary fat has also been associated with an increased risk of certain types of cancer. As in the case of coronary heart disease, risk factors are both genetic (not modifiable) and environmental (modifiable). Obesity and low blood cholesterol have also been correlated to incidence of certain cancers (e.g., of the breast and colon), but there is considerable controversy over the degree to which these components contribute to cancer.

It appears that dietary fat does not initiate or cause cancer but rather, it promotes the growth of cancer cells once the malignancy has been initiated. The connection with fat may be related to its high energy concentration compared to protein or carboyhydrates on a gram-for-gram basis.

Some studies have shown an inverse relationship between the level of blood cholesterol and cancer, i.e., lower blood cholesterol is associated with higher incidence of mortality from cancer. However, results from studies in this area are not consistent. It may be that low blood cholesterol is a result, rather than a cause, of cancer.

There appears to be an association between cancer and heavy use of salt-cured, salt-pickled and smoked foods. The NAS/NRC report, *Diet, Nutrition* and *Cancer,* recommends reduction in the consumption of cured foods such as sausages, smoked fish, hams, bacon, bologna and hot dogs. The basis for these recommendations were studies of widespread consumption of smoked fish in Iceland, and pickled and heavily salted vegetables in the orient. U.S. processed meat products are not heavily smoked or pickled.

Sodium nitrate and sodium nitrite, discussed in Chapter 4, have been considered to be possible carcinogens because of their relation to formation of nitrosamines in food products. Nitrates are not just found in processed meat, they also occur naturally in most vegetables. Beets, spinach, lettuce and radishes can contain as much as 2000 parts per million (PPM) of nitrate. Processed meat contains approximately 100 PPM (or less) of nitrite. Therefore, food scientists and other researchers believe the inhibition of botulism spores resulting from the use of nitrites in cured meat far outweighs any health risks that could result from their use.

Hypertension (High Blood Pressure)

The standard treatments for those with high blood pressure include reduction of sodium intake, drug therapy and, in the case of obese patients, weight loss. However, the degree to which sodium intake influences the development of hypertension is now questioned.

Fresh meat is naturally low in sodium. Processed, prepared and "fast" food meat products (sausages, deli meats, etc.) have more sodium than the fresh meat from which they are made. However, many new processed meat products are available with reduced or low sodium contents.

Hormones

Some individuals and consumer groups have expressed concern about the use of hormones (growth promotants) in animal feeding. Hormones are produced naturally by plants, animals and humans and are required for normal healthy functioning of the organism. Growth-promoting products must be approved for use by the FDA. Included in this class are some hormones that are produced naturally by cattle, but in lesser quantities, which are administered to cattle to increase lean tissue growth and decrease fat deposition.

At the time of slaughter, the hormone content of beef muscle from cattle that receive these hormone products is only slightly higher than that of beef from animals that do not receive them.

Conditions for the use of drugs in animal feed are prescribed by law. Animals are processed in federally inspected facilities and carcasses are randomly sampled for residue testing to monitor residues. These procedures help assure that safe levels of drug residues are not exceeded. Such testing is done under the supervision of the FDA.

Antibiotics

The use of antibiotics in animal feeds is also carefully monitored by the FDA. Antibiotics have been used for the last 50 years to treat disease in humans and animals. Sub-therapeutic doses of antibiotics are sometimes added to animal feeds as a method of promoting growth and preventing disease; such use increases the amount of meat available and decreases prices of meat for consumers. However, use of antibiotics for this purpose has been sharply curtailed due to concerns that antibiotic-resistant strains of bacteria might be transferred to man if they appear within the livestock population. The rationale is that, if resistant strains of bacteria develop from such use of antibiotics in animal production, the therapeutic use of antibiotics for the treatment of people with medical problems might then be ineffective. Most livestock producers have voluntarily stopped using antibiotics to decrease the likelihood of developing this problem even though a 1989 study by the NAS reported that they were "unable to find data directly implicating the subtherapeutic use of feed antibiotics in human illness."

FOOD SAFETY CONCERNS

The two most common safety concerns regarding meat are the use of hormones (growth promotants) and antibiotics in animal feeds.

For many consumers, cuts of meat are as confusing as pieces of a jigsaw puzzle. Like a puzzle, the shapes and sizes of the pieces begin to make sense when they are seen in relation to the whole. If a shopper can identify the source (beef, veal, pork or lamb) and primal (wholesale) cut of origin (shoulder/chuck, rib, loin, round/leg), he or she is more likely to be able to select and prepare a variety of quality meat cuts to meet his or her needs.

UNIFORM RETAIL MEAT IDENTITY STANDARDS (URMIS) PROGRAM

The need for a standardized system for naming cuts of meat has been accentuated in recent years by the mobility of the U.S. population. In the past, meat cuts could have different names depending on the city or store in which the meat was sold. Because many people identify meat cuts by name rather than sight, meat shopping was difficult if meat was purchased in a different city or store, where different names were used.

The URMIS Program

To reduce meat counter confusion, a standardized nomenclature system was developed in the early 1970s through an industrywide committee, coordinated by the National Live Stock and Meat Board. This system is called the Uniform Retail Meat Identity Standards (URMIS) program. This committee was composed of representatives from the retail and meat packing industries and from several federal agencies. The development of a master list of over 300 standardized names for retail cuts of beef, veal, pork and lamb resulted in a uniform method for labeling meat throughout the U.S.

Figure 3-1
URMIS Label

1. **The kind of meat**
   BEEF, VEAL, PORK or LAMB.
   It is listed first on every label.
2. **The primal (wholesale) cut**
   CHUCK, RIB, LOIN or
   ROUND—tells where the
   meat comes from on the
   animal.
3. **The retail cut**
   BLADE ROAST, SPARERIBS,
   LOIN CHOPS, etc.— tells from
   what part of the primal cut
   the meat comes.

With few exceptions, a specific cut of meat now can have a "unique" name and the "same" name, wherever it is sold. For example, "Beef Ribeye Steak" (the URMIS nomenclature) may be colloquially described as a "Delmonico Steak" in one area, a "Filet Steak" in another area, a "Spencer Steak" or "Beauty Steak" in still another part of the country. However, many retailers now use only the URMIS label.

In the URMIS master list, any name other than an anatomical description is considered "fanciful" and, with few exceptions, is not included in the listing. The exceptions are names of cuts so widely used, accepted and recognized in the U.S. and abroad, that they are included in the URMIS listing. Among these are "Porterhouse Steak" and "Filet Mignon" for beef, "Butterfly Loin Chops" for pork and "French-Style Chops" for lamb.

URMIS uses a three-part identification system (Figure 3-1). The first part of the label names the animal source of meat (beef, veal, pork or lamb); the second part names the primal (wholesale) cut; and the third part gives the recommended retail name.

MEAT DEPARTMENT
WEIGHT   PAY   PRICE
Lb. Net   Per Lb
0.00 $0.00 $0.00

BEEF TOP ROUND STEAK

Distinguishing Characteristics

Meat cuts from the same location on different animal species are usually similar in shape, due to similarities in bone, muscle and fat depot structures, though different in size and color. In general, cuts of beef are larger than cuts of veal, lamb or pork. To identify meat according to its species-origin, differences in muscle size and color, and differences in fat color, texture and firmness are used.

SOURCES OF MEAT

Meat primarily comes from three animals — cattle, hogs and sheep. Meat producers classify animals by factors that influence the yield, tenderness and flavor of meat such as the sex, age and weight of the animal.

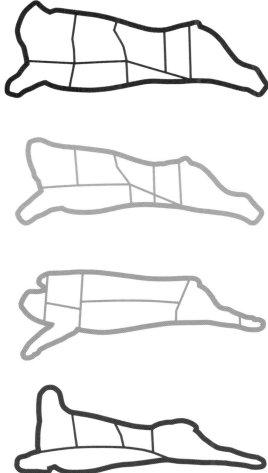

Table 3-1
Distinguishing Characteristics of Different Kinds of Meat

Kind of Meat	Lean Meat Color	Fat Characteristics
Beef	Bright, cherry-red	White or creamy-white (sometimes yellow) and firm.
Veal	Light pink	Bob veal has little or no fat cover. Special fed veal has white fat.
Pork	(Fresh) Grayish-pink (Cured) Rose	Characteristically white. The fat in pork is soft because it is relatively high in unsaturated fatty acids.
Lamb	Pinkish-red	White, brittle, rather dense, sometimes covered with the "fell," a colorless connective tissue membrane. The fat is harder than the fat in other meat because it is higher in saturated fatty acids.

The consumer who knows the location of primal cuts will have a good indication of how tender the meat will be, and how it should be prepared. For instance, the chuck, which comes from the more heavily exercised shoulder area of the beef animal, is less tender and its retail cuts should be prepared using a moist-heat cooking method.

Principles of meat cutting used in making both primal and retail cuts are:
—To separate tender portions of the carcass from less tender areas.
—To separate lean areas from the portions that have greater amounts of fat.
—To separate thicker, more heavily muscled portions of the carcass from the thin-muscled areas.
—To always cut across the grain (perpendicular to the predominant direction—longitudinally—in which muscle fibers run).

Primal cuts are often divided into smaller cuts, called subprimals, for ease and efficiency of handling and marketing. Beef tenderloin (whole) and top round are examples of subprimal cuts. Subprimals are usually boneless and are loosely wrapped in plastic film or vacuum-packaged at the processing plant before being shipped to the retailer. Vacuum-packaged beef is also known as "Beef-in-a-bag."

From the packing/processing plant, the subprimals are shipped to supermarkets (and to other places where meat is sold) in boxes, thus the term "boxed meat." After removing the cuts from the box, the retailer makes individual steaks, roasts and chops. These are then trimmed, trayed, wrapped and priced for the meat case. The meat department might also sell the meat intact in the vacuum bag with labor and packaging savings passed along to the consumer.

Consumers generally pay less for subprimal cuts packaged in vacuum bags. Meat purchased this way costs less per pound than regular cuts because there is less labor involved in preparing the meat for the meat counter display.

In recent years some impetus has developed to sell "branded" fresh meat (steaks, roasts, chops) which is processed and packaged at the packing plant and shipped to the retailer to simply place in the display case. The trend toward branded products is increasing. There is some benefit to the consumer because branded meat carries more information on the label. Historically in the U.S., only processed (cured, etc.) meat products were made into retail cuts in processing plants. These products carried the brand name of the processing company. Fresh meat (uncured) proceeds through the marketing chain in the same manner as do the commodity (unbranded) primal and subprimal cuts described above.

PRIMAL AND SUBPRIMAL CUTS

Early in the marketing chain, meat is divided into primal (wholesale) cuts (Figure 3-2). Primal cuts result from the subdivision of the carcass into more easily handled units. The meat industry in the U.S. has adopted a system of standardized primal cuts for each species. The primal cut names, which appear on the URMIS label, are important guides to meat buying.

Figure 3-2
Primal, Subprimal and Retail Cuts

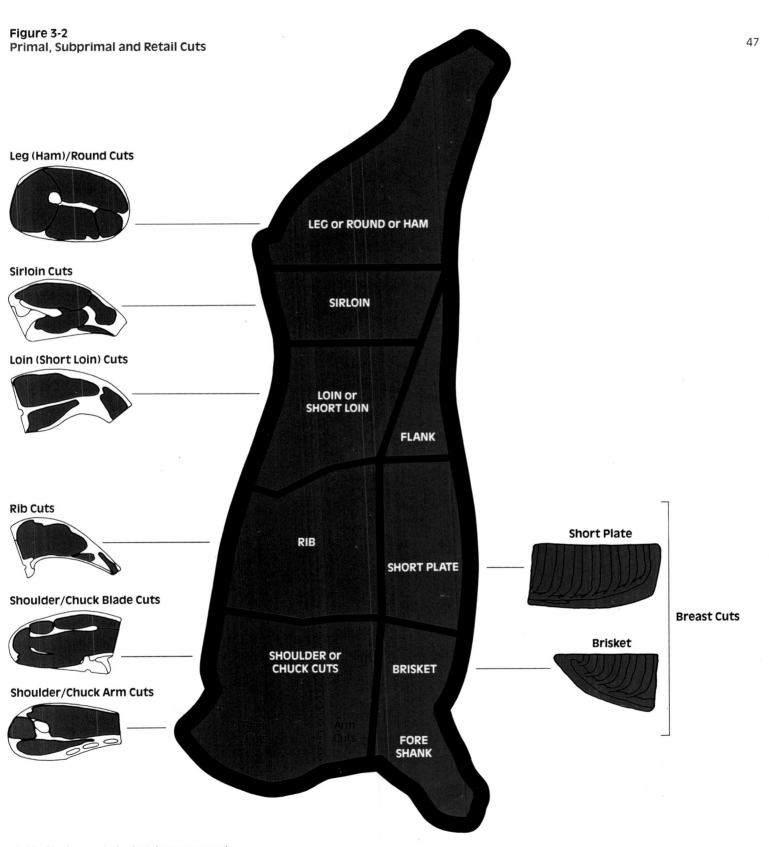

Leg (Ham)/Round Cuts

Sirloin Cuts

Loin (Short Loin) Cuts

Rib Cuts

Shoulder/Chuck Blade Cuts

Shoulder/Chuck Arm Cuts

LEG or ROUND or HAM

SIRLOIN

LOIN or SHORT LOIN

FLANK

RIB

SHORT PLATE

SHOULDER or CHUCK CUTS

BRISKET

Blade Cuts

Arm Cuts

FORE SHANK

Short Plate

Brisket

Breast Cuts

A side of beef appears in the chart above as an example.
It could just as well have been veal, pork or lamb, for
comparison purposes.

48

When a cut contains at least part of a bone, it is relatively easy to identify because most cuts have distinctively shaped bones. However, when all the bones are removed, the most important identifying factor is the configuration and relative size/shape of muscles and fat depots.

There are seven basic cuts, many of which can be identified by both bone and muscle shape (Figure 3-2). These seven basic cuts are:
—loin (short loin)
—sirloin
—leg (ham)/round
—shoulder/chuck blade
—shoulder/chuck arm
—breast (brisket, short plate)
—rib

Loin (Short Loin) Cuts

Bone-in cuts from the loin (short loin) usually contain only the back bone; the exception is a top loin steak which may include part of the 13th rib. Each back bone (vertebra) consists of three parts which are indicated in figure 3-3; these are: (a) spine bone (dorsal spinous process), (b) chine bone (body of the vertebra) and (c) finger bone (transverse process).

The three major muscles in the short loin section are illustrated in figure 3-3; these are (1) top loin or loin eye (*longissimus* muscle), (2) tenderloin and (3) flank (abdominal muscles). Pork loin chops contain very little flank meat. Porterhouse and T-bone steaks also are being sold in most stores with the less tender flank portion removed.

Similarity of muscles and bone structure among species is clearly shown when beef Porterhouse steak is compared to veal, pork and lamb loin chops from the same anatomical locations. The tenderloin is a long tapering muscle (*psoas major*) that extends through most of the length of both the short loin and the sirloin. The thick end of the tenderloin is in the sirloin.

If the short loin remains intact with the tenderloin attached and is cut into steaks, club, T-bone and Porterhouse steaks result. The difference between club, T-bone and Porterhouse steaks is the presence and size of the tenderloin muscle. The club steak has no, or a very small, tenderloin muscle. The beef loin T-bone steak contains a tenderloin which measures no less than ½ inch across, whereas, the beef loin Porterhouse steak contains a tenderloin which measures no less than 1¼ inches across. Alternatively, if the tenderloin is removed from the short loin and the short loin is cut into steaks, these steaks are all called top loin steaks. They are round to wedge shaped (in cross section). The beef tenderloin can be cut into steaks called *filet mignon*. Top loin steaks contain the top loin muscle (*longissimus*) and a portion of the backbone. Boneless beef top loin steak is known regionally by several different names including New York steak or Kansas City steak or strip steak.

Figure 3-3
Loin (Short Loin) Cuts

49

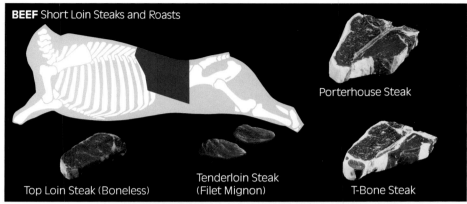

BEEF Short Loin Steaks and Roasts

Porterhouse Steak

Top Loin Steak (Boneless)

Tenderloin Steak (Filet Mignon)

T-Bone Steak

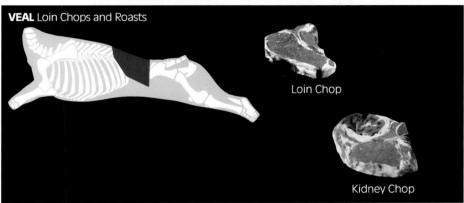

VEAL Loin Chops and Roasts

Loin Chop

Kidney Chop

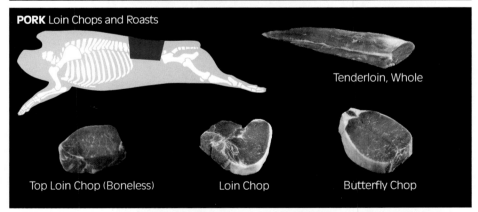

PORK Loin Chops and Roasts

Tenderloin, Whole

Top Loin Chop (Boneless)

Loin Chop

Butterfly Chop

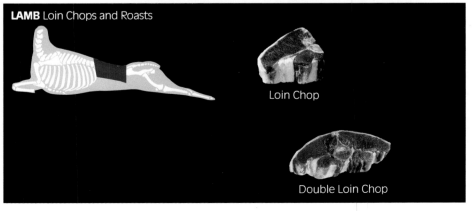

LAMB Loin Chops and Roasts

Loin Chop

Double Loin Chop

Figure 3-4
Sirloin Cuts

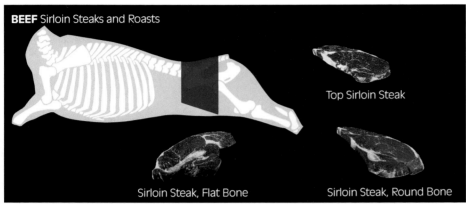

BEEF Sirloin Steaks and Roasts

Top Sirloin Steak

Sirloin Steak, Flat Bone

Sirloin Steak, Round Bone

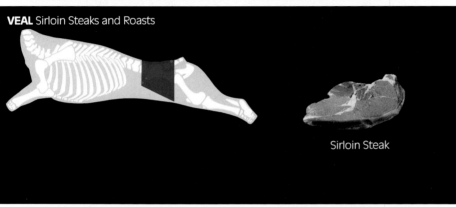

VEAL Sirloin Steaks and Roasts

Sirloin Steak

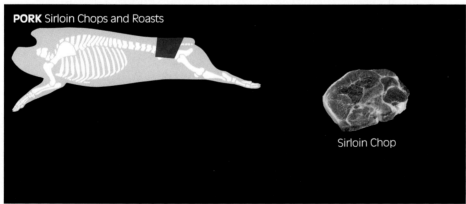

PORK Sirloin Chops and Roasts

Sirloin Chop

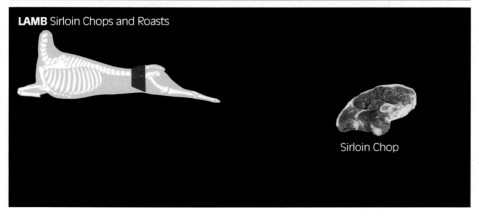

LAMB Sirloin Chops and Roasts

Sirloin Chop

Sirloin Cuts

The two bones in cuts from the sirloin are illustrated in figure 3-4. They are (a) back bone and (b) hip bone.

The muscles in the sirloin section include (1) top sirloin, (2) tenderloin and (3) bottom sirloin.

In beef, the backbone is removed from the sirloin, leaving only the hip bone in steaks. It can be seen from the charts that the hip bone is very irregular in shape. Beef is the only species where the sirloin is made into different cuts that are distinguished by bone shape. The steak nearest the round (leg) has a wedge-shaped bone (hence "wedge bone" sirloins). Just ahead are two steaks with a round or oval-shaped bone; these are called "round bone" sirloin steaks. The "flat bone" steak contains the widest section of the hip bone. A "pin bone" steak includes the front end of the hip bone, and is not offered in the market, because of the high amount of bone. It is boned out to make a boneless sirloin steak. Because boneless sirloin steaks are popular, some flat bone sirloins are converted to boneless form. The "round bone" steaks have a higher lean-to-bone ratio than the "flat bone" sirloins.

When cutting veal, pork and lamb, the backbone is left intact. Pork and lamb sirloin chops are similar but are not differentiated by bone shape; all are called "sirloin chops."

Figure 3-5
Leg (Ham)/Round Cuts

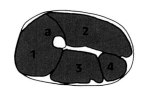

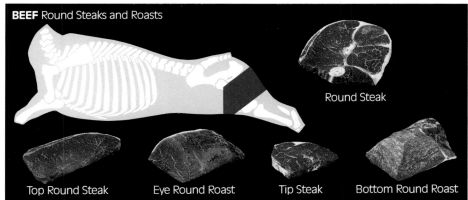

BEEF Round Steaks and Roasts

Round Steak

Top Round Steak Eye Round Roast Tip Steak Bottom Round Roast

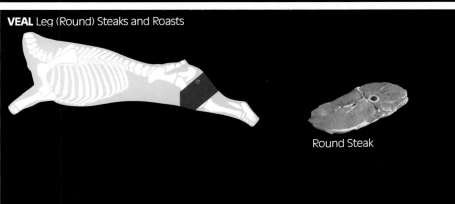

VEAL Leg (Round) Steaks and Roasts

Round Steak

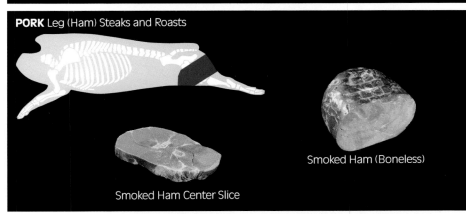

PORK Leg (Ham) Steaks and Roasts

Smoked Ham (Boneless)

Smoked Ham Center Slice

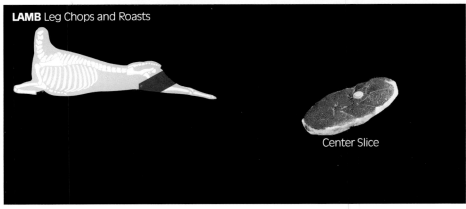

LAMB Leg Chops and Roasts

Center Slice

Leg (Ham)/Round Cuts

The leg section (back leg) is called the "round" when referring to beef primal cuts. A cross section of the leg bone is found in center cut steaks or roasts from the leg or round. The leg bone (a) appears in all of the full-cut steaks. Note the oval shape of the steaks and separating lines or layers of connective tissue and fat between muscles.

The four muscle groups in the leg are important to meat identification. As numbered in the illustration, they are (1) tip, also called the sirloin tip, (this cut is part of the round; it is adjacent to, but not part of, the sirloin); (2) top (inside) round or leg; (3) bottom (outside) round or leg; (4) eye of round or leg.

Cuts (3) and (4) sometimes are left together and sold as bottom (outside) round.

Beef full-cut round steaks may be divided into top round, bottom round and eye of round. The tip is a separate cut in beef, but is included as part of leg steaks from veal, pork and lamb. The proportion of these muscles in a round steak or roast determines the tenderness of the cut. A piece cut from near the sirloin contains some of the tip and is more tender than a piece that is cut from lower down on the leg. Cuts from the top round are more tender than those that include the bottom round. Meat from the leg contains more connective tissue and thus is less tender than cuts from the back (loin and rib cuts).

While beef, veal and lamb leg cuts are generally sold fresh, pork leg may be sold fresh or cured.

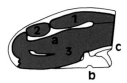

Figure 3-6
52 **Shoulder/Chuck Blade Cuts**

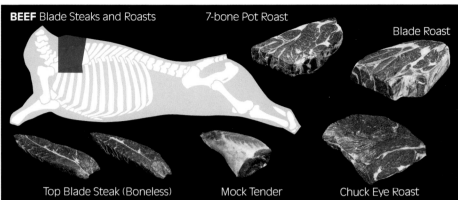

BEEF Blade Steaks and Roasts

7-bone Pot Roast

Blade Roast

Top Blade Steak (Boneless)   Mock Tender   Chuck Eye Roast

Shoulder/Chuck Blade Cuts

The shoulder section is called the chuck when referring to beef primal cuts. The chuck may be divided into blade and arm cuts. Blade cuts are usually more tender than arm cuts because blade cuts are composed of meat from less-exercised back muscles, including a small extension of the rib eye muscle (*longissimus*). The blade cuts near the rib are more tender than those near the neck. The first cut from the posterior end has a tip of white cartilage and long flat bone. It is only a knife cut away from prime rib which contains the tender rib eye steak.

Part or all of the back bone (b) and rib bone (c) in figure 3-6 may be removed by the packer or retailer so the most important identifying bone in shoulder blade cuts is the blade bone (a). In beef, the blade bone may resemble the number 7, shown in the picture of the beef chuck 7-bone steak, or it may be almost flat like the bone in the flat bone sirloin in Figure 3-4.

Several boneless cuts can be made from the blade portion of beef chuck. Their location is shown in the illustration above: (1) boneless top blade steak; (2) mock tender; and (3) boneless eye roast.

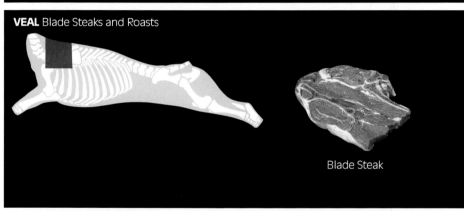

VEAL Blade Steaks and Roasts

Blade Steak

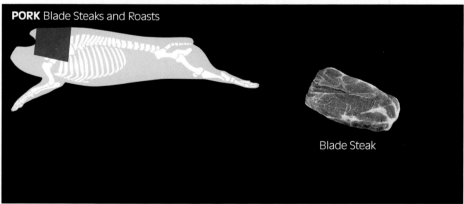

PORK Blade Steaks and Roasts

Blade Steak

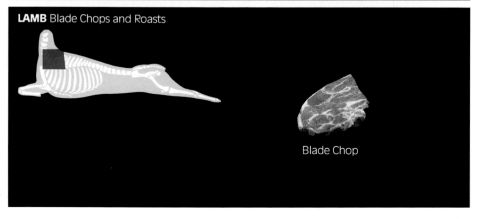

LAMB Blade Chops and Roasts

Blade Chop

Figure 3-7
Shoulder/Chuck Arm Cuts

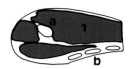

Shoulder/Chuck Arm Cuts

As shown in figure 3-7, bones found in arm cuts for all species include (a) arm bone and, in some cases, (b) cross sections of rib bones. Shoulder muscles run in different directions and a single cut of meat may contain a number of different muscles that vary in connective tissue content, fiber direction and tenderness. Therefore, different muscles, within an arm cut may differ in tenderness.

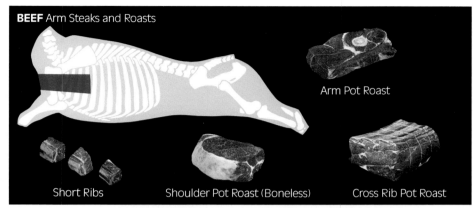

BEEF Arm Steaks and Roasts

Arm Pot Roast

Short Ribs   Shoulder Pot Roast (Boneless)   Cross Rib Pot Roast

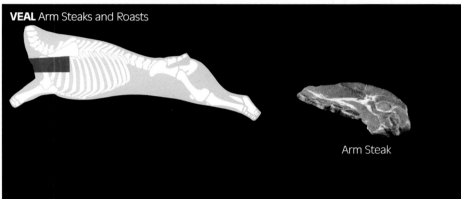

VEAL Arm Steaks and Roasts

Arm Steak

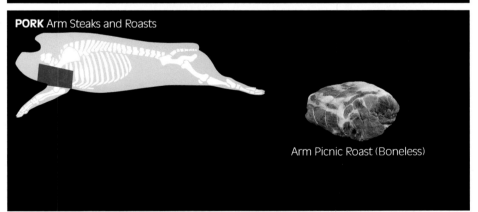

PORK Arm Steaks and Roasts

Arm Picnic Roast (Boneless)

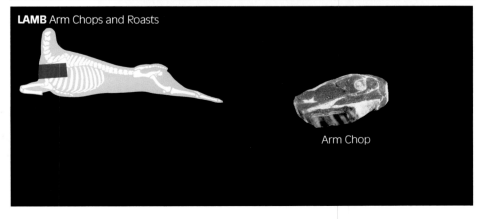

LAMB Arm Chops and Roasts

Arm Chop

Figure 3-8
Breast (Brisket, Short Plate) Cuts

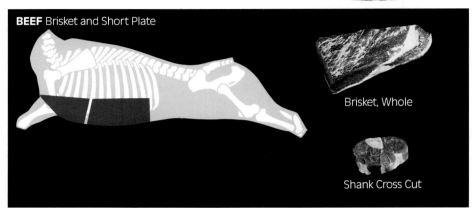

BEEF Brisket and Short Plate

Brisket, Whole

Shank Cross Cut

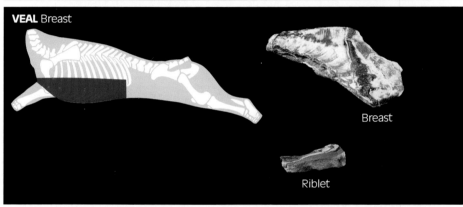

VEAL Breast

Breast

Riblet

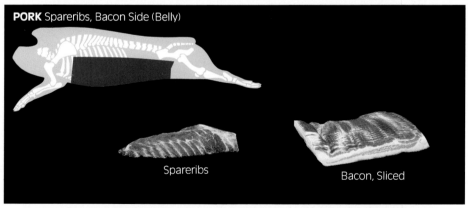

PORK Spareribs, Bacon Side (Belly)

Spareribs

Bacon, Sliced

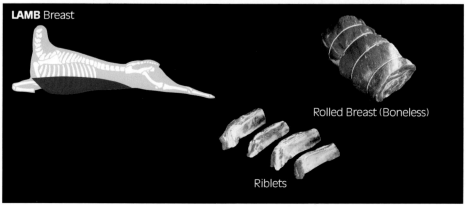

LAMB Breast

Rolled Breast (Boneless)

Riblets

Breast (Brisket, Short Plate) Cuts

Bones in the breast but not the fore shank are shown in the illustration. They are: (a) breast bone, (b) ribs and (c) rib cartilages. Breast cuts in beef come from two primal cuts—shank/brisket and the short plate. Cuts from the breast area are often cured (e.g., corned beef and pastrami) and/or used for unique merchandising (e.g., beef skirt steak). Pastrami is highly seasoned cured beef taken from the short plate, brisket or round.

The boneless side (belly) of a pork carcass is trimmed, cured, smoked and sold as bacon. The belly is also a source of fresh side pork and salt pork.

Skirt Steak—Until recently, skirt steak has not been a well known or a widely utilized beef cut. The "skirt"—named because of the muscle's appearance as it is viewed in the hanging carcass—comes from the heavily exercised diaphragm muscle, which is a part of the short plate. This makes it a less tender piece of meat which may require tenderizing before cooking. Skirt steak is either made into a Mexican-American dish known as "fajitas" (fa.hee.tas) or rolled to form pinwheels and tied or skewered and then cut to form pinwheel steaks.

**Figure 3-9
Rib Cuts**

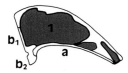

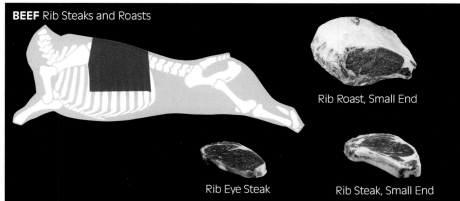

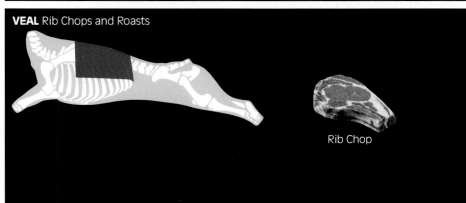

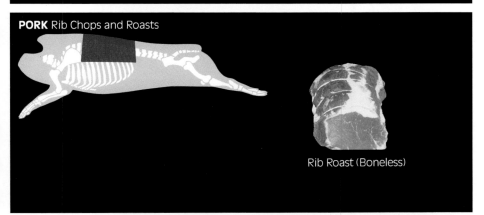

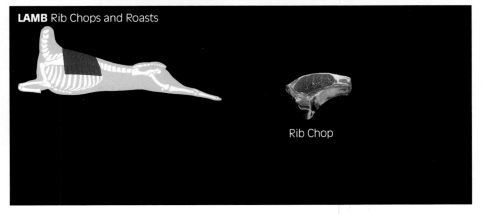

Rib Cuts

Shown in the illustration are identifying bones for retail cuts from the rib. They are (a) rib bone and the back bone, which consists of (b) feather bone (dorsal spinous process) and (c) chine bone (body of the vertebra). The chine bone is usually removed from steaks and chops. Even when all of the bones are removed, cuts from the rib are relatively easy to recognize by the appearance of the (1) rib eye which is a cross section of the muscle (*longissimus*) that lies along the back in the rib and loin.

The pork loin butterfly chop is made from a thick boneless rib chop which has the meat split nearly through in the center. When the meat is spread apart it resembles the wings of a butterfly. A pork butterfly chop can also be cut from the loin portion of the pork loin if the tenderloin is removed first. Canadian-style bacon is made from the eye muscle of the pork loin.

56

Classification

Ground (or Chopped) Beef—Ground beef is by definition, beef skeletal meat (meat that was attached to the bone) without added fat, seasoning, water, binders or extenders. The finished product contains no more than 30 percent fat if it is prepared in a state or federally inspected plant.

Hamburger—The term hamburger refers to ground beef with or without added fat or seasonings. It may not contain added water, binders or extenders.

Ground Beef or Hamburger with Soy Products—These products are combinations of ground beef or hamburger and soy products. If soy protein is added, it must be stated on the label. These combination products may not be nutritionally inferior to ground beef or hamburger.

Ground Meat—"Ground veal," "Ground pork" and "Ground lamb" products contain no more than 30 percent fat and contain no extenders, binders or water, again, if prepared in a state or federally inspected plant.

Meat Loaf—Meat loaf is a mixture of ground meat (often beef, veal and pork) plus cereal, vegetables (such as onions) and tomato products, milk or milk products and liquid. The unpublished standard specifies that the product contain at least 65 percent meat on a raw weight basis.

GROUND MEAT

Ground meat is one of the most popular meat products available. The two most important aspects of purchasing ground meat are the classification or type of meat and the lean-to-fat ratio.

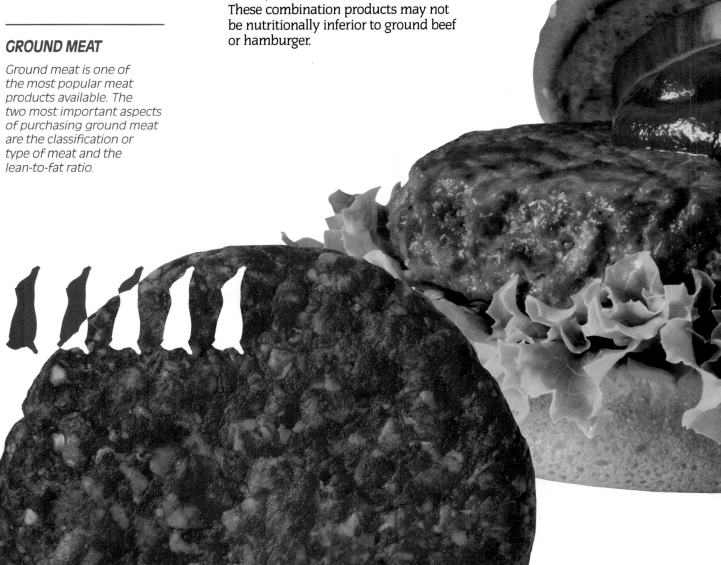

73 percent lean ground beef

80 percent lean ground beef

85 percent lean ground beef

Lean-to-fat ratio

Lean-to-fat ratio is the most important factor in determining the value differences between different types of ground beef. Lean-to-fat ratio labeling only applies to ground beef prepared under State or federal inspection or where local regulations apply. Lean-to-fat ratios and labeling styles differ from region to region and from store to store. However, according to USDA regulations, ground or chopped beef and hamburger may contain no more than 30 percent fat. With the present emphasis on reducing the fatness of meat cuts, ground beef with lean contents as high as 95 percent may be available. If labeled "lean" or "extra lean," a product must have a 25 percent *reduction* in fat from the regulated 30 percent maximum, i.e., no more than 22.5 percent fat. Percent fat must be specified to accompany any leanness claim made on the label. Many stores label ground beef by the percent lean that it contains, i.e., 70 percent lean ground beef or "not less than 70 percent lean."

If there is no lean-to-fat ratio given on the ground beef package, the label may state the primal-cut origin of the product. The primal-cut origin is usually a clue to leanness; for instance, ground beef may be identified by primal cut names such as ground chuck, ground round or ground sirloin. Ground round is the leanest, while ground chuck is the fattest. Ground sirloin falls in the middle; however, because it comes from the loin-sirloin area, it is usually the most expensive.

58

Like the other retail cuts, there is a pronounced similarity among the variety meats from beef, veal, pork and lamb. In most cases, the size of a particular variety meat is consistent with the size of the animal from which it came. For example, those from beef are the largest, those from lamb are the smallest, and those from veal and pork are intermediate in size.

Since variety meats are more perishable than other meat, they should be cooked and served soon after purchase.

Some of the choicest items on restaurant menus and in gourmet recipes are made with variety meats. However, because they have limited appeal in this country and because of their popularity in Europe and other parts of the world, most variety meats produced in the U.S. are exported.

VARIETY MEATS

Variety meats include brains, hearts, kidneys, liver, sweetbreads, tongue, tripe and others. These meat products are usually good buys for three reasons: (1) they are excellent sources of many essential nutrients; (2) they are often in less demand than other cuts of meat and, therefore, more economical; and (3) they offer many interesting variations for serving meat.

Most Common

Brains—Brains are soft in consistency, very tender and have a delicate flavor. They may be broiled, fried, braised or cooked in liquid. If brains are not to be used immediately after purchase, they should be pre-cooked regardless of the method of preparation.

Calf or Lamb Testicles—Testicles are sold fresh or frozen. When cooked, they are known as "fries" or "Rocky Mountain oysters." Generally, they are served deep-fat fried.

Chitterlings—The unqualified term "chitterlings" refers to the intestines of swine. Veal or calf chitterlings are also sold. They are thoroughly cleaned, then usually sold intact, in containers of three pounds or less, for retail use. They are normally served with sauces.

Hearts—Beef, the largest of heart meat, is usually sold cut or split. A whole beef heart can be stuffed and braised. Young lamb hearts and veal hearts are tender and can be fried.

Hog Maws—A hog maw is the stomach of a hog. It usually is stuffed with seasoned meat and vegetables and roasted.

Kidneys—Beef kidneys and veal kidneys are made up of many lobes. Lamb and pork kidneys are smaller than beef or veal. Lamb and veal kidneys are tender and delicately flavored. Beef and pork kidneys, which are stronger flavored and less tender, must be prepared by a moist-cooking method that tenderizes them. Kidneys should have a meaty fresh aroma when purchased.

Liver—The most preferred liver is that from veal, although it is sometimes referred to as calf liver. Because the demand is great, veal liver warrants a premium price. Lamb liver is equally tender and delicately flavored, but is not readily available in many parts of the U.S. Beef and pork liver, on the other hand, are more strongly flavored and firmer than veal liver. Beef liver, if sliced thinly and cooked quickly, can be delicious and tender. Fresh, uncooked veal liver should be rosy red and moist; lamb liver is redder; and beef and pork livers are a deep red-brown in color.

Beef, veal and lamb livers have two lobes, one larger than the other. Pork liver has four clearly visible lobes, about equal in size. Liver is covered with a thick membrane and has connective tissue between the lobes which should be removed prior to cooking.

Oxtails—The tails of beef are commonly used for making soups and stews. They make an attractive display when cut at each joint with the resulting segments packaged flat.

Pigs Feet, Knuckles, Ears and Snouts, and Calf's Feet—These cuts are most often pickled or used to make jellied meat loaves such as head cheese. They contain a considerable amount of connective tissue, which partially dissolves when cooked, and gels when chilled.

Sweetbreads—Veal, calf and young beef sweetbreads are thymus glands, located in the throats of young animals. As the animal matures, the gland disappears. Veal or calf sweetbreads are smooth, soft and creamy white. Beef sweetbreads are redder and less smooth than veal. Lamb sweetbreads are sometimes available, but are very small. Pork sweetbreads (the pancreas gland), not common in this country, are used in Europe for patés. Sweetbreads are usually sauteed to preserve their delicate flavor.

Tongue—Tongue is a popular variety meat that may be purchased fresh, pickled, corned, smoked or canned. Tongue is one of the less tender of the variety meats and, therefore, needs long, slow cooking in liquid. Smoked, corned, or pickled tongue may require soaking before cooking. It should be cooked slowly (simmered) in liquid (usually water) until tender. After it is cooked, the skin is removed and the tongue may be served cold or reheated (whole or sliced) in a spicy sauce.

Tripe—Tripe is the lining of the first (rumen) and second (reticulum) stomachs of cattle. The choicest is honeycomb tripe, the lining of the second stomach. Plain or smooth tripe, from the first stomach, is less tender. Tripe is available pickled, canned or fresh. Fresh tripe is usually sold partially cooked; however, it is sometimes sold fully cooked.

Variety meats—like processed meat, the subject of the next chapter—can extend food dollars and expand possibilities for creative meal planning.

Meat preservation was the primary reason processed meat was developed centuries ago. Extended shelf life is still a major asset of processed meat. Such products are popular now because they fit into today's busy lifestyle. They are easy to prepare, with little waste, and provide controlled portion sizes. Processed meat is also flavorful and provides variety to the diet.

HISTORY OF PROCESSED MEAT

Processed meat products have been favorite foods of U.S. citizens since Colonial times. In 1987, over 17.1 billion pounds of processed meat products (cold cuts, sausages, hams and bacon) were produced in the United States. In that same year approximately 2100 federally inspected processors produced 5.1 billion pounds of sausage.

Historical evidence suggests that sausage was made and eaten by the Babylonians some 3500 years ago, and that the ancient Chinese also made sausage. The earliest recorded reference to sausage was in Homer's Odyssey, written in the ninth century B.C. Sausage-making gained popularity during the Roman and Christian eras, and by the Middle Ages was popular throughout Europe. Local climate and availability of raw materials had a great deal to do with the type of products that were produced.

The warmer weather of Italy, Spain and Southern France encouraged the development of dry and semi-dry varieties, while in the cooler climates of Germany and Austria, where preservation was less of a problem, fresh and cooked sausages were produced.

Sausages frequently took the name of their town of origin: bologna from Bologna, Italy; Genoa salami from Genoa, Italy; frankfurters from Frankfurt, Germany; and Vienna sausage from Vienna, Austria, for example. When they came to the U.S., the immigrants continued to make sausages that satisfied their ethnic tastes. Their Old World recipes are the current basis of the processed meat industry in this country. Today, over 200 varieties of cold cuts and sausages, many bearing their historical names, are available in the U.S.

Table 4-1
Sausage Origins

Austria	Vienna sausage
Czechoslovakia	Jaternice, Prasky
France	D'Arles Salami
Germany	Beerwurst, Berliner sausage, Bockwurst, Bratwurst, Braunschweiger, Frankfurters, Knackwurst, Thuringer
Hungary	Blood sausage, Kiszka, Kolbase
Italy	Cappicola, Italian Salami, Mortadella, Pepperoni, Prosciutti, Salami
Mexico	Chorizo
Poland	Headcheese, Kabanosy, Polish sausage/Kielbasa
Portugal	Linguisa
Sweden	Goteborg sausage
Switzerland	Kalbsleberwurst, Landjaegar

Sources: *The Meat We Eat.* and *Principal Characteristics of Sausages of the World Listed by Country of Origin*

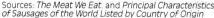

PLIMOTH PLANTATION

Processed meat is made from whole-some meat that has been inspected at every stage of manufacturing. The Food Safety and Inspection Service (FSIS) of the USDA oversees the hygiene, sanitation, labeling, packaging, refrigeration temperature and weight of processed meat from raw material to finished product. Many processed meat products utilize meat trimmings and cuts that are less demanded by consumers. If variety meats such as hearts are used, the processor must clearly state "with variety meats" or "with meat by-products" on the label and the specific variety meats must be listed in the ingredients statement. However, if all meat is muscle, no specific USDA label other than the species listing is required. Ingredients are always listed in order of prevalence (from that ingredient present in greatest quantity, to that component present in least amount).

DEFINITION OF PROCESSED MEAT

Processed meat may be defined as meat that has been changed by any mechanical, chemical or enzymatic treatment, altering the taste, appearance and often the keeping quality of the product. Approximately 35 percent of the beef, veal, pork and lamb produced in the U.S. is processed. Most of the meat which is processed (about 75 percent) is pork, and the remainder is beef with a small percentage of lamb or mutton.

METHODS USED TO MAKE PROCESSED MEAT

Some processed meat is made with seasoned fresh meat and is not further treated; others are cured, smoked and/or cooked. These methods affect both the flavor and keeping quality. Usually, more than one processing method is used to produce a single product.

Curing

Pickle Curing—In pickle curing, salt, sugar, nitrite, and often phosphate and ascorbic acid are mixed in water to form a pickle solution. This solution can be introduced into the meat in one of the following four ways:

- **Stitch Pumping**—A single needle with multiple openings or multiple needles with single openings may be used to inject the pickle solution into the meat. Most commercially produced meat is cured using the multiple needle method, which more evenly distributes the pickle solution. Curing is hastened using this method, as the curing takes place from inside as well as outside the meat. Following stitch pumping, pork bellies go directly into the smokehouse, while larger, thicker cuts (hams, etc.) may be held several hours before smoking.

- **Artery Pumping**—This procedure is limited to the curing of hams, and in some cases, arm or shoulder picnics. During processing, a pickle solution is injected into an artery and distributed throughout the cut via the vascular system. In fast-moving commercial plants, this pumping procedure requires only 24 hours.

- **Tumbling/massaging**—Many processors utilize machines that resemble a concrete mixer to tumble or massage cuts as they are cured. Tumbling/massaging hastens cure absorption and aids in extraction of the myofibrillar protein myosin, which acts as a "glue" to hold pieces of meat together. Most boneless hams are processed this way. After several hours of tumbling, the hams go directly to the smokehouse.

- **Vat Curing**—Meat is submerged in a vat containing pickle solution until the solution completely penetrates the meat. Used mostly by smaller-size processing plants, this method of curing takes more time (nine days per inch of thickness of cuts), requires more space, and necessitates higher inventories of meat than other pickle-curing methods.

Dry Curing—Water is not added to a dry cure. Rather, the dry curing ingredients, including nitrate, are rubbed onto the surface of the meat and the curing ingredients migrate into the muscle by osmosis. Excess liquids are removed as they accumulate. Meat cured by this process has an extended shelf life, even in the absence of refrigeration. To some the final product of dry-curing is considered very salty. The color of meat cured in this manner is darker and the final product is firmer and drier than pickle-cured products. Dry-cured products often command a premium price because more time is required for processing (seven days per inch of thickness), the yield is lower and the products are not as readily available as those made by the other methods described earlier.

Smoking

Originally a method of preserving meat, smoking is used today primarily to lend an appetizing, outside brown appearance and a characteristic smoky flavor to smoked products. Smoke may be applied to a product in one of two forms: natural or liquid. Wood of the hickory tree is one of the most popular sources of natural smoke. Liquid smoke, a fraction extracted from wood smoke, is more commonly used in the industry today because it is a cleaner system. Its use causes little or no atmospheric contamination.

Cooking

Generally, the objectives of the cooking step in manufacturing processed meat are to: (1) develop firmness through protein coagulation and partial dehydration, (2) fix the color of cured meat and (3) increase shelf life through pasteurization.

Sausages are cooked with either moist- or dry-heat methods. Some are cooked initially with dry heat to reduce fat and moisture content and are then exposed to steam heat. A combination of cooking methods can increase tenderness and improve flavor.

Sausages

The numerous varieties of sausages necessitate several and slightly different processing procedures. The meat can come from beef, veal, pork, lamb, poultry or a combination of these sources. Some sausages are made from meat that is cured, smoked or cooked before it is ground; other sausages are formed first, and then cured, smoked, cooked or treated by a combination of these processes. Products such as bologna, frankfurters and many loaf types of luncheon meat are made from finely ground meat emulsions. Other products, such as smoked pork sausages, or Italian and Polish sausages, are coarse in texture and do not require emulsification. Production of dry and semi-dry sausages requires carefully controlled fermentation and drying.

Types of Sausages—

■ **Fresh**—Fresh sausages are made from comminuted meat and are not cured, smoked or cooked. Therefore, they must be cooked before serving. Some examples are fresh pork sausage, fresh bratwurst, chorizo, bockwurst and Italian-style sausage.

■ **Uncooked and Smoked**—These sausages may include cured but not cooked meat. They are smoked after forming but must be cooked before serving. Smoked pork sausage, kielbasa and smoked country-style sausage are examples.

■ **Cooked**—Usually made from meat that has been cured and cooked, these sausages are ready-to-eat, although some may be heated before serving. Types of cooked sausages include precooked bratwurst, braunschweiger, liverwurst, blood sausage and tongue sausage.

■ **Cooked and Smoked**—These products are made from meat that has been cured, formed into sausages, cooked and subjected to a light smoke. This type of sausage is ready-to-eat, although some may prefer to heat certain kinds of this product before serving. Examples are bologna, cotto salami, frankfurters and Vienna sausage.

■ **Dry and/or Semi-dry**—These sausages may be smoked or unsmoked, and processing always includes curing and usually involves cooking at the plant. Carefully controlled fermentation acts as a preservative and gives these sausages their distinctive and unique flavors. Hard salami is usually in the dry-sausage category, while summer sausages are typically of the semi-dry type. Other varieties of dry and semi-dry sausages include cervelat, thuringer, pepperoni and mortadella. These sausages are ready-to-eat and do not require cooking prior to consumption.

■ **Loaves and Other Specialty Meat**—Such meat is cured and fully cooked, sometimes by baking, during processing. Examples of loaves include honey, minced ham, old fashioned, olive, pepper, and pickle and pimento; head cheese and Vienna sausage loaf are other specialty meat products. This type of sausage need not be cooked before serving.

CLASSIFICATIONS OF PROCESSED MEAT

Processed meat can be classified as sausages, cured whole muscle cuts or as restructured meat products.

Steps in Making Sausage—

■ **Comminution (Particle Reduction)—** Comminution is the process by which meat is ground, chopped, diced, emulsified, or reduced to minute particles for incorporation into sausage.

■ **Emulsification—**If a meat mixture is comminuted with salt in a bowl chopper or silent cutter, a finely chopped sausage batter is formed. In the presence of salt a meat emulsion can be formed. In meat emulsions, lean meat and fat particles are dispersed in a complex of water, proteins, cellular components, and a variety of spices and seasonings.

■ **Blending—**Ground meat or chopped meat, but not meat emulsions, can be placed in a mixer/blender to evenly distribute the lean and fat particles and any cure ingredients that are in the mixture. After blending, the mixture may be added to the revolving metal bowl of a chopper, where rotating knife blades cut through the meat mass and mix in seasonings and other ingredients. In this application, time in the bowl chopper is short and emulsification is not the desired result. After a short time in the chopper, meat to be used in ground products goes directly into the stuffer to be formed into sausages.

■ **Forming—**Some processed meat products, such as fresh pork sausage, may be sold in bulk, in chubs or formed into patties. Others are molded into loaves, but most are stuffed into casings. Comminuted products are placed in casings to give them a characteristic shape (like that of a wiener), to hold the product together, and to allow for further processing. Types of casings include:

—Animal Casings (Natural Casings)— Casings made from the gastrointestinal tract of cattle, hogs or sheep are more costly than artificial casings because their production requires more hand labor. An advantage to natural casings is that they can be consumed as part of the product.

—Cellulosic Casings—Made from a by-product of the cotton plant, cellulosic casings are uniform containers, but are not edible. They are available in a variety of sizes. Small casings are used for products like frankfurters and are removed at the processing plant prior to final packaging. Larger casings may be chemically and physically identical to the smaller casings, and may or may not be removed before sale. They are, however, removed before the sausage is eaten.

—Regenerated Collagen Casings—These edible casings have some of the properties of animal casings and some of the benefits of cellulosic casings. The production of these casings includes extraction of collagen from animal skins and hides and subsequent processing into casings of various sizes. Smaller casings are used for products such as pork link sausage and are normally eaten along with the product. Larger, thicker casings that are used on other products may be removed before the sausage is eaten.

—Fibrous Casings—Fibrous casings are the toughest of all casings and are made from a special paper-pulp base which is impregnated with cellulose, creating a strong, uniform container. Some are made easily removable by first coating the inside of the casing with a moisture-proof coating; others are processed to make the casing adhere to the sausage. Dry and semi-dry sausages typically are manufactured in non-edible, adhering, fibrous casings.

■ **Tying—**According to the type of meat product and the particular casing, the sausage may be tied at each end with string or fastened with metal clips. With smaller sausages, such as frankfurters, casings are normally twisted or drawn together either by hand or mechanically to produce links as identical in shape and size as possible.

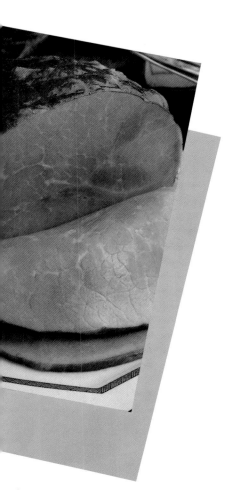

Cured Whole Muscle Cuts

Whole muscle cuts like ham, corned beef, pastrami and bacon are considered processed meat products because they have been treated with a curing solution, dry-cured, smoked and/or seasoned. These products are more popular in their processed form than as fresh cuts. A ham, for instance, is more in demand in the U.S. than a fresh leg of pork from which a ham is made.

Ham—Ham is defined as the hind leg of pork that has been cured and smoked or cured and canned. Ham, one of the more highly valued pork products, can be produced in three styles: bone-in, semi-boneless or boneless. Bone-in hams can contain four leg-bone sections including the aitch bone (a portion of the pelvic arch), the femur, the patella (the knee cap) and the fibula shank and tibia. Semi-boneless hams usually have the aitch and the shank bones removed, although occasionally the shank is left attached. Boneless hams have all the bones removed and most of the external, and as much as possible of the inter-muscular, fat trimmed away. The lean meat may be rolled, shaped or formed into a casing.

Specialty hams, such as the Smithfield Ham or Prosciutto Ham, are available regionally and by mail order. The Smithfield Ham, produced in Smithfield, Virginia, is dry-cured with salt, sugar and nitrate, then smoked and aged to give it a distinctive flavor and texture. Ham cured elsewhere by this process must be labeled "Smithfield-Style Ham" or country-style ham. Prosciutto Ham is a dry-cured Italian ham that is highly seasoned with pepper and other spices.

In order to be labeled "fully cooked," hams must be cooked to an internal temperature of 148°F. Although "fully cooked" hams require no additional heating, all hams should be cooked to 130°F to 140°F prior to consumption for optimum palatability. Hams labeled "cook-before-eating" should be cooked to an internal temperature of 160°F to 170°F before serving. If neither term appears on the label, the ham should be fully cooked before eating.

Canned hams are boneless, cured-ham sections that have been placed in metal or plastic containers, vacuum-sealed, then fully cooked. A small amount of natural unflavored dry gelatin may be added before sealing to absorb the natural juices as the ham cooks. Canned hams are produced in a variety of sizes and are ready-to-eat.

Corned (Cured) Beef—The brisket is the most popular cut of meat used for corned beef, although beef round is also used. Formerly, "corning" referred to the process of preserving beef by sprinkling it with grains ("corns") of salt. Today, corned beef is cured with a pickle solution consisting of water, salt, sugar, nitrite and spices.

Bacon—In the United States, bacon is produced primarily from pork bellies. Beef bacon is made from the boneless beef short plate (an anatomical region similar to that of the belly in pork). Canadian-style bacon is made from the top loin muscle of pork—usually that from heavier hogs. Both bacon and Canadian bacon are cured and smoked, giving them their unique flavor.

Pastrami—Pastrami is made from the brisket, plate or top round muscle of beef. After dry-curing with salt, the beef is washed, then rubbed with a paste of garlic powder, ground cumin, red pepper, cinnamon, cloves and allspice. It is then smoked and cooked.

Pork Shoulder—The pork shoulder can be divided into two major cuts, Picnic (arm) and Boston (blade). These cuts can be processed using the same techniques employed to prepare ham from the pork leg. Shoulder cuts are usually priced more economically than leg cuts due to differences in palatability and yield of edible portion.

Restructured Meat

Restructured meat products are generally made from flaked, ground or sectioned beef or pork, which is shaped into roasts, steaks or loaves. Examples of restructured meat are smoked sliced beef and most boneless hams.

The process of restructuring consists of three steps: a reduction or modification in particle size, blending and reforming into the desired product size and shape. Some restructured hams look very similar to their whole muscle counterparts. In fact, some are simply chunks of ham that have been bound together to form a larger piece.

The binding of particles in the reforming process is essential to the process of restructuring. Intracellular myofibrillar proteins (e.g., myosin) from the muscle are functional in causing meat particles to bind. Salt and phosphates, along with the proper mixing process, help bring these proteins to the surface of the particles and contribute to the binding qualities of the product (See discussion of myofibrillar proteins, Chapter 1).

INGREDIENTS IN PROCESSED MEAT

The ingredients added to processed meat are there to: enhance shelf life, perform specific functions related to the processing techniques and give the product a distinctive flavor and appearance. The USDA requires that additives be approved by the FDA and sets limits regarding the amount of an additive that can be used in a product. These additives must meet a specific, justifiable need in the product and must not be used to deceive consumers with regard to freshness, quality or weight. The USDA requires that additives be truthfully and properly listed on the product label.

Common Ingredients

Some of the common ingredients added to processed meat products are described below.

Salt—Salt is common to all curing solutions. Technically, it is the only substance required for a product to be considered cured. Composed of 40 percent sodium and 60 percent chloride, salt plays an important role in the production of processed meat. Salt serves three functions in sausages: preservation or shelf-life extension, extraction of the myofibrillar proteins needed to make the product bind and flavor enhancement.

Many companies are now producing sausage products with less salt. Sausages that state "lower salt" or "less salt" on the label must, by law, have reduced the salt level in that product by at least 25 percent compared to the "traditional" product. However, since salt is a preservative, added care must then be taken in preparation/processing and home storage of these reduced-salt products.

Phosphates—Phosphates are used in production of some sausages to retain moisture, solubilize proteins and inhibit rancidity, which often results in improved texture, juiciness and flavor. The legal limit for phosphates in finished sausages is 0.5 percent by weight, but most manufacturers use less than that because of reduced palatability.

Nitrate and Nitrite—Early European sausage-makers recognized that salts collected from certain specific geographic locations produced superior sausages. Later, it was discovered that these salts contained nitrate which was present as a natural contaminant. Nitrate (NO_3) is broken down by bacteria to nitrite (NO_2) during the curing process; it is nitrite that is responsible for the improved qualities of sausages. Nitrate is only used in the production of dry sausages, and dry-cured hams, shoulders and bellies, which require a long cure, and thus need nitrate to continually produce nitrite during the curing process. Modern meat pro-

cessors now add nitrite directly to meat or meat mixtures in very closely controlled amounts.

Of the body's exposure to nitrite, 20 percent comes from food (nitrate is found naturally in green leafy vegetables such as spinach). Of that 20 percent, only 2 percent to 3 percent comes from processed meat. An estimated 80 percent of nitrite exposure comes from that produced within the body.

In the early 1980s, there was concern over the health risks of nitrates/nitrites. Studies had shown that nitrosamines (which can be formed when nitrites combine with by-products of protein degradation—amines—in the stomach) were carcinogenic (cancer causing) in laboratory animals.

Nitrosamines were rarely found in processed meat products, although traces of these compounds had been found in bacon cooked at high temperatures to a crisp/well done state. For that reason, new processes are now used which significantly reduce the amount of nitrite used in curing bacon and minimize nitrosamine formation in cooked bacon. These processing and manufacturing procedures are monitored by USDA to help assure that nitrosamine formation is minimized.

According to a December 1981 report by the National Academy of Sciences, neither sodium nitrate nor nitrite itself has been shown to be carcinogenic.

Nitrite is used for curing meat to inhibit the growth of a number of food poisoning and spoilage microorganisms, including *Clostridium botulinum;* to retard the development of rancidity; to stabilize the color of the lean tissue; and to contribute to the characteristic flavor of cured meat. Since nitrite is an antioxidant, it helps prevent warmed-over flavor (WOF). By the time they are consumed, most processed meat products contain less than 50 parts per million of nitrite.

Water—Water serves as a carrier for salt and other ingredients permitting uniform distribution of these substances throughout the meat. Ice or cold water is often used during the chopping process to cool a meat emulsion, thus ensuring improved product stability. In most meat products the moisture:protein ratio approximates 4.0, (i.e., the meat product contains four times as much moisture as protein). When a label reads "water added," a regulated amount of water, specific for each of many products, has been added to enhance the tenderness, juiciness and overall palatability of the product. In the new, low-fat processed meat products, water is used to replace fat, which also reduces caloric density. In frankfurters and other cooked sausage items, added water can be substituted for fat, provided the combination of the two in the finished product does not exceed 40 percent. The fat content limit is 30 percent.

Sugar—A variety of sugars including molasses and other sweeteners are commonly used in the production of processed meat and sausage. Sugars used range from sucrose (cane or beet sugar) to dextrose (corn sugar). The dextrose group includes corn syrup, corn syrup solids and sorbitol. Primarily, sugar is added to cured or processed meat to counteract intense saltiness of cured meat and as a medium (food) for the microbial fermentation process used to reduce the pH of dry and semi-dry sausages. The lactic acid, produced by fermentation of the sugar, reduces the pH and gives these sausages their tangy flavor. With the exception of sorbitol, the addition of sugars or sweeteners to a product increases browning of meat during cooking. Because sorbitol has the opposite effect, it is used in frankfurters to reduce charring when the meat is grilled.

Spices—Many different spices are used to give processed meat products their distinctive flavors. Certain spices also act to inhibit bacterial growth and oxidation. Among the spices most commonly used in sausages are: red, white and black pepper, allspice, bayleaf, mustard, garlic, anise and cinnamon.

Fat—The fat content of most processed meat products is government-regulated. Some cured meat, such as whole muscle hams and corned beef made from the round, have little fat, and may be up to 97 percent fat-free. The fat content of hot dogs, bologna and most sausages, limited by the USDA to a maximum of 30 percent, is controlled during the comminution process. However, as stated earlier, added water can be substituted for fat. Sausages with a label stating "lower fat" must have 25 percent less fat than the 30 percent fat in the usual sausage product of that type (i.e., less than 22.5 percent total fat).

Mechanically Separated Meat—

High-quality meat that is mechanically separated from the bone is used in some sausages and occasionally in restructured meat. After conventional hand-deboning, machines are used to separate the meat adhering to bones, which increases the yield of meat obtained from animal carcasses. The common level of usage for mechanically separated meat (MSM) in sausage is from 5 percent to 10 percent of the weight of the product. However, USDA regulations permit use-levels up to 20 percent MSM from beef, pork or lamb if MSM is listed in the ingredient statement on the label. Although MSM is widely used around the world, its use is limited in the United States.

Extenders and Binders—Certain

sausage products may contain extenders and binders, alone or in combination, such as nonfat dry milk, dried whey, reduced lactose whey, whey-protein concentrate, calcium lactate, cereal flours, soy flour, soy-protein concentrate, isolated soy protein and/or vegetable starch at levels up to 3.5 percent of the finished product. Isolated soy protein is an exception to this regulation and may be used up to a level of 2 percent in the finished product. If soy products are used in the formulation, their presence must be reflected in the product-name label; for example, "frankfurter, cereal added" or "bologna, soy-protein concentrate and nonfat dry milk added." Some soy proteins improve binding qualities, flavor, cooking yields and slicing characteristics, while others increase protein content or are added to lower-quality products for economic reasons.

Other Ingredients

Ascorbic acid (vitamin C), erythorbic acid and their respective salts, sodium ascorbate and sodium erythorbate, are especially useful in improving and maintaining the color of processed meat. These compounds have been shown to inhibit formation of nitrosamines in cured meat.

A variety of compounds are added to fresh and dry sausage in regulated amounts to combat oxidative rancidity. The most common of these antioxidants are BHA (butylated hydroxyanisole), BHT (butylated hydroxytoluene) and propyl gallate.

Consumers make purchasing decisions on the basis of widely differing levels of knowledge about meat. Experienced consumers who understand muscle and bone structure (described in Chapter 1) can most easily identify the cuts which will best meet their demands for tenderness, leanness, ease of preparation and economy. The two things all consumers expect when purchasing meat are a guarantee that their purchase is wholesome and assurance that it meets the quality standards that justify its price. There are federally regulated programs which give consumers that assurance.

INSPECTION AND GRADING

Inspection assures that consumers receive safe and wholesome meat. Grading pertains to expected quality and yield of meat. Inspection is paid for by tax dollars, while grading is a part of the processing costs.

Inspection

The Federal Meat Inspection Act of 1906 made inspection mandatory for all meat that crossed state lines. The Wholesome Meat Act of 1967 required that inspection of meat sold within a state meet inspection requirements at least as stringent as those of the federal system. Federal meat inspection is the responsibility of the Food Safety and Inspection Service (FSIS), a division of the USDA. State meat inspection is the responsibility of each state's government with partial funding support provided by the federal government.

These inspection programs assure that only healthy animals are used for meat and guarantee that facilities and equipment meet sanitation standards. The Meat Inspection Program also includes:
—inspection of meat at various stages of processing
—temperature monitoring for both fresh and cooked meat
—review of packaging and labels used for fresh and processed meat
—control and monitoring of the use of additives
—control and monitoring of imported meat.

Any time new or revised inspection regulations or labeling rules are considered, they are published in the Federal Register and in the public press. Consumers and industry are given an opportunity to comment on them before the regulations are implemented.

A round stamp (made with purple ink) containing an abbreviation for "United States Inspected and Passed" and the official establishment number assigned to that packing/processing plant is placed on each primal cut when it passes federal inspection. The stamp must also be on every prepackaged processed meat product that has been federally inspected. If a product is packaged in a box, the inspection stamp is found on the outside of the carton and not on the meat.

State meat inspection stamps use purple ink and a symbol that is often the outline of the shape of that state, with the official establishment number within the stamp. Three stamps are illustrated in Figure 5-1. The first stamp is used for carcasses, the second is for processed meat and the third is an example of a stamp which is used for state inspection.

Kosher Inspection—The term Kosher is derived from the Hebrew word meaning "fit and proper" or "properly prepared." Kosher meat is processed under the supervision of persons authorized by the Jewish faith and meets the standards of the Mosaic and Talmudic laws.

The first requirement for Kosher meat is that it come from an animal that has split hooves and chews its cud. Since hogs do not meet this requirement, pork, ham and bacon cannot be Kosher.

A specially trained rabbi must perform the ritual slaughter and drain the blood from the animal. The fresh meat is soaked and salted on all sides and in all cuts and folds, then the meat is allowed to drain. Salting draws out the remaining blood from the meat as required by biblical law (Leviticus 17:14), "You shall not eat the blood of any creature, for the life of every creature is its blood; whoever eats it shall be cut off." Some cuts of meat, such as those from the hindquarter, are not available as Kosher meat because it is not possible to completely remove the blood from them.

The Kosher inspection stamp, which is put on meat by the rabbi, is independent of requirements for federal or state meat inspection laws and does not indicate grade. Kosher meat must also be inspected by federal or state authorities and must meet those standards prior to sale.

Figure 5-1
Meat Inspection Stamps

This stamp is used on fresh and cured meat to indicate that it has met the federal inspection requirements for wholesomeness. It is put on all primal cuts, but may not appear on every retail cut.

This stamp is used on canned and packaged meat products that have met the federal inspection standards.

State meat inspection stamps are often in the shape of the state.

Note: The number in each stamp identifies the particular meat processing facility.
Source: FSIS, USDA and Illinois Department of Agriculture

Figure 5-2
Kosher Stamp

Source: *The Meat We Eat*.

Figure 5-3
Quality Grade Stamp

Grading

Established in 1927, the USDA meat-grading system sets standards of quality and cutability (yield of edible meat) that are used in buying and selling of meat. The program is administered by the USDA but participation is voluntary; therefore, the cost of this service is borne by the meat packers. Having these standards allows livestock owners to gear production for specific grades. Packers can segregate carcasses and cuts into groups of similar grade and retailers can buy the appropriate grades of meat for their markets. For consumers, grading provides assurance that the product conforms to an established set of standards that predict palatability and/or cutability.

There are federal grades for beef, veal, pork and lamb. There are more grades for beef since the increased variation in age and weight of cattle causes quality and cutability (yield) to vary more than in other meat.

The USDA quality grade is indicated by a shield-shaped stamp, using purple ink. In addition, individual packers and retailers may use their own brand names to designate different grades of meat, such as Armour "Star," Monfort "Gold" or Safeway "Lean."

The lower beef quality grades (Commercial, Utility, Cutter, Canner) are normally not sold directly to the public. They are wholesome and nutritious, but because they are less tender, they are used in ground beef, sausages and other manufactured meat products. Some of the more tender cuts (ribs and loins) of the lower grades are tenderized and used in restaurants that feature low-cost steaks.

Beef Grading

■ **Quality Grading**—Quality grades are determined by evaluating the following components of beef:

—Marbling (Intramuscular Fat)—The amount and distribution of visible fat in lean meat is a major criterion for grading beef. Because the marbling fat melts during cooking, thereby increasing the juiciness of the meat, contributing to its flavor and increasing its perceived tenderness, very well-marbled meat is assigned the highest quality grade (Prime). Nine degrees of marbling are used to determine the USDA quality grades. The six most common degrees of marbling are illustrated in the photographs in Figure 5-4. Meat from young cattle containing the highest amount of marbling is graded Prime, followed by Choice, Select and Standard, which have progressively lower levels of marbling.

Table 5-1
USDA Grades for Beef, Veal, Pork and Lamb

Beef	Veal	Pork	Lamb
Quality Grades	**Quality Grades**	**Quality Grades**	**Quality Grades**
Prime Choice Select Standard Commercial	Prime Choice Good Standard	Acceptable—quality must be acceptable to qualify for grades 1-4 below.	Prime Choice Good
Utility Cutter Canner	Utility	Utility	Utility
	Cull		Cull
Yield Grades	**Yield Grades**	**Yield Grades**	**Yield Grades**
1 2 3 4 5	None	U.S. No. 1 U.S. No. 2 U.S. No. 3 U.S. No. 4	1 2 3 4 5

Figure 5-4
Marbling

Since marbling is such an important factor in judging and grading beef, the following pictures illustrate the lower limits of six marbling degrees: Moderately Abundant, Slightly Abundant, Moderate, Modest, Small and Slight.

It should be noted that there are nine degrees of marbling referred to in the Official United States Standard for Grades of Carcass Beef. These color photographs have been developed to assist government, industry and academia in the proper application of official grade standards.

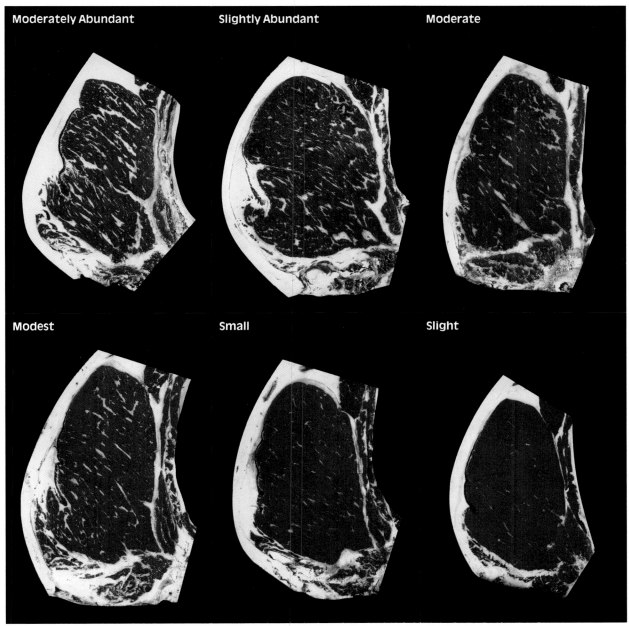

Moderately Abundant **Slightly Abundant** **Moderate**

Modest **Small** **Slight**

The above illustrations are reduced reproductions of the Official USDA Marbling Photographs prepared for the U.S. Department of Agriculture by and available from the National Live Stock and Meat Board.

—Maturity—The younger the animal the more likely that the meat will be tender. Younger cattle qualify for Prime, Choice, Select and Standard. Meat from older cattle qualify only for Commercial, Utility, Cutter or Canner grades. During the grading process, the USDA grader determines maturity (age of the animal) on the basis of skeletal characteristics and the color and texture of the ribeye muscle. The bones of young animals are soft, porous and red. As the animal gets older, bones and cartilage ossify, that is, they grow harder and turn white. The degree of ossification is best observed in the cartilage buttons on the ends (tips) of the vertebrae.

Color and texture of the lean are other indicators of maturity. Young cattle have lean that is bright red and finely textured. The color of beef becomes progressively darker and the texture coarser as the animal matures (see Chapter 1).

USDA Grade Standards are continually evaluated and periodically updated. Any time new or revised regulations for grading are considered they are published in the Federal Register and in the public press. Consumers and industry personnel are given an opportunity to comment on them before new regulations are implemented.

Figure 5-5
Relationship Between Marbling, Maturity, and Carcass Quality Grade[1]

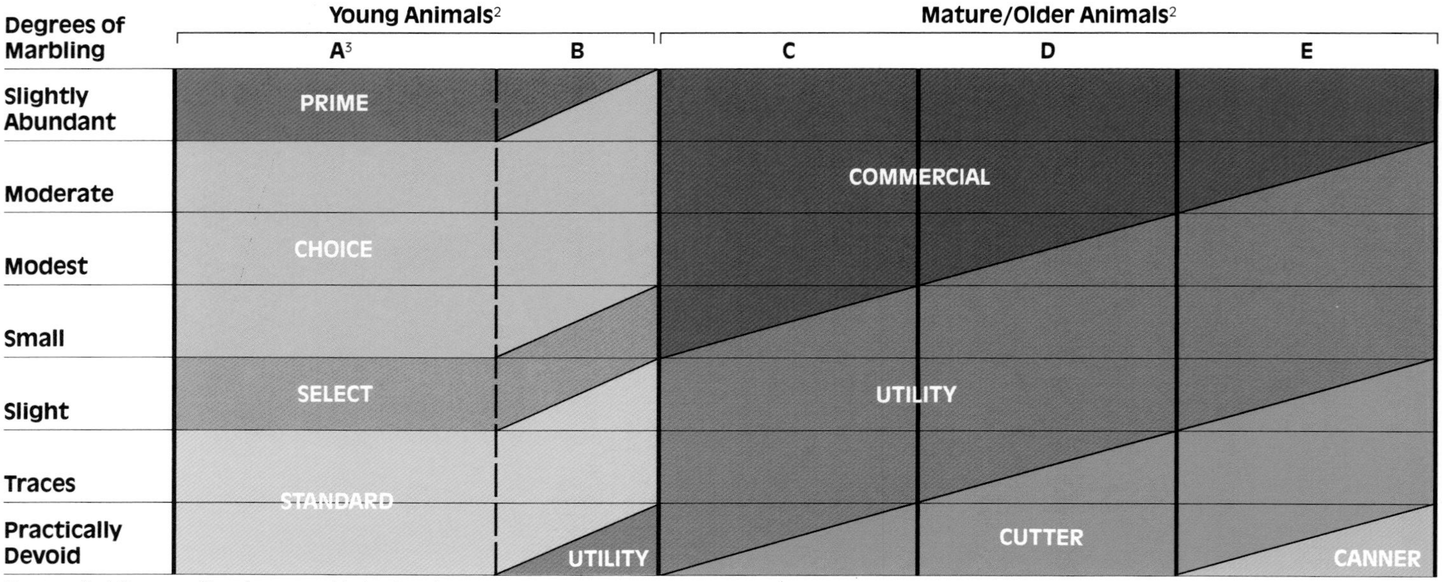

Degrees of Marbling	Young Animals[2]		Mature/Older Animals[2]		
	A[3]	B	C	D	E
Slightly Abundant	PRIME		COMMERCIAL		
Moderate	CHOICE				
Modest					
Small					
Slight	SELECT		UTILITY		
Traces	STANDARD				
Practically Devoid		UTILITY		CUTTER	CANNER

[1]Assumes that firmness of lean is comparably developed with the degrees of marbling and that the carcass is not a "dark cutter."
[2]Maturity increases from left to right (A through E)
[3]The A maturity portion of the figure is the only portion applicable to bullock carcasses.

The way in which marbling and maturity relate to the quality grades (Prime, Choice, etc.) is shown in Figure 5-5. The principles of beef quality grading are (1) palatability is determined by the relative youthfulness and relative deposition of intramuscular fat in the carcass from which the cut of meat was obtained, and (2) as maturity increases, additional intramuscular fat is required to maintain the desired level of palatability within a specific grade.

This two-part figure (Figure 5-5) is divided according to two categories of animals by age at slaughter. The first category, shown in the left section of the figure, includes only carcasses from young animals (Groups A and B). The right section of the figure includes only more mature/older animals (Groups C, D and E). Beef which comes from animals in both categories (young and mature/older), can display the full range of marbling degrees: "Slightly Abundant" to "Practically Devoid."

However, as can be seen from the figure, beef with "Slightly Abundant" marbling can only be graded as Prime if it is from very young or young (A or B) animals. Even if it has the same amount of marbling ("Slightly Abundant"), beef from older animals (C, D or E) can only be graded Commercial.

By the same token, within the young category, beef from A maturity animals will qualify for the Prime grade with "Slightly Abundant" marbling. However, beef from slightly older animals (B maturity) will only qualify for the grade of Prime if it has a higher degree of "Slightly Abundant" marbling.

—Texture—Smooth, finely textured muscle is more tender and is of a higher quality than coarser meat. The texture relates directly to the size of the muscle fiber bundles and amounts of connective tissue. In a young animal, these bundles are small but they become progressively larger as the animal grows. Generally, the older the animal, the coarser the muscle, and the lower the grade, the less tender the meat.

—Appearance—Characteristics that enhance the way meat looks to a potential buyer influence the grading of beef. Consumers want meat with color typical of the species: beef, bright, cherry-red; veal, light pink; pork, grayish-pink; lamb, pinkish-red. The exposed muscle should be firm rather than soft. In general, consumers object to dark-colored meat but not to pale-colored meat.

Figure 5-6
Yield Grade Stamp

■ **Yield Grading**—Yield Grades are useful at the wholesale level. They help identify which carcasses or cuts will provide the greatest yield of edible meat per pound. The lower the yield grade number (e.g., Yield Grade 1), the smaller the cutting losses. Yield grades are of little use to the average consumer unless they purchase sides of beef or primal cuts which have not been trimmed.

However, yield grades indirectly affect all consumer beef purchases, since cutting losses are important in determining retail price.

Yield grades identify differences in carcass cutability. "Cutability" is defined as the amount of saleable meat obtained from the carcass as boneless or semi-boneless trimmed retail cuts from the round, loin, rib and chuck. There are five Yield Grades, numbered one through five. Carcasses in the best category, Yield Grade 1, have the most saleable meat while Yield Grade 5 carcasses have the least.

Yield grades are not related to quality grades; they are based upon amount of external (subcutaneous) fat, amount of internal (kidney, pelvic and heart) fat, size of the ribeye area (REA) and carcass weight.

—Fatness (subcutaneous fat, and fat from the kidney, pelvic and heart areas)—The total amount of fat that must be trimmed from the carcass in preparing retail cuts has the greatest influence on the yield grades. A high yield grade number (4 or 5) indicates more trimmable fat and less lean meat available for sale and consumption.

—Ribeye Area (REA)—Measured at the 12th rib, REA (cross-sectional surface area in *longissimus* muscle) is considered an indication of overall muscularity. The greater the ratio of muscle to fat and bone, the lower the yield grade number, and the greater the percentage of carcass is saleable meat.

—Carcass Weight—After a certain point in development of physiological maturity, as an animal grows, the added weight is largely fat. In general, as carcass weight increases within the U.S. cattle population, the percentage of retail cuts from the carcass decreases.

Table 5-2
Percent Usable Beef

USDA Yield Grades				
1	2	3	4	5
74%	71%	68%	64%	61%

*These percentages vary depending on the spread within each yield grade and differences in the way the carcass is cut, trimmed and deboned.
Source: AMI Meat Facts

Veal and Calf Grading—The differentiation between "veal" vs. "calf" carcasses is made on the basis of the color of the lean. However, the conformation (the general shape of the carcass) and the character of the bones and fat are also considered. Typically, veal is the meat from calves up to four months of age. Veal lean color ranges from a very light pink to a darker pink. Meat that is dark grayish-pink to moderately red is designated as calf. The lighter colors generally come from the "youngest" veal and those that have been either milk-fed or formula-fed. The Quality Grades for veal and calf are established through an evaluation of the conformation of the carcass, and the quality of the lean. Quality of veal lean is determined not by marbling, as in beef, but instead, by the amount of feathering (fat intermingled within the lean between the ribs) and the amount of fat streaking within the flank muscles.

Pork Grading—The basis for grading pork is the cutability of the carcass and the quality of the meat. To qualify for any of the top grades (U.S. No. 1 through 4), pork carcasses must possess acceptable lean quality. The highest carcass yield of trimmed lean cuts is expected from carcasses of the U.S. No. 1 grade, and the lowest cutability is expected from carcasses of U.S. No. 4. In addition, a manufacturing grade of Utility is used for certain low-quality, unacceptable carcasses (assigned irrespective of expected cutability, if color/firmness are unacceptable).

In recent years, as a result of consumer demand for high-quality, lean meat, pork producers have improved the lean-to-fat ratio in U.S. hogs. In 1985, the grading standards were revised to account for the leaner type of hog being produced today.

Lamb Grading—The single most influential characteristic in evaluating the quality grade of lamb and mutton carcasses is maturity. Differentiation among the three maturity classes—lamb, yearling mutton and mutton—is based on the differences which occur in the development of muscular and skeletal systems.

There are separate grade standards for each maturity class for use in determining the grade of a carcass. Evaluations are made of: (1) Yield Grade, the percentage of trimmed, boneless, major retail cuts derived from a carcass, and (2) Quality Grade, the expected palatability of the lean and carcass conformation. Yield grading, based on relative carcass fatness and muscling, is not mandatory when lamb carcasses are quality graded, and is not commonly used.

Evaluation of the quality in lamb carcasses is based on fat streaking in the flank area, and color. Fat streaking comparable to "slight" or "traces" in beef marbling is adequate for satisfactory palatability in lamb. Fat streaking in the flank and flank firmness are evaluated because increased fat deposition and improved firmness are associated with higher quality (higher expected palatability). Lean color ranges from bright pink in lamb to dark red in mutton.

BUYING DECISIONS

An abundant variety of meat awaits consumer selection in the U.S. food market. Meat is available in many forms — fresh, cured, cured and smoked, frozen, freeze-dried, canned and ready-to-serve.

To make a wise meat purchase, a number of factors must be considered, such as: taste and nutritional needs; time and skills necessary to prepare the product; appropriateness of the cut for the recipe; and the food budget.

Personal Preferences and Nutritional Needs

Personal preferences are influenced by cultural background, flavor desires, previous exposure to a variety of foods and preparation methods, and family food customs and traditions. In addition to personal preferences, individuals have different nutritional needs based on their age and other factors.

Time Constraints

Preparation time may be limited, especially during the work week. When less-tender cuts are chosen, cooking to a tender, flavorful endpoint may require slow cooking. On the other hand, many small tender cuts and processed meat can go from the refrigerator to the table in twenty minutes or less.

Cooking Methods

Most meat can be prepared simply by broiling, pan frying, roasting, braising or cooking in liquid as described in Chapter 7. Some meat cooking techniques require special equipment such as rotisseries, crock-pots or woks, but a set of basic cooking equipment (pot, frying pan, roasting pan, broiling pan) is all that is needed to prepare most meat recipes.

Recipe Requirements

Recipes frequently call for a specific cut of meat. Cooks without extensive cooking experience may be reluctant to make substitutions. However, when the need arises, the person behind the meat counter is often able to suggest an acceptable alternative cut of meat.

Amount Needed

Since bone and fat content differ from cut to cut, the decision of how much to buy lies in the number of servings-per-pound the cut will yield. In Table 5-3, a serving is defined as three ounces (85 grams) of cooked lean meat. The servings-per-pound figures are only a guide and can be greatly influenced by differences in the amount of outside fat on the cut, as purchased; the extent of bone removal; and how great the cooking losses will be based on the time and temperature at which the meat is cooked. Because some people are likely to eat more than a standard three-ounce portion, it is wise to purchase more than the equivalent of three ounces of cooked lean meat per person.

Food Budget

Consumers who must purchase groceries on a budget will find that the cost of meat per serving is the best way to compare the price of one package of meat with another. Cost-per-serving is based on the amount of edible meat in the package and the price per pound written on the package label. To determine the cost-per-serving, divide the price-per-pound by the number of servings per pound (Table 5-3).

Lean boneless meat and processed meat which has little waste will yield from three to five servings per pound. However, meat with considerable bone and/or fat (and therefore, waste), such as pork spareribs or beef short ribs, yields only one to two servings per pound. Although the total price on the package may be lower for these cuts, they actually may be more costly when the price per portion of edible lean meat is determined.

Table 5-3
Servings per Pound

The servings per pound listed in this table are based on an average serving of 3 ounces of cooked, trimmed meat. However, it should be noted that the yield of cooked lean meat can vary depending upon the method of cooking, the degree of doneness, the size of the bone in bone-in cuts and the amount of fat that remains after trimming.

Beef

Steaks

Bnls Chuck Shoulder	3½
Chuck (Arm or Blade)	2½
Cubed	4
Flank	4
Porterhouse	2½
Rib	2
Ribeye	3
Round, Full Cut	3
Sirloin	3
T-Bone	2
Tenderloin (Filet Mignon)	3
Top Loin, bnls	3
Top Round	4

Roasts

Eye of Round	4
Rib	2
Ribeye	3
Rump, bnls	3
Tip	4

Pot Roasts

Chuck Arm	2
Chuck Blade	2½
Chuck, bnls	2½
Cross Rib, bi	2½

Other Cuts

Beef for Stew	4
Brisket	3
Ground Beef	4
Short Ribs (plate, chuck, rib)	1½–2½

Variety Meats

Brains	5
Heart	5
Kidney	4
Liver	4
Sweetbreads	5
Tongue	5

Veal

Chops, Steaks, Cutlets

Loin Chops	2
Rib Chops	2
Round Steak	3½
Shoulder Steaks	2½
Cutlets, bnls	4

Roasts

Leg	3
Shoulder, bnls	3
Rib	2

Other Cuts

Riblets	1½
Cubes	4
Bnls Breast (rolled)	3
Ground	4

Pork

Chops and Steaks

Blade Chops or Steaks	2½–3½
Chops, bnls	4
Loin Chops	2½
Rib Chops	2½
Smoked (Rib or Loin) Chops	2½
Smoked Ham (Center Slice)	3½

Roasts

Leg (Fresh Ham), bi	3
Leg (Fresh Ham), bnls	4
Smoked Ham, bi	3
Smoked Ham, bnls	4–5
Smoked Ham, Canned	4–5
Blade Shoulder (rolled) (Fresh or Smoked), bnls	3
Blade Loin	2
Top Loin, (tied), bnls (Smoked or Fresh)	3½
Center Loin	3
Smoked Center Loin	3
Arm Picnic Shoulder (Fresh or Smoked), bi	2
Sirloin, bi	2½
Smoked Shoulder Roll	3

Other Cuts

Back Ribs	1½
Bacon (Regular) Sliced	6
Country-Style Loin Ribs	2
Cubes	4
Hocks (Fresh or Smoked)	1½
Pork Sausage	4
Spareribs	1¼
Tenderloin (Whole)	4
Tenderloin (Filets)	4

Variety Meats

Brains	5
Heart	5
Kidney	5
Liver	4

Lamb

Chops and Steaks

Leg Center Slice	3
Loin Chops	2½
Rib Chops	2½
Shoulder Chops	2
Sirloin Chops	2

Roasts

Leg, bi	2½
Leg, bnls	4
Shoulder, bi	2
Shoulder, bnls	3

Other Cuts

Breast	2
Riblets	1¼
Cubes	4
Shanks	2
Ground	4

Variety Meats

Heart	5
Kidney	5

bi — bone-in
bnls — boneless

Quantity Buying

Bulk purchases can range from buying a large package of meat for several meals to buying a whole carcass. The amount of meat which can be stored per cubic foot of freezer space can vary from 35 to 45 pounds, depending on whether the meat is bone-in or boneless, and how it is wrapped. Consumers should consider available freezer space and keep only the amount of meat that can be consumed within recommended storage periods (Chapter 6). All meat must be overwrapped with freezer paper before being placed in the freezer.

One easy way to make a bulk purchase is to buy several packages of a retail cut when it is featured at a reduced price. Since prices change at the supermarket every week, it is easy to stock a freezer with a variety of cuts. Bulk meat sections or large trays of retail cuts (often referred to as family-pack trays) offer savings of five to 30 cents per pound. Prices are easy to compare, since the meat is sold as trimmed retail cuts.

Subprimals, primals, quarters, sides or whole carcasses can represent savings, but because they are priced before cutting and trimming, a direct comparison to retail prices is not easily made.

However, to estimate the comparable retail cost of a side of beef see Figure 5-7.

Figure 5-7
Calculating Price Per Pound

	Formula	Example	
Carcass Cost =	Carcass side wt. x price/lb Carcass side weight = 321 lbs Carcass price/lb = $1.00	OR 321 x $1.00	= $321.00
Processing Cost =	Carcass side wt. x processing price/lb Processing price/lb = $0.20	OR 321 x $0.20	= $64.20
Total Cost =	Carcass cost + Processing cost	OR $321.00 + $64.20	= $385.20
Est. Processed Wt. =	Carcass side wt. x Est. yield	OR 321 x .71*	= 228 lbs
Retail Price/Lb =	Total cost ÷ Est. processed wt.	OR $385.20 ÷ 228	= $1.69/lb**

*Estimated percent of usable beef in a Yield Grade 2 carcass from Table 5-2.
**Boneless, closely-trimmed product.

Subprimals, vacuum-packaged in plastic bags at the packing or processing plant, are often marketed as "beef-in-a-bag" and sold directly from the meat case (Chapter 3). Savings may be as high as 30 cents per pound for this product. Some stores will cut large pieces free of charge, while others reduce prices even further to compensate for the cutting and wrapping that will be done by the consumer.

Purchases of whole carcasses, sides of beef or pork, and quarters of beef provide a wide selection of meat cuts, but will result in real cost savings only if all the cuts are used. Buyers should be sure to specify how they want the meat to be cut (size of roasts, thickness of steaks, etc.), so that meat cuts and package sizes meet their individual needs.

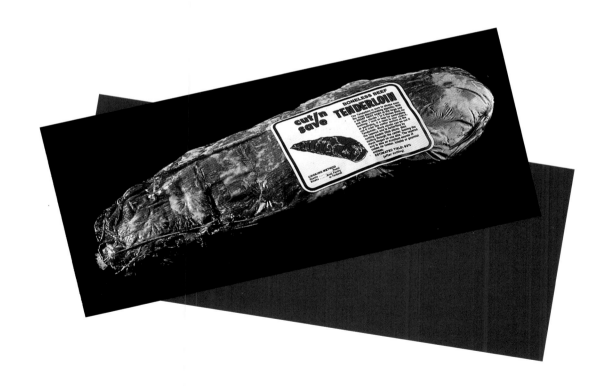

Proper storage is essential to maintain food safety and quality. Prior to the advent of modern food preservation methods, meat was preserved for future use by curing, drying and smoking, and by canning and winter freezing.

Current food preservation techniques provide practical, effective ways to store food with minimal loss of palatability, appearance and nutritive value, while at the same time retarding the growth of microorganisms.

THE GROWTH OF MICROORGANISMS

When food spoils, the color, odor and texture of the meat deteriorate, thus reducing its acceptability and providing a warning for the consumer. However, when a food has been contaminated, it is invaded with microorganisms which can cause food poisoning and infections in humans. There are usually no signs such as off-odor or color. Therefore, it is essential that such contamination be prevented.

Several types of microorganisms can grow on meat. They are fungi (which include yeasts and molds), bacteria and viruses. Parasites may also grow in animal tissue. Bacteria are clearly the most predominant and important to meat quality. Molds and yeasts are of minor importance in meat. Viruses are a potential cause of food-borne disease, but meat other than raw and undercooked shellfish has not been implicated in infections/poisonings. A few parasites are also potential problems in meat. For any of these microorganisms to thrive, there must be conditions which are conducive to growth, such as specific levels of moisture, temperature and oxygen, exposed surface area and acidity or alkalinity.

Moisture

Moisture must be present for microorganisms to multiply. Molds grow in drier environments (as low as 13 percent water content), while bacteria require at least 18 percent moisture to grow. There is enough water in most fresh meat to satisfy requirements for both molds and bacteria (Chapter 1).

The moisture level in meat is affected by air flow, humidity and temperature of the storage area. Air flow increases evaporative losses in unwrapped meat. The relative humidity of the storage area determines the amount of moisture drawn to the surfaces. When relative humidity is high, condensation occurs. If the relative humidity is low, moisture evaporates and meat surfaces stay relatively dry, inhibiting microbial growth. When the correct combination of humidity and temperature levels is employed, the surfaces remain dry enough to retard spoilage, yet moist enough to prevent shrinkage and discoloration from dehydration.

Temperature

Microorganisms that grow well at temperatures of 32°F to 68°F are known as psychrotrophs. These include bacteria and some yeasts and molds. However, most bacteria are mesophiles, which thrive at temperatures of 60°F to 104°F. A few grow at higher temperatures (104°F to 150°F) and are referred to as thermophiles. Most bacteria that can cause food poisoning cannot grow at low refrigerator temperatures. Temperatures below 40°F prevent nearly all bacterial growth. As the temperature approaches 32°F, few microorganisms grow and reproduction is greatly retarded. It is for this reason that refrigeration and freezing prolong shelf life.

Temperature is a critical factor during meat handling and storage. Meat cannot be held at temperatures higher than 40°F without compromising quality and appearance. A good rule of thumb to remember is that "life begins at 40°F" for most microorganisms.

Oxygen

Some microorganisms (aerobic) must have free oxygen to grow, others (anaerobic) grow only in its absence and some (facultative) will grow with or without oxygen. All molds and most yeasts that grow in meat are aerobic.

Aerobic conditions are present primarily on the surface of meat; thus, organisms that need free oxygen are found on the exterior, while the internal growth of microorganisms is largely anaerobic in nature. Facultative organisms exist mainly on the surface and possibly within meat tissue (usually inside chunks or blocks of ground meat but never inside intact muscle). Vacuum packaging extends shelf life by reducing the exposure of the meat to oxygen, thereby inhibiting aerobic microbial growth. Conversely, vacuum packaging creates an oxygen free environment, which allows the anaerobes to grow.

Exposed Surface Area

The interior portions of muscles are generally free of microorganisms, except in the regions of lymph nodes. Meat surfaces, however, are susceptible to exterior contamination and spoilage. Greater surface area increases the potential for microbial growth. A whole beef roast, because of its large size relative to its weight, has a minimal amount of exposed surface area, compared to the same weight of ground beef, which has much more exposed surface around each of many particles. Because of the increased potential for ground beef to become contaminated, greater care is required during handling and storage to minimize bacterial load.

Degree of Acidity or Alkalinity

For most bacteria the optimal pH (acidity) for growth is near neutral (pH 7), with minimum and maximum values of about 5.0 and 8.0. However, some bacteria will grow up to pH 11.0 and some below pH 3.0. Generally, fresh meat has a pH of between 5.3 and 6.5, which is within the range favorable for the growth of many microorganisms.

Substances which increase the acidity (pH below 7), such as vinegar or citric acid, are used in food preservation and extend the shelf life of some processed meat. Some bacteria are beneficial. For instance, in the production of fermented sausage, *lactobacillus* bacterial cultures are added to promote lactic acid production. Increased lactic acid results in a reduced pH; this creates a controlled fermentation process. Summer sausage is an example of a product that is manufactured using this process.

Food poisoning is an illness caused by the consumption of foods containing toxins produced by bacteria. Toxin-producing bacteria that can grow in meat include *Clostridium botulinum*, *Staphylococcus aureus*, and *Clostridium perfringens*. Infections occur from eating meat or other protein foods that contain organisms which multiply in the intestinal tract (*Salmonella* and *Listeria monocytogenes*) or from parasites (*Trichinella spiralis*). Proper food preservation, preparation and storage techniques minimize the possibility of food poisoning and food infection.

FOOD POISONING AND INFECTIONS

The major difference between food poisoning and food infection relates to whether the illness is caused by a toxin from bacteria or by the bacteria (or a parasite) itself. The characteristics of some common food poisonings and infections are summarized in Table 6-1.

Food Poisoning

Clostridium botulinum—Botulism, the most serious form of food poisoning, is caused by various strains of *Clostridium botulinum*, which produce toxins that attack the human central nervous system. Symptoms begin to be noticeable about 12 to 48 hours after consumption of contaminated food, for example, muscular weakness and loss of those functions which are dependent on nerve action. About two-thirds of the cases are fatal. Botulism is most often associated with improper canning of low-acid (high-pH) fruits and vegetables. *Clostridium botulinum* is an anaerobic bacteria and can grow in canned and vacuum-packed foods including meat; however, because the distribution of spores in meat is usually very low, botulism from meat sources is rare. Special care should be taken in preparing all home-canned foods, including meat.

Cans of food that show evidence of swelling or seepage should be destroyed. Processed, pre-cooked frozen, or frozen uncooked meat should not be allowed to stand at room temperature for extended periods of time. Cooking for 10 minutes at 176°F inactivates potentially harmful toxins; however, longer cooking times at higher temperatures are necessary to completely destroy botulism spores. Nitrite is added to processed meat to inhibit the reproduction of *Clostridium botulinum* spores. Information on the use of nitrite is found in Chapter 4.

Staphylococcus aureus—Staphylococcal food poisoning is serious but rarely fatal. It is caused by the heat-stable toxin produced by the bacteria *Staphylococcus aureus*, which can contaminate high-protein foods such as meat, eggs, milk and custards. The flavor, appearance and aroma of contaminated food may not be noticeably affected. The bacteria can be easily transferred from humans to meat during handling. However, the most common way *Staphylococcus aureus* toxins are produced is when cooked meat is handled and then left at room temperature for an extended period of time (over two hours). Once formed, the toxin produced by this bacteria cannot be destroyed by reheating the meat. Two to six hours after eating contaminated food, an infected individual experiences nausea, vomiting and abdominal pains. The illness usually lasts one to three days.

Clostridium perfringens—*Clostridium perfringens* may be found in fresh meat and meat-based sauces or gravies, especially if they are allowed to cool slowly after cooking. Symptoms are nausea, occasional vomiting, diarrhea and abdominal pain eight to 24 hours after eating. *Clostridium perfringens* food poisoning can be controlled by careful sanitation practices, and the rapid cooling and refrigeration of cooked foods.

Infections

Salmonella species—Salmonellosis is the most common food-borne infection in the United States. It results from eating food containing living organisms of the genus, *Salmonella*. *Salmonella* grow rapidly in contaminated protein foods, especially if they are held at room temperature or kept warm for several hours.

Symptoms of salmonellosis (nausea, vomiting, diarrhea, fever and abdominal pains) are thought to be caused by the toxin produced in the digestive tract of infected individuals. The number of organisms ingested must be high (about one million) for clinical symptoms to occur. Several days may pass between the ingestion of a contaminated food and the presence of symptoms; however, the normal incubation time is 12 to 24 hours.

Food handlers and meat-processing equipment must be scrupulously cleaned to avoid contamination. Salmonellosis can occur in the home if a cutting board and knives are not kept clean, or if the same plate is used for preparing both raw and cooked products without washing the plate between uses, or if cracked eggs are used. Heating food at temperatures and times equivalent to those used to pasteurize milk (161°F for 15 seconds or 143°F for 30 minutes) will destroy most of over 1200 species of *Salmonella*.

Cutting boards must be scrupulously cleaned after preparing raw meat products. Plastic and hard rubber cutting boards can be easily cleaned and sanitized.

Listeria monocytogenes—*Listeria monocytogenes* is a widely distributed pathogen which can be transmitted to humans through contamination of foodstuffs at any point in the food chain. Several major food commodities are implicated: milk and dairy products, meat (especially raw meat products), poultry and its products, vegetables, salads and seafoods. Unlike most other food-borne pathogens, *Listeria monocytogenes* is able to multiply at refrigeration temperatures, 40°F to 43°F. Furthermore, *Listeria monocytogenes* is about four times more heat-tolerant than *Salmonella* and it flourishes in wet conditions.

Data available at present suggest that food-borne listeriosis has a relatively low incidence, but is significant for its relatively high fatality rate. Several groups in the human population have been identified as at risk: pregnant women and their unborn children, patients receiving treatment which alters their natural immune system, alcoholics, drug abusers, diabetics, AIDS patients and the elderly. However, there have been cases of listeriosis reported in otherwise healthy individuals.

Proper heat treatment and refrigeration can reduce the number of *Listeria monocytogenes* organisms but recontamination can occur during further manipulation of the products, particularly with those foods which are not aseptically packaged immediately after the listericidal treatment. The risk of recontamination can be reduced by adherence to good hygiene practices in food manufacturing establishments, retail establishments and the home.

Trichinella spiralis—A lingering nemesis associated with pork consumption is the remote possibility of contracting an infection known as trichinosis, caused by eating undercooked pork that contains the microscopic parasite *Trichinella spiralis*. Today trichinosis is virtually nonexistent in this country because of widespread use of sanitary production conditions. Animals can acquire the parasite by feeding on uncooked garbage but federal legislation now requires that all garbage be cooked before feeding to hogs. In June 1985, the FDA established the use of low-level irradiation of pork to destroy trichinae. This was followed by USDA approval in January 1986. However, irradiated pork is not readily available. Other trichina-control measures established by USDA/FSIS include cooking pork to an internal temperature of 137°F (see Chapter 4), freezing at 5°F for at least 20 days and salting. Pork is most palatable if cooked to a final internal temperature of 160°F to 170°F.

Table 6-1
Characteristics of Some Common Food Poisonings and Infections

Illness:	**Botulism** (food poisoning)
Causative Agent:	Toxins produced by *Clostridium botulinum*
Symptoms:	Impaired swallowing, speaking, respiration, coordination. Dizziness and double vision.
Typical Time from Ingestion to Onset of Symptoms:	12 to 48 hours
Foods Usually Involved:	Canned low-acid foods including canned meat and seafood, smoked and processed fish.
Preventive Measures:	Proper canning, smoking, and processing procedures, including the use of nitrites. Cooking to destroy toxins, proper refrigeration and sanitation.
Illness:	**Staphylococcal** (food poisoning)
Causative Agent:	Enterotoxin produced by *Staphylococcus aureus*
Symptoms:	Nausea, vomiting, abdominal pain due to gastroenteritis (inflammation of the lining of the stomach and intestines).
Typical Time from Ingestion to Onset of Symptoms:	2 to 6 hours
Foods Usually Involved:	Custard and cream-filled pastries, potato salad, dairy products, cooked ham, tongue, and poultry.
Preventive Measures:	Pasteurization of susceptible foods, proper refrigeration and sanitation.
Illness:	***Clostridium perfringens*** (food poisoning)
Causative Agent:	Toxin produced by *Clostridium perfringens*
Symptoms:	Nausea, occasional vomiting, diarrhea and abdominal pain.
Typical Time from Ingestion to Onset of Symptoms:	8 to 24 hours
Foods Usually Involved:	Cooked meat, poultry and fish held at non-refrigerated temperatures for long periods of time.
Preventive Measures:	Prompt refrigeration of unconsumed, cooked meat, gravy, poultry or fish; maintenance of proper refrigeration and sanitation.
Illness:	**Salmonellosis** (food infection)
Causative Agent:	Infection produced by ingestion of any of over 1200 species of *Salmonella* that can grow in the gastrointestinal tract of the consumer
Symptoms:	Nausea, vomiting, diarrhea, fever, abdominal pain; may be preceded by chills and headache.
Typical Time from Ingestion to Onset of Symptoms:	12 to 24 hours
Foods Usually Involved:	Insufficiently cooked or warmed-over meat, poultry, eggs and dairy products; these products are especially susceptible when kept unrefrigerated for a long time.
Preventive Measures:	Cleanliness and sanitation of handlers and equipment, pasteurization, proper refrigeration and packaging.
Illness:	**Listeriosis** (food infection)
Causative Agent:	Produced by *Listeria monocytogenes*
Symptoms:	Fever, headache, nausea, vomiting, monocytosis, meningitis, septicemia, miscarriage, localized external or internal lesions, pharyngitis.
Typical Time from Ingestion to Onset of Symptoms:	Unknown, probably 4 days to 3 weeks
Foods Usually Involved:	Milk, milk products, eggs, meat and poultry.
Preventive Measures:	Use of good hygiene practices.
Illness:	**Trichinosis** (food infection)
Causative Agent:	*Trichinella spiralis* (a nematode worm) found in pork
Symptoms:	Nausea, vomiting, diarrhea, profuse sweating, fever and muscle soreness.
Typical Time from Ingestion to Onset of Symptoms:	2 to 28 days
Foods Usually Involved:	Insufficiently cooked pork and products containing pork.
Preventive Measures:	Thorough cooking of pork (to an internal temperature of 137°F or higher); freezing and storage of uncooked pork at 9°F or lower, for a minimum of 20 days; avoidance of feeding hogs raw garbage.

Source: Modified from *Principles of Meat Science.*

PREVENTION OF CONTAMINATION BY MICROORGANISMS

To prevent food poisoning or infection from occurring in meat, it should be kept clean, covered and cold. Proper wrapping assures that the meat will be clean and covered until it is cooked. Refrigeration and freezing assure that the meat will be at a cold enough temperature.

Protective Wraps for Meat

Materials designed for wrapping meat have specific functional qualities, including low moisture/vapor transmission rates, heat shrinkability, stretch, pliability, strength and the ability to retain their protective characteristics over a wide range of temperatures and conditions.

Films for fresh meat packaging are designed to allow a small amount of oxygen to pass through the film, thus maintaining the oxymyoglobin that gives meat its fresh red color (for an explanation of this refer to Chapter 1). Meat cuts wrapped in plastic film at the market can be safely stored in the home refrigerator, provided they are used within a few days. Although film-wrapped packages can be frozen as purchased for up to a week or two, the light plastic film is not designed to protect against surface dehydration, commonly known as "freezer burn." Rewrapping or overwrapping meat in a material designed for use in the freezer is a must prior to freezing it.

Some transparent wraps and food storage bags are specifically designed to be impervious to oxygen, thus making them suitable for freezer storage of meat. The package label indicates those that can be used for freezing. Any time protective wraps or bags are used, as much air as possible should be removed before sealing.

Freezer paper, commonly sold in supermarkets, is coated on one side with plastic or wax. Freezer paper is suitable for freezer storage because it creates a moisture and vapor-proof barrier. The waxed or plastic-coated side should go against the surface of the meat, and the outside of the package can be marked with the name of the meat cut, number of portions, weight and/or freezer date. Freezer tape should be used to fasten and close the package. Package tears are a potential problem with bone-in cuts. Sharp bone edges should be covered with interleafing paper or small pieces of freezer paper prior to overwrapping. A double layer of interleafing paper should be used between cuts when more than one cut is wrapped to facilitate separating the frozen or partially frozen cuts for cooking. The brown and white papers often used to wrap meat at service counters are not coated with plastic or wax, and are not designed to protect frozen foods. Therefore, meat purchased in such paper wraps should be rewrapped before freezing.

Foil can tear easily, but provides an excellent moisture and vapor-proof barrier if properly used. It is especially well suited to odd-shaped products. Foil-wrapped meat should be identified and dated on freezer tape attached around the package so that it can be used within the appropriate storage time.

Figure 6-1
Wrapping of Meat for the Freezer
(Apothecary or Drugstore Method)

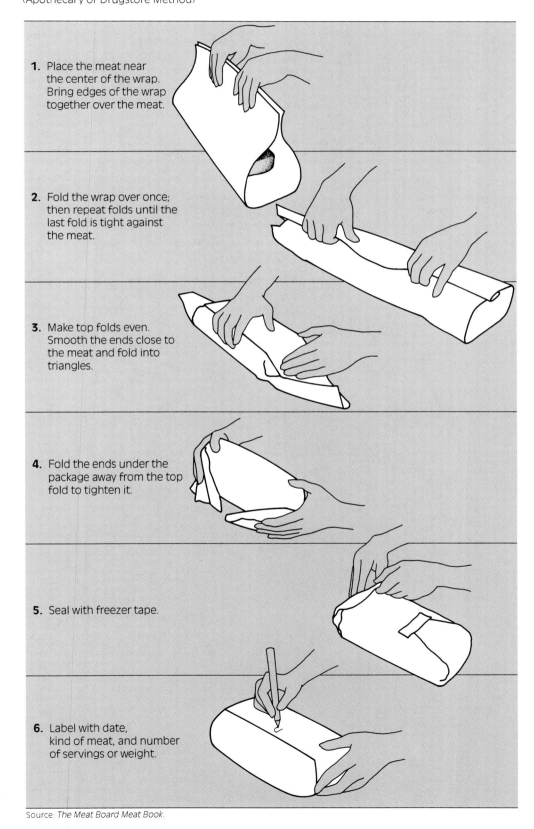

1. Place the meat near the center of the wrap. Bring edges of the wrap together over the meat.

2. Fold the wrap over once; then repeat folds until the last fold is tight against the meat.

3. Make top folds even. Smooth the ends close to the meat and fold into triangles.

4. Fold the ends under the package away from the top fold to tighten it.

5. Seal with freezer tape.

6. Label with date, kind of meat, and number of servings or weight.

Source: *The Meat Board Meat Book.*

Refrigeration

The ideal temperature for the storage of fresh meat is 28°F to 32°F. However, since home refrigerators are designed to hold a wide variety of perishable foods, temperatures of 36°F to 40°F or higher are more common. Meat should be stored in the coldest part of the refrigerator. Thermometers for both freezer and refrigerator are necessary to monitor storage temperatures. As storage temperatures approach 40°F (still considered safe for fresh meat storage), perishability increases. Rapid growth of food poisoning organisms begins at about 50°F. Meat in-transit from the place of purchase, or left to thaw at room temperature, invites the growth of spoilage organisms.

If meat is not going to be used within a few days after purchase, it should be frozen as soon as possible to preserve optimal quality.

Cured and smoked meat, including luncheon meat and canned hams, is less perishable than fresh meat. These meat products should be refrigerated in their original packaging. The general rule is that, if a product is purchased from a refrigerated section of the store, it should be refrigerated in home storage as well. In any event, follow the label instructions. Canned products such as soups or stews may remain on the pantry shelf until opened, but once the thermal seal has been broken, the can's contents should be refrigerated. Thermal processing is discussed later in this chapter.

Leftover cooked meat should be left whole, wrapped securely and stored in the coldest part of the refrigerator. Leaving the meat whole prevents dryness and inhibits bacterial growth due to recontamination. Meat cooked in liquid may be stored in the cooking liquid and then reheated in the liquid. If use is not anticipated within four to five days, liquid should be discarded and the meat immediately wrapped and frozen.

Table 6-2
Refrigerator Storage Timetable
Recommended Storage Time for Maximum Quality

Meat		Refrigerator (36°F to 40°F)
Fresh	Beef cuts	3 to 4 days
	Veal cuts	1 to 2 days
	Pork cuts	2 to 3 days
	Lamb cuts	3 to 5 days
	Ground beef, veal, pork, lamb	1 to 2 days
	Variety meats	1 to 2 days
	Leftover cooked meat	3 to 4 days
Processed	Luncheon meat*	3 to 5 days
	Sausage, fresh pork*	2 to 3 days
	Sausage, smoked	1 week
	Sausage, dry and semi-dry (unsliced)	2 to 3 weeks
	Frankfurters*	3 to 5 days
	Bacon*	1 week
	Smoked ham, whole	1 week
	Ham slices*	3 to 4 days

*If vacuum packaged, check manufacturer's date.

Freezing

Freezing is the most common method of meat preservation. Trimming excess fat and removing bones, if possible, will conserve freezer space. Meat should not be salted prior to freezing. Salting draws out moisture and oxidizes meat fat, giving it a rancid flavor and reducing the time meat can be left in the freezer.

Freezer Burn

Freezer burn is caused by loss of moisture (dehydration by sublimation) on the surface of a food. The two most common causes of surface dehydration are partial defrosting and refreezing of a frozen product and/or wrapping in such a way that air comes into contact with the surface of a food. When meat is wrapped, if all or most of the air between the surface of the meat and the wrapping materials is not removed, or, if the package is not tightly sealed, freezer burn will occur on the surface due to dehydration. Meat which has freezer burn will have a dry, discolored surface and, when cooked, it will be tough and taste bland or rancid.

Animal fats, like other lipids, are subject to deterioration over time. They are especially prone to develop oxidative rancidity which results in objectionable flavors and odors. The more unsaturated fatty acids there are in the fat, the greater is its susceptibility to oxidation and rancidity. This is why pork, which has more unsaturated fatty acids (monounsaturated and polyunsaturated) than other meats, is more perishable than beef and lamb. This fact provides the basis for limiting storage of properly wrapped pork in the freezer to six months, whereas beef and lamb may be stored in the freezer for up to 12 months (if properly wrapped). In the case of processed animal fats, rancidity is eliminated, or at least delayed, by incorporation of antioxidants, such as vitamin C, or by hydrogenation of the fat (a practice used in the production of shortening).

When meat products are reduced in size, as by grinding, the increased surface area will necessitate a shorter storage time. For this reason, ground meat and sausages cannot be left in the freezer as long as steaks and roasts. Also, salt and air that are incorporated during processing and slicing of cured and smoked meat accelerates rancidity in these products.

Table 6-3
Freezer Storage Timetable
Recommended Storage Time for Maximum Quality

Meat in Freezer Wrapping		Freezer (0°F or Colder)
Fresh	Beef cuts	6 to 12 months
	Veal and lamb cuts	6 to 9 months
	Pork cuts	6 months
	Ground beef, veal and lamb	3 to 4 months
	Ground pork	1 to 3 months
	Variety meats	3 to 4 months
	Leftover cooked meat	2 to 3 months
Processed	Luncheon meat	1 to 2 months
	Sausage	1 to 2 months
	Frankfurters	1 to 2 months
	Bacon	1 month
	Smoked ham	1 to 2 months
Frozen Combination Foods, Packaged	Meat pies	2 to 3 months
	Stews	3 to 4 months
	Prepared dinners	2 to 3 months

Freezing Methods—The faster a product is frozen, the longer its quality is maintained. A fast freeze will result in the formation of relatively small ice crystals. Large ice crystals, caused by slow freezing rates, can puncture the outer cell membranes, which will increase moisture loss when meat is thawed.

The rate of freezing is influenced by four factors:
1. Freezer temperature (colder temperatures promote faster freezing).
2. Air movement (air circulation enhances rate of freezing).
3. Temperature of meat product when placed in freezer (prechilling product reduces freezing time).
4. Size of cut (smaller cuts freeze faster).

Home freezer units provide relatively slow air movement, with temperatures ranging from about 15°F to −20°F. Therefore, they should be used for freezing only small quantities of meat.

Defrosting Frozen Meat—Meat should not be defrosted on a countertop at room temperature because the outside portion of the meat becomes warm, allowing microbes to begin to grow while the center portion of the meat is still frozen. The safest way to thaw meat is to remove it from the freezer and place it in the refrigerator. It should be put on a plate or pan to collect any juices that may leak from the package. Defrosting time is four to seven hours per pound for a large roast, three to five hours per pound for a small roast and 12 to 14 hours for a one-inch thick steak. For ground beef, gauge defrosting time by package thickness. Meat placed in a refrigerator to defrost will keep for a few days, but it should be used as soon as possible after it has thawed.

For faster thawing, frozen meat may be placed in a watertight plastic bag in cold water. The water should be changed often to keep it cold. The cold water accelerates thawing while inhibiting growth of microorganisms in the thawed portions. Meat may also be thawed in a microwave oven, following the oven manufacturer's instructions.

Once meat has been thawed, there is nothing wrong with refreezing it, providing that the temperature of the defrosted product has not risen above 40°F and the length of time does not exceed recommended storage times. Refreezing meat will not necessarily reduce palatability. However, meat that is unwrapped and thawed, then rewrapped and refrozen, may be slightly drier because of moisture loss. Meat is best thawed unopened, in its freezer packaging.

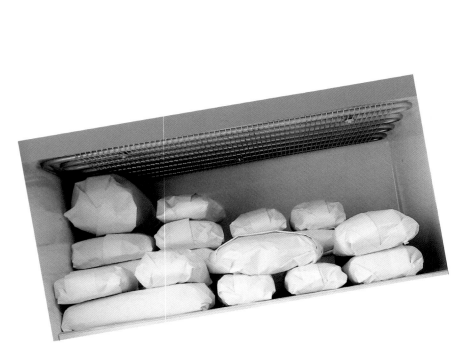

Table 6-4
Defrosting Timetable

Meat	In Refrigerator (36°F to 40°F)
Large roast	4 to 7 hrs/lb
Small roast	3 to 5 hrs/lb
1″ thick steak	12 to 14 hours

Other Methods of Preservation

Refrigeration and freezing only slow or stop growth of microorganisms but do not kill them.

Heat Processing—Heat processing will destroy microorganisms which cause spoilage or are potentially toxic. There are two types of heat treatment used to preserve meat, pasteurization and sterilization.

- **Pasteurization**—Meat is heated to 155°F to 167°F (internal temperature) to kill some of the microorganisms and to inactivate others. This process is used for most processed meat items. The shelf life is thus extended, but these products must still be stored in the refrigerator.

- **Sterilization**—Canned meat can be made shelf-stable by heating to 212°F, which kills all spoilage microorganisms. Sterilizing meat compromises its flavor and texture because protein denaturation takes place and connective tissues are broken down.

Freeze drying—Drying meat in the sun is one of the oldest methods of meat preservation. Electric drying ovens which provide a low constant heat are now available and can be used to make dried meat such as jerky. Freeze drying is a much faster process of achieving dehydration. Water is removed by transforming ice directly into vapor (without going through the liquid state). Dehydrated soup mixes often contain freeze-dried meat products. Backpackers, campers and mountain climbers can purchase a variety of shelf-stable, freeze-dried foods processed to reduce the weight and volume of their food supplies.

- **Irradiation**—Irradiation destroys microorganisms in and on meat without raising the temperature of the product. Controlled amounts of radiation can be applied to allow for unrefrigerated storage. This process is called cold sterilization. Smaller doses, called radiation pasteurization, extend refrigerator storage-life. With the exception of the use of the irradiation process to destroy *Trichinella spiralis* in pork, irradiation has not been approved by the FDA or the USDA for use with meat products. Irradiation is currently used for sterilizing spices and for preventing sprouting in potatoes, but not widely for other food preservation uses. In the future, it may be used to allow for reductions in the amount of additives used to preserve food. However, before this can occur public awareness of the safety of this process will have to be increased.

Heat changes the physical properties of meat and makes cooked meat more tender, flavorful and safe to eat. Different cooking methods are used to maximize the flavor and eating enjoyment of different cuts of meat.

TENDERNESS

When heat is applied to meat, two general changes occur: muscle fibers become tougher and connective tissue becomes more tender. During cooking, actin, myosin and other muscle-fiber proteins undergo changes. During heating, peptide chains composed of amino acids (the basic components of proteins) unfold (denaturation) and then reunite in a new form (coagulation); the end result of that process is shrinkage, moisture and fat loss, and toughening of the muscle fiber. The tenderizing effect of moist heat on connective tissue results from the conversion of collagen, a type of connective tissue (Chapter 1), to gelatin. The extent to which these changes occur in a piece of meat depends on time and temperature of cooking.

For muscles or cuts of meat with a considerable amount of collagen-containing connective tissue (e.g., the beef chuck), the toughening of the fibers is of less importance to tenderness than gelatinization of collagen. When heat is applied, the collagen is transformed into a water-soluble gel and the muscle softens. Maximum connective tissue softening is achieved using moist heat, a low temperature and a relatively long cooking period.

Cuts of meat such as rib or loin steaks, which contain small amounts of connective tissue, are most tender when cooked rapidly, with dry heat and at a higher temperature. These cuts are also more tender when cooked to rare rather than at the well done stage because toughening of muscle fibers is minimized.

Meat can be tenderized in the home with limited success by application of food acids. Most marinades contain some form of very weak, organic acid (lemon juice, tomatoes, wine, vinegar) which tenderizes the meat surfaces. Marinades penetrate only about ¼" into the interior of the meat, and thus contribute more to flavor than to tenderness.

Natural enzyme tenderizers are more effective in tenderizing than are acid marinades. Enzymes of vegetable origin that are used as tenderizers include papain, from the tropical papaya; bromelin, from pineapple; and ficin, from figs. These are available as powders or in seasoning compounds. Care must be taken to avoid over-tenderizing the meat (by using too much tenderizer or by allowing the meat to remain too long at the temperature optimal for enzyme activity). Individual steaks may be sprayed or dipped in an enzyme solution, but use on very thick cuts of meat such as roasts does little good because the enzymes only penetrate about ¼" into the meat surface.

Another method of tenderizing is to break or cut the muscle fibers and the connective tissues. This can be done by grinding, chopping, pounding or with the use of a special instrument which pierces the meat with multiple, thin needles (the terms, "needling," "blade tenderizing" and "Jaccarding" are used colloquially to describe this process). The holes made from the needles can be seen (on very close inspection) in the uncooked meat but are not visible after cooking. A version of the needle tenderizer is available for home use.

A steak macerator is used by retail stores and restaurants to make cubed steaks. Cubed steaks are made from cuts from less tender areas such as the chuck or bottom round. Sometimes steak trimmings and end pieces are formed together in a macerator to produce high-quality cubed steaks.

Aging

Within the first 10 days after slaughter, beef undergoes enzymatic changes which cause muscles to become more tender due to protein breakdown. The time between slaughter and the sale of beef to the consumer in a retail store may be as short as four days. Thus, not all beef ages long enough for optimum development of tenderness through the proteolytic action of natural enzymes. Additional tenderness and flavor development can be induced through controlled (natural) aging methods.

In natural aging, beef is held for two to four weeks at temperatures of 34°F to 38°F. Humidity is kept at about 70 percent to keep the exposed meat surfaces dry. Humidity at this level causes moisture evaporation, resulting in weight loss—a factor which increases the price-per-pound of aged beef. If a higher humidity level is used, evaporative losses are kept to a minimum, but there is greater weight loss from the trimming that must be done to remove surface spoilage. There is little or no moisture loss or spoilage when meat is aged in vacuum bags.

Pork and lamb are slaughtered at a young age, which results in inherently tender meat. Therefore, pork and lamb are usually not aged but are processed the day following slaughter. Also, pork fat is more unsaturated than beef or lamb fat and thus is more subject to development of rancid flavors unless promptly processed and packaged.

Aging requires strict control of temperature to control microbial growth, humidity and dehydration and are not recommended for consumers to use at home.

FLAVOR AND AROMA

Meat develops its desirable flavor and aroma during cooking. True meaty flavor develops with the application of heat, which speeds the rate of reactions involving nitrogenous substances, carbohydrates and fat.

The flavor of cooked meat depends in part on the amount and kind of heat applied. A cut of meat exposed to moist heat, as in cooking in liquid or braising, will develop a different flavor than one cooked by dry heat, as in roasting or broiling. Moist heat is more often used to tenderize meat than to develop its flavor, although some liquids, such as wine, will affect the flavor. For moist-heat cookery, the meat should be cooked at low temperatures for prolonged periods of time. Consequently, because small pieces of meat are often used, internal and external temperatures become equalized. The flavor which develops during moist-heat cooking is generally on the delicate side. Furthermore, exposing the meat to liquid results in leaching of water-soluble flavor components into the cooking medium; these components are retained if the cooking liquid is used in making sauces or gravies.

When meat is cooked by a dry-heat method, the temperatures exceed those used in moist-heat cooking. The surface of the cut undergoes physical and chemical changes which affect flavor development. Initially, the moisture on the surface of the meat is evaporated away; then the interior moisture, carrying with it soluble flavor components, moves to replace the surface moisture. As the concentration of these components increase, they become involved in a variety of chemical reactions, which result in changes in both flavor and color. With the increasing temperature, fat melts and covers the meat surface, and the decomposition products formed enter into reactions with other meat components, contributing to the overall flavor.

The flavor of meat during cooking is not stable. With increasing temperature, to a point, the flavor develops from bland to a more pronounced "meaty" flavor.

Meat flavor and aroma are difficult to separate because many flavor properties are the result of odor sensations. However, the contribution that aroma makes to the flavor of meat comes from a mixture of volatile organic compounds. These are produced by the partial breakdown of protein and fat caused by heating. The aroma released from fat during cooking differentiates beef, veal, pork and lamb. The flavor and aroma produced are also influenced by the age and/or sex of the animal, the type of feed it received and storage conditions of the meat.

Juiciness

The greater the degree of doneness, the less juicy a meat cut will be. An overcooked piece of meat almost always lacks juiciness. Since juiciness is closely related to the amount of moisture in a product, and also to the amount of fat, it follows that a longer, more severe cooking procedure will cause more dehydration and fat extraction, resulting in a drier final product.

The color of well-done meat from different animals is influenced by the amount of pigment in the raw meat. Well-done beef is darker than well-done pork, which changes from grayish-pink to almost white after cooking. Veal changes from light pink to brownish-gray. Pork shoulder steak and uncured ham are a dull rose-red when raw, and grayish-brown when cooked. Lamb is a pinkish-red color when raw, but it becomes grayish-brown with no traces of pink when cooked to well done. The typical bright pink color of cured meat only intensifies during cooking, since it is heat stable (Chapter 4).

Figure 7-1
Color Chart by Degrees of Doneness

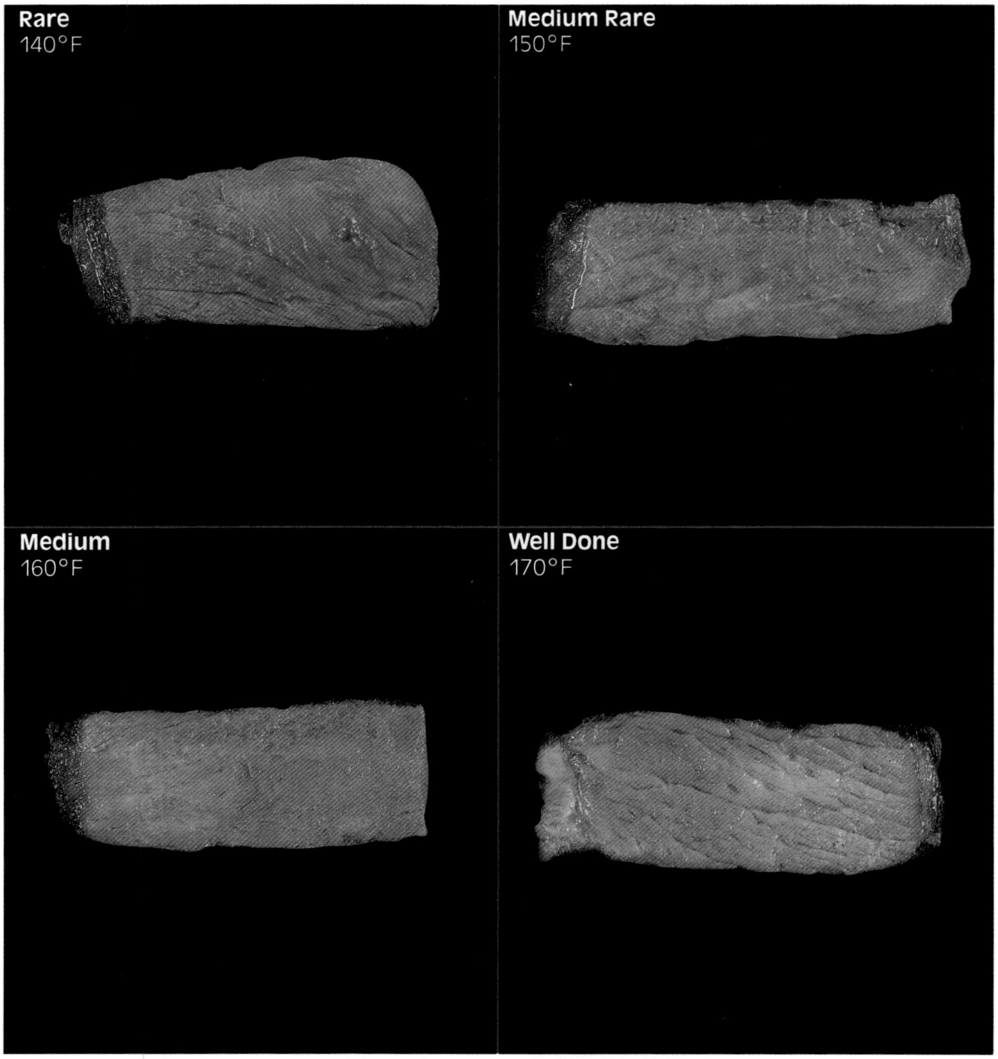

COLOR

Cooking brings about changes in the myoglobin which affects the color of meat (See Chapter 1). Because of the change in color of pigment caused by heat, the color of cooked meat is typically used as an index for doneness.

Rare 140°F — Medium Rare 150°F — Medium 160°F — Well Done 170°F

Studies of the effects of cooking (within reasonable temperature ranges) and other methods of processing show no significant alterations in the protein value of meat. The fat content, and consequently the caloric value, of meat can change substantially, depending on cooking method and time. Methods such as broiling will reduce fat content because the meat is cooked on a rack which allows the fat in the meat to drip off as it melts from the heat. Methods such as frying increase fat because the meat is cooked in added fat and the fat naturally present in the meat does not drip away as it does in broiling.

Thiamin is one of the least stable vitamins, with retentions in cooked meat reported from 90 percent (fried beef) to about 30 percent (pressure-cooked stew). Generally, more thiamin is retained in meat cooked by dry, rather than by moist, methods of cooking because, being water-soluble, thiamin tends to leach into the cooking liquid. The longer cooking time needed for moist-heat cooking methods also increases the amount of thiamin loss. Therefore, if thiamin in meat drippings is included in the analysis, the total amount of thiamin is about the same as before cooking. Meat cooked to lower internal temperatures usually retains more thiamin than meat cooked to higher internal temperatures. Other B-vitamins are fairly heat stable, but also may be transferred to the drippings or cooking liquids during preparation.

Minerals such as iron and zinc are heat-stable, so normal cooking processes do not affect the quantity or availability of minerals in meat. Small amounts do leach into the cooking liquids or juices, but if drippings or cooking liquids are consumed, the nutrients will still be retained. For effects of specific cooking methods on nutrient retention, see Chapter 2.

NUTRIENT CONTENT

Cooking time, temperature and technique can influence the nutrient content of meat.

FOOD SAFETY

Thermal destruction of microorganisms is one of the purposes of the cooking process. Refer to Chapter 6 for a more detailed discussion of meat microbiology. Both temperature and time are factors in establishing microbiologically safe conditions.

The destructive effect of elevated temperatures on pathogens and spoilage microorganisms is well established. Most yeasts and molds are inactivated by moist heat of 140°F (rare) for 10 minutes (their spores are slightly more heat-resistant). Thermal inactivation temperatures for bacteria differ. Most vegetative cells of pathogenic bacteria are destroyed at about 149°F (medium rare) for 12 to 15 minutes. Meat should never be partially cooked then finished later, because the interior temperatures may not have reached a level needed to destroy bacteria.

At an internal temperature of 165°F (medium to well done) to 212°F, most bacteria that cause food poisoning will be destroyed. When a slow process is used to cook meat, the temperature of the contents should be brought to 125°F within three hours and rise quickly to 165°F to stop bacterial growth. However, a safer and easier to implement rule-of-thumb is to be sure the internal temperature of the product rises from 40°F to 140°F within four hours.

Staphylococci toxins are so heat-resistant that once formed they will remain active regardless of the cooking technique. The best way to prevent their formation is to use strict sanitary practices and to avoid holding food in the temperature range favorable to Staphylococci toxin production (44°F to 120°F).

Trichinosis remains a remote health threat to those who eat undercooked pork (see discussion in Chapter 6). While measures have been instituted in this country to control trichinosis, it has not been completely eradicated. To be safely consumed, pork and pork products, unless labeled trichinae-free, should be thoroughly cooked to an internal temperature of 160°F to 170°F (depending on the cut). This provides a 23°F to 33°F safety margin since *Trichinella spiralis* is killed at 137°F.

Table 7-1
Changes in Meat During Heating

	Initial heating period — up to 122°F (internal temperature)	122°F to 149°F (internal temperature)	149°F and over (internal temperature)
Texture	Muscle fiber width and length gradually decreases. Collagen fibers "buckle," but tenderizing is negligible.	Muscle fiber width rapidly decreases (from 113°F to 144°F) and extensively shrinks in length (from 131°F to 149°F). Proteins coagulated by 144°F begin to break down when tissue is held 30 minutes or more at 140°F.	Muscle tissues harden and become tough. Connective tissue shrinks. Solubilization of collagen is about half completed at around 143°F (higher for meat from older animals).
Juiciness	Muscle loses a slight amount of water.	Water content of muscle decreases as proteins are broken down. Tender meat is juicy at this point.	Beef becomes less juicy as temperature increases.
Color/Odor	Center of beef becomes bright red. Outside becomes grayish-brown as temperature rises. Veal color begins as pink. Pork begins as a grayish-pink color. Pork shoulder steak and uncured ham are a dull rose-red when raw. Raw lamb begins as pinkish-red.	Beef cooked rare (140°F internal temperature) is red with a thin brown layer on surface.	Beef at 160°F is medium pink in color. Beef at 170°F is well done and brown throughout. The final color of veal is brownish-gray. Well done pork is almost white in color. Pork shoulder steak and uncured ham are grayish-brown when fully cooked. Well done lamb is a grayish-brown.
Microorganisms	Most microorganisms are still actively reproducing at these temperatures.	Most yeasts and molds are inactivated by moist heat of 140°F for 10 minutes. *Trichinella spiralis* is destroyed at 137°F.	Pathogenic bacteria destroyed at 149°F for 12 to 15 minutes. Cooking pork to 160°F to 170°F allows a margin of safety in the destruction of *Trichinella spiralis* (see text).

The rate at which meat is cooked depends upon whether it is heated in water, steam or air. Meat cooked in liquid and/or braised (moist heat) reaches a high temperature more slowly than if it is cooked in an oven surrounded by air (dry heat). This is because more energy is used in the process of raising the temperature of the moist mixture than is required to heat the dry air. Fat does not conduct heat as rapidly as muscle; roasts covered by a fat layer generally cook more slowly than those that are more closely trimmed.

Physical properties that affect heat transfer in meat include the size and shape of the cut, its thermal conductivity and its physical composition. Heating time decreases as product size and density decrease. A hamburger patty, for instance, takes less time to cook than a piece of round steak, and a thick hamburger takes longer to cook than a thin one.

THE COOKING PROCESS

The major objective when cooking meat is to achieve an internal temperature appropriate to the desired degree of doneness and the type of meat.

Methods of Heating

There are three basic mechanisms of heating: conduction, convection and radiation. Usually, more than one of the mechanisms is involved in normal food preparation processes and all three can occur simultaneously.

Conduction—In conduction, kinetic energy is transmitted from molecule to molecule without displacement of the molecules. Muscle tissues are heated primarily by conduction when there is direct contact with a heat source, such as the heated surfaces of electric range burners or the flame of gas burners.

Convection—In convection cooking, the heated air moves in currents around the piece of meat and the surrounding medium. Convection currents may occur naturally because of simple changes that occur when a gas or liquid is heated, thus becoming less dense and rising. Convection currents are mechanically stimulated by a blower in a convection oven making cooking more economical because it results in time and power savings. Since convection ovens cook 20 percent to 40 percent faster than conventional ovens, cooking times must be adjusted to avoid overcooked and dry meat.

When meat is cooked in a conventional oven, electromagnetic waves of radiant energy pass from the heat source to the pan in which the meat rests and then into the meat. Shiny surfaces tend to reflect heat, while dull or dark surfaces absorb it.

Radiation—Two types of radiation are used in meat cookery: infrared and microwave. Infrared radiation is the transfer of heat energy by long electro-magnetic waves which pass from a high-temperature surface to a low-temperature surface. The form of heat transfer is particularly important at high temperatures. Radiant energy may come from broiler units in conventional ovens or from glowing coals. This mode of heat transfer occurs through air media, and is slowed within a solid piece of meat.

In microwave radiation, energy is supplied by short electromagnetic waves. These microwaves penetrate food, causing polar molecules (e.g., water) within the food to move rapidly and to vibrate. As the molecules rub against one another, the resulting friction creates heat, which is known as thermal motion.

Microwaves denature proteins within meat, but only penetrate to a depth of about 1½ inches. When cooked in a microwave oven, the inner portion of thick cuts of meat is heated primarily through conduction. Since bone reflects microwaves, the meat nearest to the bone does not heat well. Surface evaporative cooling has been observed in microwave-cooked roasts. This may explain some of the uneven cooking that has been reported in meat prepared in a microwave oven. Because surface temperature is low and moisture is deposited on the surface of the meat, a cooked crust may not form on meat. Browning meat in a microwave oven depends upon a time/temperature relationship. For example, browning normally does not occur in small pieces of meat because they have a short cooking time. However, a 3-pound roast microwaved at 30 percent will brown because of its longer cooking time.

Microwave Ovens

Use of microwave ovens has become widespread, and they are now found in 75 percent of U.S. kitchens. In early studies, meat cooked on high power was often overdone at certain spots and underdone at others because the heat was not dissipated fast enough to reach the interior of the meat. Today's microwave ovens with variable power controls allow meat to be cooked more evenly at lower power settings.

If a crusty exterior is preferred, as for roast beef, use of the microwave oven may be less desirable than would be the conventional oven. The microwave oven will brown roasts, but not as readily as the conventional oven. A small percentage of ovens have browning devices built into them, or sauces can be put on the meat to add color. Meat will brown naturally if cooked at a low temperature for a longer period of time.

As early as the mid-1960s, experts observed that heat distribution patterns varied among microwave ovens. These early investigations led to questions of whether *Trichinella spiralis*, if present in pork, might survive when pork was cooked by this method.

To address this problem, a new procedure for cooking pork in the microwave oven was developed. The meat is placed in a closed container, such as a loosely sealed, oven-cooking bag or a covered microwave-safe container, and microwaved at a reduced power setting. This procedure produces a vaporous atmosphere and reduces temperature variations, thereby producing a consistently, properly done pork cut.

The microwave oven successfully reheats previously cooked foods, including meat. Microwave reheated meat retains aroma and flavor, and has higher acceptability than meat reheated in a conventional oven. Microwaving reduces cooking time by about 50 percent and uses correspondingly less energy. Refer to the manufacturer's guidelines for your unit for listings of specific microwave cooking times.

Methods of Cooking Meat

Methods of cooking meat include dry heat (roasting, broiling, panbroiling, panfrying, stir-frying and outdoor grilling) or moist heat (braising and cooking in liquid). Methods should be selected based on initial tenderness of the cut, desired quality characteristics of the resulting product, available cooking facilities and equipment, and the amount of time available for preparation.

Tender cuts of meat, cooked by dry-heat methods, result in tender and juicy products. Less-tender cuts must be cooked for longer periods of time by moist-heat methods, to soften the connective tissue, prevent surface drying and to develop flavor. Some less tender cuts such as beef top round and chuck arm can be cooked by a dry heat method if marinated before cooking.

The degree of doneness can easily be determined by measuring internal temperature, using a standard meat thermometer or a quick recovery/instant read thermometer. The more tender the cut, the lower the internal temperature needed to produce a satisfactory product.

A meat thermometer is the most accurate guide to the doneness of roasts. The thermometer should be inserted into the roast surface at a slight angle or through the end of the roast so the tip of the thermometer is in the thickest portion of the cut, but not resting in fat, against the bone, or on the rotisserie rod. When using the rotisserie, the thermometer must clear the cooking unit and drip pan while the meat is turning.

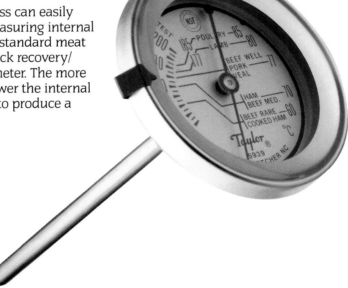

Table 7-2
Temperature Chart

Degree of Doneness

	Rare	Medium Rare	Medium	Well Done
Beef	140°F	150°F	160°F	170°F
Veal	***	***	160°F	170°F
Pork	***	***	160°F	170°F
Lamb	140°F	150°F	160°F	170°F

***Veal and pork are seldom cooked to these degrees of doneness.
Source: National Live Stock and Meat Board in cooperation with Texas Agricultural Experiment Station, 1979.

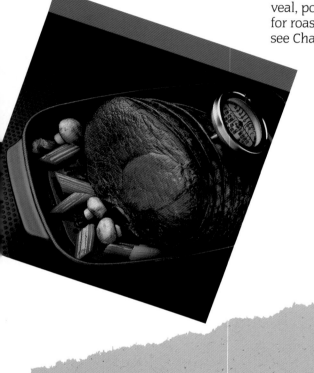

Dry Heat—

Dry heat methods of cooking are suitable for tender cuts of meat or less tender cuts which have been marinated. Dry heat methods include roasting, oven broiling, grilling, panbroiling, panfrying and stir-frying.

■ **Roasting**—This method of cooking is recommended for larger cuts of beef, veal, pork and lamb. For cuts suitable for roasting and other cooking methods, see Chapter 3.

Searing

Searing is used to develop aroma and flavor in outside surfaces of a roast and to produce drippings of a rich brown color. When roasts are seared they are browned with a short application of intense heat. Searing can be done either at the beginning or end of a roasting period. Roasts which are seared are similar in cooking losses, cooking time and palatability to roasts cooked the entire roasting time at a low to moderate oven temperature.

If the searing method for roasting meat is used, the searing period should be short and a low, constant oven temperature should be maintained throughout the remaining cooking period. A constant oven temperature has many advantages—the meat is evenly cooked, requires less attention, and there is minimal spattering of grease.

Table 7-3
Steps for Roasting Meat

1. Season meat with spices, herbs, salt or other seasonings before, during or after cooking, as desired. Meat should be taken directly from the refrigerator and placed in a cold oven.

2. Place the meat with the fat side up, on a rack (to hold the roast out of the drippings) in an open, shallow roasting pan. The fat on top lets the meat baste itself as it cooks, so further moistening of the surface is unnecessary. In roasts such as a beef rib, a pork loin or a rack of lamb, the ribs form a natural rack.

3. Insert a meat thermometer so the tip is in the center of the roast. The tip should not touch bone or rest in fat.

4. Add no water and do not cover. Roasting is a dry-heat method of cooking and if the pan is covered or water is added, the meat will be cooked by moist heat rather than roasted.

5. Roast in a slow oven — 300°F to 325°F. It is not necessary to preheat the oven.

6. Remove the meat from the oven when the thermometer registers five degrees lower than the desired level of doneness. The meat will continue to cook as it stands. The use of a meat thermometer will help avoid overcooking or undercooking. Roasts are easier to carve if allowed to "set" for 15 to 20 minutes after removing them from the oven so juices can set up.

7. Roasting for a longer time and at a low temperature, 250°F to 300°F, is an acceptable method for less tender cuts of meat, such as bottom round roast, although surface drying may occur if there is little fat covering.

Table 7-4
Timetable for Roasting

Cut			Approximate Weight (pounds)	Oven Temperature (degrees F)	Rare	Medium	Well
					— Approximate Cooking Time (minutes per pound)		
Beef	**Rib roast**		6 to 8	300 to 325	23 to 25	27 to 30	32 to 35
			4 to 6	300 to 325	26 to 32	34 to 38	40 to 42
	Rib Eye roast		4 to 6	350	18 to 20	20 to 22	22 to 24
	Boneless Rump roast		4 to 6	300 to 325	—	25 to 27	28 to 30
	Round Tip roast		3½ to 4	300 to 325	30 to 35	35 to 38	38 to 40
			6 to 8	300 to 325	22 to 25	25 to 30	30 to 35
	Top Round roast		4 to 6	300 to 325	20 to 25	25 to 28	28 to 30
	Tenderloin roast	Whole	4 to 6	425		45 to 60 (total)	
		Half	2 to 3	425		35 to 45 (total)	
	Ground Beef Loaf	(9" x 5")	1½ to 2½	300 to 325		1 to 1½ hrs (total)	
Veal	**Loin roast**	(bone-in)	3 to 4	300 to 325	—	34 to 36	38 to 40
		(boneless)	2 to 3	300 to 325	—	18 to 20	22 to 24
	Rib roast		4 to 5	300 to 325	—	25 to 27	29 to 31
	Crown roast	(12 to 14 ribs)	7½ to 9½	300 to 325	—	19 to 21	21 to 23
	Rib Eye roast		2 to 3	300 to 325	—	26 to 28	30 to 33
	Rump roast	(boneless)	2 to 3	300 to 325	—	33 to 35	37 to 40
	Shoulder roast	(boneless)	2½ to 3	300 to 325	—	31 to 34	34 to 37
Pork	**Loin roast**	Center (bone-in)	3 to 5	325	—	20 to 25	26 to 31
		Blade Loin or Sirloin (boneless, tied)	2½ to 3½	325	—	—	33 to 38
		Top (double)	3 to 4	325	—	29 to 34	33 to 38
		Top (single)	2 to 4	325	—	23 to 33	30 to 40
	Crown roast		6 to 10	325	—	—	20 to 25
	Leg roast	Whole (bone-in)	12	325	—	—	23 to 25
		Top (inside)	3½	325	—	—	38 to 42
		Bottom (outside)	3½	325	—	—	40 to 45
	Blade Boston roast	(boneless)	3 to 4	325	—	—	40 to 45
Lamb	**Leg roast**	Whole (bone-in)	7 to 9	325	15 to 20	20 to 25	25 to 30
			5 to 7	325	20 to 25	25 to 30	30 to 35
		(boneless)	4 to 7	325	25 to 30	30 to 35	35 to 40
		Shank half	3 to 4	325	30 to 35	40 to 45	45 to 50
		Sirloin half	3 to 4	325	25 to 30	35 to 40	45 to 50
	Shoulder roast	boneless	3½ to 5	325	30 to 35	35 to 40	40 to 45
		bone-in, pre-sliced	3½ to 5	325	35 to 40	40 to 45	45 to 50

Cut			Weight	Oven Temp	Rare	Medium	Well
					— Approximate Cooking Time (total minutes)		
Pork	**Tenderloin roast**	Whole	½ to 1	425	—	27 to 29	30 to 32
	Ground Pork Loaf		1 to 1½	350	—	—	55 to 65
	Backribs			325	cook until tender		1½ to 1¾ hrs
	Country-style Ribs	1 inch slices		325	cook until tender		1½ to 1¾ hrs
	Spareribs			325	cook until tender		1½ to 1¾ hrs

Cut			Approximate Weight (pounds)	Oven Temperature (degrees F)	Final Thermometer Reading (degrees F)	Approximate Cooking Time (minutes per pound)
Pork, smoked	**Ham** (cook-before-eating)	Whole (boneless)	8 to 12	300 to 325	160	17 to 21
		(bone-in)	14 to 16	300 to 325	160	18 to 20
		Half (bone-in)	7 to 8	300 to 325	160	22 to 25
		Portion (bone-in)	3 to 5	300 to 325	160	35 to 40
	Loin		3 to 5	300 to 350	140	20 to 25
	Ham (fully-cooked)	Whole (boneless)*	8 to 12	300 to 325	140	13 to 17
		**(bone-in)	14 to 16	300 to 325	140	12 to 14
		Half (boneless)*	6 to 8	300 to 325	140	17 to 20
		**(bone-in)	6 to 8	300 to 325	140	14 to 17
		Portion (boneless)	3 to 4	300 to 325	140	20 to 23
	Canadian-style Bacon	(fully-cooked)	2 to 4	300 to 350	140	20 to 30

Note: Smaller roasts require more minutes per pound than larger roasts.
*Add ½ cup water, cover tightly and cook as directed.
**Cover tightly and cook as directed.

■ **Broiling**—Broiling is suitable for tender beef steaks; beef and lamb kabobs; veal, pork and lamb chops; pork ribs; sliced ham; bacon; butterflied lamb leg and ground beef, pork and lamb. Steaks and chops should be at least ¾ inch thick and ham should be at least ½ inch thick for successful broiling.

Less tender cuts such as beef flank steak, beef top round, and veal, pork and lamb shoulder chops, may also be broiled when marinated. Marinating can increase the tenderness of these cuts but only to a limited degree.

The same tender cuts suitable for oven broiling can be pan- or griddle broiled. This method is especially good for meat ¾ inch or less in thickness; very thick cuts of meat may become overcooked on the outside before the middle has reached the desired degree of doneness.

Table-7-5
Steps for Oven Broiling

1. Set the oven regulator for broiling. The broiler may be preheated but this is not essential.

2. Place meat on the rack of broiler pan. For steaks, chops or patties ¾ to 1 inch thick, position the pan so surface of meat is 2 to 3 inches from the heat. Place thicker cuts 3 to 6 inches away from heat. Broiler heat may vary causing a modification of the recommended distances.

3. Broil until top side is brown. Cured meat and smoked pork should be cooked until lightly brown. The meat should be approximately half-done by the time it is browned on top.

4. Turn and brown other side. Table 7-6 offers a guide for broiling times. For the most accurate determination of the degree of doneness of a thick steak or chop, a meat thermometer (quick-recovery) should be inserted horizontally into the center of the cut. The steak or chop should be tested shortly before the end of the estimated total broiling time. Do not leave the thermometer in meat during broiling. To test for doneness of steaks or chops, cut a small slit in the center or close to a bone and observe the color of the meat.

5. Season, if desired, and serve at once.

Table 7-6
Timetable for Oven Broiling

Cut		Approximate Thickness (inches)	Approximate Weight (pounds)	Distance From Heat (inches)	Approximate Cooking Time (total minutes)		
					Rare	Medium	Well
Beef	**Chuck shoulder steak*** (boneless)	¾	¾ to 1	2 to 3	12	14	—
		1	1 to 1¼	3 to 4	14	18	—
	Rib steak	¾	11 to 14 oz	2 to 3	8	12	—
		1	1 to 1½	3 to 4	10	15	—
		1½	1½ to 2	4 to 5	20	25	—
	Rib Eye steak	¾	7 to 8 oz	2 to 3	8	12	—
		1	9 to 10 oz	3 to 4	10	15	—
		1½	12 to 14 oz	4 to 5	20	25	—
	Top Loin steak	¾	11 to 14 oz	2 to 3	8	12	—
		1	1 to 1½	3 to 4	10	15	—
		1½	1½ to 2	4 to 5	20	25	—
	Sirloin steak	¾	1¼ to 1¾	2 to 3	10	15	—
		1	1½ to 3	3 to 4	16	21	—
		1½	2¼ to 4	4 to 5	21	25	—
	Porterhouse steak	¾	12 to 16 oz	2 to 3	8	12	—
		1	1½ to 2	3 to 4	10	15	—
		1½	2 to 3	4 to 5	20	25	—
	Tenderloin (Filet Mignon)		4 to 8 oz	2 to 4	10	15	—
	Ground Beef patties	½ x 4	4 oz	3 to 4	—	10**	—
		1 x 4	5⅓ oz	3 to 4	—	14**	—
	Top Round steak*	1	1¼ to 1¾	3 to 4	15	18	—
		1½	1½ to 2	4 to 5	20	25	—
	Flank steak*		1 to 1½	2 to 3	12	14	—
Veal	**Loin/Rib chop**	1	8 oz	4	—	14 to 16	15 to 17
		1½	11 oz	5	—	21 to 23	23 to 25
	Arm/Blade steak*	¾	16 oz	4	—	14 to 15	15 to 16
	Ground Veal patties	½ x 4	4 oz	4		8 to 10	10 to 12
Pork	**Loin/Rib chop**	¾		4	—	8 to 11	11 to 14
		1½		4	—	19 to 22	23 to 25
	Boneless Loin/ Butterflied chop	1		4	—	11 to 13	13 to 15
		1½		4	—	16 to 18	18 to 20
	Butterflied single loin roast (boneless)		3	4	—	22 to 24	26 to 28
	Blade chop (bone-in)	¾		4	—	—	13 to 15
		1½		4	—	—	26 to 29
	Shoulder chop* (bone-in)	¾		4	—	—	16 to 18
		1		4	—	—	18 to 20
	Cubes for kabobs, Loin/Leg	1		4	—	9 to 11	11 to 13
	Tenderloin	1		4	—	12 to 14	16 to 18
	Tenderloin		½ to 1	4	—	16 to 21	20 to 25
	Ground Pork patties	½ x 4	4 oz	4	—	—	7 to 9
	Country-style Ribs	1		5	cook until tender		45 to 60
	Backribs/Spareribs			5	cook until tender		45 to 55
Lamb	**Shoulder chop***	¾ to 1	5 to 9 oz	3 to 4	—	7 to 11	—
	Loin/Rib chop	1	3 to 5 oz	3 to 4	—	7 to 11	—
		1½	4½ to 7½ oz	4 to 5	—	15 to 19	—
	Sirloin chop	¾ to 1	6 to 10 oz	3 to 4	—	12 to 15	—
	Butterflied Leg (sirloin removed, boneless)		4	5 to 7	40 to 46	47 to 53	54 to 60
	Leg steak	¾ to 1	11 to 18 oz	3 to 4	—	14 to 18	—
	Cubes for kabobs	1 to 1½		4 to 5	—	8 to 12	—
	Ground Lamb patties	½ x 4	4 oz	3	—	5 to 8	—

		Approximate Thickness (inches)				Total Cooking Time	
Pork, smoked	**Ham slice**	½				—	8 to 10	—
		1				—	14 to 16	—
	Ham kabobs	1 to 1½				—	8 to 12	—
	Loin chop	½ to 1				—	15 to 20	—
	Canadian-style Bacon	½				—	6 to 8	—

*Marinate 6 hours or overnight, if desired.
**USDA/FSIS recommends ground beef patties be cooked to 160° F.

■ **Grilling (Barbecuing)**—The technique we call grilling is thought to have originated in the Caribbean, where natives smoke-dried meat over hot coals on wood-frame "grills." Early Spanish explorers called this the "barbacoa," which evolved into the modern-day word "barbecue."

Due to the method of heating, grilling is actually a method of broiling. Meat can be grilled on a grid or rack over coals, heated ceramic briquets or an open fire. While it is usually done outdoors, grilling can be done in the kitchen with special types of range tops or newer, small appliances.

Standard charcoal briquets are the most common fuel for grilling. High-quality briquets burn evenly and consistently. Flammable material for quick-start fires may be added. It takes longer for natural lump charcoal to get hot, but it provides heat for a longer period of time.

Woods like mesquite, apple, cherry and grapevine—in chip or briquet form—give unique flavors to grilled beef and lamb. Hickory generally is best for smoking beef and pork. Wood chips are first soaked in water about 30 minutes, drained, and then placed on the burning coals. (Softwoods and evergreens should *not* be used; they can impart a bitter flavor and leave a residue in the grill.)

Grilling is often used to cook kabobs. Kabobs are pieces of meat, or a combination of meat and vegetables, or meat and fruit pieces, alternated on a skewer.

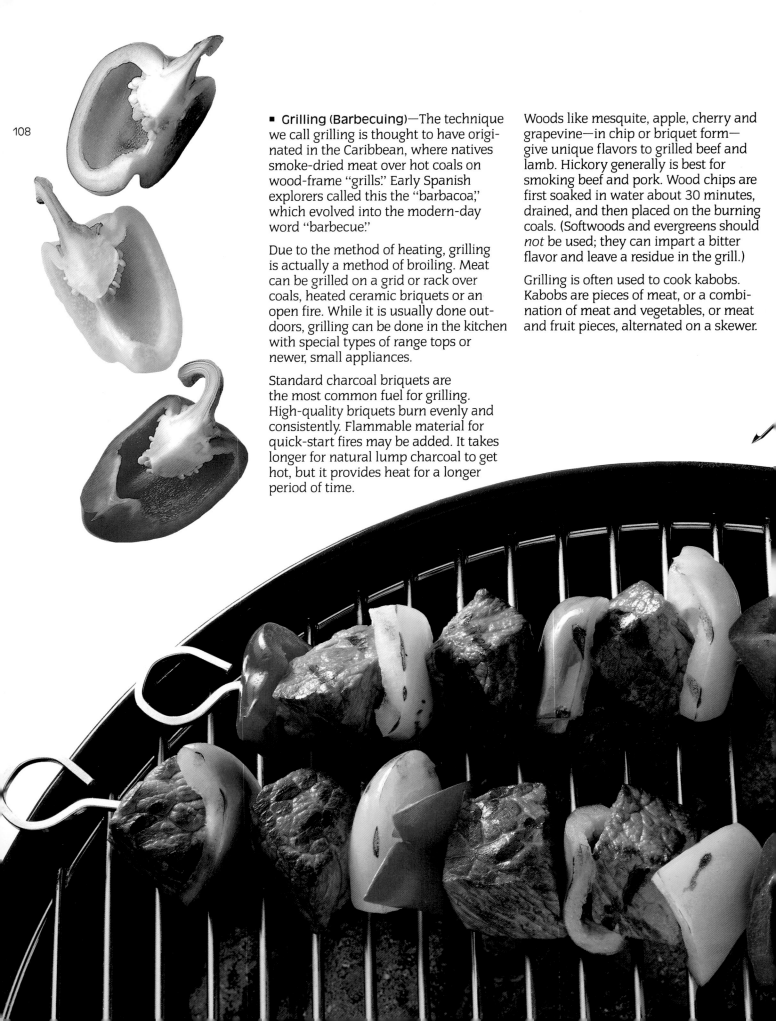

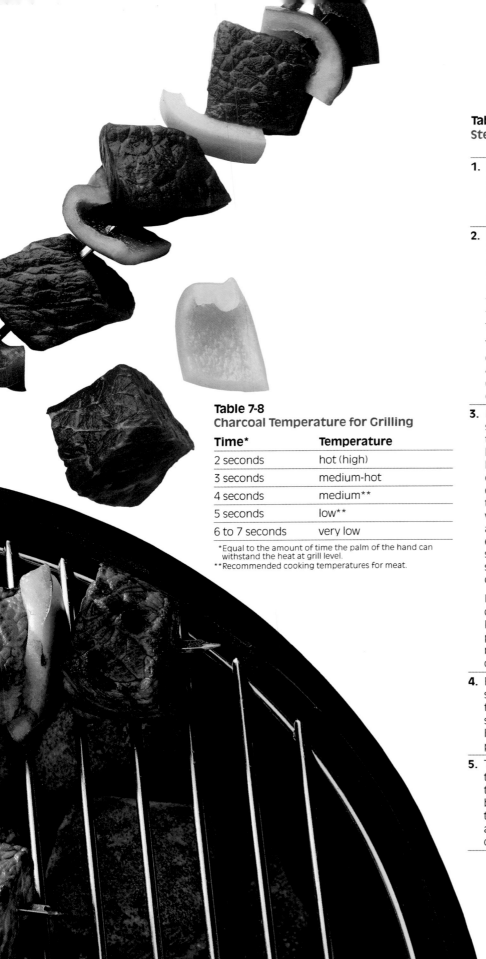

Table 7-7
Steps for Grilling

1. If using a tenderizing marinade, marinate meat in the refrigerator at least six to eight hours in acidic liquid such as wine, vinegar or lemon juice to tenderize meat and add flavor.

2. Start fire according to grill manufacturer's instructions. Spread coals in a single layer after they reach the gray ash stage. Low to medium cooking temperatures should be used. To lower the temperature, spread coals farther apart or raise the grid. To make the fire hotter, move coals closer together and tap off ash.

   To check the temperature of the coals, cautiously hold the palm of your hand about 4 inches above the coals. Count the number of seconds before the heat forces removal of the hand (See Table 7-8).

3. For direct cooking, arrange coals in a single layer directly under the food. Use this method for steaks, ham slices, chops, kabobs and other quickly cooked foods. For larger roasts and steaks which require longer cooking at lower temperatures, use indirect cooking. This method cooks food by reflective heat, similar to the way in which a conventional oven cooks. For indirect cooking, arrange an equal number of briquets on each side of the fire grate. Ignite, and make sure the coals are burning equally on both sides. If necessary, move the coals from one side to the other.

   Place an aluminum foil drip pan in the center of the fire grate between the coals. Place the meat on the grid above the drip pan. Cover (with damper open) and cook as recipe directs. Turning meat during indirect cooking is not usually necessary.

4. Baste meat with marinade or seasoned sauce throughout cooking time, if desired. If the basting sauce contains a large amount of sugar or other ingredients which burn easily, limit basting to the last 15 to 20 minutes to prevent excessive browning.

5. The cooking time required depends on the variety, size and shape of the meat cut; the temperature of the meat when cooking begins; the equipment used; the cooking temperature maintained, which may be affected by the weather; and the desired degree of doneness.

Table 7-8
Charcoal Temperature for Grilling

Time*	Temperature
2 seconds	hot (high)
3 seconds	medium-hot
4 seconds	medium**
5 seconds	low**
6 to 7 seconds	very low

*Equal to the amount of time the palm of the hand can withstand the heat at grill level.
**Recommended cooking temperatures for meat.

■ Panbroiling—Panbroiling is a faster and more convenient method than oven broiling for cooking thinner steaks or chops.

Table 7-9
Steps for Panbroiling

1. Place meat in a preheated heavy frying pan or on a griddle. Most meat cuts have enough fat to prevent sticking; however, the cooking surface may be lightly brushed or sprayed with oil when panbroiling very lean cuts. No oil is needed when a nonstick frying pan is used.

2. Do not add oil or water and do not cover.

3. For cuts thicker than ¼ inch cook at medium heat, turning occasionally. Cuts less than ¼ inch should be cooked at medium-high. Turn more than once to assure even cooking.

4. Remove fat as it accumulates. If fat is permitted to collect, the meat will be fried instead of panbroiled.

5. Cook until brown on both sides. Do not overcook. Season, if desired, and serve at once. Count on about one-third to one-half the time for panbroiling or griddle broiling as required for regular broiling. To test for doneness of steaks or chops, cut a small slit in the center or close to the bone and observe the color of the meat.

Table 7-10
Timetable for Panbroiling

Cut			Approximate Thickness (inches)	Range Temperature	Approximate Cooking Time (total minutes) Rare	Medium	Well
Beef	**Rib Eye steak**		½	Medium-high	3 to 5	—	—
	Top Loin steak		¼	Medium-high	2 to 3	—	—
	Eye Round steak		½	Medium-high	2 to 4	—	—
			1	Medium	8 to 10	—	—
	Tenderloin		¾ to 1	Medium	6 to 9	—	—
	Round Tip		⅛ to ¼	Medium-high	1	—	—
	Sirloin	(boneless)	¾ to 1	Med-low to med	10 to 12	—	—
	Top Round		1	Medium	13 to 16	—	—
	Ground Beef patties		½ x 4	Medium	—	7 to 8**	—
Veal	**Loin/Rib chop**		¾ to 1	Med-low to med	—	10 to 12	12 to 14
	Blade/Arm steak*		¾	Med to med-high	—	13 to 14	14 to 15
	Ground Veal patties		½	Med-low to med	—	6 to 7	8 to 9
Pork	**Loin/Rib chop**	(bone-in)	½	Medium	—	7 to 8	9 to 10
			1	Medium	—	12 to 14	15 to 17
	Loin chop	(boneless)	½	Medium	—	7 to 8	9 to 10
			1	Medium	—	10 to 12	12 to 14
	Butterflied chop		½	Medium	—	8 to 9	10 to 11
			1	Medium	—	12 to 14	15 to 17
	Ground Pork patties		½ x 4	Medium	—	—	7 to 8

*Marinate 6 hours or overnight, if desired.
**USDA/FSIS recommends ground beef patties be cooked to 160°F.

- Panfrying—Panfrying differs from panbroiling in that a small amount of fat is added first, or allowed to accumulate during cooking.

Panfrying is a method suitable for ground meat, small or thin cuts of meat, thin strips, and pounded, scored or otherwise tenderized cuts that do not require prolonged heating for tenderization.

Table 7-11
Steps for Panfrying

1. Brown meat on both sides in small amount of oil. Some cuts will cook in the fat that comes from the meat. Lean cuts such as cubed steak or liver, and cuts which are floured or breaded, require additional oil on the surface of the frying pan to prevent sticking.

2. If the meat is cooked with a coating, seasoning may be added to the coating ingredients. Otherwise, the meat may be seasoned after browning.

3. Do not cover the meat. If covered, the meat is braised and will not have the crisp texture inherent to frying. In frying, there may be some sacrifice of tenderness for crispness and flavor.

4. Cook at medium heat, turning occasionally. The temperature should be kept below the smoke point of the fat. The object in frying is to cook the meat through while it is browning. Turning occasionally is necessary to promote even (uniform) cooking.

Table 7-12
Timetable for Panfrying

Cut			Approximate Thickness (inches)	Approximate Cooking Time (total minutes)		
				Rare	Medium	Well
Beef	**Flank strips**		⅛ to ¼	1	2 to 3	—
	Sirloin strips		⅛ to ¼	1	2 to 3	—
	Top Round strips		⅛ to ¼	1	2 to 3	—
Veal	**Cutlets**		⅛	—	3 to 4	—
			¼	—	5 to 6	—
	Ground veal patties		½	—	5 to 7	—
Pork	**Loin/Rib chop**	(bone-in)	¼	tender	4	—
			½	—	5 to 6	7 to 8
			¾	—	8 to 10	11 to 13
			1	—	13 to 15	15 to 18
	Boneless Loin/ Butterflied chop		½	—	5 to 6	7 to 8
			¾	—	10 to 13	14 to 16
			1	—	17 to 19	19 to 22
	Sirloin chop		¾	—	—	14 to 15
	Tenderloin		¼	tender	3 to 4	—
			½	—	4 to 5	6 to 7
	Ground pork patties		½	—	—	7 to 9
	Loin chop	(boneless)	¼	tender	4	
	Sirloin cutlet		¼	tender	4	
	Cubed steak			tender	6 to 7	
Lamb	**Leg**		⅛ to ¼	2	3	—

- **Stirfrying**—Stirfrying is similar to panfrying except that the food is stirred almost continuously. Cooking is done with high heat, using small or thin pieces of meat.

- **Deep-fat frying**—When meat is cooked immersed in fat, the process is called deep-fat frying. This method is only used with very tender meat. Usually, meat to be deep-fat fried is coated with egg and crumbs or a batter, or it is dredged in flour or corn meal (breaded). This method of cooking is sometimes used for brains, sweetbreads, liver and croquettes; however, a number of other meat products are suitable for deep-fat frying.

Table 7-13
Steps for Stirfrying

1. Partially freeze meat to facilitate slicing.

2. Slice meat across the grain into thin, uniform slices, strips or pieces.

3. If desired, marinate while other ingredients are prepared.

4. Cook meat and vegetables separately and then combine.

5. Place meat in a small amount of hot oil in wok or large frying pan. Stirfry about half a pound at a time.

6. Cook at high temperature.

7. Slide spatula under meat and turn continuously with a scooping motion.

Moist Heat—Moist-heat methods of cooking are suitable for less tender cuts of meat. Moist-heat cooking helps to reduce surface drying in those cuts requiring prolonged cooking times. Unless a pressure cooker is used, cooking temperature is usually low, but heat penetration is faster than in dry-heat methods because steam and water conduct heat rapidly.

With moist-heat cookery, meat may lose some water-soluble nutrients into the cooking liquid. However, if the cooking liquids are consumed, as in stews or soups, nutrients are transferred and not totally lost.

- **Braising**—In some regions of the country the term "fricassee" is used interchangably with braising. Pot roast and Swiss steak are popular examples of braised-meat dishes.

In addition to the method described in Table 7-16, meat can be braised in cooking bags designed specifically for use in the oven. Use of oven-cooking bags can reduce cooking time for larger cuts of meat. No additional water is needed, as moisture is drawn out of the meat due to the atmosphere created by the cooking bag.

Table 7-14
Steps for Braising

1. Brown meat slowly on all sides in a heavy pan in just enough oil to prevent the meat from sticking. Cuts with sufficient fat require no added fat unless they are coated with flour or crumbs. The browning develops flavor and color. A slow browning adheres to the meat better than quick browning at a high temperature. Drain drippings after browning.

2. Season meat with salt, herbs or spices after browning unless seasoning is added to the coating.

3. Add a small amount of liquid [as little as two tablespoons may be used, however, ¼ to ½ cup (maximum) is recommended], such as water, tomato juice, wine, meat stock or other seasoned liquid.

4. Cover tightly to provide a moist atmosphere for cooking.

5. Simmer at low heat until the meat is tender. This may be done on top of the range or in an oven at 300°F to 325°F. Use Timetable 7-17 as a guide to total cooking time.

6. Sauce or gravy may be made from the liquid in the pan.

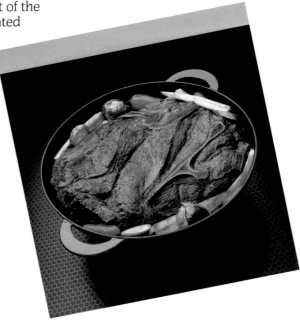

Table 7-15
Timetable for Braising

Cut			Approximate Thickness (inches)	Approximate Weight (pounds)	Approximate Cooking Time (total hours)
Beef	**Blade pot roast**			3 to 5	1¾ to 2¼
	Arm pot roast			3 to 5	2 to 3
	Chuck roast	(boneless)		3 to 5	2 to 3
	Short ribs		2 x 2 x 4		1½ to 2½
	Flank			1½ to 2	1½ to 2½
	Round steak		¾ to 1		1 to 1½
	Swiss steak		1½ to 2½		2 to 3
Veal	**Boneless Breast**	(stuffed)		2 to 2½	1¼ to 1½
				4 to 4½	2 to 2½
	Boneless Breast	(rolled & tied)		2 to 3	1½ to 2½
	Riblets				50 to 70 min.
	Arm/Blade steak		¾ to 1		45 to 60 min.
	Round steak		¼		30 min.
			½		45 min.
	Shoulder roast	(boneless)		3½ to 4	2 to 2½
	Loin/Rib chop		½		8 to 10 min.
			¾ to 1		20 to 25 min.
Pork	**Chops**	Rib, Loin	¾		30 min.
		Boneless Loin	1½		45 min.
	Spareribs/Backribs				1½
	Country-style Ribs				1½ to 2
	Tenderloin	Whole		½ to 1	40 to 45 min.
		Slices	½		25 min.
	Shoulder steak		¾		40 to 50 min.
	Cubes		1 to 1¼		45 to 60 min.
	Leg steak*	(inside)	⅛ to ¼		5 to 7 min.
	Blade Boston	(boneless)		2½ to 3½	2 to 2½
		(bone-in)		3 to 4	2¼ to 2¾
	Sirloin	(boneless)		2½ to 3½	1¾ to 2¼
	Arm Picnic Shoulder	(boneless)		2 to 4	2½ to 3
		(bone-in)		4 to 8	2¼ to 2¾
Lamb	**Breast**	(stuffed)		2 to 3	1½ to 2
		(rolled)		1½ to 2	1½ to 2
	Riblets			¾ to 1 each	1½ to 2
	Neck slices		¾		1
	Shanks			¾ to 1 each	1 to 1½
	Shoulder chop		¾ to 1		45 to 60 min.
	Lamb for stew		1½		1½ to 2

*Marinate 6 hours or overnight, if desired.

■ **Cooking in Liquid**—Less tender cuts of meat can be covered with liquid and gently simmered until tender. Care should be taken not to let the temperature of the liquid exceed 195°F, because boiling (212°F) toughens meat protein. When the liquid is used as a base for soup it is called meat stock (also called broth or bouillon). Meat that is partially cooked in liquid before cooking by another method is called "parboiled."

The three ways to cook in liquid are simmering, stewing and poaching. Simmering and stewing are used for less tender cuts of meat while poaching is used for tender cuts. Also, poaching is only appropriate for beef while any type of meat (beef, veal, pork or lamb) can be simmered. The difference between simmering and stewing is that simmering is used with whole cuts of meat while stewing is used with small pieces of meat. Steps for stewing are identical to steps for simmering shown in Table 7-16, below.

Poaching has been a traditional way of cooking poultry and fish. However, beef roasts can also be successfully poached if they come from tender cuts. Appropriate roasts for poaching are beef eye round, rib eye and tenderloin.

After an initial browning period, the poaching liquid is added and the roast is then gently simmered until it reaches 130°F. A combination of beef broth or consommé, red wine and herbs makes a flavorful poaching liquid. After cooking, the liquid can be used to make a simple sauce for the roast or it can be strained and frozen for later use as a soup base or stewing liquid.

Poaching takes one third less time than roasting. (A beef roast will poach to rare in about 20 to 30 minutes.) In addition to cooking more quickly, poaching helps to keep shrinkage of the meat to a minimum. A poached beef roast is also just as tender, juicy and flavorful as one which has been conventionally prepared.

Table 7-16
Steps for Cooking in Liquid — Simmering

1. Brown meat on all sides, if desired. The browning develops flavor and color. Drain drippings after browning. Corned beef, and cured and smoked pork are not browned before simmering.

2. Cover the meat with water or stock. The liquid may be hot or cold. Entirely covering the meat with liquid assures uniform cooking without the necessity of turning the meat.

3. If desired, season with salt, herbs, spices and vegetables. Cured and smoked meat and corned beef do not require added salt.

4. Cover tightly and simmer (do not boil) until meat is tender. Overcooking will shrink the meat and make it dry, detract from flavor and texture, and make carving difficult.

5. When vegetables are to be cooked with the meat, as in "boiled" dinners, add them whole or in pieces, near the end of cooking time.

6. When cooked, remove meat and vegetables to a pan, platter or casserole and keep hot.

7. If desired, the cooking liquid may be thickened to make gravy.

8. Serve the hot gravy over the meat and vegetables or serve separately in a sauce boat.

Table 7-17
Steps for Cooking in Liquid — Poaching

1. Rub beef roast with seasonings, if desired. Tie roast with heavy string at 2-inch intervals, if necessary. Brown on all sides in a small amount of oil.

2. Pour off excess drippings.

3. Cover with liquid. Season with additional ingredients, if desired.

4. Bring to a boil. Reduce heat, cover and simmer until internal temperature of roast registers 10°F below doneness desired.

5. Remove roast to carving board. Cover tightly with plastic wrap or aluminum foil and allow to "stand" 10 minutes before carving. Remove string from roast and carve into thin slices.

Table 7-18
Steps for Making Soup Stock

1. Place meat and meat bones in a large kettle. Meat may be cut into small pieces and the bones are often cracked to release soft marrow, which adds flavor to soup. In soup, the flavor should leach into the broth.

2. Add water or vegetable juices to cover. The amount of water added determines the strength of the stock.

3. Add vegetables and seasonings and bring to a boil; reduce heat, and simmer covered for about three hours.

4. If a large proportion of bone is used, the collagen may rise to the top and form a scum. Skim it off as it accumulates.

5. Strain the broth, cover and refrigerate. The fat that rises to the top can be discarded before stock is reheated.

6. Clarified broth is called consommé. It is made by removing all fat, then bringing the broth to a boil with one egg white and one crushed egg shell added for each quart of stock, stirring constantly. (The egg binds to small particles in the broth.) Remove broth from heat and let stand five minutes. Pour through a strainer lined with cheesecloth.

Table 7-19
Timetable for Cooking in Liquid

Cut		Approximate Thickness (inches)	Approximate Weight (pounds)	Approximate Cooking Time (total hours)
Beef	**Fresh or Corned Beef Brisket**		4 to 6	3½ to 4½
	Shank Crosscuts		¾ to 1¼	2½ to 3½
	Beef for stew			2 to 3
Veal	**Boneless Breast**	1		1¼ to 1½
	Shank Crosscuts	1½		1 to 1¼
	Veal for stew	1 to 1½		45 to 60 min.
Pork	**Spareribs**			2 to 2½
	Country-style Ribs			2 to 2½
	Cubes	1 to 1¼		45 to 60 min.
Lamb	**Lamb for stew**	1 to 1½		1½ to 2
Pork, smoked	**Ham, Country or**		10 to 16	4½ to 5
	Country-style Half		5 to 8	3 to 4
	Arm Picnic Shoulder		5 to 8	3½ to 4
	Shoulder roll		2 to 4	1½ to 2
	Hocks			2 to 2½

Cooking Meat
from the Frozen State

Frozen meat may be cooked satisfactorily either by defrosting it prior to cooking or by cooking it directly after removing it from the freezer. To defrost meat before cooking, see Chapter 6.

Additional cooking time is needed when cooking frozen meat. Frozen roasts require approximately 30 percent to 50 percent longer total cooking times than roasts started at refrigerator temperature. The additional time required for cooking steaks and chops differs according to the surface area and thickness of the meat, as well as the temperature used during cooking.

Thick frozen steaks, chops and ground meat patties must be broiled further from the heat than those that have been defrosted. This allows the internal temperature to reach the desired level without excessive browning of the outside. When steaks or chops are to be coated with eggs and crumbs, the meat should be partially defrosted so the coating will adhere to the meat.

When panbroiling frozen steaks and chops, a heated frying pan should be used to rapidly defrost the surface, enabling it to brown. The heat should be reduced after browning and the meat turned often so that it will cook evenly.

In medieval times, part of every nobleman's education was learning to become a skillful meat carver. Until recently, meat carving has been a skill passed down from generation to generation. Carving is an art that should be preserved. Well-carved meat, attractively arranged on a platter or serving plate, contributes to the presentation and enjoyment of a meal.

CARVING TECHNIQUES

The structure of meat determines how it should be carved. Careful examination of bones and muscle fiber alignment (grain) before cooking can be a guide. Bones outline the cutting plan, while the direction of slicing is based on muscle grain.

Most meat is sliced across the grain. Cutting through the outer connective tissue membrane of the fiber bundles and through the fibers shortens the fibers into segments and makes the meat easier to chew. Some cuts (e.g., corned beef brisket and flank steaks) are too thin to be sliced across the grain, so they are sliced diagonally across the grain. Most steaks, including tenderloin and rib steaks, have already been cut across the grain when the steaks were cut from the primal or subprimal cut.

Large cuts such as roasts are firmer and easier to carve if they stand (set) for a few minutes after cooking is completed. If carved immediately, there will be a significant loss of meat juices. Rare roasts should be covered loosely and allowed to remain in the open oven or some other warm place for 15 to 20 minutes before carving. The medium and well-done roast should be allowed to stand seven to 10 minutes. The internal temperature rises about 5 degrees (Fahrenheit) during the standing time, which should be included when cooking time is calculated. Steaks and chops do not need to set, and can be served immediately after cooking.

Uniform slices are the result of holding the knife at the same angle (generally 90° or perpendicular to the cutting surface) for each cut. The more tender the roast, the thicker the slices can be. A rib roast, for example, can be sliced as thick as ½ to ¾ inch, whereas bottom round roast slices should be no more than ⅛ to ¼ inch thick.

Slices should be placed neatly to one side on the carving board if there is room, or arranged in an overlapping row on a warmed serving platter. Many carvers prefer to carve all the meat needed for the first serving before serving anyone, so the slices are evenly divided. If leftovers are anticipated, some meat should be left unsliced because a solid piece of meat normally stays moist longer than do slices.

Figure 8-1
Carving

Carving Across the Grain

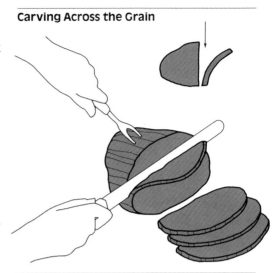

Carving Across the Bias of the Grain

Figure 8-2
Carving Certain Cuts of Meat

Beef Rib Roast

1. When necessary, remove wedge-shaped slice from large end so roast will stand firmly on this end. Insert fork below top rib. Carve across "face" of roast to rib bone.

2. Cut along rib bone with tip of knife to release slice.

3. Slide knife back under slice and, steadying it with fork, lift slice to side of carving board or to an auxiliary platter.

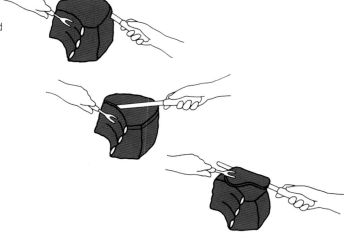

Lamb Leg Roast

1. With lower leg bone to right, remove two or three length-wise slices from thin side of leg. This side has the kneecap.

2. Turn roast up on its base and, starting where shank joins the leg, make slices perpendicular to leg bone or lift off cushion.

3. Loosen slices by cutting under them, following closely along top of leg bone. Lift slices to platter for serving.

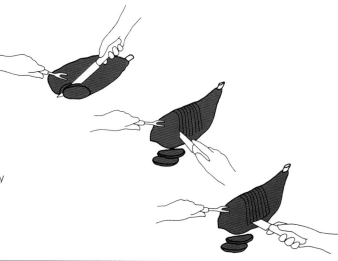

Shank Half of Ham

1. With shank at carver's left, turn ham so thick cushion side is up. Cut along top of leg and shank bones and under fork to lift off boneless cushion.

2. Place cushion meat on carving board and make perpendicular slices as illustrated.

3. Cut around leg bone with tip of knife to remove meat from this bone. Turn meat so that thickest side is down. Slice in same manner as cushion piece.

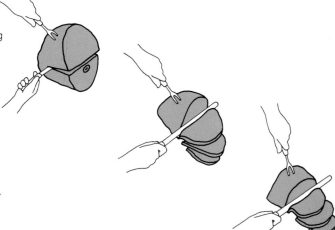

Meat is not as apt to slide on a wooden cutting board, and the surface is less likely to damage the knife's edge. Care must be taken when cleaning wooden boards because juices can lodge in crevices and slits in the board and create a favorable environment for bacterial growth. All wooden cutting boards or carving surfaces should be washed with hot soapy water and sanitized after each use with a mild bleach solution. Wooden cutting boards should never be submerged in water. Excessive moisture will cause them to warp and crack. Rubbing a board with coarse salt and lemon juice may help to remove stubborn grease stains.

Some health departments require food preparation surfaces made of materials approved by the National Sanitation Foundation (NSF). Plastic and hard-rubber cutting surfaces that can be easily cleaned and sanitized may be required for institutional use and are also available for home kitchens.

The NSF requires that materials be "corrosion resistant, nonabsorbent, smooth, easily cleanable and durable under conditions of normal use." Hard maple, plastic, rubber and rubberlike materials that meet these requirements may be used. Cutting surfaces must be resistant to scratching, scoring, decomposition, cracking, chipping and distortion. They must also have sufficient thickness and weight to permit cleaning and sanitizing.

The cutting board or carving platter should be firmly placed and, if possible, anchored so it does not slip when meat is carved. Many carving boards and platters have an indented well to catch juices, or are designed on a slant with a raised rim so juices can collect at the back of the board.

THE CARVING SURFACE

For all perpendicular carving, meat should be on a cutting board. Traditionally, cutting boards are made of wood, however, plastic or hard rubber surfaces may also be used.

Care of Knives

Knives should not be cleaned in a dishwasher unless the instructions indicate that they are dishwasher safe. The heat of a dishwasher affects the strength and elasticity of metal blades, and the repeated exposure to hot water is not good for either carbon steel or wooden handles. Knives should be carefully washed by hand in hot soapy water, rinsed well and dried immediately.

Knives should be stored in a box with individual knife slots or hung in a knife rack where they will not be dulled by rubbing against each other. The safest racks are slotted and should be securely attached to a wall or drawer, out of the reach of young children. If a magnetic rack is used, the magnets must be strong enough to hold the knives in place. A greasy knife will not adhere properly to a magnetic rack. If a knife holder is not available, knives should be stored in the protective jackets in which they were purchased.

KNIVES

Knives are designed for particular functions. For meat, a chef's knife is used for chopping, cubing, mincing and dicing; a narrow thin-bladed knife for boning; and a cleaver for cutting through bone and for tenderizing. A knife with an 8 to 9 inch curved blade is used to carve roasts. The carving knife is usually part of a set which includes a matching fork and a steel for sharpening the knife. The slicer is used with a carver's helper, which holds the meat steady during cutting.

Figure 8-3
Knives Used for Meat Cutting/Carving

Chef's Knife

Boning Knife

Cleaver

**Roast Slicer
with Carver's Helper**

**8" to 9" Carving Knife with
Fork and Sharpening Steel**

Steeling

A sharpening steel (butcher's steel) is used to keep a sharp edge on a quality knife over time if used regularly. The steel aligns the microscopic "teeth" of a knife edge which are bent during use, making the knife dull.

Sharpening steels are made of substances harder than the knife blades. They range in length from 8 to 14 inches, lengths of 10 and 12 inches being the most popular. A steel should have a protective guard by the handle.

KNIFE SHARPENERS

It is important to distinguish between methods used to maintain a knife's sharpness after the time it is professionally sharpened and those methods used to grind a new edge. Methods described here will apply to maintaining a knife's sharpness because grinding a new edge is a difficult, technical procedure that is best done by a professional.

Figure 8-4
Using a Sharpening Steel

123

How to Steel a Knife

Hold steel firmly in left hand, thumb on top of handle. Place heel of blade against far side of steel, with steel and blade of knife making a 25° angle.

Bring blade down along steel to the left with a swinging motion of right wrist. Entire length of blade should pass lightly over steel.

Bring knife back into starting position, but this time with blade on near side of steel making the 25° angle. Repeat stroking motion. Continue alternating strokes until edge is trued.

American Meat Institute (AMI), *Meat Facts*, 1989 ed., Washington, D.C.: AMI, August, 1989.

Anderson, J. and Chen, W., "Plant Fiber: Carbohydrate and Lipid Metabolism," *American Journal of Clinical Nutrition*, Vol. 32, 1979.

Block, B. *The Meat Board Meat Book*, New York: McGraw Hill, 1977.

Breidenstein, B.C. "The Meat We Really Eat," *Food and Nutrition News*, Vol. 56, No. 3, May-June, 1984.

Breidenstein, B.C. and Cannon, C.L., *Diet, Blood Lipids and Atherosclerosis*, Chicago: National Live Stock and Meat Board, 1985.

Breidenstein, B.C. and Williams, J.C., *Contribution of Red Meat to the U.S. Diet*, Chicago: National Live Stock and Meat Board, 1986.

Bryan, F.L. *Diseases Transmitted by Foods*, U.S. Department of Health and Human Services, 1982.

Buege, D.R., et. al., "A Nationwide Survey of the Composition and Marketing of Pork Products at Retail," University of Wisconsin, Madison, Wisconsin, 1990. Conducted in cooperation and with the guidance of the U.S. Department of Agriculture to provide the data base for the revision of USDA Agriculture Handbook 8-10, which will be published in 1991.

Bunch, K.S., *Food Consumption, Prices, and Expenditure, 1985*. Statistical Bulletin 749, Economic Research Service, U.S. Department of Agriculture, Washington, D.C.: U.S. Government Printing Office, 1987.

Campbell, A.M., et al., *The Experimental Study of Foods*, Boston: Houghton Mifflin Company, 1979.

Carroll, M.D., et al., Dietary intake source data: United States, 1976-80. *Vital and Health Statistics*. Series 11- No. 231. Public Health Service, Washington, D.C.: U.S. Government Printing Office, March, 1983.

Center for Human Nutrition, University of Texas Health Science Center at Dallas, "Monounsaturates Challenge Polyunsaturates' Superiority in Fight Against Cholesterol," *Nutrition and Health News*, Vol. 2, No. 2, Spring, 1985.

Charley, H., *Food Science*, New York: The Ronald Press Company, 1970.

Cook, J.D. and Monsen, E.R., "Food Iron Absorption in Human Subjects. III. Comparison of the Effect of Animal Proteins on Non-heme Iron Absorption," *American Journal of Clinical Nutrition*, Vol. 29, August, 1976.

deHoll, J.C. and deHoll, J.F., *Encyclopedia of Labeling Meat and Poultry Products*, 8th ed., Meat Plant Magazine, 1987.

Farm & Food Facts, Washington, D.C.: Kiplinger Agriculture Letter, 1989.

Federation of American Societies for Experimental Biology, *Assessment of the Iron Nutritional Status of the U.S. Population Based on Data Collected in the Second National Health and Nutrition Examination Survey, 1976-1980*. Washington, D.C.: U.S. Government Printing Office, August, 1984.

Forrest, J.C., et al., *Principles of Meat Science*, San Francisco: W.H. Freeman and Company, 1975.

Greger, J.L., "Nutrient Interactions Involving Iron and Zinc," *Food and Nutrition News*, Vol. 55, No. 3, May-June, 1983.

Guthrie, H.A., *Introductory Nutrition*, 7th ed., St. Louis: Times Mirror/Mosby, College Publishing, 1989.

Hallberg, L. and Rossander, L. "Absorption of Iron from Western-type Lunch and Dinner Meals," *American Journal of Clinical Nutrition*, Vol. 35, March, 1982.

"Irradiation in the Production, Processing and Handling of Food," *Federal Register*, Vol. 50, Number 140, July 22, 1985.

Krause, M.B. and Mahan, L.K., *Food, Nutrition and Diet Therapy*, Philadelphia: W.B. Saunders, 7th ed., 1984.

Lawrie, R.A., *Meat Science*, New York: Pergamon Press, 4th ed., 1985.

Lehninger, A.L., *Biochemistry*, New York, Worth Publisher, 1981.

Levie, A., *Meat Handbook*, 4th ed., Westport, CT: AVI Publishing Company, Inc., 1979.

Lundberg, D.E. and Kotschevar, L.H., *Understanding Cooking*, Holyoke, MA: Marcus Printing Company, 1976.

Mattson, F.H. and Grundy, S.M., "Comparison of Effects of Dietary Saturated, Monounsaturated, and Polyunsaturated Fatty Acids on Plasma Lipids and Lipoproteins in Man," *Journal of Lipid Research*, Vol. 26, 1985.

The Meat Evaluation Handbook, Chicago: National Live Stock and Meat Board, 1983.

Mertz, W., "Mineral Elements: New Perspectives," *Journal of the American Dietetic Association*, Vol. 77, September, 1980.

Monsen, E.R., et al., Estimation of Available Dietary Iron. *American Journal of Clinical Nutrition*, Vol. 31, 1978.

National Research Council, *Designing Foods*, Washington, D.C.: National Academy Press, 1988.

National Research Council, 10th ed., *Recommended Dietary Allowances*, Washington, D.C.: National Academy Press, 1989.

1982 Yearbook of Agriculture, Food from Farm to Table, Washington, D.C.: U.S. Government Printing Office, 1982.

Paddleford, C., *How America Eats*, New York: Charles Scribner's Sons, 1960.

Perkins, E.G. and Visek, W.J., "Dietary Fats and Health," Champaign, IL: American Oil Chemists Society, 1983.

Potter, N. N., *Food Science*, 4th ed., Westport, CT: AVI Publishing Co., 1986.

Price, J.F. and Schweigert, B.S. eds. *The Science of Meat and Meat Products*, Wesport, CT: Food and Nutrition Press, Inc., 1978.

Romans, J.R., et al., *The Meat We Eat*, 12th ed., Danville, IL: The Interstate Printers and Publishers, Inc., 1985.

Root, W. and deRochement, R., *Eating in America—A History*, New York: William Morrow and Company, Inc., 1976.

"Scientific Status Summaries of the Institute of Food Technologists' Expert Panel on Food Safety and Nutrition, Mechanically Deboned Red Meat, Poultry and Fish," Chicago: Institute of Food Technologists, March, 1979.

Shaping a Nation, The Role of the Livestock and Meat Industry in History and Economics, Chicago: National Live Stock and Meat Board, 1984.

Sinclair, U., *The Jungle*, 1906, New York: Penguin, 1980 Edition.

Spencer, H., et al., "Further Studies of the Effect of a High Protein Diet of Meat on Calcium Metabolism," *American Journal of Clinical Nutrition*, Vol. 37, June, 1983.

Trager, J., *The Food Book*, New York: Grossman Publishers, 1970.

Uniform Retail Meat Identity Standards, Chicago: National Live Stock and Meat Board, 1973.

U.S. Bureau of the Census. *Statistical Abstract of the United States: 1988*, 108th ed., Washington, D. C., 1987.

USDA, *Composition of Foods: Beef Products—Raw, Processed, Prepared, Agriculture Handbook No. 8-13*, Washington, D.C.: U.S. Government Printing Office, 1986.

USDA, *Composition of Foods: Dairy and Egg Products—Raw, Processed, Prepared, Agriculture Handbook No. 8-1*, Washington, D.C.: U.S. Government Printing Office, 1976.

USDA, *Composition of Foods: Fats and Oils— Raw, Processed, Prepared, Agriculture Handbook No. 8-4*, Washington, D.C.: U.S. Government Printing Office, 1979.

USDA, *Composition of Foods: Finfish and Shellfish Products—Raw, Processed, Prepared, Agriculture Handbook No. 8-15*, Washington, D.C.: U.S. Government Printing Office, 1987.

USDA, *Composition of Foods: Fruits and Fruit Juices—Raw, Processed, Prepared, Agriculture Handbook No. 8-9*, Washington, D.C.: U.S. Government Printing Office, 1979.

USDA, *Composition of Foods: Lamb, Veal and Game—Raw, Processed, Prepared, Agriculture Handbook No. 8-17*, Washington, D.C.: U.S. Government Printing Office, 1989.

USDA, *Composition of Foods: Pork Products—Raw, Processed, Prepared, Agriculture Handbook No. 8-10*, Washington, D.C.: U.S. Government Printing Office, 1983.

USDA, *Composition of Foods: Poultry Products—Raw, Processed, Prepared, Agriculture Handbook No. 8-5*, Washington, D.C.: U.S. Government Printing Office, 1983.

USDA, *Nutrition and Your Health, Dietary Guidelines for Americans*, Home and Garden Bulletin No. 232-1, Washington, D.C.: U.S. Government Printing Office, April, 1986.

USDA, *Nutritive Value of Foods*, Home and Garden Bulletin No. 72, Washington, D.C.: U.S. Government Printing Office, 1981.

USDA, *Provisional Table on the Fatty Acid and Cholesterol Content of Selected Foods*, March, 1984 (Slightly revised June, 1984).

USDA, *The Safe Food Book*, Home and Garden Bulletin No. 241, Washington, D.C.: U.S. Government Printing Office, July, 1984.

Wentworth, E.N., *American Sheep Trails*, Ames, IA: The Iowa State College Press, 1948.

Wilson, George D., *Listeria Monocytogenes*, Reciprocal Meat Conference Proceedings, Vol. 41, 1988.

World Health Organization, *Foodborne Listeriosis*, Report of a WHO Informal Working Group, Geneva, 15-19 February, 1988.

Appendix

NUTRIENT VALUE TABLE

Nutrient Values for 3 oz Portions, Lean Only

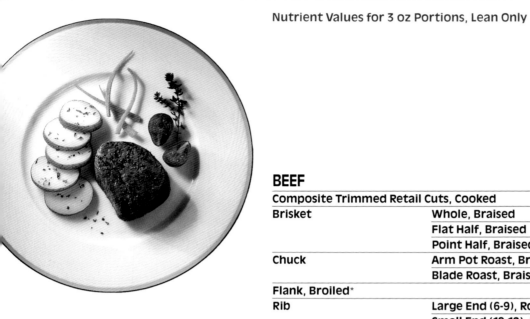

BEEF

		Food Energy (kcal)	Protein (g)	Total Fat (g)	Ash (g)
			Proximate		
Composite Trimmed Retail Cuts, Cooked		183	25.14	8.42	1.02
Brisket	Whole, Braised	206	25.29	10.85	0.88
	Flat Half, Braised	189	26.79	8.24	0.93
	Point Half, Braised	222	23.84	13.34	0.83
Chuck	Arm Pot Roast, Braised	183	28.07	7.05	0.94
	Blade Roast, Braised	213	26.40	11.13	0.84
Flank, Broiled*		176	23.01	8.60	1.73
Rib	Large End (6-9), Roasted	201	23.40	11.22	0.92
	Small End (10-12), Broiled	188	23.83	9.52	1.05
Short Ribs, Braised*		251	26.14	15.41	0.83
Round	Full Cut, Broiled*	162	24.83	6.22	1.20
	Bottom Round, Braised	178	26.85	6.97	0.97
	Eye of Round, Roasted	143	24.64	4.16	1.03
	Tip Round, Roasted	157	24.41	5.86	1.00
	Top Round, Broiled	153	26.93	4.16	1.17
Shanks, Crosscuts, Simmered*		171	28.63	5.41	2.03
Short Loin	Porterhouse Steak, Broiled*	185	23.94	9.18	1.05
	T-Bone Steak, Broiled*	182	23.91	8.81	1.05
	Tenderloin, Broiled	179	24.01	8.50	1.10
	Top Loin, Broiled	176	24.33	7.99	0.99
	Top Sirloin, Broiled	165	25.81	6.12	1.16
Ground Beef	73% Lean, Broiled, med.	246	20.46	17.59	0.85
	80% Lean, Broiled, med.	231	21.01	15.69	0.92
	85% Lean, Broiled, med.	217	21.59	13.88	0.86
Variety Meats	Brain, Panfried	167	10.68	13.46	1.34
	Heart, Simmered	148	24.47	4.77	0.92
	Kidneys, Simmered	122	21.66	2.92	1.10
	Liver, Braised	137	20.72	4.16	1.20
	Tongue, Simmered	241	18.80	17.63	0.65

*Nutrient information given is for cuts which grade Choice.
All other beef cut information uses All Grades data.

		Minerals						Vitamins							Fatty Acids			
Iron (mg)	Magnesium (mg)	Phosphorus (mg)	Potassium (mg)	Sodium (mg)	Zinc (mg)	Copper (mg)	Manganese (mg)	Thiamin (mg)	Riboflavin (mg)	Niacin (mg)	Pantothenic Acid (mg)	Vitamin B$_6$ (mg)	Folacin (mcg)	Vitamin B$_{12}$ (mcg)	Saturated, Total (g)	Monounsaturated, Total (g)	Polyunsaturated, Total (g)	Cholesterol (mg)
2.54	22	198	306	57	5.89	0.106	0.014	0.08	0.21	3.51	0.34	0.32	7	2.24	3.22	3.54	0.29	73
2.39	20	205	242	60	5.85	0.101	0.014	0.06	0.19	3.15	0.30	0.25	7	2.21	3.87	4.99	0.33	79
2.41	21	218	253	54	5.41	0.105	0.014	0.06	0.19	3.28	0.32	0.26	7	2.24	2.70	3.68	0.31	81
2.37	19	192	232	65	6.28	0.098	0.014	0.06	0.19	3.03	0.29	0.24	7	2.19	5.01	6.25	0.34	77
3.22	20	228	246	56	7.36	0.139	0.016	0.07	0.25	3.16	0.33	0.28	9	2.89	2.56	2.95	0.28	86
3.13	20	200	224	60	8.73	0.126	0.015	0.07	0.24	2.27	0.30	0.25	5	2.10	4.32	4.80	0.36	90
2.19	20	201	352	70	4.08	0.084	0.013	0.09	0.16	4.28	0.30	0.29	7	2.77	3.70	3.46	0.34	57
2.40	21	178	303	62	6.34	0.089	0.014	0.07	0.19	3.78	0.38	0.22	8	2.22	4.48	4.69	0.32	69
2.18	23	177	335	59	5.94	0.085	0.014	0.09	0.18	4.08	0.29	0.34	7	2.82	3.85	4.02	0.27	68
2.86	19	199	266	50	6.63	0.091	0.015	0.06	0.17	2.73	0.29	0.24	6	2.94	6.58	6.78	0.47	79
2.29	24	218	359	54	3.95	0.091	0.013	0.09	0.19	3.62	0.35	0.34	9	2.69	2.18	2.63	0.26	66
2.94	21	231	262	43	4.66	0.114	0.015	0.06	0.22	3.47	0.36	0.31	9	2.10	2.35	3.05	0.27	82
1.66	23	192	336	53	4.03	0.085	0.014	0.07	0.15	3.19	0.39	0.32	6	1.84	1.51	1.76	0.13	59
2.50	23	206	328	55	6.01	0.106	0.014	0.08	0.23	3.18	0.40	0.34	7	2.46	2.05	2.33	0.23	69
2.45	26	332	376	52	4.73	0.105	0.014	0.10	0.23	5.13	0.42	0.48	10	2.11	1.43	1.62	0.19	71
3.28	25	224	380	54	8.92	0.146	0.017	0.12	0.18	5.01	0.35	0.31	8	3.22	1.94	2.43	0.18	66
2.55	25	181	346	56	4.59	0.122	0.013	0.09	0.21	3.94	0.29	0.34	7	1.93	3.67	3.68	0.34	68
2.55	25	177	346	56	4.59	0.122	0.013	0.09	0.21	3.94	0.28	0.33	7	1.93	3.53	3.54	0.33	68
3.04	25	202	356	54	4.75	0.152	0.014	0.11	0.25	3.33	0.32	0.37	6	2.18	3.18	3.21	0.32	71
2.10	23	185	337	58	4.44	0.091	0.014	0.08	0.17	4.54	0.31	0.36	7	1.70	3.05	3.21	0.26	65
2.86	27	207	343	56	5.54	0.124	0.014	0.11	0.25	3.64	0.33	0.38	8	2.42	2.38	2.61	0.24	76
2.07	17	144	248	70	4.40	0.070	0.014	0.03	0.16	4.91	0.28	0.23	8	2.49	6.91	7.70	0.66	76
1.79	18	134	256	65	4.56	0.056	0.012	0.04	0.18	4.39	0.32	0.22	8	2.00	6.16	6.87	0.58	74
2.00	18	137	266	59	4.63	0.060	0.014	0.05	0.23	4.21	0.30	0.23	8	1.84	5.45	6.08	0.52	71
1.89	12	328	301	134	1.15	0.187	0.027	0.11	0.22	3.21	0.49	0.33	5	12.92	3.18	3.38	1.96	1696
6.38	22	213	198	54	2.66	0.629	0.050	0.12	1.31	3.46	0.74	0.18	2	12.16	1.43	1.06	1.16	164
6.21	15	260	152	114	3.59	0.578	0.157	0.16	3.45	5.12	1.44	0.44	83	43.61	0.93	0.63	0.63	329
5.75	17	343	200	59	5.16	3.835	0.351	0.17	3.48	9.11	3.88	0.77	184	60.35	1.62	0.55	0.91	331
2.88	14	121	153	51	4.08	0.187	0.022	0.03	0.30	1.83	0.44	0.14	4	5.02	7.59	8.05	0.66	91

Nutrient Values for 3 oz Portions, Lean Only

		Proximate			
		Food Energy (kcal)	Protein (g)	Total Fat (g)	Ash (g)

VEAL

Retail Composite, Cooked		166	27.11	5.59	1.05
Leg, Cutlets, Breaded, Panfried		175	24.15	5.33	1.99
Loin, Whole, Braised		192	28.53	7.78	0.98
Rib, Whole, Roasted		151	21.89	6.32	0.92
Shoulder	Whole, Braised	169	28.62	5.19	1.08
	Arm, Braised	171	30.37	4.53	1.11
	Blade, Braised	168	27.76	5.50	1.06
Sirloin, Whole, Braised		173	28.86	5.53	1.02
Cubed Lean, Braised		160	29.70	3.66	1.61
Ground Lean, Broiled		146	20.72	6.43	1.11
Variety Meats	Brain, Braised	115	9.76	8.18	1.19
	Heart, Braised	158	24.76	5.74	1.54
	Kidneys, Braised	139	22.37	4.81	1.23
	Liver, Braised	140	18.38	5.87	1.19
	Tongue, Braised	171	21.98	8.59	0.77

PORK

Ham	Whole, Roasted	187	24.07	9.38	0.94
	Rump Half, Roasted	187	24.77	9.06	1.01
	Shank Half, Roasted	183	23.98	8.92	0.89
Loin	Blade, Roasted	203	22.61	12.58	1.00
	Center Loin Chop, Broiled	165	25.67	6.89	1.02
	Center Rib Chop, Broiled	179	25.08	8.50	0.99
	Sirloin Chop, Broiled	156	26.44	5.70	1.16
	Tenderloin, Roasted	133	23.89	4.08	1.11
	Top Loin Chop, Broiled	165	26.44	6.63	0.99
Shoulder	Arm Picnic, Roasted	194	22.68	10.73	0.90
	Blade Steak, Broiled	187	22.70	10.63	0.93
Variety Meats	Brains, Braised	117	10.32	8.09	1.19
	Heart, Braised	126	20.06	4.29	0.85
	Kidneys, Braised	128	21.59	4.00	1.11
	Liver, Braised	141	22.12	3.74	1.28
	Tongue, Braised	230	20.49	15.81	0.68

	Minerals								Vitamins							Fatty Acids			
Iron (mg)	Magnesium (mg)	Phosphorus (mg)	Potassium (mg)	Sodium (mg)	Zinc (mg)	Copper (mg)	Manganese (mg)	Thiamin (mg)	Riboflavin (mg)	Niacin (mg)	Pantothenic Acid (mg)	Vitamin B_6 (mg)	Folacin (mcg)	Vitamin B_{12} (mcg)	Saturated, Total (g)	Monounsaturated, Total (g)	Polyunsaturated, Total (g)	Cholesterol (mg)
0.99	24	213	288	76	4.33	0.10	0.03	0.05	0.29	7.16	1.13	0.28	13	1.41	1.56	2.00	0.50	100
1.39	27	219	326	387	2.44	0.06	0.12	0.14	0.31	9.18	0.94	0.36	17	1.09	1.36	1.84	1.15	96
0.93	23	201	253	71	3.47	0.08	0.03	0.04	0.28	8.54	0.72	0.24	13	1.12	2.17	2.78	0.70	107
0.82	20	176	264	82	3.81	0.09	0.03	0.05	0.25	6.37	1.17	0.23	12	1.34	1.77	2.26	0.57	97
1.23	24	221	271	83	5.95	0.14	0.03	0.05	0.30	5.68	1.37	0.22	14	1.65	1.45	1.85	0.47	110
1.20	26	234	295	76	5.30	0.12	0.03	0.05	0.28	9.11	1.18	0.26	16	1.55	1.26	1.62	0.41	132
1.25	23	214	259	86	6.28	0.15	0.03	0.05	0.31	4.82	1.35	0.21	13	1.71	1.54	1.97	0.49	135
1.05	25	220	288	69	4.04	0.12	0.03	0.05	0.32	6.00	0.92	0.32	13	1.35	1.54	1.98	0.50	96
1.23	24	203	291	79	5.10	0.13	0.03	0.06	0.34	7.05	1.01	0.33	14	1.42	1.10	1.18	0.38	124
0.84	20	184	287	70	3.29	0.09	0.03	0.06	0.23	6.83	0.98	0.33	10	1.08	2.59	2.41	0.47	87
1.42	14	327	181	133	1.37	0.22	0.03	0.07	0.17	2.07	0.85	0.14	3	8.20	—	—	—	2635
3.67	16	213	169	50	1.90	0.37	—	0.30	0.79	4.15	1.40	—	—	—	1.54	1.21	1.52	150
2.58	20	316	135	93	3.61	0.31	0.11	0.16	1.69	3.94	0.73	0.15	18	31.36	1.48	1.05	0.96	672
2.23	16	271	174	45	8.09	6.76	0.10	0.11	1.65	7.21	1.94	0.42	645	31.02	2.18	1.26	0.93	477
1.78	15	141	138	54	3.83	0.18	0.04	0.06	0.30	1.25	0.63	0.13	7	4.50	—	—	—	—
0.95	21	239	317	55	2.77	0.09	0.03	0.587	0.297	4.195	0.570	0.38	10	0.61	3.23	4.21	1.14	80
0.96	24	242	332	55	2.56	0.09	0.02	0.648	0.303	4.267	0.638	0.26	5	0.62	3.12	4.07	1.10	81
0.95	21	236	306	54	2.93	0.09	0.03	0.538	0.292	4.149	0.582	0.39	5	0.61	3.07	4.01	1.08	78
0.92	22	208	347	65	3.22	0.09	0.01	0.646	0.323	3.970	0.697	0.37	4	0.88	4.55	5.84	0.87	76
0.78	25	208	357	66	1.89	0.07	0.01	0.977	0.262	4.711	0.587	0.40	5	0.63	2.47	3.17	0.47	70
0.69	25	226	373	57	2.02	0.07	0.02	0.760	0.275	4.446	0.634	0.34	7	0.59	3.03	3.92	0.54	69
0.75	29	225	369	51	2.01	0.09	0.01	0.876	0.342	4.049	0.770	0.46	5	0.72	1.88	2.48	0.45	78
1.31	21	245	457	57	2.55	0.14	0.03	0.799	0.332	4.003	0.584	0.36	5	0.47	1.40	1.62	0.35	67
0.69	25	226	373	57	2.02	0.07	0.02	0.760	0.275	4.446	0.634	0.34	7	0.59	2.32	3.15	0.36	68
1.55	10	187	166	77	1.26	0.22	0.07	0.066	0.190	2.831	1.550	0.12	—	1.21	3.70	4.82	1.30	81
1.36	17	186	300	62	3.71	0.11	0.01	0.502	0.315	3.655	0.485	0.26	4	0.82	3.66	4.92	0.88	80
1.55	10	187	166	77	1.26	0.22	0.07	0.066	0.190	2.831	1.550	0.12	—	1.21	1.82	1.46	1.25	2169
4.96	20	151	175	30	2.63	0.43	0.06	0.472	1.447	5.143	2.100	0.33	3	3.22	1.14	1	1.11	188
4.50	15	204	121	68	3.53	0.58	0.13	0.337	1.348	4.917	2.442	0.39	35	6.62	1.28	1.31	0.32	408
15.23	12	205	128	42	5.71	0.54	0.26	0.219	1.867	7.170	4.058	0.48	139	15.87	1.20	0.53	0.90	302
4.24	17	148	201	93	3.85	—	—	0.269	0.434	4.539	—	.20	—	2.03	5.48	7.47	1.64	124

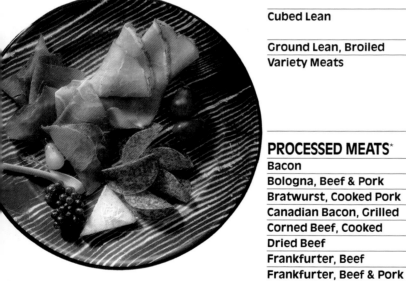

Nutrient Values for 3 oz Portions, Lean Only

		Food Energy (kcal)	Protein (g)	Total Fat (g)	Ash (g)
LAMB					
Retail Composite, Cooked		175	23.99	8.09	0.97
Foreshank, Braised		159	26.36	5.12	0.80
Leg	**Whole, Roasted**	162	24.05	6.58	0.93
	Shank Half, Roasted	153	23.94	5.67	0.93
	Sirloin Half, Roasted	173	24.10	7.80	0.93
Loin, Whole, Broiled		183	25.49	8.27	1.06
Rib, Whole, Roasted		197	22.23	11.32	0.91
Shoulder	**Whole, Braised**	241	27.89	13.51	1.49
	Arm, Braised	237	30.21	11.97	1.04
	Blade, Broiled	179	21.66	9.62	1.07
Cubed Lean	**Braised**	190	28.64	7.48	1.51
	Broiled	158	23.86	6.23	1.25
Ground Lean, Broiled		240	21.04	16.70	0.97
Variety Meats	**Brain, Braised**	124	10.66	8.64	1.16
	Heart, Braised	158	21.22	6.73	0.84
	Kidneys, Braised	117	20.10	3.08	1.10
	Liver, Braised	187	25.98	7.49	1.21
	Tongue, Braised	234	18.34	17.24	0.62
PROCESSED MEATS*					
Bacon		163	8.63	13.96	1.92
Bologna, Beef & Pork		89	3.31	8.01	0.84
Bratwurst, Cooked Pork		85	3.99	7.33	0.52
Canadian Bacon, Grilled		52	6.87	2.39	1.21
Corned Beef, Cooked		71	5.15	5.38	0.74
Dried Beef		47	8.25	1.11	2.53
Frankfurter, Beef		89	3.41	8.09	0.82
Frankfurter, Beef & Pork		91	3.20	8.26	0.89
Ham	**Extra Lean (5%), Roasted**	41	5.93	1.57	1.24
	Regular (11%), Roasted	50	6.41	2.56	1.12
	Whole, Lean Only, Roasted	45	7.10	1.56	1.06
Italian Sausage		92	5.68	7.29	0.80
Pastrami, Beef		99	4.89	8.27	1.08
Pepperoni		141	5.94	12.47	1.47
Polish Sausage		92	4.00	8.14	0.68
Pork Sausage		105	5.57	8.83	1.02
Salami	**Cooked, Beef & Pork**	71	3.95	5.70	0.94
	Hard, Pork & Beef	118	6.46	9.72	1.55
Smoked Link Sausage, Pork		110	6.29	9.00	1.34
Thin Sliced Beef		50	7.97	1.09	1.20
Thuringer, Summer Sausage		95	4.47	8.37	1.04

Proximate

*Processed meat servings are 1 oz portions.

	Minerals							Vitamins							Fatty Acids			
Iron (mg)	Magnesium (mg)	Phosphorus (mg)	Potassium (mg)	Sodium (mg)	Zinc (mg)	Copper (mg)	Manganese (mg)	Thiamin (mg)	Riboflavin (mg)	Niacin (mg)	Pantothenic Acid (mg)	Vitamin B_6 (mg)	Folacin (mcg)	Vitamin B_{12} (mcg)	Saturated, Total (g)	Monounsaturated, Total (g)	Polyunsaturated, Total (g)	Cholesterol (mg)
1.74	22	179	293	64	4.48	0.11	0.02	0.09	0.24	5.37	0.58	0.14	19	2.22	2.89	3.55	0.53	78
1.93	20	149	227	63	7.36	0.11	0.02	0.04	0.16	4.31	0.54	0.09	16	1.92	1.83	2.24	0.34	89
1.81	22	175	287	58	4.20	0.10	0.02	0.09	0.25	5.39	0.60	0.14	20	2.24	2.35	2.88	0.43	76
1.75	22	177	291	56	4.27	0.10	0.02	0.09	0.24	5.43	0.60	0.14	21	2.30	2.03	2.49	0.37	74
1.87	22	173	283	60	4.12	0.10	0.02	0.10	0.26	5.33	0.59	0.14	18	2.20	2.79	3.42	0.51	78
1.70	24	192	320	71	3.51	0.12	0.02	0.10	0.24	5.82	0.56	0.14	21	2.14	2.95	3.62	0.54	80
1.50	20	165	268	69	3.80	0.11	0.02	0.08	0.20	5.24	0.56	0.13	19	1.84	4.04	4.96	0.74	74
2.27	23	173	222	67	6.39	0.11	0.03	0.05	0.20	5.07	0.53	0.10	16	2.47	5.24	5.48	1.17	99
2.30	25	197	287	64	6.20	0.13	0.02	0.06	0.23	5.38	0.53	0.11	19	2.25	4.28	5.24	0.79	103
1.54	22	184	312	75	5.51	0.11	0.02	0.08	0.23	5.16	0.59	0.14	18	2.39	3.44	4.22	0.63	78
2.38	24	174	221	60	5.59	0.12	0.03	0.06	0.20	5.05	0.51	0.10	18	2.32	2.68	3.01	0.68	92
1.99	26	190	285	65	4.90	0.13	0.02	0.09	0.25	5.62	0.59	0.12	19	2.58	2.23	2.51	0.57	77
1.52	21	171	288	69	3.97	0.11	0.02	0.09	0.22	5.69	0.56	0.12	16	2.22	6.90	7.07	1.19	82
1.43	12	286	175	114	1.16	0.18	0.05	0.09	0.21	2.10	0.84	0.09	4	7.86	2.21	1.57	0.89	1737
4.69	21	216	160	54	3.13	0.52	0.05	0.14	1.01	3.71	1.16	0.25	2	9.52	2.67	1.89	0.66	212
10.54	17	246	151	128	3.23	0.31	0.12	0.30	1.76	5.10	1.73	0.10	69	67.06	1.04	0.66	0.57	481
7.04	18	357	188	48	6.71	6.01	0.44	0.20	3.43	10.33	3.37	0.42	62	65.02	2.90	1.56	1.12	426
2.24	14	114	134	57	2.54	0.18	0.03	0.07	0.36	3.14	0.29	0.14	2	5.35	6.66	8.50	1.06	161
0.46	7	95	138	452	0.92	0.05	0.01	0.196	0.081	2.076	0.299	0.077	1	0.496	4.94	6.72	1.65	24
0.43	3	26	51	289	0.55	0.02	0.01	0.049	0.039	0.731	0.080	0.050	1	0.380	3.03	3.80	0.68	16
0.36	4	42	60	158	0.65	0.03	0.01	0.143	0.052	0.907	0.090	0.060	—	0.270	2.64	3.46	0.78	17
0.23	6	84	111	438	0.48	0.02	0.01	0.234	0.056	1.960	0.147	0.130	1	0.220	0.81	1.15	0.23	16
0.53	3	35	41	321	1.30	0.04	0.01	0.007	0.048	0.859	0.119	0.070	—	0.460	1.80	2.61	0.19	28
1.28	9	49	126	984	1.49	0.05	—	—	—	—	—	—	—	—	0.45	0.46	0.06	—
0.41	1	25	47	291	0.62	0.02	0.01	0.014	0.029	0.685	0.082	0.030	1	0.440	3.42	3.86	0.39	17
0.33	3	24	47	318	0.52	0.02	0.01	0.056	0.034	0.747	0.099	0.040	1	0.370	3.05	3.88	0.77	14
0.42	4	56	81	341	0.82	0.02	0.02	0.214	0.057	1.141	0.114	0.110	1	0.180	0.51	0.74	0.15	15
0.38	6	80	116	425	0.70	0.04	0.01	0.207	0.094	1.744	0.204	0.090	—	0.200	0.88	1.26	0.40	17
0.27	6	64	90	376	0.73	0.03	0.01	0.193	0.072	1.423	0.141	0.130	1	0.200	0.52	0.72	0.18	16
0.43	5	48	86	261	0.67	0.02	0.02	0.177	0.066	1.181	0.128	0.090	—	0.370	2.57	3.38	0.93	22
0.54	5	43	65	348	1.21	—	—	0.027	0.048	1.436	—	0.050	—	0.500	2.95	4.10	0.28	26
0.40	5	34	98	578	0.71	0.02	—	0.091	0.071	1.406	0.530	0.070	—	0.710	4.57	5.98	1.24	—
0.41	4	39	67	248	0.55	0.03	0.01	0.142	0.042	0.976	0.130	0.050	—	0.280	2.93	3.83	0.87	20
0.35	5	52	102	367	0.71	0.04	0.02	0.210	0.072	1.281	0.204	0.090	—	0.490	3.06	3.94	1.08	24
0.76	4	33	56	302	0.61	0.06	0.02	0.068	0.107	1.007	0.240	0.060	1	1.040	2.29	2.61	0.57	18
0.43	5	40	107	527	0.92	0.02	0.01	0.170	0.081	1.380	0.301	0.142	—	0.540	3.46	4.85	0.91	22
0.33	5	46	95	425	0.80	0.02	—	0.198	0.073	1.285	0.221	0.100	—	0.460	3.21	4.15	1.07	19
0.76	5	48	122	408	1.13	0.01	0.01	0.023	0.054	1.494	0.167	0.100	—	0.730	0.47	0.47	0.06	12
0.72	4	31	77	352	0.72	0.04	—	0.043	0.094	1.222	—	0.070	—	1.560	3.41	3.68	0.34	21

Beef and Veal (Bovine)

Veal	An immature male or female bovine animal, up to four months of age, that has been fed primarily milk or milk replacers.
Bob veal	Bob veal or Bobby veal are very young beef or dairy animals (usually less than 21 days of age at slaughter and weighing less than 150 pounds).
Special-fed veal	Special-fed veal are beef or dairy animals that are fed scientifically controlled liquid diets to produce pale, fine-textured meat. Such animals are generally slaughtered from five to 16 weeks of age or 150 to 400 pounds live weight. Such animals are also referred to as Formula-Fed, Milk-Fed or Nature-Fed Veal.
Calf	An immature bovine animal four to nine months old that can be slaughtered, as such, or designated either for breeding or fed in a feedlot for subsequent slaughter. Calves normally weigh more than 400 pounds and, if slaughtered at live weights of 400 to 800 pounds, are called "baby beef." Calf meat is normally differentiated from veal on the basis of lean color. Calf has a grayish red to moderately red lean color, while veal is usually grayish pink.
Heifer	A young female bovine animal that has not borne a calf. Heifers produce high grade meat which is superior to that of cows.
Cow	A female bovine animal that has borne one or more calves. Cows are mainly used for milk production; however, when they are no longer productive, they are sold for beef.
Steer	A male bovine animal that has been castrated as a calf and which has not developed secondary physical characteristics of a bull. Castration is performed to improve the quality of the meat. Beef steers (15 to 24 months old) typically furnish more than 2/3 of the high grade beef on the market.
Bullock	A young bull, under 24 months of age (castrated or uncastrated at the time of slaughter) which has developed or has begun to develop the secondary physical characteristics of a bull.
Bull	A fully developed, mature (24 months of age or older) male bovine animal.
Stag	A male bovine animal that has been castrated after reaching sexual maturity.

Pork (Porcine)

Pig	A porcine animal that is less than 4 months of age and/or which weighs less than 120 pounds
Hog	A porcine animal that is more than 4 months of age and which weighs more than 120 pounds.
Barrow	A male porcine animal castrated when young.
Gilt	A female porcine animal that has not had offspring or has not reached an evident stage of pregnancy. Gilts and barrows that are from 5 to 7 months of age produce the highest quality pork.
Shoat	A young feeder pig. Shoats usually weigh 40 to 100 pounds.
Feeder pig	A barrow or gilt that will be raised for meat. Purchased after weaning, a feeder pig weighs about 40 pounds. It is fed until it reaches about 220 pounds, at which time it is marketed as a butcher hog.
Sow	An adult female hog that is in an evident stage of pregnancy or has borne at least one litter of pigs. A sow usually produces large cuts of meat.
Boar	An adult male hog that is used for breeding. Most boar meat has a strong undesirable odor and flavor.
Roaster pig	A barrow, gilt or boar weighing 30 to 60 pounds, although weights outside of this range are common. The carcasses are sold whole without splitting to allow for stuffing or spit roasting.

Lamb (Ovine)

Ewe	A female ovine animal.
Wether	A castrated male ovine animal which has not reached sexual maturity or developed the physical characteristics of a ram.
Ram	An uncastrated male ovine animal of any age. Sometimes referred to as a "buck."
Hothouse lamb	A young ovine animal between 6 and 10 weeks old, weighing between 25 and 60 pounds. Can be ewe, wether or ram lambs but they are almost always reared in a closed area—e.g., in a "hot house"—hence the name.
Spring lamb	An ovine animal ranging in age from 3 to 7 months and in weight from 70 to 120 pounds. Sex class is unimportant in spring lambs due to their young age, therefore, they can be ewes, wethers or rams.
Lamb	Ovine animals which are under 1 year of age including, but not restricted to, those classified as either hothouse or spring lambs. They are normally marketed at 7 to 12 months of age.
Yearling	A male or female ovine animal approximately 12 to 24 months of age at slaughter.
Mature sheep	Ovine animals that are 2 years of age or older.
Mutton	Meat from sheep that are considered physiologically mature.

Temperature

°C	°F
100	212
90	194
80	176
70	158
60	140
50	122
40	104
35	95
30	86
25	77
20	68
15	59
10	50
5	41
0	32
−5	23
−10	14
−15	5
−20	−4
−25	−13
−30	−22
−40	−40

*(9/5 C) + 32

*Multiply the System Internationale (SI) units (degrees Centigrade or Celsius) by this factor to convert to Farenheit.

Length

inch	cm	feet
0.4	1	
0.8	2	
1.2	3	0.1
1.6	4	
2	5	
2.4	6	0.2
2.8	7	
3.1	8	
3.5	9	
3.9	10	0.3
7.9	20	0.6
12	30	1
16	40	1.3
20	50	1.6
24	60	2
28	70	2.3
32	80	2.6
36	90	3
39	100	3.3
79	200	6.6
118	300	9.8
157	400	13
197	500	16
236	600	20
276	700	23
315	800	26
354	900	30
394	1000	33

*0.3937 ____ *0.0328

*Multiply the System Internationale (SI) units (centimeters) by this factor to convert to inches or feet.

Volume

qt	L	gal
1	1	0.3
2.1	2	0.5
3.2	3	0.8
4.2	4	1.1
5.3	5	1.3
6.3	6	1.6
7.4	7	1.8
8.5	8	2.1
9.5	9	2.4
11	10	2.6
21	20	5.3
32	30	7.9
42	40	11
53	50	13
63	60	16
74	70	18
85	80	21
95	90	24
106	100	26
211	200	53
317	300	79
423	400	106
528	500	132
634	600	159
740	700	185
846	800	211
951	900	238
1057	1000	264

*1.057 ____ *0.264

*Multiply the System Internationale (SI) units (liters) by this factor to convert to quarts or gallons.

Weight

lb	kg	ton	g	oz
0.2	0.1		1	0.04
0.4	0.2		2	0.07
0.7	0.3		3	0.1
0.9	0.4		4	0.14
1.1	0.5		5	0.18
1.3	0.6		6	0.21
1.5	0.7		7	0.25
1.8	0.8		8	0.28
2	0.9		9	0.32
2.2	1		10	0.35
4.4	2		20	0.7
6.6	3		30	1.1
8.8	4		40	1.4
11	5		50	1.8
13	6		60	2.1
15	7		70	2.5
18	8		80	2.8
20	9		90	3.2
22	10		100	3.5
44	20		200	7.1
66	30		300	11
88	40		400	14
110	50		500	18
132	60		600	21
154	70		700	25
176	80		800	28
198	90		900	32
220	100	0.1	1000	35
441	200	0.2		
661	300	0.3		
882	400	0.4		
1102	500	0.5		
1323	600	0.7		
1543	700	0.8		
1764	800	0.9		
1984	900	1		
2205	1000	1.1		
4410	2000	2.2		
6615	3000	3.3		
8820	4000	4.4		
11025	5000	5.5		
13230	6000	6.6		
15435	7000	7.7		
17640	8000	8.8		
19845	9000	9.9		
22050	10000	11		
*2.205		*0.0011		*0.0353

*Multiply the System Internationale (SI) units (kilograms or grams) by this factor to convert to pounds, tons, or ounces, as appropriate.

actin	a protein of muscle that is active in muscular contraction
actomyosin	the complex of actin and myosin with ATP that is involved in muscular contraction
collagen	one of the three stromal proteins; strands of collagen are dispersed in the connective tissues to give them strength. Collagen is white in color and is susceptible to solubilization (being converted to gelatin) during cooking of meat (almost completely, in meat from young animals; less so, progressively, in meat from older animals).
connective tissue	body tissues which surround, support and harness the activity—usually—of muscle fibers, muscle bundles and whole muscles (in which case they are named edomysium, perimysium and epimysium, respectively). Other forms of connective tissue attach muscles to bones (periosteum, tendons), bones to bones (ligaments) or form broad sheets (fascia) which collectivize activities of one or several muscles. Connective tissue is comprised of a watery substance (water plus proteins, lipids, etc.) into which is dispersed a matrix of stromal protein fibrils made up of collagen, elastin and reticulin.
cytochrome protein	respiratory pigments are parts of the electron transport system inside individual cells. Myoglobin gives up its oxygen to cytochrome pigments; the oxygen is then used for oxidative phosphorylation to create energy (as ATP) inside the cell.
elastin	one of the three stromal proteins; strands of elastin (as fibrils) are dispersed in the connective tissues to give them strength. Elastin is yellow in color and is not solubilized during cooking. Elastin is most prevalent in ligaments (e.g. *ligamentum nuchae*) and in connective tissues from mature animals (e.g., old cows, etc.).
endogenous	produced or synthesized within the cell, tissue, or body
endomysium	the connective tissue sheath or layer surrounding individual muscle fibers
epimysium	the connective tissue sheath or layer that surrounds an entire muscle
exogenous	produced outside the cell or body and transported into the body or cell via osmosis, ingestion, inhalation, etc.
fascicule	a bundle (usually, of muscle fibers)
fasciculus	a slender bundle of anatomical fibers
hemoglobin	a red, iron-containing protein in blood. Its function is to transport oxygen from the lungs, through the vascular system, to the cells where hemoglobin gives up its oxygen to myoglobin for subsequent use in the cells.
myofibril	any of the longitudinal parallel contractile elements of a muscle cell that are composed of myosin and actin
myofibrillar	an adjective used to define the location of some other thing (noun); e.g., the myofibrillar proteins (that is the proteins found in the myofibril)
myofilament	either of the individual filaments (actin or myosin) that, together make up the bulk of a myofibril
myoglobin	a red, iron-containing protein, that is a part of the red-colored pigment in muscles. It is similar to hemoglobin, but only one-fourth as large. Its function is to accept oxygen from hemoglobin and to deliver oxygen to the electron transport system in the cell.
myosin	a fibrous globulin protein of muscle that can split ATP and that reacts with actin to form actomyosin
oxymyoglobin	name for myoglobin when the free binding site on heme (in the myoglobin molecule) is occupied by molecular oxygen
perimysium	the connective tissue sheath or layer that surrounds muscle bundles (groups of muscle fibers)
reticulin	one of the three stromal proteins; strands of reticulin are dispersed in the connective tissues. Often called "pre-collagen," reticulin behaves, upon cooking, as would collagen from immature animals.
sarcolemma	the thin transparent homogeneous sheath surrounding a striated muscle fiber
sarcomere	a repeating structural unit of striated muscle fibers
sarcoplasm	the cytoplasm of a striated muscle fiber
stroma	the supporting framework of an animal organ, typically consisting of connective tissue
stromal	an adjective used to define the location of some other thing; e.g. the stromal proteins